# The Middle Ages in Modern Culture

*New Directions in Medieval Studies*

Series Editors:
Helen Young (Deakin University, Australia)
Andrew Elliott (University of Lincoln, UK)

This wide-ranging monograph series responds to emerging themes and interdisciplinary research methods in medieval scholarship, including the reception and reworking of the medieval in the post-medieval period. Particular concerns involve cataloguing the rich variety of experience of medieval people and exploring cultural transfer across different periods, places and groups. In doing so, *New Directions in Medieval Studies* seeks to contribute to the future directions and debates of medieval studies.

**Published Titles**

*The Middle Ages in Popular Imagination*, Paul Sturtevant
*Medieval Literature on Display*, Alexandra Sterling-Hellenbrand
*Cultures of Compunction in the Medieval World*, Graham Williams and Charlotte Steenbrugge (eds.)
*The Middle Ages in Modern Culture*, Karl C. Alvestad and Robert Houghton (eds.)

**Upcoming Titles**

*Constructing Viking History*, Thomas Smaberg
*Laughter and Awkwardness in Late Medieval England*, David Watt
*The Cult of Thomas Becket*, Paul Webster
*Medieval Radicalism*, Daniel Wollenberg
*Medievalism in Finland and Russia*, Reima Välimäki (ed.)

# The Middle Ages in Modern Culture

*History and Authenticity in Contemporary Medievalism*

Edited by
Karl C. Alvestad and Robert Houghton

BLOOMSBURY ACADEMIC
LONDON • NEW YORK • OXFORD • NEW DELHI • SYDNEY

BLOOMSBURY ACADEMIC
Bloomsbury Publishing Plc
50 Bedford Square, London, WC1B 3DP, UK
1385 Broadway, New York, NY 10018, USA
29 Earlsfort Terrace, Dublin 2, Ireland

BLOOMSBURY, BLOOMSBURY ACADEMIC and the Diana logo are trademarks
of Bloomsbury Publishing Plc

First published in Great Britain 2021
Paperback edition first published 2023

Copyright © Karl C. Alvestad and Robert Houghton, 2021

Karl C. Alvestad and Robert Houghton have asserted their right under the Copyright,
Designs and Patents Act, 1988, to be identified as Editors of this work.

Cover image: © Hulton Deutsch / Getty Images

Series design by Tjaša Krivec

This work is published open access subject to a Creative Commons
Attribution-NonCommercial-NoDerivatives 4.0 International licence (CC BY-NC-ND 4.0,
https://creativecommons.org/licenses/by-nc-nd/4.0/). You may re-use, distribute,
and reproduce this work in any medium for non-commercial purposes, provided
you give attribution to the copyright holder and the publisher and provide a link
to the Creative Commons licence.

Bloomsbury Publishing Plc does not have any control over, or responsibility for, any
third-party websites referred to or in this book. All internet addresses given in this
book were correct at the time of going to press. The editors and publisher regret any
inconvenience caused if addresses have changed or sites have ceased to exist,
but can accept no responsibility for any such changes.

Every effort has been made to trace copyright holders and to obtain their permissions
for the use of copyright material. The publisher apologizes for any errors or omissions
and would be grateful if notified of any corrections that should be incorporated
in future reprints or editions of this book.

A catalogue record for this book is available from the British Library.

Library of Congress Cataloging-in-Publication Data

Names: Alvestad, Karl C., editor. | Houghton, Robert (Robert E.), editor.
Title: The Middle Ages in modern culture: history and authenticity in contemporary
medievalism / edited by Karl C. Alvestad and Robert Houghton.
Description: London; New York: Bloomsbury Academic, 2020. | Series: New directions
in medieval studies | Includes bibliographical references and index. |
Identifiers: LCCN 2021012894 (print) | LCCN 2021012895 (ebook) | ISBN 9781788314787
(hardback) | ISBN 9781350167469 (epub) | ISBN 9781350167476 (ebook)
Subjects: LCSH: Medievalism. | Middle Ages in popular culture. |
Authenticity (Philosophy) in mass media.
Classification: LCC CB353 .M525 2020 (print) | LCC CB353 (ebook) | DDC 940.1–dc23
LC record available at https://lccn.loc.gov/2021012894
LC ebook record available at https://lccn.loc.gov/2021012895

ISBN: HB: 978-1-7883-1478-7
PB: 978-1-3502-6600-1
ePDF: 978-1-3501-6747-6
eBook: 978-1-3501-6746-9

Typeset by Deanta Global Publishing Services, Chennai, India

To find out more about our authors and books visit www.bloomsbury.com and
sign up for our newsletters.

# Contents

| | |
|---|---|
| List of illustrations | vii |
| List of contributors | viii |
| Acknowledgements | xi |

Introduction: Accuracy and authenticity – interactions in contemporary medievalism  *Robert Houghton and Karl C. Alvestad* — 1

### Part I  Claiming authenticity

1. The 'accurate' deeds of our fathers: The 'authentic' narrative of early Norway  *Karl C. Alvestad* — 15
2. Race and historical authenticity: *Kingdom Come: Deliverance*  *Helen Young* — 28

### Part II  Exploring authenticity

3. 'Contrary to common sense': The impact of the depiction of William Wallace's longsword  *Laura S. Harrison* — 43
4. Misdiagnosing medieval medicine: 'Magical' Muslims, metanarrative and the modern media  *April Harper* — 58
5. Audience perceptions of historical authenticity in visual media  *Sian Beavers and Sylvia Warnecke* — 74
6. *La posta di falcone* and *la porta di ferro*: Representations and receptions of historical fighting practices in medieval media and contemporary popular culture  *Jacob Henry Deacon* — 90
7. Malevolent and marginal: The feminized 'Dark Ages' in modern card game cultures  *Daisy Black* — 105

### Part III  Creating authenticity

8. The tourist gaze and the 'medieval' landscape  *Megan Arnott* — 121
9. Playing at the crossroads of religion and law: Historical milieu, context and curriculum hooks in *Lost & Found*  *Owen Gottlieb* — 140
10. Modding and authentic, gritty medievalism in *Skyrim*  *Victoria Cooper* — 161

11  Playing with taskscapes: Representing medieval life through
    video games technologies  *Juan Hiriart*                              174
12  If you're going to be the king, you'd better damn well act like the king:
    Setting authentic objectives to support learning in grand strategy
    computer games  *Robert Houghton*                                     186

Bibliography                                                              211
Filmography                                                               234
Ludography                                                                235
Mods cited                                                                236
Index                                                                     238

# Illustrations

## Figures

| | | |
|---|---|---|
| 3.1 | Statue of William Wallace at Dryburgh, Berwickshire | 47 |
| 3.2 | Statue of William Wallace at Edinburgh Castle | 48 |
| 3.3 | Statue of Robert the Bruce at Edinburgh Castle | 49 |
| 3.4 | Memorial to Wallace in Elderslie | 50 |
| 3.5 | Statue of William Wallace at the Scottish National Portrait Gallery, Edinburgh | 51 |
| 3.6 | Processional frieze in Scottish National Portrait Gallery featuring William Wallace, Edinburgh | 52 |
| 5.1 | Perceptions of historical authenticity across media forms with % adjustments | 78 |
| 6.1 | Various low guards from Fiore dei Liberi's fight book | 91 |
| 8.1 | Sign to Vinland along Hwy 430, Newfoundland, Canada | 133 |
| 9.1 | Card back showing architectural patterns from Fatimid Fustat in *Lost & Found* | 144 |
| 9.2 | Card back showing architectural patterns from Fatimid Fustat in *Lost & Found* | 145 |
| 9.3 | Card back showing architectural patterns from Fatimid Fustat in *Lost & Found* | 146 |
| 9.4 | Card from *Lost & Found* illustrating objects, garments and milieu | 147 |
| 9.5 | Card from *Lost & Found* illustrating objects, garments and milieu | 147 |
| 9.6 | Plague card from *Lost & Found* | 148 |
| 9.7 | Monsoon card from *Lost & Found* | 148 |
| 9.8 | Bumper Crop card from *Lost & Found* | 149 |
| 9.9 | *Ketubah* card in *Lost & Found* | 151 |
| 9.10 | Dinarim card from *Lost & Found* | 152 |
| 9.11 | Dinarim card from *Lost & Found* | 153 |
| 9.12 | Train a Judge card from *Lost & Found* | 154 |
| 9.13 | Train a Teacher card from *Lost & Found* | 154 |
| 9.14 | Honey Jar Cracks event card from *Lost & Found* | 155 |
| 9.15 | Abandoned Cow event card in *Lost & Found* | 155 |
| 9.16 | Rulings cards in *Lost & Found* | 157 |
| 9.17 | Explanations cards in *Lost & Found* | 158 |

## Table

| | | |
|---|---|---|
| 5.1 | Demographic of Survey Respondents by Gender and Age | 76 |

# Contributors

**Karl C. Alvestad** is Associate Professor in Social Studies at the University of South-Eastern Norway, Norway. His work explores Norwegian political culture in the Viking Age, and the reception of the Viking Age in the later Norwegian culture and politics. His recent publications include 'Olavian Treaces in Post-Medieval England' in *The Land of the English Kin* (2020) and 'A Kingdom for My Bed: Marriage, Sexuality, and Power in Harald Fairhair's Conquest of Norway' in *Royal Studies Journal* (2019).

**Megan Arnott** is PhD Candidate at Western Michigan University, United States, and Contract Lecturer at Lakehead University, United States, and Seneca College, United States. Her recent publications include '"Viking tough": How Ads Sell Us Medieval Manhood' in *The Public Medievalist* (2019) and 'King Sverrir and the First Baglar War' in *Medieval Warfare* (2018). She is currently working on a chapter for *Vikings! A Public History: Museums, Recreations and Reenactments*. She has research interests in Old Norse literature, politics in literature, commemoration and tourism, medievalism, medieval kingship and early Scandinavian society.

**Sian Beavers** is PhD Graduate in Classical Reception, Game studies and Educational Technology at The Open University, UK. Her doctoral thesis, *The Informal Learning of History with Digital Games* (2020), addresses players' online and offline learning habits in relation to ancient Rome. She has recently published 'The Representation of Women in *Ryse: Son of Rome*' in *Classical Antiquity in Video Games: Playing with the Ancient World* (2020). Her research interests focus on digital media with a particular emphasis on the reflexive creation of meaning from interactions with digital tools.

**Daisy Black** is Lecturer in English Literature at the University of Wolverhampton, UK. She has published works on the use of space and authority in medieval performance; gender and medieval drama; and the senses and medievalism in modern tabletop gaming. Her monograph *Play Time: Gender, Anti-Semitism and Temporality in Medieval Biblical Drama* (2020) examines time, gender and anti-Semitism in medieval drama. Her next major research project will examine the use of food on the medieval stage. Daisy has produced creative work for diverse bodies, including museums, cathedrals, folk and storytelling festivals and the Royal College of Physicians. She is a BBC/AHRC new generation thinker.

**Victoria Cooper** teaches English literature in Beijing, China. She has recently published, with Andrew B.R. Elliott, '"I braved in my youth-days battles unnumbered": Beowulf, Video Games and Hack-and-Slash Medievalism' in *Beowulf in the Media*, edited by David Clark. Her research interests include medievalism in video games;

ideas of heritage, identity and whiteness in medievalism, fantasy and politics; Vikings in popular culture; and Old Norse-Icelandic romance. She is currently writing a monograph from her doctoral thesis on medievalism in *Skyrim* and is working on translations of some lesser-studied Old Norse Romances into English.

**Jacob Henry Deacon** is PhD Student at the Institute for Medieval Studies, University of Leeds, UK, and Assistant Editor for *Acta Periodica Duellatorum*, whose doctoral research explores fencing knowledge, practices and cultures in late medieval and early modern England. His research interests encompass the creation and transmission of embodied knowledge, violence in late medieval and early modern urban centres, and the development and use of arms and armour. He has recently published 'Reaching Excellence: Staff Weapon Typologies, Contexts, and Fighting Techniques in the *Collectanea* of Pietro Monte', *Acta Periodica Duellatorum* (2019), with Iason-Eleftherios Tzouriadis.

**Owen Gottlieb** is Associate Professor of Games and Interactive Media at the Rochester Institute of Technology, United States. He is Founder (2015) and Lead Research Faculty at the Initiative in Religion, Culture, and Policy at the RIT MAGIC Center. Gottlieb's team have received international prizes at venues including the Serious Play Conference (2019) and Indiecade (2019). His most recent publication is an article with Ian Schreiber in *International Journal of Designs for Learning* (2020). Gottlieb's research addresses history education; learning games in religion, culture, and policy; interactive media and wellness; and Cold War instructional design influences on contemporary interactive learning media.

**April Harper** is Associate Professor of Ancient and Medieval History at SUNY Oneonta, United States. Her recent publications include 'Punishing Adultery: Private Violence, Public Honor, Literature, and the Law' in *Haskins Society Journal* (2017); 'Silencing Queens' in *Pre-modern Rulers and (Post)modern Viewers: Gender, Sex and Power in Popular Culture* (2017); and (with Sally Dixon-Smith) 'The Ties That Bind' in *The Cultural History of Marriage* (2019). She is currently working on a primary source collection for the history of medicine in pre-modern Europe titled *Sickness and Society: Medieval Medicine and Medical Practice before 1600*.

**Laura S. Harrison** is Cultural Resources Advisor at Historic Environment Scotland, UK. Her recent publications include '"That famous manifesto": The Declaration of Arbroath, Declaration of Independence, and the power of language' in *Scottish Affairs* (2017) and 'Beyond the Cannon: The methodological underpinnings of War Through Other Stuff' in *Critical Military Studies* (Forthcoming). She is currently preparing a monograph presenting a framework for understanding the role of local identity in commemoration, an article on using technology to increase engagement with neglected heritage sites, and a co-authored book on participatory medievalism.

**Juan Hiriart** is Senior lecturer in Interactive Media Arts and Design at the University of Salford, UK. His research interests lie in the intersections between games, digital heritage and education with particular emphasis on the development and use of games for the meaningful and critical understanding of subjects across disciplines. Recent publications include 'How to be a 'Good' Anglo-Saxon: Designing and Using Historical Video Games in Primary Schools' in *Communicating the Past in the Digital Age* (2020) and 'Designing and Using Digital Games as Historical Learning Contexts for Primary School Classrooms' in *Historia Ludens* (2019).

**Robert Houghton** is Senior Lecturer in Early Medieval History at the University of Winchester, UK. His work addresses political and social systems in Italy c.800–c.1125 and the representation of the Middle Ages in modern games. Recent publications include 'Hugh, Lothar and Berengar: The Balance of Power in Italy 945-950' in *Journal of Medieval History* (2020) and 'World, Structure and Play: Digital Games as Historical Research Tools' in *Práticas da História* (2018). He is currently writing a volume addressing the interactions between medievalism and computer game tropes and their implications for teaching and researching the Middle Ages.

**Sylvia Warnecke** is Senior Lecturer in Languages at The Open University, UK. Her recent publications include 'Researching Participatory Literacy and Positioning in Online Learning Communities' in *Routledge Handbook of Language Learning and Technology* (2016) and 'Uncovering Reader Expectations and Concepts of Readers in Children's Literature of the Digital Age' in *Children as Readers in Children's Literature: The Power of Texts and the Importance of Reading* (2016). Her current research incorporates languages for well-being pedagogy in online and distance learning contexts; digital tools and engagement for language learners; and digital storytelling and multimodality.

**Helen Young** is Lecturer in the School of Communication and Creative Arts at Deakin University, Australia. Her research interests include medievalism, race and popular culture. She has recently published on gendered aesthetics of whiteness in *postmedieval* (2019, with Stepahnie Downes), on racialization of the Middle Ages during the late eighteenth century in *Literature Compass* (2019), and on race, gender and sexuality and the politics of choice in *Continuum* (2019, with Rowan Tulloch and Catherine Hoad). Her latest monograph is *Race and Popular Fantasy Literature: Habits of Whiteness* (2016).

# Acknowledgements

We need to thank our friends and colleagues for their help in the creation and development of this volume, including most notably Tobias Winnerling, Iain Donald, Katherine Lewis, Jeremiah McCall, Andrew Elliott, Derek Fewster, Jamie Wood, Usha Vishnuvajjala, Heta Aali, Ryan Lavelle and Katherine Weikert.

We would also like to thank all of our contributing authors and our contacts at I. B. Tauris and Bloomsbury – Anna Henderson, Joanna Godfrey, Rhodri Mogford and Laura Reeves – for their patience and perseverance with this volume.

Finally, we want to thank our partners Bracken and Varan for their unwavering and constant support in this and everything else. Without them none of this would have been possible.

*

This title has been made Open Access with the generous support of Knowledge Unlatched (KU).

# Introduction

## Accuracy and authenticity – interactions in contemporary medievalism

Robert Houghton and Karl C. Alvestad

The Middle Ages are an important cultural reference within both popular and high modern culture. The medieval and medievalism is common in contemporary culture in almost every genre and media format. Numerous TV series including *Game of Thrones*, *Vikings* and *Tudors* draw on medieval stories and imagery.[1] Films from *Lord of the Rings* to any of the range of Robin Hood films have followed the same trend.[2] Tabletop and computer games increasingly engage with the Middle Ages, either directly or through fantasy settings, and draw growing audiences.[3] There is a growing trail of tourism to sites of real or imagined historical significance.[4] Medieval historical and fantasy literature has undergone something of a renaissance in recent years.[5] This all implies a broad interaction with the Middle Ages and a complex and changing construction of cultural perceptions of the period.

In recent years, a concern for an accurate or authentic representation of the Middle Ages has formed a core element of this popular interaction.[6] There is a substantial demand for 'historical accuracy' among the audiences of modern media concerning the Middle Ages, and presenting an 'authentic experience' can have considerable commercial value. Popular discussion around depictions of the Middle Ages in modern media is often dominated by arguments about the authenticity of a particular work or element of a work. Critique of accuracy has also formed a core element of academic interaction with popular medievalism.[7]

On the surface, this drive for accuracy appears harmless or even beneficial. An apparently authentic environment can support audience immersion in any form of media. Medieval stories can act as the basis for entertaining retellings through modern media. The draw of an 'authentically' historical site may expose a greater portion of the public to the period. More generally, much of the appeal of historical media is its ability to convey knowledge of the past. A degree of historical accuracy is clearly desirable for these purposes.

However, these demands for accuracy and authenticity are often problematic. Those demanding accuracy are sometimes incompletely informed about the Middle Ages and demands for authenticity are based on modern perceptions of the Middle Ages rather than the reality of the period.[8] There is also substantial debate over the definition of historical accuracy and authenticity across and within media forms:[9] Are they the slavish recreation of the past? Or the creation of a believable setting for a story? Moreover, and most problematically, 'historical accuracy' is frequently used to justify the proliferation of racist, sexist and nationalist rhetoric.

## The democratization of popular medievalism

Scholarly discussion around the medieval in modern culture has grown and evolved significantly in recent years, contributing to a vibrant and active debate around modern medievalism. Key voices in this discussion have been presented in a series of edited volumes including *History and the Media*,[10] *Playing with the Past*[11] and *Neomedievalism in the Media*.[12] More recently, Andrew Elliott's *Medievalism, Politics and Mass Media* (Boydell & Brewer, 2017) has nuanced the debate with a concise and detailed piece about the importance of mass media in modern medievalism.[13]

Popular interaction with the medieval and medievalism is not a new phenomenon, but it has changed substantially in recent decades. Paralleling the rise of mass tourism in the second half of the twentieth century, popular demand for and interaction with the medieval through commercialization and innovation has changed the form and use of the medieval in modern culture. A broader spectrum of audiences seek out new experiences and interactions with the medieval through tourism, amusement parks, films and games. This growing demand for opportunities to experience the medieval or medievalism is perhaps demonstrated most strongly through the emergence and popularity of 'medieval' pilgrimage routes throughout Europe and the guided tours dedicated to themes such as *Game of Thrones* and the Viking Age in relevant sites as discussed by Megan Arnott in her chapter in this book.

Technological and social changes have simultaneously altered the way in which audiences interact with popular medievalism. Media of all formats is more readily available to growing audiences as access to TV and the internet widens. Social media allows the near endemic spread of medieval tropes, and it positions users as the constructors and curators of the medievalism in which they participate.[14] Digital games allow immersive interaction with the past in a different way from other modern media and very much centre the player within their medieval and medievalist worlds.[15]

In short, popular medievalism has become democratized to a quite substantial extent. Audiences have transitioned from a relatively passive role as recipients of knowledge dispensed by the creators of popular media to a more active role, by driving the discussion and shape of medievalism to a much greater degree.

This democratization has shaped the messages and cultural relevance of popular medievalism, and, in conjunction with changing cultural and political environments, this process has contributed to several negative trends within contemporary medievalism. The use of the Middle Ages as a backdrop for the presentation of race,[16] nationality,[17] gender[18] and other key contemporary issues in modern media has been critically analysed through various methods within numerous disciplines, as has the impact of these representations on modern society and their role in broader cultural issues. In many cases, whether intentionally or coincidentally, the use of the medieval and medievalism within popular media upholds regressive social values and contributes to harmful political agendas. Many of these modern appropriations of the medieval past have roots in earlier academic and political approaches to the period, although in each case contemporary variations have emerged around the broad themes. The substantive change here is not so much that of ideas or ideals, but of audience size and participation. The democratization of popular medievalism has allowed the unprecedented spread and mutation of this rhetoric.

However, despite the severe and widespread negative trends associated with popular medievalism, there still exist several positive elements within some modern media's representation of the Middle Ages. The educational potential of social media and digital games is increasingly acknowledged, and these systems are being deployed more frequently and with greater success in classrooms at every level of study.[19] There are commercial, artistic and social benefits to the greater engagement with the medieval period, which is prompted by the democratization of medievalism and history more generally.[20] The more active engagement with history encouraged by much of this media may promote a more critical approach to modern political issues.[21] Most significantly, several media have exploited the engagement potential of popular medievalism to challenge popular misconceptions of the period and to dispute harmful modern rhetoric.[22]

## Accuracy and authenticity

Within this broader trend, a reoccurring topic of discussion within and outside the academy is the issue of authenticity and accuracy in presentation and depiction of the medieval.[23] Absolute historical accuracy is an impossible goal for academic history, much less for popular history. It is impossible to recreate the past as our knowledge is inevitably incomplete. Sources do not survive; those that do distort events to suit the goals of their authors. The histories presented by modern authors are dictated to a large extent by their choice of sources, parsing of said sources and construction of arguments influenced by their own ideologies, social backgrounds and prejudices.[24] The creators of popular historical works must contend with these issues, and their ability to produce historical accuracy is further limited by the necessity of producing an entertaining (and often profitable) output. They are further limited by the restrictions of their genre and media format and by the expectations of their audiences. While academic and popular histories in any format may provide plausible versions of events, they can never reliably reconstruct the past.

It should not be surprising therefore that contemporary medievalism across media formats generally have little relation to the medieval reality. Instead medievalism tends to reiterate popular stereotypes and tropes of the Middle Ages: the period was the 'Dark Ages';[25] medieval is synonymous with violent;[26] Europe was socially isolated and ethnically and racially homogenous.[27] Elliott has demonstrated through a series of case studies that the use of the medieval and medievalism within modern mass media rarely has a substantive connection with an academic understanding of the period.[28] He contends that medievalist imagery and narrative is often separated from its original meaning through a lengthy and sometimes passive process, which ultimately allows its use as a supporting structure in modern ideologies and rhetoric.[29]

These representations are potent in their influence and resistant to academic scrutiny and sanction, because they create worlds which feel authentic to their audiences.[30] The use of reductive and accessible medievalist tropes provides a much more convenient and recognizable shorthand than complex and nuanced academic considerations, and hence allows the communication of a clearly understood message.[31] Attempts to counter the misconceptions perpetuated by these contemporary media often enjoy limited success as their nuanced counter-narrative and acknowledgement of unknowns produce a substantially less accessible story.[32]

Despite their inevitable and often unavoidable shortcomings in this regard, appeals to historical accuracy can certainly be powerful marketing tools for contemporary media.[33] Many digital games set within the Middle Ages, including the *Total War* and *Assassin's Creed* franchises, lay claim to historical accuracy founded on academic research and this forms a core component of their appeal to a large portion of their player base.[34] The advertising for numerous films set in the period including *King Arthur* (2005) and *Robin Hood* (2010) takes the presentation of a 'real' story as their core element.[35]

These appeals to accuracy can act in more insidious ways. In recent years, the longstanding use and appropriation of the Middle Ages by nationalist, racist and misogynist groups highlighted earlier has increasingly turned to claims of historical accuracy to grant authority to their rhetoric and media. The ubiquity of white characters within digital games set in the Middle Ages or medievalist fantasy worlds has been justified on the grounds of 'historical accuracy' by players and designers alike.[36] The absence of women from films such as *The Lord of the Rings* and casual sexualization and abuse of women in shows such as *Game of Thrones* have been highlighted in academic and popular circles, but have been justified as 'historically accurate'.[37] The overt and covert narratives of nationalism, colonialism and imperialism present within many museums and historical sites are well documented and the authority and impact of these narratives are driven by the implicit and explicit claims to 'historical accuracy' made by the curators of these sites. Historical accuracy may be an impossibility, but claims to this authority are nevertheless incredibly powerful.

The audiences of these contemporary medievalisms should not be viewed as passive consumers: they play a pivotal role in parsing the vision of the Middle Ages presented through these media. This role is perhaps most obvious within digital and physical games, where the user takes an active role in the outcome of the narrative through interactive play.[38] However, audiences of all media formats consume and construct the Middle Ages through their preconceptions of the period.[39] Their understanding of what is authentic to the period contributes to their interpretation of the story and its representation of the medieval. The simple act of setting a book, film or game in the Middle Ages establishes assumptions in the minds of the audience based on their conception of the period. They will often expect a violent and regressive society which may drastically alter their comprehension.

The ideas and debates concerning authenticity and inauthenticity that surround contemporary medievalism illustrate contemporary cultural perceptions of the medieval both among consumers and producers; hence these ideas and appeals to historical accuracy and authenticity may be used to gauge wider cultural values, developments and sensitivities. Discussions about the perceived authenticity and inauthenticity within the audiences of this popular medievalism, and about the steps through which authenticity is constructed by their creators, illustrate the ways in which contemporary society relates to and interacts with the medieval. They reveal nuances and trends within modern culture.

This poses difficulties for the creators of contemporary medievalist media. There is a growing demand for historical accuracy, but absolute accuracy is impossible to deliver and, in any case, will not be recognized as historically authentic by a sizeable portion of the audience. These creators must contend with vocal claims to an exclusionary Middle Ages as the 'accurate' version of the past as well as less divisive but more widespread misconceptions about the 'authentic' Middle Ages. Many creators of contemporary medievalist media certainly have the desire to create worlds close to the medieval reality, for both commercial and artistic purposes, but the desire is often stymied by practical requirements and by popular misconceptions of the period.[40]

The production of medievalist media which approaches the medieval reality can be a worthwhile pursuit, however. From an educational perspective, popular media has a substantial impact on audience's perceptions of the Middle Ages and hence can be a valuable tool for influencing these perceptions.[41] By challenging the misappropriation of the Middle Ages in this manner, these media could be used to challenge the ideologies which make use of misrepresentations of the period for their rhetoric.[42]

Conversely, a number of academics and creators have promoted the opposite approach: deliberately eschewing the rigidity of claims to historical accuracy and instead employing anachronisms and medievalist tropes as part of their means of countering harmful ideologies in the modern world.[43] To this end, the presentation of progressive viewpoints and messages regarding politics, racial and sexual identities, and other issues within media which draws upon medieval themes could be considered to be of greater importance than meticulously crafting a simulacrum of the past. This line of reasoning is particularly powerful within works of fantasy fiction: worlds of magic and dragons already break from medieval reality and hence should not be subject to the more mundane tropes associated with the period.

In sum, the debate over historical accuracy and authenticity within popular medievalism is complex and nuanced and is far from resolved. It remains an important issue within the academy, within the classroom, and, above all, in the wider world.

## Interactions in contemporary medievalism

This book addresses several issues of great significance within and outside the academy. In a world where the understanding of 'historical truth' is simultaneously becoming more fluid and authoritative, where 'alternative facts' dominate the news cycle, where authors of fiction and fantasy insist on the 'historical authenticity' within their works and where the validity of expert opinion, research data and reasoned analysis is rejected by those in power, the debates around historical accuracy have never been more relevant. The popularity of games, films, books and other media with medieval or medievalist themes combined with a less-than-comprehensive popular understanding of the period and extremist groups and politicians willing to exploit these perceptions to further their rhetoric makes issues of historical accuracy and authenticity particular relevant to works which are set in or draw upon the Middle Ages. By employing the expertise of a large and international range of scholars, the book demonstrates the great variance and nuance of thinking surrounding ideas and ideals of historical accuracy and authenticity across disciplines and audiences.

In doing so, this work meshes with a substantial and growing body of research into the use of the medieval in the modern world. Many of these works focus on one (or at most two) variety of media. The study of medievalism in contemporary literature is well established with recent key works including monographs by Young and Carroll, and the edited volume *Medieval Science Fiction*.[44] Among many others, Aberth, Haydock, Bildhauer and Sturtevant have produced learned volumes addressing the use of the medieval in film.[45] Canadine's edited volume *History in the Media* and Elliott's *Medievalism, Politics and Mass Media* provide deep considerations of medievalism in news media.[46] A number of recent volumes address medievalism in television – often in comparison with other media forms.[47] Medievalism in digital games remains an embryonic subfield, but is represented by a growing number of scholarly works.[48] Several important works have been produced addressing medievalism across media more generally, including recently the edited volumes *The Cambridge Companion to Medievalism*, *The Middle Ages in the Modern World* and monographs by Fitzpatrick and Utz.[49]

In contrast to much of this previous scholarship, this book considers a diverse range of media and hence provides an important and underutilized interdisciplinary angle of enquiry. Through a focus on the key issue of accuracy and authenticity across media formats and by drawing together a range of perspectives from different elements of the academy, this work highlights new connections, comparisons and contrasts. Further, this book provides an important bridge across the divide between academia and industry through the inclusion of chapters by the creators of medievalist media in various forms (Black, Theatre; Gottlieb, Board Games; Hiriat and Houghton, Digital Games).

This book explores definitions, claims and uses of historical authenticity around the Middle Ages and medievalism across a range of modern media formats (literature, heritage, tourism, politics, film, TV, board games and digital games). As highlighted previously, numerous authors have demonstrated the importance of this issue both within and outside the academy. Several scholars have conducted work within this area previously, but this is the first book dedicated to the theme.

To this end, the chapters of this book address three interconnected issues: claims to authenticity, deployment of known inaccuracies and methods of creating authenticity. Each of these issues is addressed within a dedicated selection of chapters which cohere around this common theme.

Part I addresses claims to authenticity within contemporary medievalism. The chapters in this section consider the notion and ideology behind purportedly authentic works. They consider the appeals to authority, which these claims represent, and underline the importance of the acceptance of a piece of media's historical authenticity in ensuring the effective transmission of its ideas. Karl C. Alvestad's chapter addresses the national foundation narratives of post-war Norway and considers the changing approaches employed by the creators of various media and the changing comprehension of historical accuracy among the audiences of these media. Helen Young's chapter uses a case study of the recent digital game *Kingdom Come: Deliverance* to highlight the trend within popular medievalism to promote a vision of a racially homogenous Middle Ages and to tie this image firmly to claims of authenticity.

The chapters in Part II explore the willing misrepresentation of the Middle Ages within modern media. They consider why particular inaccuracies emerge and remain in these works, despite repeated refutations from the academic community, and explore audience perceptions of these discrepancies. Laura S. Harrison's chapter addresses the commonplace anachronism within modern media representations of William Wallace's two-handed longsword and argues that while the representation is certainly inaccurate, this does not undermine its perception as an authentic part of Wallace's story or broader ideology surrounding Scottish independence. In her chapter on medieval medicine in modern film, April Harper demonstrates the disconnect between popular representations of medieval doctors as backwards, superstitious and ineffective, with the dominant academic narrative of practical, if limited, medical practice. She argues that this wilful misrepresentation forms part of a broader tendency to present the Middle Ages as primitive and violent, which has substantial application within modern political rhetoric. The chapter by Sian Beavers and Sylvia Warnecke employs a deep and methodical survey of audience perceptions of authenticity in visual media relating to the Middle Ages to demonstrate a strong perception that violent and regressive representations of the period are the most authentic. In his chapter on medieval combat in modern media, Jacob Henry Deacon argues that medieval fighting practices are deliberately ignored or marginalized within popular medievalism in order to create more visually spectacular set pieces. Daisy Black's chapter on medieval gender in modern card games concludes the section and demonstrates the marginalization and trivialization of women within these games before highlighting the negative impact this may have on gender relations in contemporary society.

Part III considers the methods employed by creators of modern media to produce medieval environments, which will be perceived as accurate or authentic by their audience. The chapters in this section address the limitations of various media forms and consider the benefits and pitfalls associated with the creation of authentic portrayals of the Middle Ages. The section opens with a chapter by Megan Arnott, which considers the impact of tourist expectations on the presentation of the medieval within museums and at historical sites. Owen Gottlieb's chapter describes the development of an education card game designed to broaden discourse around religious legal systems and considers the methods used to incorporate historical accuracy within this medium. In her chapter on user modifications of the digital game *Skyrim*, Victoria Cooper discusses the work of players who strive for a more historically realistic and authentic game, noting that most of this work focuses on creating a more violent environment, but highlighting a number of mods which take a more mature and constructive approach. Juan Hiriart's chapter details his construction of an educational digital game about Anglo-Saxon daily life and discusses the difficulties faced when using this medium alongside the opportunities it presents for educational and outreach purposes. Robert

Houghton's chapter engages with the impact of victory conditions and other objectives on the behaviour of players of strategy games, argues that unrealistic objectives can negatively impact their educational utility and suggests methods through which this issue can be overcome in and around the classroom.

Each chapter builds its own argument on the depiction of the medieval and its relationship to authenticity. However, an overarching thesis emerges: claims to historical authenticity are powerful tools in any media format and these claims may have both positive and negative influences on the consumers of these media and the history they present. The volume in no way claims to be the final word on this subject, but contributes to a diverse and growing field of interdisciplinary study.

## Notes

1. Meriem Pagès and Karolyn Kinane, eds, *The Middle Ages on Television: Critical Essays* (Jefferson, NC: McFarland, 2015); Carolyne Larrington, 'Mediating Medieval(Ized) Emotion in Game of Thrones', in *Authenticity, Medievalism, Music*, Studies in Medievalism XXVII (Woodbridge: Boydell and Brewer, 2018); KellyAnn Fitzpatrick, 'Game of Thrones: Neomedievalism and the Myths of Inheritance', in *Neomedievalism, Popular Culture, and the Academy* (Woodbridge: Boydell and Brewer, 2019).
2. Nickolas Haydock, *Movie Medievalism: The Imaginary Middle Ages* (Jefferson, NC: McFarland, 2008); Stephen Meyer, 'Soundscapes of Middle Earth: The Question of Medievalist Music in Peter Jackson's Lord of the Rings Films', in *Defining Medievalism(s) II*, Studies in Medievalism XVIII (Woodbridge: Boydell and Brewer, 2009); Andrew B. R. Elliott, *Remaking the Middle Ages: The Methods of Cinema and History in Portraying the Medieval World* (Jefferson, NC: McFarland, 2011); Bettina Bildhauer, 'Medievalism and Cinema', in *The Cambridge Companion to Medievalism*, ed. Louise D'Arcens (Cambridge: Cambridge University Press, 2016); Paul B. Sturtevant, *The Middle Ages in Popular Imagination: Memory, Film and Medievalism*, New Directions in Medieval Studies (London: I.B. Tauris, 2018).
3. Carol L. Robinson, 'An Introduction to Medievalist Video Games', in *Medievalism in Technology Old and New*, Studies in Medievalism XVI ( Rochester, NY: D.S. Brewer, 2008); Oliver M. Traxel, 'Medieval and Pseudo-Medieval Elements in Computer Role-Playing Games: Use and Interactivity', in *Medievalism in Technology Old and New*, Studies in Medievalism XVI (Cambridge ; Rocheter, NY: D.S. Brewer, 2008); William J. White, 'The Right to Dream of the Middle Ages Simulating the Medieval in Tabletop RPGs', in *Digital Gaming Re-Imagines the Middle Ages*, ed. Daniel T. Kline, Routledge Studies in New Media and Cyberculture 15 (New York, NY: Routledge, 2014).
4. John Urry and Jonas Larsen, *The Tourist Gaze 3.0: Theory, Culture & Society* (London: SAGE, 2011); Ewa Skowronek et al., 'What Is the Tourist Landscape? Aspects and Features of the Concept', *Acta Geographica Slovenica* 58, no. 2 (1 January 2018): 73–85.
5. Shiloh Carroll, *Medievalism in A Song of Ice and Fire and Game of Thrones*, Medievalism, volume 12 (Rochester, NY: D.S. Brewer, 2018).
6. Tara Jane Copplestone, 'But That's Not Accurate: The Differing Perceptions of Accuracy in Cultural-Heritage Videogames between Creators, Consumers and Critics', *Rethinking History* 21, no. 3 (3 July 2017): 415–38.
7. Elliott, *Remaking the Middle Ages*, 11–33.

8    Ibid., 178; Konstantinos Andriotis, 'Genres of Heritage Authenticity: Denotations from a Pilgrimage Landscape', *Annals of Tourism Research* 38, no. 4 (October 2011): 1613–33; Tison Pugh and Angela Jane Weisl, *Medievalisms: Making the Past in the Present* (London: Routledge, 2013), 110–11.
9    Urry and Larsen, *The Tourist Gaze 3.0*, 10–11; Jonathan Stubbs, *Historical Film: A Critical Introduction*, Bloomsbury Film Genres Series (New York, NY: Bloomsbury, 2013), 46; Copplestone, 'But That's Not Accurate'.
10    David Cannadine, ed., *History and the Media* (Basingstoke: Palgrave Macmillan, 2004).
11    M. Kapell and A. Elliott, eds *Playing with the Past: Digital Games and the Simulation of History* (New York, NY: Bloomsbury, 2013).
12    Carol L. Robinson and Pamela Clements, eds *Neomedievalism in the Media: Essays on Film, Television, and Electronic Games* (Lewiston, NY: Mellen, 2012).
13    Andrew B. R. Elliott, *Medievalism, Politics and Mass Media: Appropriating the Middle Ages in the Twenty-First Century*, Medievalism, volume X (Woodbridge: D. S. Brewer, 2017).
14    Ibid., 7–8.
15    G. Frasca, 'Simulation versus Narrative', in *The Video Game Theory Reader*, ed. M. Wolf and B. Perron (New York, NY: Routledge, 2003); Espen Aarseth, 'Playing Research: Methodological Approaches to Game Analysis', *Game Approaches/SPil-Veje. Papers from Spilforskning.Dk Conference* (2004); Jesper Juul, *Half-Real: Video Games between Real Rules and Fictional Worlds* (Cambridge, MA: MIT Press, 2005); Adam Chapman, 'Privileging Form Over Content: Analysing Historical Videogames', *Journal of Digital Humanities* 1, no. 2 (2012): 42–6.
16    Helen Young, 'Whiteness and Time: The Once, Present and Future Race', in *Medievalism on the Margins*, Studies in Medievalism XXIV (Woodbridge: Boydell and Brewer, 2015); Lynn Tarte Ramey, *Black Legacies: Race and the European Middle Ages* (Gainesville, FL: University Press of Florida, 2016); Andrew B. R. Elliott, 'Internet Medievalism and the White Middle Ages', *History Compass* 16, no. 3 (March 2018): e12441-n/a; Matthew X Vernon, *The Black Middle Ages: Race and the Construction of the Middle Ages* (New York, NY: Palgrave, 2018); Helen Victoria Young, *Race and Popular Fantasy Literature: Habits of Whiteness* (London: Routledge, 2018).
17    Patrick J. Geary, *The Myth of Nations: The Medieval Origins of Europe* (Princeton, NJ: Princeton University Press, 2003); John Coakley, 'Mobilizing the Past: Nationalist Images of History', *Nationalism and Ethnic Politics* 10, no. 4 (January 2004): 531–60; Richard Utz, 'Academic Medievalism and Nationalism', in *The Cambridge Companion to Medievalism*, ed. Louise D'Arcens (Cambridge: Cambridge University Press, 2016).
18    Jane Tolmie, 'Medievalism and the Fantasy Heroine', *Journal of Gender Studies* 15, no. 2 (July 2006): 145–58; Megan L. Morris, 'Chivalric Terrors', in *Defining Neomedievalism(s) II*, Studies in Medievalism XX (Woodbridge: Boydell and Brewer, 2011); Serina Patterson, 'Women, Queerness, and Massive Chalice: Medievalism in Participatory Culture', in *Medievalism on the Margins*, Studies in Medievalism XXIV (Woodbridge: Boydell and Brewer, 2015).
19    Harry J. Brown, *Videogames and Education* (Armonk, NY: M.E. Sharpe, 2008); Simon Egenfeldt-Nielsen, *Beyond Edutainment: Exploring the Educational Potential of Computer Games* (S.l.: Selbstverlag bei www.lulu.com, 2010); Mariruth Leftwich, 'New Intersections for History Education in Museums', *Journal of Museum Education* 41, no. 3 (2 July 2016): 146–51; Pablo Álvarez, Paulí Dávila, and Luis M. Naya, 'Education Museums: Historical Educational Discourse, Typology and Characteristics. The Case

of Spain', *Paedagogica Historica* 53, no. 6 (2 November 2017): 827–45; Alan S. Marcus, et al., *Teaching History with Film: Strategies for Secondary Social Studies* (London: Routledge, 2018).

20  Laura King and Gary Rivett, 'Engaging People in Making History: Impact, Public Engagement and the World Beyond the Campus', *History Workshop Journal* 80, no. 1 (October 2015): 218–33; Scott Robertson, 'Social Media and Civic Engagement: History, Theory, and Practice', *Synthesis Lectures on Human-Centered Informatics* 11, no. 2 (23 May 2018): i–1123.

21  Richard Utz, *Medievalism: A Manifesto* (Amsterdam: Arc Humanities Press, 2017).

22  Tara Foster, '"Kaamelott"'s Global Fifth Century', *Arthuriana* 25, no. 1 (2015): 5–21.

23  Christoph Classen and Wulf Kansteiner, 'Truth and Authenticity in Contemporary Historical Culture: An Introduction to *Historical Representation and Historical Truth*', *History and Theory* 48, no. 2 (May 2009): 1–4; Dominic Lees, 'Cinema and Authenticity: Anxieties in the Making of Historical Film', *Journal of Media Practice* 17, no. 2–3 (September 2016): 199–212; Copplestone, 'But That's Not Accurate'.

24  Edward Hallett Carr, *What Is History?* (New York: Vintage, 1961).

25  Amy S. Kaufman, 'Our Future Is Our Past: Corporate Medievalism in Dystopian Fiction', in *Corporate Medievalism II*, Studies in Medievalism XXII (Woodbridge: Boydell and Brewer, 2013); Frank M. Turner, 'Medievalism and the Invention of the Renaissance', in *European Intellectual History from Rousseau to Nietzsche*, ed. Richard A. Lofthouse (New Haven, CT: Yale University Press, 2014); Louise D'Arcens, 'The Past Is a Different and Fairly Disgusting Country', in *Comic Medievalism: Laughing at the Middle Ages* (Woodbridge: Boydell and Brewer, 2014).

26  James L. Smith, 'Medievalisms of Moral Panic', in *Medievalism and Modernity*, Studies in Medievalism XXV (Woodbridge: Boydell and Brewer, 2016).

27  Ramey, *Black Legacies*; Vernon, *The Black Middle Ages*.

28  Elliott, *Medievalism, Politics and Mass Media*.

29  Ibid., 6.

30  Ibid., 8.

31  Ibid., 38–54.

32  Smith, 'Medievalisms of Moral Panic', 170.

33  Erik Champion, *Critical Gaming: Interactive History and Virtual Heritage*, Digital Research in the Arts and Humanities (Farnham: Ashgate, 2015); Copplestone, 'But That's Not Accurate', 430–3.

34  Robert Houghton, 'World, Structure and Play: A Framework for Games as Historical Research Outputs, Tools, and Processes', *Práticas Da História* 7 (2018): 11.

35  Bettina Bildhauer, *Filming the Middle Ages* (London: Reaktion Books, 2011), 20.

36  Lisa Nakamura, 'Race in/for Cyberspace: Identity Tourism and Racial Passing on the Internet', in *Reading Digital Culture*, ed. David Trend, Keyworks in Cultural Studies 4 (Malden, MA: Blackwell, 2001); T. Higgin, 'Blackless Fantasy: The Disappearance of Race in Massively Multiplayer Online Role-Playing Games', *Games and Culture* 4, no. 1 (2008): 3–26; Young, 'Whiteness and Time'; Dennis Jansen, 'How Fantasy Games Deal with Race: As Demonstrated by The Elder Scrolls', *First Person Scholar*, 12 December 2018. Available online: http://www.firstpersonscholar.com/how-fantasy-games-deal-with-race/ (accessed 5 April 2019).

37  Valerie Estelle Frankel, *Women in Game of Thrones: Power, Conformity and Resistance* (Jefferson, NC: McFarland, 2014); Debra Ferreday, 'Game of Thrones, Rape Culture and Feminist Fandom', *Australian Feminist Studies* 30, no. 83 (2 January 2015): 21–36; Carroll, *Medievalism in A Song of Ice and Fire and Game of Thrones*.

38 Jeremy Antley, 'Going Beyond the Textual in History', *Journal of Digital Humanities* 1, no. 2 (2012); Adam Chapman, 'Is Sid Meier's Civilization History?', *Rethinking History* 17, no. 3 (September 2013): 312–32.
39 Elliott, *Medievalism, Politics and Mass Media*, 7–8.
40 Robert Houghton, 'Crusader Kings Too? (Mis)Representations of the Crusades in Grand Strategy Games', in *Playing The Crusades*, ed. Robert Houghton, Engaging the Crusades 7 (London: Routledge, 2021).
41 Brown, *Videogames and Education*; Egenfeldt-Nielsen, *Beyond Edutainment*; Leftwich, 'New Intersections for History Education in Museums'; Robert Houghton, 'Where Did You Learn That? The Self-Perceived Educational Impact of Historical Computer Games on Undergraduates', *Gamevironments* 5 (2016): 8–45; Álvarez, Dávila, and Naya, 'Education Museums'; Marcus et al., *Teaching History with Film*.
42 Smith, 'Medievalisms of Moral Panic', 170.
43 Steven Poole, *Trigger Happy: The Inner Life of Videogames* (London: Fourth Estate, 2000), 77; Bildhauer, *Filming the Middle Ages*, 20–1.
44 Carl Kears and James Paz, eds *Medieval Science Fiction*, King's College London Medieval Studies, XXIV (London: King's College London, Centre for Late Antique & Medieval Studies, 2016); Young, *Race and Popular Fantasy Literature*; Carroll, *Medievalism in A Song of Ice and Fire and Game of Thrones*.
45 John Aberth, *A Knight at the Movies: Medieval History on Film* (New York: Routledge, 2003); Haydock, *Movie Medievalism*; Bildhauer, *Filming the Middle Ages*; Sturtevant, *The Middle Ages in Popular Imagination*.
46 Cannadine, ed., *History and the Media*; Elliott, *Medievalism, Politics and Mass Media*.
47 Pagès and Kinane, *The Middle Ages on Television*; Carroll, *Medievalism in A Song of Ice and Fire and Game of Thrones*; Janice North, Karl Alvestad, and Elena Woodacre, eds *Premodern Rulers and Postmodern Viewers* (New York, NY: Springer, 2018).
48 Karl Fugelso and Carol L. Robinson, eds *Medievalism in Technology Old and New*, Studies in Medievalism 16 (Rocheter, NY: D.S. Brewer, 2008); Daniel T. Kline, ed., *Digital Gaming Re-Imagines the Middle Ages*, Routledge Studies in New Media and Cyberculture 15 (New York: Routledge, 2014); Robert Houghton, ed., *Playing The Crusades*, Engaging the Crusades 7 (London: Routledge, Forthcoming).
49 Louise D'Arcens, ed., *The Cambridge Companion to Medievalism* (Cambridge: Cambridge University Press, 2016); Bettina Bildhauer and Chris Jones, eds *The Middle Ages in the Modern World: Twenty-First Century Perspectives*, Proceedings of the British Academy 208 (Oxford: Oxford University Press, 2017); Utz, *Medievalism*; KellyAnn Fitzpatrick, *Neomedievalism, Popular Culture, and the Academy: From Tolkien to Game of Thrones*, Medievalism, volume XVI (Rochester, NY: D.S. Brewer, 2019).

# Part I

# Claiming authenticity

# 1

# The 'accurate' deeds of our fathers

## The 'authentic' narrative of early Norway

### Karl C. Alvestad

*The archaeological traces leave little doubt about the fact that several generations of Iron Age chieftains of the same calibre as Raudr have lived in Skjerstad.*[1]

This quote by Heim Bjartman Bjerck, taken from the programme of the 2010 performance of the site-specific play *Ragnhilds Drøm* (*Ragnhild's Dream*), directed by Ronald Rørvik and written by Anne Helgesen and Lyder Verne,[2] refers to the cultural landscape of the Skjerstad fjord area, a landscape consisting of a significant selection of burial mounds from the Viking Age. In his statement, Bjerck claims that this landscape gives evidence of the existence of a series of strong chieftains in the region during the Viking Age. The inclusion of Bjerck's quote in the programme is meant to legitimize and authenticate the narrative of *Ragnhilds Drøm* and to anchor it in the physical landscape surrounding the production. However, this use of the landscape raises a number of questions: first, what function does the landscape and landscape references, like those used by Helgesen and Verne, play in the production and experience of Norwegian medievalism? Second, what does this tell us about Norwegian medievalism? And third, what, if anything, does this have to do with the ideas of accuracy and authenticity within medievalism in Norway after 1945? These questions are interlinked and require a comparative analysis of the changing attitudes to accuracy and authenticity within mainstream medievalism in Norway between 1945 and 2015. I have elsewhere explored the role of Norwegian medievalism in the cultural construction of Norway in the period 1770–1940,[3] but in this chapter, I wish to explore how these mythologies were extended in the post-1945 Norwegian medievalist corpus of historical plays and books, and how they construct and validate their ideas and notions of accuracy and authenticity.[4]

Exploring these questions will help us better understand the strategies used to validate and construct authentic and 'accurate' medieval experiences in non-Anglophone contexts and will give a comparison for contemporary interaction with the medieval and medievalism in places such as the British Isles, France, the United States and Australia, as well as in the virtual world. In their 2013 study of Medievalism, Tison Pugh and Angela Weisl noted that authentic representation of the medieval is 'what successive periods have chosen to make of this period' and that the experience of this authenticity is the sharing in 'the sense of fantasy' that is drawn from this post-medieval construct of the medieval.[5] In the Norwegian context, an authentic experience of the Viking Age, which serves as the context for *Ragnhilds Drøm*, would be dependent on the transmission of historical scholarship, popular understanding and cultural mythologizing of the period and its imagery through which the audience can directly draw on their own pre-existing understanding of what makes a 'Viking' and what constitutes the Viking Age. Similar to Pugh and Weisl's observation of experiencing 'medieval' music,[6] the audience needs to be directly exposed to features that to them are perceived as distinctly 'Viking' or medieval to not feel cheated in their experiences. This experience does not have to be an accurate depiction of the medieval, as the concerns and thoughts of people of the medieval period might not be familiar or recognizable to a popular audience, but instead the experience needs to express at least a veneer of 'authenticity'; that is, it must make reference to commonly held understandings of the period displayed, to veil modern concerns and attitudes as authentic for the audience. This veneer, or 'fantasy', as Pugh and Weisl call it, is needed to bridge the gap between the present and the past, and in their words sends the audience on a 'direct experience, of an emotional journey [. . .] to take [the audience] out of the contemporary world, into [. . .] a nostalgic past'.[7] In other words, the foundations of authenticity of the medieval and Viking Age in Norwegian post-1945 medievalism are those elements that validate and project individuals that are engaging with the medievalism from their contemporary time into the past; these aspects do not need to be accurate or based in actual historical evidence. Instead they need to be based on aspects that are commonly held as representative of the period with which the medievalism interacts. The role of the bridge between present and past can be fulfilled most easily by visual clues such as buildings like a castle, medieval church, ruins, the costumes used by the actors, sounds or even social interaction or gender norms.

Unfortunately, a combination of historical developments, demography, geography and climate contributes to the reality that the Norwegian landscape today lacks distinctly medieval structures or remains that can function as mnemonic devices and backdrops for medievalism. The few surviving medieval churches, including the Stave Churches,[8] are among the rare physical remains of the middle ages in Norway. Instead, sites of memory linked to events in the sagas of Snorri Sturluson, like the fields of Stiklestad or the fjords and landscape itself, take on this authenticating function through the actions of men. This use of memory sites and the landscape is also advocated by Birger Sivertsen, through the website *spelhåndboka.no*, as part of a guide to producing historical plays, but Sivertsen also stresses that a play will appear more trustworthy and authentic if it draws on local historical sources or oral traditions.[9] Such local historical plays are usually site-specific, preformed in open-air theatres and are rarely, if ever preformed, outside the locality with which their narrative is concerned. This means that the landscape surrounding the theatre grounds the narrative spatially as is the case with *Ragnhilds Drøm*.

A common source to use as a foundation for the plays is Snorri's *Heimskringla*, as it chronicles the story of the Norwegian kingdom and its people, and it forms the foundations for early Norwegian history. Snorri's importance for Norwegian history and nationalism has been discussed elsewhere, but for the clarity of this chapter it is worth noting that from the nineteenth century onwards, stories from *Heimskringla* formed a crucial part of the Norwegian history textbooks making children and adults alike aware of the ethno-genesis of the Norwegian nation as told by Snorri.[10] Beyond this, *Heimskringla* actively uses the landscape and place names to validate its own narratives and stories, and these references are in modern times used as the geographical foundations for productions like *Ragnhilds Drøm*, while the society and gender balance described in the saga form the foundation of a popular historical understanding of the gender relations of the Viking Age. These gender relations are integrally connected with the idea of the division of labour in Viking Age society, with women being responsible for cooking, childcare and textile production – all indoor pursuits – whereas men were responsible for farming, hunting, fishing and trade. These stereotypes are reproduced in textbooks and provide a 'universal' historical 'truth' alongside landscape references that artists and authors can use to construct a medieval feeling for those interacting with their productions. These are the 'universal' myths of the gender roles of the pre-industrial past, with women working indoors and men outside, and the timelessness of the Norwegian landscape. It has elsewhere been argued that Snorri was used by modern historians during the nineteenth century and the early twentieth century to define the Norwegian nation and to transmit the idea of Norway as a coherent natural unit.[11] As an extension of this mythology of the Norwegian 'homeland', the local and regional cultural landscape became the local representation of the wider nation and a touchstone for the self in the national narrative of the Norwegians. Because of this, the landscape of Norway is almost a nationwide site of memory connecting the nation with the former inhabitants of the land.

This national reading of the landscape and nation is, and has been, focused on the Norse or Norwegian historical continuity, which has excluded indigenous traditions such as that of the Sami and Finnish populations of modern Norway. The historical erasure of the Sami was until the late 1980s part of an official cultural policy of the Norwegian state which sought the cultural assimilation of the Sami.[12] Similar to the Norwegian narratives of historical continuity in a historical homeland of fjords and farms, the Sami preserved and maintained an identity closely linked to the landscape and the lifestyle it supported. This is partly due to the romanticization of the Sami, which, according to Kjell Olsen, is defined by their relationship with the region and landscape of Finnmark and its wilderness.[13] This connection is reflected in the few films produced about events in Sami history, such as *The Pathfinder* (1987)[14] and *The Kautokeino Rebellion* (2008),[15] where the landscape and its distinctive features play an integral role. Such landscape-based identities are not unique to Norway, but have been recognized also by Miroslav Hroch, Ruby Koshar, Serhii Plokhy and Adrian Hastings, who acknowledge that similar trends can be found elsewhere in Europe.[16] In the Norwegian case, it can be argued that the whole Norwegian landscape is steeped in memories and narratives, like a promised land, causing the landscape of 'land of the Norwegians',[17] according to Inger Birkeland, to become part of the cultural heritage of the nation and causing the landscape and culture to influence each other.[18] Nevertheless, within this landscape there are certain sites and places, like Stiklestad, where the historical narrative of the past condenses and thus they become symbolically more important than others; such places can best be understood as a site of memory in the manner described and theorized by Pierre Nora.[19] As such, both the landscape overall and the specific sites within it are anchors that can validate and authenticate medievalism by creating a link between the now and then.

The foundation for the continued appreciation of the Norwegian landscape is the curriculum in Norwegian schools, which directly informs contemporary understanding of the landscape.[20] The curriculum has also influenced how the modern audience interact and engage with pre-industrial gender roles. Nanna Løkka noted in 2014 that modern research into gender and gender roles in the Viking Age has not influenced the popular understanding of the period, but that instead the persistent image in popular culture depicts gender relations in accordance to who women are to their male relatives.[21] As such, it is reasonable to claim that Norwegian medievalism, as popular culture, perpetuates a simplified depiction of Viking Age gender and thus caters to the pre-existing expectations of its audience rather than taking on board new research. Løkka's main argument is that women's societal role in the Viking Age is undervalued in popular representations and that there are modern cultural and societal barriers against depicting female agency outside the household and farm.[22] This assumption and representation also flavour what is perceived as natural for men and the masculine – that men are responsible for social, cultural and political interests of the family in the wider socio-political environment in which they live. Løkka's assessment of the gender bias in popular culture, and the reliance on Snorri's work in Norwegian medievalism, help focus this study of the use of landscape and gender in medievalism. On the basis of Løkka's critique and the use of Snorri's narratives, this chapter will focus on popular medievalism in the forms of historical plays, novels and films that draws on or is set in the period 800–1200 and was produced in post–Second World War Norway. For the sake of brevity, this chapter will focus its analysis on a small corpus of representative examples that reflect the wider trends of the period, but which also have significant circulation and cultural impact compared to other examples of post-war medievalism. The sample has been selected on the basis of experiential interaction with text and the past and will consist of the site-specific plays *Spelet om Heilag Olav* (*The Drama of Saint Olaf*) and *Ragnhilds Drøm*, and Vera Henriksen's trilogies *The Sigrid Trilogy* and *The Ship Without a Dragon*. These texts and plays represent a wider context of medievalism in Norway, but to best illustrate the relationships of the sample with the rest of post-war Norwegian medievalism a chronological overview of medievalist trends has been included.

Following the Second World War, Norwegian culture and society underwent a process of cleansing and rehabilitation from the influence of the occupation years and their cultural production. This rehabilitation was a reaction against the Norwegian fascist party *Nasjonal Samling*'s use of medieval sites like Stiklestad and Borre for their political rallies and monuments.[23] The fascist use of these two sites was part of a wider trend of using Viking and medieval history to further the party's racial and social ideals. The destruction of *Nasjonal Samling*'s monument at Stiklestad in 1945 and the demonstrations against Quisling's visit to the Norwegian coronation church Nidarosdomen in 1942 illustrate how *Nasjonal Samling*'s medievalism did not sit well with the majority population. Following the surrender of German forces in Norway in May 1945, the Norwegian resistance removed the traces of *Nasjonal Samling*'s monument at Stiklestad, and physically cleansed the site of its fascist past. In the wake of this process, the publication of medievalism in Norway fell to almost nothing.[24]

However, those works, such as Olav Gullvåg's book *Menneske og Helgen Olav Haraldsson (Olaf Haraldson: Man and Saint)* from 1946[25] and the completion of Oslo City Hall in 1947,[26] resemble the 1930s aesthetics and understanding of Olaf II and the Norwegian past, meaning the Second World War was not a definite moment of change in Norwegian culture and consciousness. This trend of limited production of medievalism changed with the 1954 premiere of Gullvåg and Paul Okkenhaug's *Spelet om Heilag Olav*, which was the first play of its type in Norway and started a trend of locally grounded saga plays known as *Spel*.[27] These *Spel*, or history plays, draw extensively on local history or myths, are often connected to a particular site and are immensely popular. According to Solveig Nessa, these plays first emerged in Norway with Gullvåg and Okkenhaug's play in 1954.[28] However, these plays in general, and Gullvåg and Okkenhaug's play in particular, are part of a longer tradition of folk theatre. In addition, *Spelet om Heilag Olav* draws extensively on Gullvåg's previous work on Olaf II such as his 1946 book and the 1930 cantata *Heimferd*,[29] and translates his ideas to a wider audience. The similarities between Gullvåg's three visions of Olaf are striking, and perpetuate a set of core ideas. First, the idea of Olaf as a national hero; second, Olaf's religious awakening the night before the battle of Stiklestad was the light that converted Norway; and third, that Olaf the saint was more important to Norway than Olaf the king.[30] All of these readings of Olaf emerge from Gullvåg's texts and reflect the wider historical understanding of Olaf popularized around the 900-year anniversary of his death in 1930: namely Olaf as a national saint and hero. The key to the success of this play, and the historical plays in general in Norway, might be due to two factors: the population's widespread historical knowledge and the relationship of the plays with an authoritative narrative of the national past.

Snorri's perceived 'authoritative' status served Gullvåg, as well as later authors, with a historical text they could use as basis for 'authoritative' narratives about the medieval past. It is, therefore, not surprising that many of the most famous and successful productions of late twentieth-century medievalism in Norway draw directly on this text, such as Henriksen's debut novel *The Silverhammer* in 1961, the first volume of the *Sigrid-trilogy* (1961–3).[31] With the publication of Henriksen's novels, medievalism and the medieval – and especially the Norse medieval – regained some traction in Norwegian cultural production, first and foremost as a comparison to and critique of the contemporary industrial society, but also as escapism from the dire post-war economic reality.

Following this revival, during the 1970s and 1980s, medievalism diversified and benefited from new critical approaches in historical thought and perspectives with regard to local and regional history and sought to recover the medieval past of the districts rather than a nationally based one. This meant that medievalist historical plays drew inspirations from local medieval legends and historical events as well as references from *Heimskringla*. This strain in Norwegian medievalism seems to have grown out of a growing local historical consciousness that underpins local identities. As a result of this, local medieval history is still a strong trend in Norwegian medievalism; among the many products of this period are Helgesen and Verne's play *Ragnhilds Drøm* and Rolf Losnegård's play about St Sunniva at Kinn.[32] The late 1980s also saw the production of the movie *Pathfinder* (1987),[33] which shows the pre-industrial Sami society under the threat of raids from the East. The historical foundation for this production is based in many local legends from Northern Norway about the man who led the raiding party to their death, while he himself survived by tricking them and defending his community. This film can be seen as an attempt by the Sami community to de-colonize their historical past as it seeks to depict and engage with their own indigenous historical experience. *Pathfinder* must be read in the wider context of the post-colonial rebellions of 1980s Norway and the fight for Sami representation and identity; in this context, the film follows the wider patterns of the 1970s and 1980s, by deconstructing the national narratives and its universality as historical truths for the people of Norway. Yet the national narrative still had its appeal, and in 1994 the Winter Olympics at Lillehammer and the EU referendum saw a revival of ethnic nationalism and historicism using symbols taken from the Middle Ages. But unlike the pre-1980s national focus, the 1994 nationalism acknowledged that Norway was a land of two peoples – the Norwegians and the Sami.[34]

This ethnic-national focus also spilled over in literary medievalism such as Henriksen's youth trilogy *Skipet uten drage* (*The Ship without a Dragon*) (1990–2). Although the book series engages with contemporary questions of identity, migration, the other, the self, religion and the gender balance of society, it also perpetuates the national myth that the original populations of the North Atlantic Islands were Norwegian. The books are set in the late ninth century and follow the migration of the family of Aud 'the Deepminded' from Caithness to Iceland via Orkney, Shetland and the Faeroe Islands and give an account of their experiences of the migration. The 1980s and 1990s also saw the rise of pockets of far-right nationalism and medievalism in Norway. These communities and their uses of the past will not be explored here, but they are worth a more detailed analysis in the future. Compared to this, Norwegian post-2000 medievalism is both tamer and more extreme; for one cannot ignore the medievalism of Anders Behring Breivik, which already has been examined by Andrew Elliott and Daniell Wollenberg.[35] Conversely, the 2000s saw an increase in popularity of historical productions that draw on the medieval past. One example is the opera production *Quirini* at the small island community of Røst. *Quirini* commemorates the visit of the Venetian merchant, Pietro Querini, to the island in the fifteenth century and his introduction to the Norwegian stockfish – an event which local merchants, in the Lofoten Islands, herald as the origins of profitably modern stockfish trade with Italy.[36] Within these trends, Gullvåg's work represents the early stages of Norwegian re-engagement with the medieval following the Nazi abuse of the past. Whereas the early works of Henriksen illustrate the broader appeal of the medieval in the 1960s and 1970s, these books, along with her later work, also reflect the ideas of second-wave feminism by seeking to reclaim women's history. Helgesen and Verne's works also represent a similar trend of reclaiming the past, but this time in the 1970s–2000s local and regional revival, which is intrinsically bound to the relationship between the local and the national. Among these samples, this study will explore how authenticity and notions of accuracy are presented and validated to the audience by the uses of landscape and gender norms.

Of all of these examples, Gullvåg and Henriksen's works can, on the basis of their popularity, be claimed to have been both the best received and the most influential and for this reason this chapter will focus on these works. As Gullvåg and Henriksen utilize gender and the landscape slightly differently, a closer examination of their works will highlight the variations in the use of landscape and gender in Norwegian medievalism.

## Authenticity and grounding of Gullvåg's work

In his play *Spelet om Heilag Olav*, Gullvåg focuses on presenting Olaf II Haraldsson and the transformation of the King in the last hours on earth, but at the core of the text, and the performances of the play, is the presentation of Olaf's masculinity. The actors who have been selected to play Olaf since the premier in 1954 have consistently been men whose charisma and acting skills construct a rugged hyper-masculine look trying to embody a sense of stereotypical 'Vikingness'. Actors such as Erik Hivju and Nils Ole Oftebro were exceptional in highlighting this in their presentations of Olaf.[37] This role presents Olaf as a hard man unable to overcome his differences with the farmers and aristocracy at the beginning of the play;[38] at the end of the play Olaf's stubbornness mellows due to the individuals and situations he encounters through the narrative. These encounters expose the role of Olaf to the nuanced reality of conversion and cultural syncretism in late Viking Age Norway. This awakening to the cultural syncretism of the age foreshadows in many ways Olaf's role as a cultural guardian and patron saint of the people, protecting them from their old pre-Christian beliefs and practices following his death.[39]

The role and development of Olaf in this play develop particularly through his interaction with Gudrun, one of the leading female characters; she is a nominal Christian youth who has been baptised but also instructed in pre-Christian folklore by her grandfather and her father's pagan servants. Her character relies extensively on her presentation as an escapist child trying to deal with her parents' problematic relationship and the infanticide of her brother. In her escapism, she finds solace in dance, play and song: activities all presented as distinctly feminine and opposite to Olaf's warrior masculinity when read through her body and movements. During the course of the play, Olaf becomes aware of Gudrun's play and recital of traditional lore, and questions this in a show of force and dominance critiquing Gudrun for not being a proper Christian. Gudrun's innocence along with her femininity contributes to the change in Olaf, mellowing his harshness and converting the Viking to a saint. By emphasizing the shift in Olaf, Gullvåg's Olaf engages directly with the literary presentations of Viking behaviour, as well as *Heimskringla* accounts of Olaf's personality. In doing so, he caters to the pre-conceptions of the audience and their understandings. By emphasizing the overt masculinity of Olaf, and the military behaviour of other male characters in the play, the play conforms to comfortable stereotypes of historical gender norms among the audience. At the same time of the fictive setting of the narrative, the farm Suul, reimagined on the slopes of the fields of Stiklestad, also contributes to a historical grounding for the play. By producing the play at Stiklestad, the play projects the events at the real local farm of Suul (sometimes spelled Sul) onto the site of Stiklestad, re-enforcing its narrative through the direct interaction with the site.

Yet what is this site and landscape the play is using? And why is it important? The short answer is that it is the site of the battle itself, while the more complicated version is the play draws on the pre-existing emotional narratives and energy connected with the site of Stiklestad through the invocation of the Olavian narrative and later the re-telling of the battle through a nationalist prism. Such an invocation is consciously and unconsciously done through the site's use as the backdrop of the play, while the battle in 1030 forms the culmination of the play narrative. This invocation of the site and its narrative is particularly visible in the play programmes issued each year, and the 2015 programme is no exception. In it, we find a statement which links the site, the history and its legacy, and invokes this in the mind of the audience:

> The state, the monarchy, and the church in Norway have their origin in the events at Stiklestad.[40]

As such, the site of Stiklestad as a site of memory is itself invoked as a particular validating factor for the events and interactions in the play, a validation not unlike that which we find in Helgesen and Verne's use of the archaeological landscape in Skjerstad as mentioned earlier. This use of masculinity and a particular site and landscape differs from the tactics employed by Henriksen in her work.

## Henriksen's attempts at accuracy and connectivity to experiences

In her writings, Henriksen develops her own literary expression and interaction with the past through the use of 'timeless' experiences of life and the natural landscape, the perspectives of gender and use of historical records. For like her predecessor Sigrid Undset, Henriksen masters the balancing act between fidelity to sources and creating engaging narratives set in the past. Henriksen painstakingly matches her narrative up to her sources. This is evident in the third book of both the *Sigrid-trilogy* and *Skipet uten drage*, where she includes a detailed analysis of the relationship between the sources and her novels.[41] By including this she helps readers to navigate the past, but also helps us understand the methodology behind her work, including the use of gender and landscape. Due to the attention to detail in her work, by including detailed accounts of the role of women in the conversion to Christianity and the experiences of growing up fast in a harsh and cruel world, Henriksen attempts to construct a medieval realism and a relatability of the human experience across eons. Henriksen's attempts to construct a relatable medieval world is a product of her mind, thus the relatability to the characters and experiences she writes are entirely dependent on her own mitigation of the historical sources and understanding of the human condition. In depicting the experiences of Sigrid, Aud and Aud's adolescent grandson, Olav Torsteinsson, Henriksen gives agency and voices to individuals whose stories are included in the

Norse literature, but whose voices, thoughts and feelings are lost to us. In her 1982 book *Sjebneveven: Om Sagaen kvinner* (*Fate: About the Saga Women*) Henriksen explores the rationale behind her medievalism and wider literary work, claiming that she seeks to explore how the women of the sagas would have experienced their own time and its relationship with our experiences of our own context.[42] Through giving agency to her characters, she uses gender and a gendered experience of life to bring realism and relatability into her texts, which grounds them in a feeling of authenticity. In doing so, Henriksen constructs an 'authentic' past by drawing on commonly held ideas and myths about gender, and as such she invokes the readers preconceptions about the age and projects her own stories into the readers' existing frame of reference. Thus, presenting her characters' fairly modern lives and concerns through the frame of the Viking Age gives her texts an 'authentic' feel. The idea that these historical experiences and behaviours are authentic is furthered by Henriksen through her extensive use of notes and sources, among which is Snorri's *Heimskringla*, which again lends her a veneer of historical accuracy through the popular acceptance of Snorri's status as an authority on early Norwegian history.

As her medievalism is designed to be read rather than watched, Henriksen uses landscape descriptions and place names to create a sense of place as a setting for her books. Furthermore, she also references ideas of a shared cultural and linguistic community in the North Atlantic, making her texts sit in a wider cultural narrative and thus relatable to a wider audience familiar with the myths of cultural kinship among the Norse settlements in the North Atlantic. While Gullvåg's landscape is an authenticating anchor for his narrative connecting the audience to the here and now, Henriksen's landscape contributes to the realism of her narratives by reminding the reader of the vastness of the Norse world, while also re-affirming the imagined community[43] between Norway and the Atlantic colonies and drawing on the emotional bond related to the Norwegian membership in this community to authenticate her narrative set in the medieval. Through the use of these emotional narratives and active agency based on experiences, she uses gender and landscape as tools to capture the readers in grounded and experientially relatable stories about human lives not dissimilar to those of the readers of Henriksen's own time.

## Imagining a relatable past in Helgesen and Verne

Similar to Henriksen's work, Helgesen and Verne extrapolate their narrative from a short reference found in Snorri's *Heimskringla* about the conversion of Salten in Hålogaland. In this reference, Snorri informs us that Olaf Tryggvason fought and captured the chieftain Raudr *inn rammi* (the Powerful) 'before giving him the choice of conversion or death'.[44] In the Saga, Raudr's choice of death and Olaf's execution of Raudr by snake stand out as one of the more memorable episodes of the Norwegian conversion, causing the subsequent conversion of Raudr's former home region Salten.[45] In his account Snorri uses specific landscapes and place names to validate his own narrative, including a reference to the maelstrom Godøystraumen, which blocks the entry to the Skjerstadfjord, heart of Salten and Raudr's home.[46] Building on Snorri's name-dropping, Helgesen and Verne link the references in Heimskringla with the archaeological landscape at the site of Godøystraumen and the fjord within to validate the narrative in their play. As with Stiklestad, the landscape of Northern Norway, and the Skjerstadfjord in particular, is integral to the local culture, self-understanding and identity, thus tying *Ragnhilds Drøm* to a specific site in the landscape anchors it in the shared historical experience and cultural consciousness of the North.[47] Quite practically the play, like Snorri, name-drops the locations of the events accounted in the Saga, while at the same time uses the actual landscape for the stage and backdrop of the performance. Not unlike Stiklestad, Helgesen and Verne's play uses a specific historical landscape as their stage and the play is performed among some boathouses near the traditionally important and powerful Skjerstad village, the site of the medieval parish church and home to a significant collection of Viking Age burial mounds. By staging the play here, the play uses the fjord and its role as a temporal anchor in the lives of the people of the fjord. The fjord and mounds make up for the lack of other recognizable medieval structures, such as Stave Churches, Castles or Manors in the district, and take on the role of the visual veneer transporting the audience into a moment where they are familiar with and open to the authenticity of the play and its content. Consequently, Bjerck's quote about the mounds can be read as setting the scene for this experience, and helps to prepare the audiences' mindset for the play by reminding them of the antiquity of their land and its people.[48]

Within this landscape, Helgesen and Verne's play contains a broad spectre of characters, including Raudr, his daughter Ragnhild and her husband, and the people of the farm and chiefdom. Like the landscape they live in, their behaviour and interaction reflect the historical experience of life in the North, which also helps to transport the audience back through the years and authenticate their experience of the play. For instance, Ragnhild, like many North-Norwegian women through the centuries, is a strong independent woman left in charge of the farm and its people while worrying about the future of her child and the likelihood of her husband and father returning from their expedition at sea. Her gender is, as Løkka suggested, defined by her relationship to her father, husband and child,[49] but also references the reality of pre-industrial gender roles in her management of the farm – in the temporary absence of her male kin during the opening scenes of the play. Ragnhild's gender is further elaborated through her style of dress and by her mother's life story; the audience are introduced to the story during the performance and are told that Ragnhild's mother was kidnapped from her family in Ireland to become wife to a chieftain in the North of Norway. In telling this story, Helgesen and Verne introduce the audience to the reality of human trafficking during the Viking Age and at the same time add to the image of the brutality of the pre-Christian period. At the same time, they also engage with the myth of the impact of the Irish church on the conversion of Norway through cultural contact. For as the play develops, Ragnhild starts to remember an Irish lullaby which she learned from her mother about the Virgin Mary and it helps her in her role as cultural mediator to guide her people to accept the new faith and the authority of King Olaf I Tryggvason. Through this journey of remembering, Ragnhild is given agency and a voice to impact the future of her people within the confines of the societal norms of a patriarchal society and within the perceived norms of the Viking Age.

## Conclusion – gender, visibility and narrative

As suggested earlier, the narratives of modern Norwegian medievalism are infused by images of and references to landscapes and sites of cultural significance. By including these features, the authors and producers push the audience to remember and connect with the cultural heritage of the Norwegian nation. Via these invocations of the sites and landscapes of memory, the consumers of medievalism are shown a past by the invisibility of historical markers and encounter the past in the mundanity of their day-to-day landscape. With the landscape being a historically important factor in the human experience of Norway, the use of the cultural landscape as an authenticator and foundation for 'accuracy' in medievalism furthers the Norwegian relationship with the landscape, but also re-emphasizes the idea of Norway as an ancient and natural cultural unit that has stood the test of time. These reiterations and uses of the landscape suggest that an underlying feature of these productions is the constant reaffirming of national unity and cohesion continuing the trends from the nineteenth century. The slight shift from a male-dominated corpus to a slightly more nuanced gender landscape implies that the concerns of national unity and provision of an authentic and immersive depiction of the deeds of past generations will continue to shape Norwegian medievalism, even if it makes space for new voices.

The depiction of Helgesen and Verne's Ragnhild shares key similarities with Aud, Sigrid and Gudrun, and with Olaf and Raudr in that, beyond their costumes, these characters are meant to give the audience an illusion of having stepped into a premodern patriarchal society where both men and women are tough, and the history is real. The increased visibility and agency of female characters within Norwegian medievalism has asserted the realism of the narrative, but also regurgitated the illusion of the limitations of political and economic agency for women in a premodern world. Giving medievalism more depth and experiential grounding for the audience, and thus making it more relatable, the narrative remains the 'accurate' actions of our father, but it is now seen and authenticated through the lives of our mothers.

## Notes

1. Hein Bjartman Bjerck, *Programme for Ragnhilds Drøm: Sagaspillet 2010* (Skjerstad, 2010); all translations are my own.
2. Ibid.
3. Karl Christian Alvestad, *Kings, Heroes and Ships: The Use of Historical Characters in Nineteenth – and Twentieth – Century Perceptions of the Early Medieval Scandinavian Past*, Unpublished PhD Thesis (Winchester: University of Winchester, 2016).
4. The gap in analysis for the period 1940–5 is due to a number of reasons; chief among them is the political complexity that impacts the corpus of sources in the period as this makes the analysis a coherent analysis difficult to complete and to include in the context of this chapter.
5. T. Pugh and A. J. Weisl, *Medievalisms: Making the Past in the Present* (Abingdon: Routledge, 2013), 110.

6 Ibid., 111.
7 Ibid.
8 Birger Sivertsen, 'Historisk materiale, myter, sagn', *spelhandboka.no* (2018) https://spelhandboka.no/historisk-materiale-myter-sagn-2/, accessed 1 October 2018.
9 Ibid.
10 Alvestad, *Kings, Heroes and Ships*, 70.
11 Karl Christian Alvestad, 'Neither Dane, Nor Swede, and Definitely Not Finn; Transmission of Narratives of Otherness in 19th- and Early 20th-Century Norwegian Historiography', *Revue d'Histoire Nordique* 23, no. 2 (2016): 105–20.
12 Kjell Olsen, *Identities, Ethnicities and Borderzones* (Stamsund: Orkana Akademisk, 2010), 14.
13 Ibid., 30.
14 *Veiviseren [The Pathfinder]*. Norway: Filmkameratene A/S, Norway Film, 1987.
15 *Kautokeino Opprøret [The Kautokeino Rebellion]*. Norway: Borealis Production, Filmlance International AB; Metronome Productions, Rubicon TV AS, 2008.
16 Miroslav Hroch, *European Nations: Explaining Their Formation* (London: Verso, 2015), 258–9; Ruby Koshar, *From Monuments to Traces: Artifacts of German Memory 1870-1990* (London: University of California Press, 2000), 68; Serhii Plokhy, *The Origins of the Slavic Nations: Premodern Identities in Russia, Ukraine, and Belarus* (Cambridge: Cambridge University Press, 2006), 333–7; Adrian Hastings, *The Construction of Nationhood: Ethnicity, Religion and Nationalism* (Cambridge: Cambridge University Press, 1997), 27.
17 J. Bately, 'Text and Translation: The Three Parts of the Known World and the Geography of Europe North of Danube According to Orosius' Historiae and Its Old English Version', in *Ohthere's Voyages*, ed. J. Bately and A. Englert (Roskilde: Viking Ship Museum, 2007), 46.
18 Inger Birkeland, *Kulturelle Hjørnesteiner: Theoretiske og Didaktiske Perspektiver på Klimaomstilling* (Oslo: Cappelen Damm Akademisk, 2014), 64; it is worth noting that this romantic view of the Norwegian landscape has its roots in the nineteenth century, not in the Middle Ages.
19 P. Nora, 'Between Memory and History: Les Lieux de Mémoire', *Representations* 26 (1989): 7–24.
20 Alvestad, 'Neither Dane', 105–20.
21 Nanna Løkka, 'Vikingtidskvinnen I ettertidens lys', in *Kvinner i Vikingtid*, ed. Nancy Coleman and Nanna Løkka (Oslo: Scandinavian Academic Press, 2014), 12.
22 Ibid., 13.
23 Tor Einar Fagerland and Trond Risto Nilssen, 'The Norwegian Fascist Monument at Stiklestad 1944-45', in *Historicizing the Uses of the Past,* ed. Helle Bjerg, Claudia Lenz and Erik Thorstensen (Bielefeld: Transcript-Verlag, 2011), 77; Bjørn Myhre, 'The Significanse of Borre', in *Heritage and Identity: Shaping the Nations of the North*, ed. J. M. Fladmark (Shaftsbury: Donhead, 2002), 22–3.
24 The completion of Oslo City Hall and Olav Gullvåg's 1946 book *Menneske og Helgen: Olav Haraldsson* are the exceptions here, but the overarching cultural trends of the nine years was functionality and efficiency in the reconstruction of Norway after the war.
25 Olav Gullvåg, *Menneske og Helgen Olav Haraldsson* (Oslo: Olaf Nordli, 1946).
26 Ulf Grønvold, 'Oslo Rådhus', in *Store Norske Leksikon på Nett*, https://snl.no/Oslo_r%C3%A5dhus, accessed 19 August 2018.

27 Maria Danielsen, 'Den eventyrlege historia' [The Enchanting History], in spelhandboka.no (2018) https://spelhandboka.no/den-eventyrlege-historia/, accessed 1 October 2018.
28 Solveig Nessa, *Utviklinga av historiske spel i Noreg* (Stavanger: University of Stavanger, 2009), 25.
29 Yngve Kvistad, *Stiklestad Spelet* (Oslo: Schibsted, 2003), 32.
30 Alvestad, *Kings, Heroes and Ships*, 156.
31 Karl C. Alvestad, 'Seeing Him for What He Was: Reimagining King Olaf II Haraldsson in Post-War Popular Culture', in *Premodern Rulers and Postmodern Viewers: Gender, Sex, and Power in Popular Culture*, ed. Janice North, Karl C. Alvestad and Elena Woodacre (London: Palgrave Macmillan, 2018), 286.
32 [Anon.] 'Om Oss' on *Kinnaspelet.no* (Online), http://kinnaspelet.no/omoss/index.html, accessed 1 October 2018.
33 *Veiviseren [The Pathfinder]*.
34 The historical erasure of the Finnish, Kven and other minority groups in this narrative is significant and suggests that Norway still has yet to engage with its colonial past.
35 Andrew Elliott, *Medievalism, Politics and Mass Media: Appropriating the Middle Ages in the Twenty-First Century* (Woodbridge: Boydell and Brewer, 2017), 132–54; Daniel Wollenberg, *Medieval Imagery in Today's Politics* (Leeds: ARC Humanities Press, 2018), 23–6.
36 Finn H. Eriksen, 'Røst og Pietro Querinis «bidrag» til tørrfiskeksporten', in *Fiskeribladet* (29. oktober 2017), https://fiskeribladet.no/nyheter/?artikkel=56300, accessed 1 October 2018.
37 Kvistad, *Stiklestad Spelet*, 190.
38 Olav Gullvåg, Paul Okkenhaug, *Mus.ms.a 5967 Paul Okkenhaug: «songar til Spelet om Heilag Olav»* (1954), 4.
39 L. R. Langslett and K. Ødeggård, *Olav den Hellige; Spor etter Helgenkongen* (Oslo: Oslo Press, 2011), 20.
40 Stiklestad Nasjonale Kultursenter, 'Historisk bakgrunn', in *Programme for Spelet om Heilag Olav* (Stiklestad: Stiklestad Nasjonale Kultursenter, 2015), 3.
41 Vera Henriksen, *Helgenkongen* (Oslo: Den norske bokklubben, 1962), 275; Vera Henriksen, *Skipet uten Drage: Vest i Havet* (Oslo: Aschehoug, 1992), 150.
42 Vera Henriksen, *Skjebneveven: om sagaens kvinner* (Oslo: Grøndahl, 1982), 7.
43 Benedict Anderson, *Imagined Communities* (London: Verso, 1991), 6.
44 Snorri Sturluson, *Heimskringla volume 1: The Beginnings to Olafr Tryggvason*, ed. and trans. A. Finlay, and A., Faulkes (London: Viking Society for Northern Research, 2011), 204.
45 Ibid., 203–5.
46 Ibid., 205.
47 Harald Rinde, *Nordlands Historie Volume 3: Etter 1900: Det Moderne Fylket* (Bergen: Fagbokforlaget, 2015), 14.
48 Bjerck, *Programme for Ragnhilds Drøm: Sagaspillet 2010*.
49 Løkka, 'Vikingtidskvinnen I ettertidens lys', 12.

# 2

# Race and historical authenticity

## *Kingdom Come: Deliverance*

### Helen Young

## Introduction

In February 2018, Czech developer Warhorse Studios released its long-awaited medievalist game *Kingdom Come: Deliverance*[1] to initial commercial success.[2] The game had been touted as 'realistic' by its makers since the very early stages of development in 2011,[3] including in a hugely successful Kickstarter campaign that raised about USD2.5 million in 2014. The Kickstarter campaign used the tagline 'Dungeons and no Dragons' to differentiate the games from fantasy roleplaying games (RPGs) such as Bethesda's *The Elder Scrolls*, Blizzard's *World of Warcraft*, Bioware's *Dragon* Age and Wizard of the Coast's *Dungeons and Dragons* franchises. Historical authenticity was credited with at least some of the game's early success,[4] but was also a charged issue in discussions of race and representation during the development process. A Tumblr-user, @medievalpoc, was targeted with a barrage of rape and death threats after suggesting that it might include diverse characters without being historically inaccurate during the 2014 Kickstarter campaign.[5] In 2015, Daniel Vávra, the lead designer on the game tweeted, 'would you please explain to me whats racist about telling the truth? There were no black people in medieval Bohemia. Period'.[6] He also insisted on the game's historical accuracy linking 'realism' to representation of race and gender in *Kingdom Come* in an interview with the alt-right outlet *Breitbart*.[7] The game and its makers were also praised in other venues for 'resisting' what Vávra had positioned as modern identity politics.[8] A number of reviewers who credited the games' success to its realism also pointed out that that inclusion of historical detail was selective and used to justify its ideological position.[9]

*Kingdom Come* is one of many medievalist popular culture texts about which claims to historical accuracy have been made to justify *not* representing people of colour; other games include CD Projekt RED's *Witcher 3: Wild Hunt*[10] and, more recently, Triternion's *Mordhau*.[11] Games and their makers have also been criticized on the same grounds for *including* characters of colour, for example, Bioware's *Dragon Age* franchise.[12] The discourse of historical authenticity is also deployed by those who argue *for* racial diversity in medievalist texts;[13] this was the case for @medivealpoc and others' comments about *Kingdom Come*. Claims about historical authenticity are made (with or without supporting evidence) in polar-opposite arguments about representing race; these are not limited to being about medievalist texts.[14] The question then is not 'why are the Middle Ages so strongly associated with racial whiteness?' but 'what connects ideas about historical authenticity and race?' In order to answer, this chapter now offers outlines of these core concepts, followed by a case study centred on *Kingdom Come* which explores what was said about the game during production and early release by its makers, audiences and in games media and the ways which that commentary generates a discourse of historical authenticity.

Race is a system of social categorization in that it is produced by collective belief, and because it structures relationships between people.[15] Kalpana Seshadri-Crooks argues that race is a semiotic system in which Whiteness is 'a master signifier (without a signified) that establishes a structure of relations, a signifying chain that through a process of inclusions and exclusions constitutes a pattern for organizing human difference'.[16] Without Whiteness at its centre, both the system and the raced subjectivities it produces collapse. 'Visual difference', Seshadri-Crooks argues, 'is critical to securing the power of race: 'the phenotype secures our belief in racial difference'.[17] Race literally appears to be real because physical features of the body (skin tone, hair, eye colour etc.) that have been assigned significance in a semiotic system are *seen* and thus seem to be empirically verifiable. The observable reality of signifying phenotypical features is (incorrectly) taken to verify the reality of the signified race. Visual representations of the past, such as historical film and videogames, are thus particularly powerful media sites for generation and perpetuation of racial subjectivities and of race as a semiotic social system. When phenotypical features (signifiers) are seen in historical games (and other visual media), they seem to attest to the existence of the signified – specific racial subjectivities – and the system of race itself as an ontological given. Constructing a text as 'historically authentic' reinforces this appearance of reality.

'Accuracy' and 'authenticity' are often used interchangeably in popular culture. It is axiomatic among scholars that historical fictions in any medium represent the past 'within the constraints of the chosen form and style';[18] representation is always selective. As the following case study shows, creators and audiences are quite willing to acknowledge this within certain parameters. Historical authenticity has little to do with verifiable historical fact even though it is predicated as a concept on existence of an objective and knowable historical truth. Contemporary scholarly approaches to historical authenticity are generally rooted in theories of reception. In his important work on medievalist film, Andrew B. R. Elliott draws on the ideas of Hans Robert Jauss to argue that 'to be authentic a film need not conform to historical reality (whatever this might have been) but only to what audiences think the period looked like'; those expectations are shaped by genre and habit, and can encompass both outright inventions and inaccuracies.[19] Historical authenticity, however, is not a quality of the text created by its producers through their aesthetic, formal and content choices more or less successfully depending on how well they have understood and met the expectations of their audience. Rather it is a discourse that circulates through processes of production and consumption to manage anachronisms and inventions and the constraints of form, genre and audiences' expectations, resulting in representation that is 'historical' in the sense that it has the character of History: it is socially and culturally constructed but also widely understood as objectively true. The discourse of historical authenticity manages what can and cannot be represented without drawing attention to the constructed nature of the text and thus disrupting truth-claims about both the past and the text.

Nickolas Haydock, writing of medievalist cinema, argues that claims to historical authenticity are made 'to lay the framework for the film's reality effects and to authorize it as a site of what Lacan calls "imaginary identifications" for a mass audience'.[20] Such an approach suggests that the textual Whiteness of the typical popular culture medievalism is a fantasy of racial purity which organizes the White identity of the (imagined ideal) spectator who recognizes a Self in it. Seshadri-Crooks, however, argues that ideological readings are based on an overly simplistic understanding of the Lacanian mirror stage and require race to be accepted as 'an *a priori* fact of human difference' with the result that there is no possibility of interrogating the underlying racial system.[21] Rather, the (at times violent) debates about race and representation in *Kingdom Come* and other texts like it are symptoms of what Seshadri-Crooks terms 'racial anxiety',[22] which is initiated by 'the subject's encounter with the historicity of Whiteness'.[23] The core challenge is not the suggestion that people of colour may have been present in medieval Bohemia but rather an imminent realization that race is a culturally and historically produced social category.[24] The threat of such a realization is the fragmentation not only of a particular White identity but of the entire system that produced raced subjectivities. Arguing that characters of colour should be included on the grounds of historical accuracy ultimately gives the same support to the social system of race as arguing that they should be excluded on the grounds of historical authenticity, because both work to suggest that racial subjectivities are ahistorical – essentially stable and consistent over time rather than contextually constructed.

## *Kingdom Come: Deliverance*

*Kingdom Come* is what Adam Chapman terms a 'realistic simulation', a category that refers to 'stylistic approach to representation rather than [...] historical content'.[25] Such games tend to take a 'reconstructionist' approach to historical epistemology which positions (and understands) itself as objective and untouched by ideology; claims to represent a single, true narrative; and masks its condition as a representation.[26] They historicize the represented world by making truth-claims about and through representation of the past. Discourses of historical authenticity are easily deployed around realistic simulations, although they are not limited to realist genres. The following paragraphs explore how key narrative, ludic and technical elements of *Kingdom Come* function in both the text and discussions of it to historicize the game world through a discourse of historical authenticity.

*Kingdom Come* is set in 1403 in a sixteen-square-kilometre rural part of Bohemia, then part of the Holy Roman Empire (now in the Western Czech Republic).[27] The action of the game takes place against the backdrop of an invasion by King Sigismund of Hungary, half-brother of the ruling King Wenceslaus the Fourth. The player's character is Henry, who believes he is the son of a blacksmith in the games' early stages, but is later revealed to be the bastard of a local lord, Sir Radzig Kobyla. The narrative is precipitated when a band of Sigismund's mercenaries raid Henry's home town, Skalitz. Henry escapes but sees both his parents murdered, and swears vengeance on their killer. Henry joins Radzig's retinue (although he is unaware of his parentage at the time), and although he is initially restricted to being a regular soldier because of his peasant background, through courage and by befriending and saving the lord's heir, he becomes Radzig's envoy. At the end of the game, the fate of the kingdom of Bohemia is still undecided; it closes with Henry being sent as part of a delegation with an offer to end the war.

A blacksmith's son becoming a knight is one of the anachronisms that backers – and the game developers – typically elide in their discussions of historical authenticity. This is fundamentally a modern neoliberal storyline. Henry is rewarded – able to advance socially – because he is useful to the ruling classes in their quests for power at both a local and national level, and not because he is one (illegitimately) of them. Although he is notionally motivated by revenge, that quest is unfulfilled at the end of the game, and the personally motived actions that he takes as a specific result of it end badly. A return to Skalitz motivated by a desire to see his parents properly buried, made against his lord's orders, sees the loss of the sword his father had been making, and he is almost killed. It is only through a governmental process of reshaping his peasant self into a fighter who is useful and has value in the feudal political system and war-torn context, underpinned by the mechanics of the game (discussed further below), that Henry and the player are rewarded: Henry by improving his social position, and the player through progress in the central narrative of the game.[28] Poor decisions (not understanding the logic of the game) and execution (insufficient expertise or knowledge) can lead to frustration for the player as they struggle to complete quests. Within the game itself, however, while Henry may die, he is always respawned at the last save point and thus effectively insulated – as the privileged are in reality – from the consequences of 'wrong' choices. This is a narrativized and gamified version of neoliberal discourse which, as Eduardo Bonilla-Silva argues, is closely linked to colour-blind racism through its erasing of the realities of unequal social power.[29] Henry achieves his goals in a neoliberal medievalist world. The form and content of the game insert a noticeably modern neoliberal subjectivity into a representation of the past which hides its constructedness by insisting on its own reality through discourses of historical authenticity.

The Kickstarter campaign positioned player choice and agency as a major drawcard: 'Enjoy a world of endless options. [. . .] Overcome objects in multiple ways whether by diplomatic skills or brute force.'[30] The design of the game functions to bolster the players' sense of agency. *Kingdom Come* is a first-person, non-linear roleplaying game (RPG) with an open-world environment. These design decisions maximize the realism of the game by masking the constructedness of the digitally represented world, as does the game play. Through the first-person positioning, the player has what Chapman terms 'spatial agency', that is, control (within the limits of the game world) over movement and field of vision.[31] The player's freedom to go anywhere in the sixteen-square-kilometre game world, and to act as they choose in pursuing quests, contributes to the sense of free agency for players. Agency, as in all games, is inherently constrained by the scope and rules of *Kingdom Come* (despite the emphasis in publicity on openness and choice).[32] In *Kingdom Come*, players can take Henry anywhere within the game world, but only by choosing to be in the right place at the right time can they progress the central quest.

The mechanics of the game are complex and require players to manage multiple systems including weapons, clothing, building skills and stamina, and managing food and rest. A range of weapons can be used in fight sequences, for example, and the combat system is designed so that each is effective in different situations; the player must decide. Clothing and weapons require repair, and food rots. *Kingdom Come* is designed so that player choices – including but not limited to weapons, whether clothing is repaired, conversations in dialogue cut scenes and interactions with non-player characters (NPCs) – have lasting effects within the game world. When Henry is clean and well-dressed, for example, NPCs with whom he interacts are more likely to treat him with respect. Learning to manage those systems, and doing so throughout the game, is a key element of the governmental formation of neoliberal subjectivity: the player must continually work at keeping their character valued and useful within the game world in ways that are not typically part of active play in RPGs. The game is designed to mimic the quotidian complexities of everyday life, but as is typical of realistic simulations, successful play depends on understanding the internal logic and systems of the game rather than those of the external world (either medieval or modern).[33] The game mechanics connect to the discourse of historical authenticity: one reviewer said it is 'designed to deliver an authentic medieval experience'. although the effect 'can be more than a little confusing'[34] even for an experienced player because of the complexity and number of the systems.

Primary sources like photographs are often used to construct realism within historical games set in the relatively recent past, and in their publicity material.[35] The fifteenth-century setting of *Kingdom Come* precludes this, so the game instead represents other physical remnants of the past, particularly buildings. Warhorse's PR Manager, Tobias Stolz-Swilling, claimed: 'all of the buildings really existed.'[36] Vávra commented that the setting was close to the studio in Prague and said:

> our team has had chance to visit those castles, churches, landscapes and deep forests. We are talking to locals and we take as many reference pictures as possible to use in bringing our world to life. [. . .] We actually want to show how 15th century life looked like.[37]

The comments collapse time, constructing the game world as a complete digital recreation of a past that has survived to the present only in part. They function to link the game directly to historical reality, not least by minimizing the role of the developers.[38] Warhorse is positioned as a faithful transmitter of past reality rather than creative agents making specific and deliberate choices about the digital representation of an imagined past. In-game representations of buildings that stood in the Skalitz area in 1403, such as the Sasau Monastery and Rovna Church, avoid anachronistic recreation of post-medieval additions and renovations that are found in other games which use architecture in similar ways.³⁹ This avoidance of visual anachronism might be considered an historical authenticity effect; the digital representations seem accurate because they do not include post-medieval features, but are still based on, at best, educated guesswork about what the buildings looked like in the early fifteenth century.

Warhorse's commitment to creating a realistic fifteenth-century Bohemian rural setting was presented as the key factor in technical decision-making: 'Being that KCD's environment was supposed to be a dense forest with lots of grass, CryEngine 3 was the only way to go. It handled our test scenes with a much higher framerate.'⁴⁰ Warhorse insisted throughout the production process that *Kingdom Come* would visually represent the material world of fifteenth-century Bohemia, intimately linking this to broader claims of historical authenticity. Vávra, for example, commented:

> When a swordsman plays our game, he should feel that the combat is as authentic as everything else – architecture, flora, the way people lived and spoke. It's like a time machine. A historian's dream come true [. . .] And we don't try to hide anything, we are showing it with all the dirt as it really was.⁴¹

This emphasis on graphics and the visual world reinforces the positioning of the game and its makers as transmitters of historical realities rather than imaginative, agential creators. The detailed digital visual landscape with its de-modernized medieval buildings functions to lend credence to Warhorse's claims to have represented past reality. This discourse of historical authenticity around what is seen in the game works to reify the digital representation of somatic markers of race, perpetuating its function as a semiotic system in which, as discussed earlier, visible signifiers are understood as evidence of the (arbitrarily and socially assigned) signified. That is, seeing 'race' represented in a game world that purports to visual historical authenticity makes it appear real.

Warhorse was, however, also willing to acknowledge that its commitment to faithful representation of the past was selective at times. In a late-2016 interview, Stolz-Swilling said: 'we had real sword fighters who came to the studio. [. . .] These professionals told us exactly how a fight would look in real life [. . .] this is not possible in a game, from a technical standpoint [. . .] we have to adjust the idea to make it playable.'⁴² This acknowledgement that the game sacrificed accuracy for playability was uncontroversial to the interviewer who wrote: 'Warhorse is still pretty confident with how legitimate the game's combat is.'⁴³ The deviation from detail functioned as a pivot to reinforce the claim to authenticity. The move can be understood through Elliott's work on historical cinema: 'deviations from the historical record when there is either a narrative necessity [. . .] or in which there is simply no historical record'.⁴⁴ In the case of gaming, the technical limitations of game systems and considerations of playability may be added to these.

The discussion boards of the Kickstarter campaign, where potential players who had backed the project financially interacted with each other and (less frequently) Warhorse employees, demonstrate that consumers are aware of the technical and practical limits of historical representations and see them as acceptable constraints in the space between strict (perceived) accuracy and historical authenticity. This comment exemplifies common themes:

> that's the whole dilemma. Whether to use actual authentic period language (medieval German/Czech/etc.), pseudo-'Shakespearean' English [. . .] or just straight-up modern languages. Each have their gameplay and marketing advantages and disadvantages, I guess.[45]

The discussion boards also highlight how broader ideological discourses shape historical authenticity. A thread asking backers what they did not want to see in the game included multiple comments arguing against racial and cultural diversity posted over the span of almost two years, for example:

> Please do not destroy it with mostly unnecessary political correctness. In the 15th century in Bohemia region there certainly was not some 'Babilon' with a multicultural society and equal opportunities for men and women! Middle age was not perfect, but it was as it was.[46]

The unsupported truth-claims about racial composition and gendered roles in medieval Bohemia resonate closely with statements from Warhorse employees throughout the game's production.

Warhorse employees were willing to abandon 'accuracy' when doing so met their needs, but were equally willing to fall back on it as a justification for other design and content decisions. In January 2018, just prior to the game's release, studio co-founder Martin Klíma said: 'after more than four years of intensive research, it can be stated that there is no proof that there were no dark-skinned people in Bohemia and vice versa.'[47] Vávra invoked historical accuracy to explain the racial composition of the game in a statement released alongside Klíma's, saying *Kingdom Come* does not

> limit itself to any ethnic group. In the course of history, based on our knowledge of historical events, there are, besides Czechs, Germans and Jewish residents, the largest grouping in the game, the Kumans (in German also Kipchak) a Turkic tribe from the Eurasian steppe.[48]

The Kuman (commonly spelled Cuman) are invading mercenaries hired by Sigismund to invade Bohemia in *Kingdom Come*. The linguistic descriptor 'Turkic' emphasizes that they are not Slavic people like the Czechs who mainly populate *Kingdom Come*; the resonance with 'Turkish' – a people strongly Othered in contemporary discourses of European identity – is notable. The Kuman are outsiders, foreign invaders who are driven away or killed in the game, thus preserving the cultural and racial purity of rural Bohemia. This type of plot device is typical of medievalist popular culture in which the presumed exclusive presence of White bodies means that all other bodies must be narratively explained.[49]

Arguments *for* including people of colour in popular culture representations of the European Middle Ages also typically invoke historical authenticity and detail to support their cause. In the case of *Kingdom Come*, a 2018 *Eurogamer* review quoted historian Sean Miller as saying:

> we know of African kings in Constantinople on pilgrimage to Spain; we know of black Moors in Spain; we know of extensive travel of Jews from the courts of Cordoba and Damascus; we also know of black people in large cities in Germany.[50]

The reviewer added: 'Czech cities Olomouc and Prague were on the famous Silk Road which facilitated the trade of goods all over the world. If you plot a line between them, it runs directly through the area recreated in *Kingdom Come*.'[51] In 2014, @medievalpoc had offered evidence based on fifteenth-century Bohemian art as well as scholarship to argue that the game could include racial and ethnic diversity – including but not limited to representing people of African origin.[52] Such details can temporarily disrupt fantasies of racial and cultural purity; the statements by Klíma and Vávra quoted earlier, however, demonstrate that those fantasies are relatively easily maintained by dismissing such evidence as, for example, inaccurate, poorly researched, politically motivated or too specific.

## Whiteness and the Middle Ages

Historical authenticity discourse places the digital world of the game within the past but outside history through its claims to represent minimally or un-mediated reality. Although it is deployed to rationalize white-centric representations of many places and times, I would argue that the discourse resonates particularly with medievalisms; the European Middle Ages have been understood since their inception as a 'simpler, more organic past', that is, a time of 'wholeness' un-constructed (or re-constructed) by civilized modernity.[53] As a result, in the racial medievalisms of White identity formations, the European Middle Ages hold out a (false) promise of White racial completeness and purity.[54] The Western 'cultural archive'[55] works to create belief in the European Middle Ages as a naturally and genuinely 'Whites-only' place and time; historical authenticity discourse orients texts to 'conform to custom and audience expectation'[56] – in medievalist texts this includes centring Whiteness.

The logic of race, and mastering significance of Whiteness within that logic, depends on the apparent ahistoricity of racial categorization, that is, on the belief that racial identity is fixed among individuals who share it in all places and times. Race must 'deny knowledge of its own historicity or risk surrendering [. . .] the possibility of wholeness and supremacy'.[57] Race refuses to acknowledge own historicity as a crucial aspect of refusing its own unreality; it can maintain social power only through 'international belief in race as real'.[58] For Whiteness (and the system of race constructed around it) to exist in the present, it must have existed in the past. To maintain its place as the master signifier, Whiteness must be simultaneously pan-historical (existing in all times), historical (have existed) and ahistorical (denying its own temporality and socially contextual nature). Even the suggestion that people of colour might be represented in a text that claims to be an historically accurate recreation of the European Middle

Ages, such as *Kingdom Come*, makes the historicity of race imminent. Representation of people of colour in medievalist texts in ways that disrupt historical authenticity discourse threatens not only fantasies of White purity but the entire social semiotic system of race. Their presence (and its possibility) makes visible the lack of signified behind the master signifier of Whiteness not only in iterations of race that are directly predicated on the supposed racial purity of the European Middle Ages but on all iterations. If pure Whiteness cannot be located there, it cannot be located anywhere and the fraudulence of its offer of wholeness to the subject is revealed.

## Notes

1. *Kingdom Come: Deliverance* (Deep Silver, 2018).
2. Sherif Saed, 'Kingdom Come Deliverance Has Sold 1 Million Copies', *VG24/7*, 22 February 2018. https://www.vg247.com/2018/02/22/kingdom-come-deliverance-has-sold-1-million-copies/; this early success was not sustained, see Shabana Arif, 'Kingdom Come: Deliverance's Player Base Has Dropped by 95% on Steam', *IGN India*, 22 February 2018. https://in.ign.com/kingdom-come-deliverance/122081/news/kingdom-come-deliverances-player-base-has-dropped-by-95-on-s.
3. Jim Rossignol, 'Czech Veterans Form New Studio, Warhorse', *Rock, Paper, Shotgun*, 26 July 2011. https://www.rockpapershotgun.com/2011/07/26/czech-veterans-form-new-studio-warhorse/.
4. Phil Iwaniuk, 'The Obsessive Historical Accuracy of Kingdom Come: Deliverance, and How It Makes for a Better RPG', *PCGamesN*, 2016. https://www.pcgamesn.com/kingdom-come-deliverance/kingdom-come-deliverance-historical-accuracy?amp; Nathan Grayson, 'Kingdom Come Owes Its Popularity to "Realism" and Conservative Politics', *Kotaku Australia*, 2018. https://www.kotaku.com.au/2018/03/kingdom-come-owes-its-popularity-torealism-and-conservative-politics/.
5. @medievalpoc, 'On Telling the Truth', *People of Colour in European Art History*, 2014. http://medievalpoc.tumblr.com/post/88796194073/on-telling-the-truth; @medievalpoc, 'Hi! I've Been Looking at a Kickstarter for a 'Realistic' Medieval-Era Game Called 'Kingdom Come: Deliverance' and Realized It Looked Rather . . . White', *People of Colour in European Art History*, 2014. http://medievalpoc.tumblr.com/post/75252294049/hi-ive-been-looking-at-a-kickstarter-for-a; Gavia Baker-Whitelaw, 'Is a Medieval Video Game Historically Accurate without People of Color?' *The Daily Dot*, 2014. http://www.dailydot.com/gaming/reddit-tumblr-medieval-video-game-poc/.
6. A similar statement was made on the Kickstarter page in 2014. Daniel Vávra, 'Tweet', *Twitter*, 2015. https://twitter.com/DanielVavra/status/569686445344079872.
7. Robert Shimshock, 'Developer Speaks Out Over Claim "Historical Accuracy" Pushes White Supremacy in Games', *Breitbart*, 2015. http://www.breitbart.com/big-hollywood/2015/07/28/developer-speaks-out-over-claim-historical-accuracy-pushes-white-supremacy-in-games/.
8. 'Kingdom Come: Deliverance – Historical Accuracy Isn't Whitewashing : Kingdomcome', *Reddit*, 2018. https://www.reddit.com/r/kingdomcome/comments/7zgt4f/kingdom_come_deliverance_historical_accuracy_isnt/; other examples are noted in Grayson, 'Kingdom Come Owes Its Popularity to "Realism" and Conservative Politics'.
9. Grayson, 'Kingdom Come Owes Its Popularity to "Realism" and Conservative Politics'; Robert Purchese, 'Kingdom Come: Deliverance Review - History Is a

Double-Edged Sword', *Eurogamer*, 20 February 2018, https://www.eurogamer.net/articles/2018-02-20-kingdom-come-deliverance-review; Alice Bell, 'The 5 Most Extremely Historically Accurate Things in Kingdom Come: Deliverance - VideoGamer.Com', *VideoGamer*, 2018. https://www.videogamer.com/features/the-5-most-extremely-historically-accurate-things-in-kingdom-come-deliverance.

10  *The Witcher 3: Wild Hunt* (CD Projekt, 2015); Tauriq Moosa, 'Colorblind: On The Witcher 3, Rust, and Gaming's Race Problem', *Polygon*, 6 March 2015. https://www.polygon.com/2015/6/3/8719389/colorblind-on-witcher-3-rust-and-gamings-race-problem.

11  *Mordhau* (Triternion, 2019); Douglas Dante, '"Mordhau" and the Fantasy of an All-White Middle Ages', *Vice*, 2019. https://www.vice.com/en_us/article/8xzpeg/mordhau-and-the-fantasy-of-an-all-white-middle-ages?__twitter_impression=true.

12  Helen Young, '"It's the Middle Ages, Yo!": Race, Neo/Medievalism, and the World of Dragon Age', *The Year's Work in Medievalism* 27 (2012). https://sites.google.com/site/theyearsworkinmedievalism/all-issues/27-2012.

13  Helen Young, *Race and Popular Fantasy Literature: Habits of Whiteness* (London and New York: Routledge, 2016), 71–6.

14  See, for example, 'Pharos: Doing Justice to the Classics', 2019. http://pages.vassar.edu/pharos/. The blog tracks examples of far-right appropriations of the Classical Greek and Roman past, including although not limited to in popular culture.

15  Eduardo Bonilla-Silva and Tukufu Zuberi, 'Toward a Definition of White Logic and White Methods', in *White Logic, White Methods: Racism and Methodology*, eds Eduardo Bonilla-Silva and Tukufu Zuberi (New York: Rowman & Littlefield, 2008), 7.

16  Kalpana Seshadri-Crooks, *Desiring Whiteness: A Lacanian Analysis of Race* (New York and London: Routledge, 2000), 3.

17  Ibid., 21.

18  Adam Chapman, *Digital Games as History: How Video Games Represent the Past and Offer Access to Historical Practice* (New York: Routledge, 2016), 63. See also Andrew J. Salvati and Jonathan M. Bullinger, 'Selective Authenticity and the Playable Past', in *Playing with the Past: Digital Games and the Simulation of History*, eds Matthew Wilhelm Kappell and Andrew B. R. Elliott (New York: Bloomsbury, 2013), 153–63.

19  Andrew B. R. Elliott, *Remaking the Middle Ages: The Methods of Cinema and History in Portraying the Medieval World* (Jefferson: McFarland, 2011), 215–16. The genre conventions of fantasy, for example, allow creators and fans to argue against inclusion of people of colour on the grounds of historical authenticity in the examples given earlier, even when those texts include magic, dragons and other supernatural elements typical of the genre.

20  Nickolas Haydock, *Movie Medievalism* (Jefferson: McFarland, 2008), 7.

21  Seshadri-Crooks, *Desiring Whiteness: A Lacanian Analysis of Race*, 31.

22  Ibid., 32.

23  Ibid., 21.

24  Ibid., 21.

25  Chapman, *Digital Games as History: How Video Games Represent the Past and Offer Access to Historical Practice*, 61.

26  Ibid., 66–8.

27  This is a much more specific setting than most medievalist games, which are commonly much more expansive. C. San Nicolas Romera, M. A. Nicolas Ojeda and J. Ros Velasco, 'Video Games Set in the Middle Ages: Time Spans, Plots, and Genres', *Games and Culture*, 2016, 18. https://doi.org/10.1177/1555412015627068.

28  Michel Foucault conceptualized governmentality as a particularly neoliberal mode of power. See, for example, Andrew Baerg, 'Governmentality, Neoliberalism, and the Digital Game', *Symploke* 17, no. 1–2 (2009): 115–27.
29  Bonilla-Silva and Zuberi, 'Toward a Definition of White Logic and White Methods', 1–27.
30  https://www.kingdomcomerpg.com/, accessed 8 August 2016.
31  Chapman, *Digital Games as History: How Video Games Represent the Past and Offer Access to Historical Practice*, 66.
32  Rowan Tulloch argues that agency and rules are not oppositional, but rather part of a 'constructive process' of play. Rowan Tulloch, 'The Construction of Play: Rules, Restrictions, and the Repressive Hypothesis', *Games and Culture* 9, no. 5 (2014): 348. https://doi.org/10.1177/1555412014542807.
33  Chapman, *Digital Games as History: How Video Games Represent the Past and Offer Access to Historical Practice*, 62–3.
34  James Billcliffe, 'Kingdom Come Deliverance Guide', *VG24/7*, 2018. https://www.vg247.com/2018/03/01/kingdom-come-deliverance-guide-tips-walkthrough/.
35  Chapman, *Digital Games as History: How Video Games Represent the Past and Offer Access to Historical Practice*, 67.
36  Iwaniuk, 'The Obsessive Historical Accuracy of Kingdom Come: Deliverance, and How It Makes for a Better RPG.'
37  Adam Cook, 'Kingdom Come: Deliverance Beta – Dan Vávra Interview', *Red Bull*, 2016. https://www.redbull.com/au-en/kingdom-come-deliverance-dan-vavra-interview.
38  Chapman, *Digital Games as History: How Video Games Represent the Past and Offer Access to Historical Practice*, 67, emphasizes the role of primary sources and minimization of the mediating role of the developer in realistic simulations.
39  Douglas M. Dow, 'Historical Veneers: Anachronism, Simulation, and Art History in Assassin's Creed II', in *Playing with the Past: Digital Games and the Simulation of History*, eds Matthew Wilhelm Kappell and Andrew B. R. Elliott (New York: Bloomsbury, 2013), 215–32.
40  Poorna Shankar, 'Kingdom Come: Deliverance – The Tech Behind Henry's Quest', *amespace.com*, 2018. https://www.gamespace.com/featured/kingdom-come-deliverance-the-tech-behind-henrys-quest/.
41  Shimshock, 'Developer Speaks Out Over Claim "Historical Accuracy" Pushes White Supremacy in Games'.
42  Dom Peppiatt, 'Kingdom Come: Deliverance Is So Historically Accurate Historians Are Consulting the Dev Team', *XboxAchievements.com*, 2016. https://www.xboxachievements.com/news/news-25767-Kingdom-Come--Deliverance-Is-So-Historically-Accurate-Historians-Are-Consulting-The-Dev-Team.html.
43  Ibid.
44  Elliott, *Remaking the Middle Ages: The Methods of Cinema and History in Portraying the Medieval World*, 215–16.
45  Mike, 20 February 2014, in Various, 'Kingdom Come: Deliverance', *Kickstarter*, 2018. https://www.kickstarter.com/projects/1294225970/kingdom-come-deliverance/comments.
46  Various, 'What Do You Want NOT to See in Kingdome Come: Deliverance?', *Kingdom Come: Deliverance Community Forum*, 2014. http://forum.kingdomcomerpg.com/t/what-do-you-want-not-to-see-in-kingdome-come-deliverance/2106/240.
47  Martin Klíma and Daniel Vávra, 'Statement by Daniel Vávra and Martin Klíma Regarding Racism/Nazism Accusations (Gamestar.De)', *ResetEra*, 2018. https://www

.resetera.com/threads/statement-by-daniel-vávra-and-martin-klíma-regarding-raci sm-nazism-accusations-gamestar-de.17259/.
48 Ibid.
49 For explorations of narrative justifications for the presence of non-white bodies in medievalist representations of Europe and its fantasy analogues, see Kathryn Wymer, 'A Quest for the Black Knight: Casting People of Color in Arthurian Film and Television', *The Year's Work in Medievalism* 27 (2012); Stephanie Downes and Helen Young, 'The Maiden Fair: Nineteenth-Century Medievalist Art and the Gendered Aesthetics of Whiteness in HBO's Game of Thrones', *Postmedieval* (2019): 219–35.
50 Purchese, 'Kingdom Come: Deliverance Review - History Is a Double-Edged Sword'.
51 Ibid.
52 @medievalpoc, 'Hi! I've Been Looking at a Kickstarter for a "Realistic" Medieval-Era Game Called "Kingdom Come: Deliverance" and Realized It Looked Rather… White.'
53 Laurie A. Finke and Martin B. Shichtman, 'Inner-City Chivalry in Gil Junger's Black Knight: A South Central Yankee in King Leo's Court', in *Race, Class, and Gender in "Medieval" Cinema*, eds Lynn Ramey and Tison Pugh (Basingstoke: Palgrave Macmillan, 2007), 105.
54 See, for example, Amy Kaufman, 'Purity', in *Medievalism: Key Critical Terms*, eds Elizabeth Emery and Richard Utz (Cambridge: D. S. Brewer, 2014), 199–206.
55 Tuhiwai Smith, *Decolonizing Methodologies: Research and Indigenous Peoples*, 2nd edn (London and New York: Zed Books, 2012), 95.
56 Elliott, *Remaking the Middle Ages: The Methods of Cinema and History in Portraying the Medieval World*, 216.
57 Seshadri-Crooks, *Desiring Whiteness: A Lacanian Analysis of Race*, 8.
58 Bonilla-Silva and Zuberi, 'Toward a Definition of White Logic and White Methods', 7.

# Part II

# Exploring authenticity

# 3

# 'Contrary to common sense'

## The impact of the depiction of William Wallace's longsword[1]

Laura S. Harrison

On the 28th of January 1912, G. Baldwin Brown of the University of Edinburgh wrote to the newspaper *The Scotsman* in support of the two-handed longsword that was to be depicted on the proposed statue of Sir William Wallace at Edinburgh Castle.[2] Brown argued that 'the sword is here as a symbol, not an effort at prosaic historical verity'.[3] With this, Brown summarized the argument surrounding the ongoing depiction of Wallace with a longsword: despite a lack of evidence for Wallace having such a sword, he is almost exclusively portrayed with one. This chapter will consider depictions of Wallace with a longsword in order to consider where this legend may have come from, why it continues, and what affect this has on the overall Wallace tale, particularly in terms of his depiction as an idealized medieval masculine hero. It will also explore why the sword is considered to be authentic as Wallace's weapon, despite widespread knowledge of its inaccuracy.

Wallace has become a common topic of commemoration in Scotland, reflecting the near-mythic status he achieved following his rebellion and eventual execution during the first Scottish War of Independence (1296–1328). The nineteenth and twentieth centuries see the rise of modern nationalism in Scotland, which partially involved the reframing of Scottish history to reflect Scotland as an entity that was historically separate from England. Certain periods and characters from history therefore became touchstones for Scottish nationalism, and Wallace's failed rebellion during the medieval Wars of Independence was reframed with him in a martyr role fighting for Scottish independence. Though the history of the Wars of Independence is, inevitably, considerably more complicated, Wallace as a martyr for the Scottish cause has become the common narrative. The focus of this chapter will be on depictions of Wallace since 1800, which was the most popular period of commemoration for the medieval hero. In particular, the focus will be on showing the prevalence of his portrayal with a longsword. Several scholars have shown that it is not feasible for Wallace to have possessed a longsword during his lifetime, particularly because two-handed longswords did not appear in Scotland until the late fifteenth century, and the first definite use of them in a Scottish army was at the battle of Flodden in 1513, more than two hundred years after Wallace's death.[4] This has been the extent to which scholars have considered depictions of Wallace with a longsword, to indicate that it is inherently anachronistic. The goal of this chapter, then, is to go beyond this to illustrate the power of these ongoing depictions on the popular memory of Wallace.

It is in this dichotomy – that Wallace is often portrayed with a longsword despite the reality that he likely never even encountered one – that the difference between accuracy and authenticity can be seen. The question of accuracy versus authenticity has been common within the field of medievalism in terms of film, gaming and other forms of modern media, but it is less common in studies specifically on commemorations of medieval figures and events.[5] One benefit of making a distinction between accuracy and authenticity is that it leaves room for the role of myth in commemoration. 'Myth-busting', as Stephanie Trigg has pointed out, is 'an easy temptation for historians'.[6] However, when looking at commemorations, what people believe happened in the past is often more pertinent than what actually occurred. Whatever transpired in the Middle Ages, the fact that people believe certain stories makes those stories real for purposes of commemoration. Though something may not be technically 'accurate' in a historic sense, if it feels authentic then it can swiftly become part of the historic landscape. Raphael Samuel and Paul Thompson have argued that historians should not discount the role of myths, saying 'persistent blindness to myth undeniably robs us of much of our power to understand and interpret the past'.[7] To study how people interact with the past, one has to embrace the role of myth.

There have been a number of studies that have specifically considered the myth of Wallace's longsword. David Caldwell and Magnus Magnusson have both examined the veracity of the 'Wallace Sword' on display since the late nineteenth century at the National Wallace Monument. The history of this sword, as compiled by Charles Rogers in the late nineteenth century, is that following Wallace's capture by English forces the sword was taken to Dumbarton, Scotland, where it was kept for 600 years until it was given to the National Wallace Monument by the commander of the garrison at Dumbarton in the mid-nineteenth century.[8] Both Caldwell and Magnusson, however, have expressed doubts about this account. The sword only appears twice in the written record at Dumbarton, in 1505 and 1825, and there is uncertainty that these entries refer to the same sword.[9] Work done on the sword has also shown it is a compilation of at least four swords. Three of these date from later than Wallace, but one of these may have come from the approximate time of the Wars of Independence. The best that can be said, then, is that this sword is perhaps the 'ghost' of Wallace's sword, with the oldest part having potentially belonged to Wallace, though it is highly unlikely that will or could ever be proven.[10] As Caldwell has suggested, 'no serious scholar has in recent times been inclined to give the Wallace Sword any credence as the hero's own.'[11] No scholar has gone further in considering the sword than Caldwell and Magnusson, and they themselves have not examined the depictions contained in this chapter beyond the Wallace Sword itself. Though the realization that the Wallace Sword, both in theory and practice, is historically inaccurate is important, not going beyond that minimizes the lengths to which Wallace has been shown with the sword. As Andrew Elliott and Matthew

Kapell have argued, 'it is less interesting to note where and whether a given product deviates from the historical record, but rather for what reason it does so and what effect this might have.'[12] This chapter, then, will address the reason and effect of this deviation.

Ultimately, this chapter will consider the impact the depictions of Wallace with a longsword have on his legacy and commemorations. The first section will briefly outline the potential origin of this myth, before the second section examines examples of the ways in which Wallace is shown with a longsword, in order to show the scale to which this occurs. These examples are a representative sample of the types of commemorations that show Wallace with a longsword, including monuments, art, texts, stained glass, films and public events. Though the time period of this study is from 1800 to the present, it is noteworthy that there is a significant lack of examples from the middle of the twentieth century. The Second World War marked a temporary departure from the trend of using the medieval past to rationalize events in the present.[13] Following the First World War, there was a lot of effort to understand the conflict as part of a series of large-scale conflicts that occurred through history, including in the Middle Ages.[14] The Second World War disrupted this theory, as it occurred so soon after the First World War, and interest in the medieval past generally decreased for several decades. It may also have been that the medieval history of Scotland seemed less relevant in light of the recent near-global conflict. A crucial change in this level of interest, particularly in terms of the Wars of Independence, was the release of the film *Braveheart* in 1995. Finally, the third section will then consider the ways in which these depictions influence how Wallace is remembered and memorialized in Scotland, in order to show how authenticity can become accuracy in commemorations. In particular, how it reinforces Wallace as an ideal of medieval military masculinity.

## Origins of the Myth

The first question in considering the impact of Wallace's longsword is where this myth began. Many point to the fifteenth-century minstrel Blind Hary's poem *Wallace*, one of the best primary sources available for the life of Wallace, though it was written more than a century following his death. The text makes several references to Wallace's sword, including describing 'his good sword, that heavy was, and long.'[15] However, Hary always describes Wallace using the sword one-handed, such as, 'except a sword . . . which he took in his hand.'[16] Hary's suggestion that Wallace's sword was 'heavy and long' could still have been the beginnings of this myth, however, as it is possible the heavy/long sword became a two-handed longsword once these were introduced in Scotland. Another potential source for the myth of Wallace's longsword is the influence of the trope of the Highland warrior in Scotland. Depictions of Wallace, as well as another hero from the Wars of Independence King Robert I (Robert the Bruce), have often been used to draw a line between medieval military heroes and the idea of a historic Scottish military prowess. In addition, two-handed swords, most notably the claymore, are often attached to the image of the ideal Highland warrior. Perhaps to best frame Wallace as this idealized warrior, he needed to be shown with certain types of weapons.

Yet another origin for this myth could be the significant number of two-handed swords that belonged to important families within Scotland in this period. For example, at the laying of the foundation stone at the National Wallace Monument in 1861, there were six swords in attendance that were thought to date to the time of the Wars of Independence. These included the aforementioned 'Wallace Sword' that now resides in the monument itself; two swords said to be used by Sir John de Graeme, who fought alongside Wallace; a sword used in a battle during the Wars of Independence; a sword that apparently belonged to Robert the Bruce, which is still held by the Elgin family, descendants of Bruce; and a sword belonging to James Douglas, who fought with Bruce.[17] The accuracy of all of these swords is now questioned by scholars, as they are all much larger than swords thought to be used during the period. As the Wars of Independence were one of the more popular historical periods during this time, perhaps there was a natural inclination to attempt to link these swords to Wallace and Bruce, rather than recognizing them as being from a later period.

Caldwell points to this wider popularity of historical relics in the nineteenth century as the origin of the 'Wallace Sword' myth, suggesting that the National Wallace Monument 'clearly needed a relic of the nation's favourite hero to heighten the feeling of awe and reverence amongst visitors'.[18] Since the weapon now known as the Wallace Sword had a potential connection, it is clear this history was prioritized in order to help advertise the monument itself. In the nineteenth century, there were many more objects that were thought to date from this period than there are today. Teresa Barnett has suggested that while relics often only represent disparate random moments in history, 'collectively they articulated a coherent historical vision'.[19] The Wallace Sword helped people feel connected to wider Scottish history. A clear comparison to these historical relics is saints' relics. Objects associated with saints were cherished because they are a potential source of sacred power, rather than as historical objects.[20] However, both types of relics are similar in that they are seen as allowing for a direct connection between the past and the present.

## Depictions of the longsword

Regardless of how the myth began, by the beginning of the nineteenth century, Wallace was almost exclusively shown with a longsword. One of the earliest examples of Wallace with the longsword is a statue erected by David Steuart Erskine, the eleventh earl of Buchan, on his lands in Dryburgh in the Scottish borders (Figure 3.1). This 6.6-metre statue was built in 1814 and features possibly the largest of all Wallace's swords. Monuments and statues are by far the richest examples in terms of the types of commemorations that include Wallace with a longsword, and he is also shown with one on at least four other statues in Scotland. One such example is a statue of Wallace erected in Aberdeen in 1888. The design was decided through public competition, for which twenty designs were submitted from both within the UK and internationally.[21] The committee released a letter of support for the chosen

**Figure 3.1** Statue of William Wallace holding the longsword with the point resting on the ground in Dryburgh, Berwickshire.

design, stating, 'the statue is 16ft. in height, being the largest and most important figure yet erected in Scotland'.[22]

Another example is the aforementioned statues of Wallace and Bruce that sit at the entrance to Edinburgh Castle (Figures 3.2 and 3.3). During the debates surrounding the form and placement of these statues, Stanley Cursitor, a member of the committee responsible for the statues, wrote to *The Scotsman*, 'Wallace should not have a sword unknown in Scotland till 150 years after his death. It appears the deliberate perpetuation of a mistake is contrary to common sense.'[23] The Wallace statue at Edinburgh Castle is displayed with one of the shortest swords of any of the examples, so Cursitor appears to have succeed with his concerns. That being said, Wallace's sword is still larger than Bruce's, which reinforces the idea that Wallace had a larger sword than was standard at the time. As will be seen in subsequent examples, this is a relatively common practice when both Wallace and Bruce are portrayed together with swords – Wallace's tends to be larger than Bruce's.

**Figures 3.2** Statue of William Wallace holding a longsword at entrance to Edinburgh Castle.

Though statues of Wallace use quite literal representations of the longsword, it can also be depicted on monuments in a more abstract manner. The Wallace Memorial (Figure 3.4) was built in 1912 in Elderslie in the west of Scotland, which is Wallace's disputed birthplace. The design features a six-sided pedestal and a central column, which is entwined with a garland that is supposed to symbolize Wallace's sword.[24] Therefore, even when the longsword is not shown explicitly, it still features in the design process as a symbol that should be associated with Wallace.

The longsword also appears in other decorative acts of commemoration. Stained glass windows became popular in Scotland following the Disruption of the Kirk in 1843, when new churches were being built that incorporated stained glass into the design.[25] James Ballantine & Sons were asked to create four windows to be installed in the National Wallace Monument in 1885.[26] They are located on the second floor, in the Hall of Heroes. The Hall features sixteen busts of notable Scots, including Bruce. These windows feature Wallace, Bruce and two medieval warriors – a spearman

**Figure 3.3** Statue of Robert the Bruce wearing a shorter sword in his belt at entrance to Edinburgh Castle.

and an archer. A guide from 1909 suggests the windows 'exhibit carefully studied representations of the clothing and arms of the Scottish fighting men at the time of the War of Independence'.[27] In the window dedicated to Wallace, the focal point is the outsized longsword he carries. This is particularly fitting as the Hall of Heroes and is also where the 'Wallace Sword' is kept. Wallace is shown in full armour, including a helmet and shield. He also carries a horn with him. The background is simple, and he is depicted standing on a small grassy hill.

Wallace is also shown with the longsword twice in the Scottish National Portrait Gallery, the red sandstone Gothic building located in New Town in Edinburgh was built between 1885 and 1890. The funder and the architect for the project both envisaged that the building would be a 'tribute to Scotland's heroes'.[28] This focus on celebrating Scotland's history and heroes is indeed clear throughout the exterior and interior of the building. The exterior of the building is decorated with statues of figures from Scottish history. Wallace appears as a larger-than-life figure flanking the main entrance doors

**Figure 3.4** Memorial to Wallace in Elderslie, his disputed birthplace. The garland that circles the central column symbolizes his sword.

(Figure 3.5). He is pictured wearing chainmail and holding the longsword. The theme of celebrating Scotland's heroes continues inside the gallery. The entrance hall is heavily decorated with murals, which were the responsibility of William Brassey Hole.[29] Wallace is included in the processional frieze, which features 155 figures from Scottish history (Figure 3.6). The frieze has perhaps been most accurately described as 'a confection of didacticism, antiquarian enthusiasm and a little artistic license'.[30] Wallace is one of ten figures from the Wars of Independence depicted among these 155 figures from Scottish history. The weaponry included alludes to legends about the figures – Wallace is in possession of a longsword and Bruce has an axe, referencing the story of him killing Henry de Bohun with one stroke of an axe at the beginning of the Battle of Bannockburn. Bruce is also shown with a sword, though it is significantly smaller than Wallace's.

There are also specific instances where the longsword is mentioned in texts. In the 1825 *Popular Ballads and* Songs, there is a song called 'The Dirge of Wallace', which contains the line 'For his lance was not shiver'd on helmet or shield – And the sword

**Figure 3.5** Statue of William Wallace holding a longsword at entrance to the Scottish National Portrait Gallery, Edinburgh.

that seem'd fit for Archangel to wield, Was light in his terrible hand!'.[31] This suggests his sword was much larger than a standard sword but he was able to wield it, again likely alluding to his supposed height. Another example is the 1909 tourist book *Guide to the National Wallace Monument*, where William Middleton suggested the Wallace Sword used to be even larger, but that the point was broken off when it was sent to London for repair in 1825 and thus had to be shortened.[32] Middleton did acknowledge that there was some doubt about the accuracy of the sword, but suggested these concerns were 'without sufficient reason'.[33]

More recently, the myth of the sword has been propagated by the 1995 film *Braveheart*. In the film, the character of Wallace carries a 1.4-metre sword, and it also featured prominently in the official poster for the film. On a website that sells a replica of the sword, the inaccuracies of its use were justified by saying, 'like the movie itself, it may not be historical – but it is inspired. It may not have been carried by heroes in the past, but it is representative of the swords they would have carried – an idealized weapon for an idolized character in film history.'[34] Perhaps the best example of how associated the sword has become with Wallace comes from the slogan for the 700th

**Figure 3.6** Processional frieze in Scottish National Portrait Gallery featuring Wallace (centre-left) holding a long gold and red sword and Bruce (left) carrying an axe with a smaller sword in his belt, Edinburgh.

anniversary celebrations of the Battle of Stirling Bridge in 1997, 'Big man, Big sword, Big FUN'.[35] This is clearly alluding to the popular idea that Wallace was much taller than the average man, which will be discussed below.

What is perhaps most astonishing is that in many of these examples people acknowledge the inaccuracies of portraying Wallace with a longsword, though that did not stop these depictions. This issue was particularly clear during the Glasgow International Exhibition in 1888 which brought together a large number of relics from the Scottish historical past, though there were no relics on display that were associated with Wallace. A newspaper article from August 1888 addressed this, saying, 'there is not in the Bishop's Castle a single relic associated with the name of Wallace, but that may be explained by the circumstance that it is doubtful whether any genuine personal memorial of that great chief really exists.'[36] The article went on to discuss the existence of the Wallace Sword in the National Wallace Monument, explaining why it was not included, 'but we fear the evidence which favours the claim would not be accepted by the modern investigator'.[37] This article reveals that the authenticity of the relics in the exhibition was important to the public and it is clear there was some level of curation, as objects like the Wallace Sword were not admitted. That being said, there were objects included that were clear anachronisms, such as other two-handed swords apparently from the Wars of Independence. The same article reveals the important distinction between accuracy and authenticity,

> With these relics certificates of authenticity are really a matter of secondary importance. There they are, objects which have been cherished with religious care for centuries. . . . Around them have clustered many traditions, and these traditions have so penetrated national life that they have attained the consistency and virtue of truth. It matters little now although we may be told by high authority that these things are not what they purport to be; they are sanctioned with the faith of centuries, their traditions would cling to them in spite of the clearest demonstration, and they will remain in all times the most cherished monuments of the great men with whose names they have so long and so intimately been associated.[38]

This author is arguing a point that historians of commemoration today still argue – that though objects may be historically inaccurate, they can gain authenticity over time.

Looking at depictions of Wallace in this period as a whole, despite the known inaccuracies he is shown with a longsword far more often than not. I gathered a collection of fifty depictions of Wallace for my doctoral thesis, representing the time period from 1800 to 1939.[39] Of these, 75 per cent of the depictions show him with a longsword. This illustrates the sheer scale of these depictions. The 25 per cent that do not depict him with one are largely text-based sources, which is significant as it is easier to identify Wallace by name in texts, rather than relying on iconography to reveal his identity. This is the first way the image of Wallace's longsword impacts his legacy, which will be the focus for the remainder of this chapter.

## Impact of the longsword

The inclusion of a longsword with depictions of Wallace is important because it helps to identify who he is. In general, symbols are particularly useful when commemorating historical figures whose appearance was not captured in contemporary paintings. These symbols indicate identity when one's physical appearance cannot. Therefore, the longsword is a clear indicator of Wallace's identity, and is one of the key symbols through which he can be identified. To give a relevant comparison, Bruce is nearly always shown with a crown, especially when he is pictured alongside Wallace. This helps differentiate each man from the other. This also reveals why Wallace's sword is often longer than Bruce's when they are shown together – it helps to reveal his identity. For example, in the aforementioned processional frieze at the Scottish National Portrait Gallery in Edinburgh both Wallace and Bruce are shown with swords, though Wallace's is significantly longer than Bruce's (Figure 3.6).

This also reveals why some types of commemoration show Wallace with a longsword more than others. In physical commemorations such as monuments and stained glass windows, there is a nearly equal spread of times he is shown with a longsword versus the times when he is not. In texts, however, it is much more rare for the longsword to be mentioned, since an author can identify Wallace, whereas with other forms of commemoration there needs to be signs and symbols to reveal this information to the audience. Again, this reveals the role of the longsword as an indicator of Wallace's identity.

The second way in which depictions of Wallace with the longsword impacts his legacy is that it helps to reinforce other ideas about him. Previously, I mentioned that Wallace is often described as being of above-average height. Caldwell begins his chapter on the history of the Wallace Sword by saying, 'big men have big swords. None comes any bigger for the Scots than William Wallace.'[40] In terms of historical figures, it is true that no one comes bigger in terms of historical figures of Scotland than Wallace. He has dominated interest in the Scottish medieval past for much of the period since 1800. However, the statement also alludes to this idea that Wallace was very tall. The sword helps reinforce this. The information panel beside the Wallace Sword in the National Wallace Monument says, 'it is reasonable to assume that, in order to wield a sword of this size, Wallace would have had to be of considerable stature – at least six foot six inches in height.'[41] *Braveheart* even addressed the fact that Mel Gibson, who played Wallace, is of average height. There is a scene in the film where a Scottish solider points out Wallace to another man, who says 'can't be, not tall enough.'[42] The character of Wallace also references this himself, after a solider says, 'William Wallace is seven feet tall!' he replies, 'Yes, I've heard.'[43]

In terms of historical veracity for Wallace's height, it is difficult to determine. Hary's *Wallace* and the fifteenth-century *Scotichronicon* both mention that he was taller than the average man, 'he was a tall man with the body of a giant, cheerful in appearance with agreeable features, broad-shouldered and big-boned.'[44] However, being tall is also a common trait for a medieval heroes. Gerald of Wales recounted how King Arthur's bones were apparently recognized in the Middle Ages because of their sheer size.[45] From Wallace's own period Edward I, also known as Edward Longshanks, was apparently very tall. Edward (1330–76), the so-called Black Prince, was also thought to have been taller than average, or at least is portrayed as such on his funeral effigy and a surviving lead badge, ensuring that this would be the enduring memory of him.[46] Even Bruce is often described as being of above-average height, and after the discovery of his bones in 1818 it was estimated he had been about six feet tall, though today that has been changed at 5'6" to 5'9".[47] The longsword may be a marker for apparent height, as Bruce is also displayed with a longsword in a number of occasions, though only about 17 per cent of the time, as opposed to Wallace's 75 per cent. Clearly, one of several prerequisites for being a medieval hero is height, and every effort has been made to prove that Wallace fits that criterion. Wallace's apparent height also helps reinforce the image of him as an ideal masculine hero, which is the final way the longsword impacts his memory.

The representation of Wallace as a large man with a large sword has obvious gender implications. Swords are often seen as a phallic symbol of masculinity, and Goran Stanivukovic has described the sword as 'the archetypal masculine symbol of sexual prowess'.[48] This can be seen in many studies of medieval literature, both from a medievalist and a medievalism angle. For example, Jennifer Dukes-Knight has examined masculinity in the early Irish text *Táin Bó Cúailnge*.[49] She compares the depiction of Fergus in other texts in the Ulster Cycle when he is the epitome of masculinity, particularly due to his 'enormous size and sexuality, and the *Tidings of Conchobar Mac Nessa* lists . . . the amount of food and women required to satisfy his various appetites . . . .'[50] In *Táin*, however, Fergus' sword is stolen and his story is one of emasculation and overall decline as both a hero and a lover.[51] To take a more modern example, Andrea Wright has written about Sonja from the 1985 film *Red Sonja*, who is the victim of sexual and other violence in childhood and becomes an accomplished swordswoman.[52] She makes 'a vow not to form an intimate relationship with any man until she finds one who can beat her in a fight with the phallic sword . . . .'[53] Wright makes the argument that despite her masculinized appearance and actions, she is still sexualized as a character, illustrating how powerful masculinity and a sexual appetite go hand in hand.

Wallace, with the longsword, is the epitome of medieval military masculinity – in terms of his height, the size of his sword, his military prowess in life, and also his influence since death. This is particularly important in terms of the Scottish identity, as it reinforces a strong martial history. It also acts as a symbol of his status. Richard Boothby has argued that 'traditions of costume have long required the man in charge to carry a big stick.'[54] Depictions of Wallace with the longsword reinforce the popular notion that he was an ideal military hero in the Middle Ages, placing him as an important player in the history of Scottish militarism.

It is clear the longsword plays a crucial role in how Wallace is remembered. It helps to identify who he is; it reinforces aspects of his appearance and strengthens his image as an ideal solider. Elliott coined the word 'historicon' to describe 'an indicator of a historical period'.[55] Wallace's longsword could easily fall into this category – it is immediately recognizable as signalling not only Wallace's identity but also the wider period of the Wars of Independence, and also alludes to the tradition of Scottish military prowess that is still so relevant in Scotland.

## Conclusion

Overall, the example of Wallace and the longsword shows the difference between accuracy and authenticity. Though it is not accurate for Wallace to be portrayed with a longsword, it is authentic due to the sheer amount of representations. This case study of the impact of one relic on wider commemoration also shows the intricate ways in which commemorations relate to each other. As more commemorations were created that depicted Wallace with the longsword, it further enforced that this was the 'correct' image of him. Wallace's sword is not just a weapon but rather a symbol of the popular assumptions of who he was and what he stood for. What is particularly interesting about this is the dichotomy that people are often very invested in historical accuracy when undertaking commemorative acts, though they are often actually referring to authenticity. The title of this chapter refers to the quote from Stanley Cursitor about the Wallace statue located at Edinburgh Castle, suggesting that perpetuating a known myth is against common sense. Though this is a logical view, it is clear that the image of Wallace with a longsword is much more nuanced then this. The image impacts his legacy in three ways: it indicates who he is in commemorations, it reinforces other myths about him, and it alludes to his reputation as an ideal example of military masculinity. It is clear that simply relegating Wallace's longsword as a myth is missing its profound impact on his legacy. Indeed, though Wallace did not have a longsword in the fourteenth century, he certainly does in the twenty-first.

## Notes

1. National Records of Scotland: 'Wallace and Bruce Memorial: Edinburgh Castle', RF2/14; A note on terminology: the term 'longsword' is being used here because it describes the sword – it is longer than the average sword, and thus would need to have been used with both hands.
2. G. Baldwin Brown, 'Letters from Readers', *The Scotsman*, 12 January 1912.
3. Ibid.
4. David Caldwell, 'The Wallace Sword', in *The Wallace Book*, ed. E .J. Cowan (Edinburgh: Birlinn Limited, 2007), 172; Magnus Magnusson, *Scotland: The Story of a Nation* (London: HarperCollins, 2000).
5. See: Andrew B. R. Elliott, *Remaking the Middle Ages: The Methods of Cinema and History in Portraying the Medieval World* (Jefferson: McFarland, 2011); A. Keith Kelly, 'Beyond History Accuracy: A Postmodern View of Movies and Medievalism', *Perspicuitas* (2004).
6. Stephanie Trigg, 'Medievalism and Convergence Culture: Researching the Middle Ages for Fiction and Film', *Parergon* 25, no. 2 (2008): 109.
7. Raphael Samuel and Paul Thompson, 'Introduction', *The Myths We Live By*, ed. Raphael Samuel and Paul Thompson (London: Routledge, 1990), 4–5.
8. Charles Rogers, *The National Wallace Monument* (Edinburgh: John Menzies, 1860).
9. Ibid.; Caldwell, 'The Wallace Sword', 172.
10. Magnusson, *Scotland: The Story of a Nation*.
11. Caldwell, 'The Wallace Sword', 172.
12. Andrew B. R. Elliott and Matthew Wilhelm Kapell, 'Introduction: To Build a Past That Will "Stand the Test of Time"—Discovering Historical Facts, Assembling Historical Narratives', in *Playing with the Past: Digital Games and the Simulation of History*, ed. Matthew Wilhelm Kapell and Andrew B. R. Elliott (New York and London: Bloomsbury Academic, 2013), 8.
13. Stefan Goebel, *The Great War and Medieval Memory* (Cambridge: Cambridge University Press, 2007), 13.
14. Ibid., 14.
15. William Hamilton, *Blind Harry's Wallace* (Edinburgh: Luath Press Ltd, 1998), 7:1, 101.
16. Ibid., 2:4, 23.
17. William Middleton, *Guide to the National Wallace Monument* (Stirling: W. Middleton, 1909), 10–11.
18. Caldwell, 'The Wallace Sword', 169.
19. T. Barnett, *Sacred Relics: Pieces of the Past in Nineteenth-Century America* (Chicago: University of Chicago Press, 2013), 28.
20. Ibid., 18.
21. 'Competitive Designs for the Wallace Statue in Aberdeen', *Aberdeen Weekly Journal*, 5 July 1884.
22. Ibid.
23. National Records of Scotland: 'Wallace and Bruce Memorial: Edinburgh Castle', RF2/14.
24. 'Wallace Memorial at Elderslie', *Aberdeen Daily Journal*, 25 September 1912.
25. Michael Donnelly, *Scotland's Stained Glass: Making the Colours Sing* (Edinburgh: The Stationery Office /Historic Scotland, 2007), 25.
26. The National Wallace Monument, 'Stained Glass Windows', http://www.nationalwallacemonument.com/the-monument/stained-glass-windows/, accessed 31 January 2017.

27  Middleton, *Guide to the National Wallace Monument*, 23.
28  National Galleries Scotland, 'About the Portrait Gallery', https://www.nationalgalleries.org/visit/about-the-portrait-gallery/, accessed 15 November 2016.
29  Elizabeth S. Cumming, 'Hole, William Fergusson Brassey', *Oxford Dictionary of National Biography*, http://www.oxforddnb.com.ezproxy.is.ed.ac.uk/view/article/100749.
30  Helen E. Smailes, 'A Pride of Lions: Noel Paton and the National Wallace Monument', *Architectural Heritage* 25 (2014): 85.
31  Author unknown, *Popular Ballads and Songs, from Tradition Manuscripts, and Scarce Editions* (Paris, 1825).
32  Middleton, *National Wallace Monument*, 22.
33  Ibid., 22.
34  Darksword Armoury, 'The William Wallace Scottish Claymore Sword – Braveheart Sword (#1362)', http://www.darksword-armory.com/medieval-weapon/medieval-swords/william-wallace-scottish-claymore-sword-braveheart-sword-1362/, accessed 30 March 2018.
35  Graeme Morton, *William Wallace: A National Tale* (Edinburgh: Edinburgh University Press Ltd, 2014), 70.
36  'Glasgow International Exhibition', *Glasgow Herald*, 29 August 1888.
37  Ibid.
38  Ibid.
39  This information is taken from my PhD thesis, which was submitted to the University of Edinburgh in March 2018.
40  Caldwell, 'The Wallace Sword', 169.
41  Magnusson, *Scotland: The Story of a Nation*, 126.
42  *Braveheart*, dir. Mel Gibson, Paramount Pictures (1995).
43  Ibid.
44  Walter Bower, *A History Book for Scots: Selections from Scotichronicon*, ed. D. E. R. Watt (Edinburgh: Mercat Press, 1998), 186.
45  Richard White, ed., *King Arthur in Legend and History* (London: Routledge, 1997), 517.
46  R. Barber, 'Edward, Prince of Wales and of Aquitane', *Oxford Dictionary of National Biography*, http://www.oxforddnb.com/view/10.1093/ref:odnb/9780198614128.001.0001/odnb-9780198614128-e-8523.
47  'Royal Dunfermline: King Robert the Bruce', Royal Dunfermline website, accessed 3 December 2016. http://www.royaldunfermline.com/Resources/DUNFERMLINE_AND_ROBERT_THE_BRUCE.pdf.
48  Goran Stanivukovic, '"The Blushing Shame of Soldiers": The Eroticism of Heroic Masculinity in John Fletcher's *Bonduca*', in *The Image of Manhood in Early Modern Literature*, ed. Andrew P. Williams (London: Greenwood Press, 1999), 46.
49  Jennifer Dukes-Knight, 'The Wooden Sword: Age and Masculinity in "*Táin Bó Cúailnge*"', *Proceedings of the Harvard Celtic Colloquium* 33 (2013): 107–22.
50  Ibid., 111.
51  Ibid., 111–12.
52  Andrea Wright, 'A Sheep in Wolf's Clothing? The Problematic Representation of Women and the Female Body in 1980s Sword and Sorcery Cinema', *Journal of Gender Studies* 21, no. 4 (2012): 403.
53  Ibid., 403.
54  Richard Boothby, *Sex on the Couch* (London: Routledge, 2005), 4.
55  Elliott, *Remaking the Middle Ages*, 210–11.

# 4

# Misdiagnosing medieval medicine

## 'Magical' Muslims, metanarrative and the modern media

### April Harper

In 1952, Charles Singer published his great criticism of medieval medicine in which he set the tone for the treatment of the subject for the next two, and arguably four decades. He decried it as 'the last stage of a process that has left no legitimate successor, a final pathological disintegration of the Greek system of medical thought'.[1] A decade later he had not changed his mind when he wrote that medieval medicine was 'demonstrative of the wilting mind of the dark ages'.[2] He argued it 'lacked any rational element which might mark the beginnings of scientific advance'.[3] Medical historians, especially from the 1990s onward, have challenged Singer's assertions and successfully shown the efficacy of many medieval medical treatments and recipes. Perhaps more importantly, they have sought to reconstruct the history of Western medicine, not as a series of peaks and troughs, in which the Middle Ages represents the greatest nadir, but as a transformation of theories connecting the practices of ancient, medieval and Renaissance medicine, in order to accurately portray the development of the field.[4] While important work is being done to strip the prejudice and stigma from the subject, it is the inaccuracies in the portrayal of medieval medicine, science and technology that provide key insight into modern fears and conflicts. The inaccuracies function on a series of imbricated planes, with interwoven agendas acting: on the most basic level, as a signifier of the medieval in modern media and the imagination; on a more complex level, as a means to reinforce a comfortable narrative of historical progress in which the primitive and barbarous medieval is comfortably dissimilar to our own modern world; and lastly, at a deeper and arguably far more disturbing level, is the means by which these inaccuracies allow us to portray the Middle East as a backward place that has refused to develop past the medieval and by its rejection of the modern, has rejected the science, technology and philosophy that has defined humanism and humanity in the West and therefore validates the dehumanization of Muslims who, having once been on the forefront of all scientific advancement, chose to remain medieval, rather than embrace Renaissance and Enlightenment.

Singer's argument that medieval medicine was 'the last stage of a process that has left no legitimate successor'[5] establishes an estrangement so severe between the science, medicine and technology of the modern world and that of the medieval, that there is no discernible link between the two periods. It is what the most obvious and common use of medicine in modern media (especially television and film in which the time available for world-crafting is limited) likewise accomplishes – the immediate acknowledgement that the audience is experiencing a radically different time and mindset that is nothing like our own. It is immediately foreign and immediately medieval in the depiction of its lack of scientific technology and the ubiquitous image of its medicine as brutal, superstitious and often magical. This is important for what Andrew Elliott describes in his *Remaking the Middle Ages* as 'authenticity' – part of a medieval imaginary in which certain sets of signs form a recognizable idea. It creates a 'feel' of medieval.[6] Science and technology, or the lack thereof, are just as important as signifiers of what is medieval as depicted in modern media as is a castle, knights on horseback, dirty peasants or even dragons. Science and technology are a key divide between the perceived medieval and modern.

As a signifier of the medieval, medical treatment in modern media productions is often depicted to compliment a perceived brutality of medieval life. The medieval reality of hospitals (depending on time period and geographic location), educated practitioners, medication and even cleanliness must remain absent from this constructed medieval world entirely in order for the medieval imaginary to be fully constructed.[7] For example, in the popular TV show *Vikings*, a character named Torstein is hit with an arrow in the upper arm and in a very masculine fashion, breaks it off, but the wound becomes infected and one afternoon, while sitting around the fire, he asks his friends to cut off his arm 'because he never liked it anyway'.[8] Several men stand up, ready to do the procedure, but he asks for one man in particular to do the job, not because of his medical knowledge but because he had wronged him before and it seems to be a kind of statement of trust. The patient is held down by multiple men, an axe is heated red hot to cauterize the wound, and a successful amputation is done in a few neat whacks. The cinematic demands to showcase brutality and primitivism and celebrate the hyper-masculinity of the battlefield and Viking culture are satisfied.

Chronicles and other non-medical texts of the Middle Ages, such as those by Jean de Joinville, the crusader and author of *The Life of Saint Louis* who was excited to have returned from battle with 'only five arrows' stuck in him,[9] and the poetry of Norman poet Ambroise, who describes King Richard looking 'like a hedgehog' from the amount of arrows in him, detail just how common arrow wounds were and that soldiers, and indeed their medieval audience knew better than to break off an arrow.[10] Arrowhead extraction, though painful, was common and largely successful, as was treatment of infection. The texts of battlefield surgeons illustrate the wide variety of arrowheads and other ballistics that any surgeon needed to know how to remove. The battlefield often proved a fertile ground to train in surgery, to pioneer new techniques of arterial stitching and wound management. Battlefield weaponry was changing as fast as battlefield medicine could adapt, though arrows remained a core concern and standard subject in all surgical texts. Detailed procedures clearly show an understanding of the nature of such wounds and their particular risks, depending on whether they had targeted flesh, artery, joint, nerve or bone. The surgeon John Bradford's innovative solution in extracting the head of a bodkin that had come loose from its shaft after penetrating the future Henry V of England's face and lodging in the interior bone of his skull shows not only a deep understanding and familiarity with arrow wounds but also the understanding that the worst case scenario was an arrowhead that had come loose from a shaft, or a broken shaft left in the body.[11] Amputation, that the character of Torstein so easily embraced, was a last resort and would have been carried out by a specialist. Evidence of this kind of specialization and practice exists in Scandinavia and England as early as the ninth century. By the eleventh century, the Muslim physician Al-Zahrawi, latinized as Albucasis, wrote a detailed procedure for amputation, describing the process of ligature and the problems and necessary procedural differences depending on the location of amputation, different tissues and the presence of a healthy or bad bone.[12] While the inaccuracy in the presentation of Torstein's amputation is deeply problematic for historians of medicine, as it continues and reinforces the misinformed image of the brutal ignorance of medieval medicine, for medievalists, it is the power of this image combined with other signifiers, such as the hyper-masculinity of the Vikings, the adherence to codes of honour, rules of feuding and even choice of weaponry, that provides valuable insight into the creation of the 'medieval'.

While brutality is one of the common ways in which the medicine of the Middle Ages is instantly identifiable to a modern audience, the medieval imaginary is often crafted through a complete sacrifice of both logic and realism in the depiction and acceptance that the only effective medieval medicine is linked to magic. There are many examples of this, from the slight to the fantastical. In the TV series *Merlin*, for example, the young sorcerer is given a book of magic in the first episode.[13] As he thumbs through it, he is amazed by the spells and the screen settles on a particular page of the magical text that historians of medicine will recognize as the entry for the herb henbane in the Old English Herbarium, a ninth-century, Anglo-Saxon medical text. The vibrant colours; spidery, calligraphic Anglo-Saxon written text, and images of plants and animals seem to be enough to render it suitably magical in the audience's mind. Countless other television shows and films rely on the connection between medicine and sorcery ranging from the simple references akin to that in *Merlin* to the wilder images and dangerous necromancy of shows like *Game of Thrones*. Many recent television miniseries, including *The Last Kingdom*, *Game of Thrones* and *The World Without End*, have developed this trend to tap into a kind of pseudo-feminist Romanticism of the imagined medieval pagan past. In these productions, the inadequate medieval medicine practiced is the preserve of men whose patriarchy proves impotent in the face of real disaster. The only capable healers in these dramas are female, often greatly sexualized, pagan priestesses or witches, who wield true, though often dangerous, power. Extremes are often taken to craft this image that seems far more unbelievable than the efficacy of medieval medicine. Yet, the power of these signifiers is such that directors, writers and audiences readily engage in a kind of suspension of disbelief that renders them willing to accept that this period is so removed from history that it has also become removed from reality and that in this imaginary, magic was more real, more common and more efficacious than actual medieval medicine.

The second, and more complex level at which the images of medieval medicine interact is upon historical narrative. While the inaccuracies functioning as signifiers create the idea of the Middle Ages as comfortingly dissimilar from our own, they are also able to function simultaneously at deeper levels, to reinforce a false narrative of historical progress that allows us to avoid our own scientific shortcomings by giving credence to Singer's next claim – that medieval medicine 'lacked any rational element which might mark the beginnings of scientific advance'.[14] This narrative is usually promoted by the use of two major themes in medicine: the incurable medieval disease that is easily cured in the modern period and ineffective and/or dangerous medicine of the Middle Ages.

The first of these themes – the incurable – is especially effective as it plays upon the universal human fears of the unknown and death. These scenes are often highly emotionally charged by a seeming senselessness to deaths that are easily preventable in the modern world. While many advancements in medicine were made within the Middle Ages that improved the quality of life and in some cases, even saved the lived of patients, such as fistula, hernia and cataract surgeries, and skin grafting, modern media rarely focuses on highly risky surgeries, such as bladder stone removal to illustrate historical progress. Instead, it is the inability to help the most vulnerable that helps further this agenda the most. This may account for why images of sick children and especially women dying in childbirth feature prominently in this category. The trope is a common backstory for tragic male figures who have lost their families in childbirth-gone-wrong and, as most famously depicted in *Robin Hood Prince of Thieves* (1991), provides a dramatic scene in which even the martial prowess of a story's hero cannot save a woman who struggles to give birth.

Outside of TV and film, there are webpages, blog and articles devoted to a similar image of medieval childbirth as terrifying and deadly. Supposedly historical blogs feature titles such as 'The Historical Horror of Childbirth';[15] a popular health magazine runs the story 'Medieval Pregnancy Advice That Is Beyond Disturbing';[16] and the *Daily Mail* headlines an article 'Medieval Woman Gave Birth After Death'.[17] The goal of these sensationalist headlines and the images of the inability of medieval medicine is to save these women through what by modern standards is seen as a simple caesarean delivery, to disparage the Middle Ages and comfort the audience with the knowledge that progress has been made. Indeed, each of the written sources – blog, journal and newspaper – ends with an assurance that things are better today. However, childbirth is still one of the most dangerous events in a woman's life, with approximately 143 deaths per 100,000 live births, making it the fifth greatest cause of death for women, according to global data collected for the year 2015.[18]

Childbirth was dangerous in the Middle Ages, and although access to medical care varied due to financial status, social class and even geography, women were commonly attended by midwives and royal women often had personal surgeons and physicians who were well-educated in gynaecology. Physicians and midwives were familiar with the various fetal presentations, including dangerous positions, such as a breech birth.[19] While caesarean births were originally developed as a means to save a baby after the death of the mother during labour, by the fifteenth century, caesarean births in which the mother and child could both be saved are recorded in texts.[20]

There may be evidence of successful surgeries being practiced earlier, as rabbinical texts describe the practice carried out with both maternal and child survival in Jewish communities as early as the second century AD.[21] Midwives who were ignorant of possible complications of childbirth could be found guilty not only of malpractice but of murder if their actions or lack of skill was at fault in a maternal death, as illustrated in the fourteenth-century case of a French midwife named Philipa, who attempted to remove the afterbirth of a woman by pulling on the still-anchored umbilical cord. The legal text in which this case is recorded describes her actions as 'crude [. . .] brutal and cruel', implying that this kind of ignorance was against standards of practice and certainly not the norm.[22] By not waiting for the arrival of a more experienced midwife and carrying out actions that led to the death by haemorrhage of the mother, Philipa found herself on trial for murder. Despite the historical reality of obstetric good practice, film, television and the media continue to conflate many images of life in the Middle Ages with that of the American Wild West and it is especially evident in the erroneous depiction of women giving birth in isolation and the dehumanized, uncaring treatment given to women in childbirth that is more akin to the treatment of livestock than one's wife. This portrayal has little in common with the medieval reality of village life, the community nature of childbirth and the common presence of educated and/or experienced female attendants, midwives and/or physicians.[23] The inaccurate portrayal of hopelessness and tacit acceptance of needless death is critical, though, in forming the narrative of progression, even when the same condition remains a threat to the modern audience. As long as there are perceived differences or the option of scientific recourse, there is a distinguishable difference and the narrative can be confirmed.

This highly effective imagined combination of despair and inadequate medical response can be combined with an additional attribute that signifies historical progress – compassion, or rather the medieval lack thereof, in order to create a powerful 'proof' of not only our scientific, but moral distance from the medieval. Perhaps the best example of this is in the image of the Plague. Understandably, filmmakers and screenwriters are intrigued by the plague, just as historians, and especially historians of medicine, are profoundly interested in the impact it had upon medical practice, theory and regulating institutions. The actual terror the Black Death inspired in medieval people cannot be understated. Contemporary chroniclers, such as the Irish friar John Clynn, described himself as 'waiting among the dead for death to come'. He ends his work by stating, 'I leave parchment for continuing the work, in case anyone should still be alive in the future and any son of Adam can escape this pestilence and continue the work thus begun.'[24] Fear led many of the wealthy to flee the cities for their countryside estates, hoping to outrun the outbreaks, as the setting of Boccaccio's Decameron illustrates. Some left their homes entirely and, as the Bishop of Bath and Wells bemoaned, it was impossible to recruit new priests to replace those who had died while tending to the ill.[25] The misunderstanding of the plague's origin led to outbreaks of violence against minorities and strangers.[26] The problem of the inaccuracies of modern media is not that it portrays some or even all of these responses in its depiction of the Black Death but that it presents these very real fears as the *status quo* in the Middle Ages, not the world-upside-down experience it really was.

The use of the plague, in film and television particularly, is disturbing as it seems to have become an all-inclusive image of life in the Middle Ages, especially in Hollywood blockbuster culture. Indeed, there often seem to be two overarching themes for medieval productions: war or plague and sometimes war and plague as shown in films such as *The Seventh Seal* (1957) and *Season of the Witch* (2011) among others. The combination of themes presents a past in which life was held cheaply and those who did survive lived in squalor, filth and abject fear. The perceived baseness of human nature in the Middle Ages that is portrayed in these films is shown through terrifying acts of violence and the wholesale neglect of the ill and destitute. Even comedies that address the Black Death, such as Monty Python's *Holy Grail*, show a disregard for life, the elderly are depicted as a burden, children are too many and entirely replaceable and no one mourns the dead.

It also shows little of the attempts to deal with this epidemic. While films like *Season of the Witch* link the plague to the revenge of downtrodden pagans and portray the authorities as crazed zealots hunting down young women, in reality, the greatest medical minds in Europe's leading universities were attempting to find scientific rationale for the plague.[27] Historical outbreaks of other plagues were studied; surgeons and physicians, including the Pope's own physician, began to write treatment protocols that advocated frequent bathing, the use of vinegar washes, frequent washing of clothing and so on, and civil government began to step in to regulate at-risk areas and implement quarantines, waste disposal and mandate that bodies must be placed in a coffin before leaving the house, the coffin must be sealed with nine-inch nails to prevent it from coming open during burial or in high water table areas and that all graves be dug a minimum of six feet deep in order to not interfere with drinking water.[28] The terror of the Black Death was deeply felt, and while a cure evaded medieval physicians, fifteenth-century Europe was far from the Monty Python-esque image of a mud-soaked hovel. Rather, at the onset of the plague, Europe was stable, prospering, enjoyed a level of education previously unknown, had seen the establishments of universities as well as hospitals and had experienced four renaissances. While the objective of creating a myth of historical progress is achieved through inaccuracy, it is interesting to note that the image of the period as one in which primitivism supersedes all rational thought and humanity reverts to some imagined dark age in which hunger, filth and a mass grave await us all as far more in common with images of the holocausts and post-apocalyptic, dystopian nightmares of our postmodern society than it does with an accurate medieval past. The power of this 'authentic' rather than 'accurate' image may be two-edged at this level – providing comfort in the historical narrative of progress, but also admonitory in purpose, warning what should befall us if we cease to continue to progress.

The second of these is themes is historical narratives promoting the ineffective or dangerous nature of medieval medicine. While audiences are often willing to suspend disbelief in order to accept magical medical cures, when pressed to witness real medieval medical treatment, the media images of doctors as bumbling fools, or pedantic churchmen, whose treatment is quite commonly ineffective or even counter-productive, seem to resonate so strongly that modern audiences are averse to admit any value to the practice. Instead, emphasis is given to the futility of the treatments: the perceived disgusting nature of suitably 'medieval' ingredients such as dung, beer and grease, and the copious amount of praying that often accompanies certain procedures or processes. Even today, when some medieval medical treatments are found to be most efficacious, with better results than modern medicine, acceptance and enthusiasm are low. For example, in 2015, the University of Nottingham combined experts in molecular biology and Anglo-Saxon studies to work on a recipe for eye salve from *Bald's Leechbook*, a ninth-century Anglo-Saxon medical text. The simple ingredients of onion, garlic and wine were mixed with gall from the stomach of an ox and allowed to sit in a brass container for nine days. The resulting mixture has proven to be an incredibly strong antibacterial tincture that has proven more effective at fighting MRSA than modern medicines. Interestingly, however, media attention has focused on the humble and medievally 'gross' ingredients and the shock of the researchers involved at its efficacy. The pejorative presentism surrounding the medieval nature of the recipe is found in titles of articles such as 'Getting Medieval on Bacteria', The *Smithsonian*'s 'This Nasty Medieval Remedy Kills MRSA' and from *The Conversationalist*, an academic online journal, the article 'Why I wasn't excited about the medieval remedy that works against MRSA'. The latter, written by the well-respected classicist Helen King, employs an argument from fallacy in which she pairs a very brief summary of the project in a tone that all but denies its results, with a much longer description of the more fantastical recipes found within the *Leechbook* that include charms or supernatural elements, in an attempt to discredit the efficaciousness of Anglo-Saxon medicine and to argue for the fruitlessness of continuing such research. This is remarkably interesting, considering that the same year, the chemist Tu Youyou received the Nobel Prize in Medicine for her similar work in researching efficacious treatments from ancient Chinese medicine. However, comments on a variety of pages seem to echo those of Dr King, such as this comment from David Wright, another classicist:

> The odds are against anything spectacularly effective having been 'lost' [. . .] effort should be spent on 21st century remedies [. . .] To those who say this is 'culturally insensitive' I merely shrug and say 'Look at mortality rates for now well-understood conditions, then and now. Would you rather be treated by the old, or new, methods? And your children? I rest my case.'[29]

The appeal of the fallacious argument and fear-mongering in Wright's comment is not unlike those voiced by readers in the comments section of various articles covering this experiment:

> Find something that worked in ages past and turn it into something else that will cause 'unfortunate side effects' which will require more drugs to alleviate. Sort of explains the whole bit about Pharma (cology) originating from the Latin word for 'sorcery'.[30]

> A lot of good people died because of those treatments. That is not allowed today. They did their best, but, have you ever looked at our lifespan and compared it to the days of the healers?[31]

Let's see, possibly because its [sic] a foul nasty brew, and no one is going to apply to their skin? Also, it may not be something in itself that can be ingested, and if it possible, if it's that horrible, good luck swallowing it and not vomiting. So yes, they need to see what in the slime is doing the job and than [sic] replicate it and put it in a usable form.[32]

Why mess with stinky stuff?[33]

While we might be amused or intrigued by the efficacy of some medieval treatments, such as the Anglo-Saxon eye salve, by and large audiences can feel comforted by this topos of the ineffective, dangerous and disgusting pharmacopeia that not only acts as a signifier, creating an immediately identifiable medieval world that is comfortingly distinct from our own, but affirms the present as progressive, distinct, logical, scientific and less vulnerable. Louise D'Arcens and Clare Monagle aptly note, 'Since the Renaissance, whenever modernity has found itself in crisis – when the shibboleths of rationalism, secularism, capitalism and the nation-state seem to be coming apart at the seams – fantasies of the medieval have suggested a mostly frightening, though sometimes alluring, vision of what the alternatives to modernity might be.'[34] No matter what we face in the modern age, we have evidence that we have survived worse and we have the tools of medicine, science and technology to overcome our present challenges. By constantly portraying the Middle Ages as a period of medical and scientific backwardness, we

> affirm a progressivist model of history which emphasises the breach between periods, and arguably validates and advocates for modernity for its implicitly more evolved culture [. . .] the medieval period is evoked as a superseded age of ignorance and cruelty [. . .] provid[ing] a reservoir of images and ideas that have been crucial to defining what it is to be modern.[35]

Thirdly, and perhaps the most important level at which the inaccuracies of medieval medicine, science and technology impact the modern world is in the interaction of these deeply imbedded signifiers and narratives of modernity with the leitmotif of the medieval technologically advanced Muslim. The image of Muslims as a people who once held advanced technology and engaged in cutting-edge science but through laziness and cultural and religious prohibitions ceased to progress is more than Orientalism or even popular Islamophobic bigotry. It is far more dangerous. Andrew Elliott includes in his work, *Medievalism, Politics and Mass Media*, a political cartoon in which a directional sign that points to the 'Middle East' is vandalized to read 'Middle Ages' instead. He notes how

> such a syllogism has important ramifications in our reclassification of the world not into geopolitical entities but also into a chronological idea of progress [. . .] Even the language we use to divide the world bears witness to such chronological division when, for example, we divide the world into developed and developing worlds, a metaphor whose implicit logic is temporal and dependent on our seeing the so-called 'developed' worlds of the West teleologically as the most fulfilled and

modern point of evolution, while the others languish in a pre-modern state of ungentrified barbarity.[36]

The perceived 'barbarity' of Islam is key not just to the defamation of Islam, but to the dehumanization of all Muslims. Much attention has been given, especially in the press, in television and media, to the physical violence that the Islamic State has engaged in and even its own use of nostalgia, that consistently references the medieval. And while numerous historians and political commentators have repeatedly pointed out, as John Terry aptly states, ISIS is 'not medieval – it is viciously modern', the power of calling it and its actions 'medieval', 'tempts us to define the group's special barbarism as something from the past that should be eradicated because, by God, we've progressed and are therefore advanced as a people.'[37] Indeed groups like IS and the Taliban 'becomes something not only out of place but, more importantly, out of time'.[38] Chris Jones argues:

> to call the perpetrators of these crimes, and the societies that foster them 'medieval' is to place them on the other side of a temporal fault-line imagined to run through history. 'We' are 'modern' and therefore civilized and unable to countenance these forms of violence; 'they' are 'medieval', pre-modern, and have not progressed through the same process of historical evolution that would render such acts unthinkable. In effect 'they' are inhuman, or rather 'pre-human' if being human means having gone through the later stages of European history (and it is a metaphor which is entirely Euro-centric), which Humanists first labelled 'the Renaissance', and subsequently that most savage of times, 'The Enlightenment'. There is already a substantial history of this language of medievalism being used to describe the opponents of the West. On occasions, in denying individuals their humanity. [. . .] The medievalist academic Bruce Holsinger has analysed how the so-called 'torture memos' of the U.S. State argue that the Taliban is an apparently 'feudal' organization, and one which has therefore failed to evolve into a modern state, and as a consequence its 'medieval' members do not qualify for the protections of the Geneva Convention while under detention at Guantanamo. The logic is shockingly brutal: 'medieval' people are not modern humans; Human Rights do not need to be extended to 'pre-humans'.[39]

Interestingly, the majority of effective, non-magical, medical treatment in medieval film and TV productions is carried out by Muslims. In 2001, director Spike Lee spoke publicly on the cliché of the 'magical black man' in film and TV, noting a longstanding tradition that the only acceptable character of colour has to be the exceptional, a trope commonly referred to as 'the magical black man'.[40] In medieval film, this exceptional character is often cast as a Muslim, though Hollywood occasionally conflates the two, as found in Morgan Freeman's portrayal of the black, Muslim sidekick to Robin Hood in Kevin Costner's *Robin Hood: Prince of Thieves* (1991).[41] While we might be tempted to refer to this trope as the 'magical medieval Muslim', it is his (to date, this figure is universally male) complete lack of magic that marks him as different and exceptional. The inclusion of a non-magical though nevertheless fantastical, scientifically minded, technologically advanced Muslim often acts within the script as a kind of deus ex machina device as illustrated in Freeman's character. Azeem, with his knowledge of gunpowder and his possession of technology, such as the telescope, is an invaluable sidekick who gives Robin Hood an advantage over his less-developed, Western European foes. This superior knowledge also enables Azeem to save the life of Little John's wife, delivering her child by Caesarean. As previously noted, Caesarean sections were most likely not performed with maternal survival before the fifteenth century. Similarly, Muslims did not acquire the knowledge of gunpowder until the late thirteenth century; telescopes were first developed in the early seventeenth century in the Netherlands. If these were just isolated incidents of such misattribution, one might be tempted to just blame them on a film that is already fraught with a wide variety of inaccuracies. However, this kind of chronological misappropriation of scientific goods and technologies is not unusual and affects not just fantasy film and fiction, but has infiltrated official narratives of the history of science. Professor Nir Shafir, an expert on Ottoman science and medicine, has recently noted the production and circulation of many images that have been intentionally changed on the internet to imply Muslim technological inventions and advancements that are being attributed to the Middle Ages, though, in some cases, hundreds of years before the actual development of some technologies. While we may expect this of the unregulated nature of the internet, more disturbingly, he has also found a similar wide variety of misrepresentations in art and in heritage settings.[42] These include alterations, such as an original painting depicting an Islamic astronomer using a sextant that has now been over-painted to show him using a telescope; medical images drawn in a medieval style, but with modern knowledge of anatomy; paintings of world maps that contain details only known post-nineteenth century; and even updated recreations of supposedly medieval scientific instruments and machines. While some of these forgeries are found online or in tourist shops, others have worked their ways into museums and libraries such as the Museum for the History of Science and Technology in Islam in Istanbul and the 'Science in Islam' exhibition website at the Museum of the History of Science in Oxford. Even the Wellcome Collection in London, which specializes in the history of medicine, was found to have what Nazir describes as 'several poorly copied miniatures demonstrating Islamic models of the body, written over with a bizarre pseudo-Arabic and with no given source'.[43]

While these pseudo-scientific modernizations and forgeries may seem bizarre, they have a firm footing in medievalism from the nineteenth century onwards. In John Ganim's work, *Medievalism and Orientalism*, he notes that the

> European powers mounted enormous international exhibitions, displaying both their technological and economic power and their newly acquired colonial possessions. [. . .] As it turns out, world's fairs in the nineteenth century not only celebrated the triumph of European modernity, they also displayed aspects of Europe's own medieval past. From the Great Exhibition of 1851 onwards, medieval reconstructions were among the most popular exhibits at world's fairs.[44]

While medieval installations may seem to be out of place in such display, the fairs' focus was not only to showcase advances in technology, but to celebrate empire and Western cultural superiority over the colonized. The fairs had displays of handicrafts and items from colonized lands that stood in stark contrast to the modernity of the Western European installations, but bore striking resemblance to the mocked up Western medieval goods often showcased right next to them. The medieval and the colonized Muslim were displayed side by side.

The link between medievalism and orientalism was already well-established in art and literature, but was now connected in science as well. Ganim illustrates how firmly this connection was made in his example of an address given to the Workingman's College in 1881: 'All the heaped up knowledge of modern science, all the energy of modern commerce, all the depth and spirituality of modern thought, cannot reproduce so much the handiwork of an ignorant, superstitious Berkshire peasant of the fourteenth century, nay of a wandering Kurdish shepherd.'[45] This teaming of the modern Middle East with the Middle Ages contributed to a growing trend for scholars to shift between the two fields of study and a great deal of conflation to take place. As Ganim argues, 'The Middle Ages represented in time what the Orient represented in space, an "other" to the present development of western civilization.'[46]

While the connection between the science and technology of the East and that of the medieval was firmly established in the nineteenth-century fusion of orientalism and medievalism, it seems confusing why modern productions that embrace both these analytical approaches would choose to show Islam as advanced and even attribute developments from the European late Middle Ages and early modern period to it. The answer may lie in the West's devotion to the Whiggish narrative of progress. As Chris Jones argues, the Italian humanists' desire to separate themselves from past resulted in them:

> denigrat[ing] this 'middle age' as a period of ignorance and backwardness precisely in order to promote themselves, and the new age in which they had decided they were living, as more 'advanced'. Styling the previous ten centuries of human achievement as barbarically 'medieval' was, in short, a hugely successful piece of spin – a Public Relations coup for a new philosophical 'brand' being launched by an elite group of western Europeans, [. . .] For 'the Middle Ages' is not a neutral historical term. It's a metaphorical way of understanding history as a process of evolution, by which a less advanced culture has to (or perhaps fails to) progress from a 'medieval' period to modernity.[47]

The display of the inferior West and the technological superior, though still medieval, Islam fuels a two-fold modern desire to show the incredible progress of the West, while showing stagnation of Islam. The eagerness of the West to advance and Islam's inability to do so is especially evidenced in the films *The Physician* (2013) and in *Kingdom of Heaven* (2005).

In *The Physician*, a young Englishman travels to Persia in the eleventh century to learn from Avicenna, one of the greatest medical minds of the period. It is a deeply problematic film in many ways, for its portrayals of race, for its bizarre conflation of historical events and its complete lack of understanding of any aspect of medieval medicine. While the inaccuracies are rampant throughout the film, it is the relationship between the Englishman and his Muslim teacher that proves more important for how these inaccuracies function at this third level. The student surpasses not only all his peers in class but then begins to rival his master. He not only perfects many of Avicenna's theories, but is found arguing with his teacher when the Muslim proves too cowardly to push forward in their discoveries or to challenge previous beliefs. Avicenna is comfortable with his reputation and satisfied in achieving a high level of respect within the field, but lacks drive and bravery to continue to progress. In the end, the Englishman leaves the school, riding away as the compound slams its doors shut under the new rule of a conservative Muslim ruler. The message is clear: Islam fears modernity and it is up to the Westerner to continue the progress begun by Islam.

Similarly, in *Kingdom of Heaven*, a narrative of Western progress is set against the image of a hesitant and wilfully stagnant Muslim east. This is especially obvious in the protagonist, Balian's, first encounter with the East. As Paul Sturtevant notes:

> In this scene, Balian surveys his newly inherited lands, and, finding them well-populated but parched, orders his men to build a well. Balian himself leads the team of welldiggers [. . .]. Water is struck, and in the following scenes, his lands are transformed into and oasis paradise. This scene is controversial because it calls back to an imperialist, Orientalist and colonialist narrative wherein Europeans were needed to 'make the desert bloom' – bringing civilization to the Arab world [. . .] This sets up a problematic paradigm where without dictates from a strong (European) leader, the people are so listless that they will not even work together to provide for their most basic needs.[48]

The complete lack of a desire to progress marks the Muslims throughout the film, as does their need to have Europeans develop and even re-teach them their own once-superior science. The message is clear – Middle East is medieval and desires to remain so, while the West, even when medieval, is progressive, active and leading the way to modernity.

There is a terrible power in interpreting, labelling and portraying not only the violence perpetrated by Islamic groups as 'medieval' but also their motivations, their worldview and their culture, as 'medieval'. It marks them as hopelessly different, not human. In an age where science becomes one of our greatest signifiers between our past and present, periods such as the Renaissance and the Enlightenment act as a kind of lock in the river of progressivism, not only enabling forward momentum but raising Western culture as well and ensuring against any backslip.

In conclusion, science and technology are a key divide between the perceived medieval and modern. In the preface to his collection of essays, Jacques Le Goff describes the idea of a medieval period 'dying under the blows of the industrial revolution'[49] and no matter the inaccuracy of that statement, it does bely a pervasive image of a lack of scientific understanding or development in the Middle Ages. The inaccuracies act on the most basic level as powerful signifiers – a bubbling potion, a spell-book, the mention of a disease long-eradicated or no longer threatening, a wound from weapons no longer used; these create an immediately identifiable medieval world that is comfortingly distinct from our own. However, when applied to medicine, science and technology, inaccuracy is not only a general tool for world-crafting, but functions on far deeper emotional and cognitive levels, impacted by nationalism and fear. Accurately portraying a medieval European past that was in possession of logical, rational, scientific medicine, that was scientifically minded and technologically innovative is simply counterproductive to the progressivist, presentist narrative demanded by many modern audiences and so filmmakers, television directors and the media continue to engage in the comfortable Western narrative of progress and cultural superiority. That narrative serves to create an idea of a Middle Ages that is dissimilar enough from our present that, despite our current scientific shortcomings, we can map a trajectory of success over nature, disease and the unknown. It allows Islam's early scientific success to be not a challenge to the superiority of the West but, when paired with the image of its current state of stagnation, to become a vivid image of regression – a society that has not evolved socially, technologically, philosophically or morally. This final stage in the use of inaccuracy in the portrayal of medieval medicine is the most powerful and potentially the most destructive, as the imbrication of the various uses and effects of the inaccuracies reduces the image of the Muslim to signifiers of a past age and as evidence confirming a dangerous metanarrative that not only includes Western progress, but the admonition of what happens if the West fails to progress or tolerates those it sees as doing so.

# Notes

1. J. H. G. Grattan and Charles Singer, *Anglo-Saxon Magic and Medicine* (London: Folcroft Library Editions, 1952), 92.
2. Charles Singer, *A Short History of Medicine* (New York: Oxford University Press, 1962), 31.
3. Ibid.
4. M. L. Cameron, *Anglo Saxon Medicine* (Cambridge: University of Cambridge Press, 1993); Monica Green, *The Trotula: An English Translation of the Medieval Compendium of Women's Medicine* (Philadelphia: University of Pennsylvania Press, 2002); Mirko Grmek, ed., *Western Medical Thought from Antiquity to the Middle Ages*, trans. Antony Shugaar (Cambridge, MA: Harvard University Press, 1998); A. Wear, Lawrence Conrad, Michael Neve, Roy Porter, and Vivian Nutton, *The Western Medical Tradition: 800 BC to AD 1800* (Cambridge, MA: Cambridge University Press, 1995) and Vivian Nutton, *Ancient Medicine* (New York: Routledge, 2004).
5. Grattan and Singer, *Anglo-Saxon Magic*, 92.
6. Andrew Elliott, *Remaking the Middle Ages* (Jefferson: McFarland, 2011), 178.
7. Medical care available depended largely on geographic location and the time period in question. See Grmek, 1998 and Wear, Conrad, Neve, et al., 1995.
8. *The Vikings*, 'The Wanderer', Season 3, Episode 2, (2015), [TV programme] History Channel, 26 February.
9. Ambroise, *Estoire de la Guerre Sainte - Histoire en Vers de la Troisieme Croisade (1190-1192)*, ed. G. Paris (Paris: Imprimerie nationale, 1897), 311.

10 Jean Joinville, *The Life of St Louis* (London: Sheed and Ward, 1955), 84.
11 H. Cole and Tig Lang, 'The Treating of Prince Henry's Arrow Wound, 1403', *Journal of the Society of Archer Antiquaries* (2003): 95–101.
12 Piers Mitchell, *Medicine in the Crusades* (Cambridge: Cambridge University Press, 2005), 153.
13 Merlin, 'The Dragon's Call', Season 1, Episode 1, (2008), [TV programme] BBC One, 20 September.
14 Grattan and Singer, *Anglo-Saxon Magic*, 92.
15 Miss Cellania, 'The Historical Horror of Childbirth', *Mental Floss*, 9 May 2013. Available online: http://mentalfloss.com/article/50513/historical-horror-childbirth, accessed 13 October 2019.
16 L. Douglas, 'Medieval Pregnancy Advice That Is Beyond Disturbing', *Healthyway*, 5 April 2007. Available online: https://www.healthyway.com/content/medieval-pregnancy-advice-that-is-beyond-disturbing/, accessed 13 October 2019.
17 C. MacDonald, 'The Haunting Remains of a Medieval Woman Who Had a Hole Drilled into Her Skull at 38 Weeks Pregnant and "Gave Birth" AFTER She Was Buried', *Dailymail.com*, 10 December 2018. Available online: https://www.dailymail.co.uk/sciencetech/article-5547203/Medieval-woman-hole-drilled-skull-38-weeks-pregnant-gave-birth-death.html, accessed 13 October 2019.
18 This data is based on figures worldwide. Maternal death figures must not to be presumed to represent only the third world, as shown in the article's statistics revealing the United States to have the highest maternal death rate in the developed world with approximately nineteen maternal deaths per 100,000 live births. See Ellison, Katherine; Nina Martin, 'Lost Mothers: Severe Complications for Women During Childbirth Are Skyrocketing — And Could Often Be Prevented', *ProPublica*, 22 December 2017. Available online: https://www.propublica.org/article/severe-complications-for-women-during-childbirth-are-skyrocketing-and-could-often-be-prevented, accessed 14 July 2018.
19 Monica Green, *The Trotula* and Monica Green, *Women's Healthcare in the Medieval West* (Philadelphia: University of Pennsylvania Press, 2002).
20 Renate Blumenfeld-Kosinski, *Not of Woman Born: Representations of Caesarean Birth in Medieval and Renaissance Culture* (Ithaca: Cornell University Press, 1991).
21 Jeffrey Boss, 'The Antiquity of Caesarean Section with Maternal Survival: The Jewish Tradition', *Medical History* 5, no. 2 (1961 April): 117–31.
22 Monica Green, 'The Art of Medicine: Midwives and Obstetric Catastrophe', *The Lancet*, 372. https://www.thelancet.com/pdfs/journals/lancet/PIIS0140-6736(08)61467-1.pdf, accessed 14 July 2018.
23 Monica H. Green, *Making Women's Medicine Masculine: The Rise of Male Authority in Pre-Modern Gynaecology* (Oxford: Oxford University Press, 2008).
24 R. Butler (ed.), *Annalium Hibernae Chronicon*, Irish Archaeological Society. 1849, 35–7 in *The Black Death*, ed. Rosemary Horrox (Manchester: Manchester University Press, 1994), 84.
25 D. Wilkins, *Concilia Magnae Britanniae et Hiberniae*, 4 vols, 1739, II, 745-6 in *The Black Death*, ed. Rosemary Horrox (Manchester: Manchester University Press, 1994), 271.
26 See Rosemary Horrox, 'Human Agency', in *The Black Death*, ed. Rosemary Horrox (Manchester: Manchester University Press, 1994), 205–26.
27 R. Hoeniger (ed.), *Der Schwarze Tod*, Berlin, 1882, appendix III, pp. 152–6 in *The Black Death*, ed. Rosemary Horrox (Manchester: Manchester University Press, 1994), 158–63.

28  A. Chiappelli (ed.), 'Gli Ordinamenti Sanitari del Comune di Pistoia contro la Pestilenza del 1348', *Archivio Storico Italiano*, series 4, XX, 1887, 8–22 in *The Black Death,* ed. Rosemary Horrox (Manchester: Manchester University Press, 1994), 194–203.
29  David Wright. Richard Landes, April 2015, comment on Helen King, 'Why I wasn't excited about the medieval remedy that works against MRSA', *The Conversationalist* (blog), 9 April 2015. Available online: https://theconversation.com/why-i-wasnt-excited-about-the-medieval-remedy-that-works-against-mrsa-39719#comment_641009, accessed 8 May 2018.
30  ExpertExpat, 2017, comment on Erin Blakemore, 'This Nasty Medieval Remedy Kills MRSA', *Smithsonian* 21 March 2015. Available online: https://www.smithsonianmag.com/smart-news/nasty-medieval-remedy-kills-mrsa-180954808/#comment-3287469822, accessed 8 May 2018.
31  Cordel, 2017, comment on Erin Blakemore, 'This Nasty Medieval Remedy Kills MRSA', *Smithsonian,* 21 March 2015. Available online: https://www.smithsonianmag.com/smart-news/nasty-medieval-remedy-kills-mrsa-180954808/#comment-3287469822, accessed 8 May 2018.
32  Unthwarted, comment on Erin Blakemore, 'This Nasty Medieval Remedy Kills MRSA', *Smithsonian* 21 March 2015. Available online: https://www.smithsonianmag.com/smart-news/nasty-medieval-remedy-kills-mrsa-180954808/#comment-3287469822, accessed 8 May 2018.
33  Kathleen Marion, comment on Erin Blakemore, 'This Nasty Medieval Remedy Kills MRSA', *Smithsonian* 21 March 2015. Available online: https://www.smithsonianmag.com/smart-news/nasty-medieval-remedy-kills-mrsa-180954808/#comment-3287469822, accessed 8 May 2018.
34  Clare Monagle and Louise D'Arcens, '"Medieval" Makes a Comeback in Modern Politics: What's Going On?', *The Conversation*, 22 September 2014. Available online: https://theconversation.com/medieval-makes-a-comeback-in-modern-politics-whats-going-on-31780, accessed 8 May 2018.
35  Louise D'Arcens, *Comic Medievalism: Laughing at the Middle Ages* (Cambridge: D.S. Brewer, 2017), 12.
36  Andrew B. R. Elliott, *Medievalism, Politics and Mass Media: Appropriating the Middle Ages in the Twenty-First Century* (Cambridge: D.S. Brewer, 2017), 200–201.
37  John T. R. Terry, 'Why ISIS Isn't Medieval', *Slate,* 19 February 2015. Available online: http://www.slate.com/articles/news_and_politics/history/2015/02/isis_isn_t_medieval_its_revisionist_history_only_claims_to_be_rooted_in.html, accessed 14 August 2018.
38  Elliott, *Medievalism, Politics,* 66.
39  Chris Jones, 'Is the Islamic State Medieval?', *The Research Headlines*, 18 September 2014. Available online: https://researchtheheadlines.org/2014/09/18/is-islamic-state-medieval/, accessed 16 June 2018.
40  Susan Gonzalez, 'Director Spike Lee Slams "Same Old" Black Stereotypes in Today's Films', *Yale Bulletin & Calendar* (Yale University), 2 March 2001. See also Matthew Hughey, 'Cinethetic Racism: White Redemption and Black Stereotypes in "Magical Negro" Films', *Social Problems* 25, no. 3 (August 2009): 543–77.
41  See *The Public Medievalist*. Available online: https://www.publicmedievalist.com/race-racism-middle-ages-toc/ for an ongoing series on the topic of race and medievalism.

42  Nir Shafir, 'Why Fame Miniatures Depicting Islamic Science Are Everywhere', *Aeon*, 11 September 2018. Available online: https://aeon.co/essays/why-fake-miniatures-depicting-islamic-science-are-everywhere, accessed 1 October 2018.
43  Ibid.
44  John Ganim, *Medievalism and Orientalism* (New York: Palgrave Macmillan, 2005), 84.
45  Ibid., 42.
46  Ibid., 85.
47  Jones, 'Is the Islamic State Medieval?'.
48  Paul Sturtevant, *The Middle Ages in Popular Imagination: Memory, Film and Medievalism* (New York: I.B. Tauris, 2018), 139.
49  Jacques Le Goff, *Time, Work, and Culture of the Middle Ages* (Chicago: The University of Chicago Press, 1980), ix.

# Audience perceptions of historical authenticity in visual media

Sian Beavers and Sylvia Warnecke

Historical media, in this context the fictive representations of history in television (TV), film and video games, have most commonly been researched in terms of their uses and formal applications in learning contexts such as schools.[1] There is limited empirical research that investigates informal engagements with historical film and television,[2] with the momentous research by Rosenzweig and Thelen carried out in 1995, before the emergence of the widespread use of digital historical games, which were therefore not included in their investigation. Additionally, while their research remains a seminal study for understanding informal historical engagements both with history, and with fictive representations of history, in the twenty-three years since their data was collected, historical media production and consumption practices have changed drastically. Consequently, more up-to-date research is needed to capture these developments.

While Rosenzweig and Thelen investigated the perceived trustworthiness or authenticity of historical film and TV, they did so in relation to other historical practices and activities such as visiting heritage sites or talking with family members, with their study participants classifying these different ways of experiencing the past based on perceptions of their trustworthiness. However, this means that the elements specifically within historical media that contributed to their participants' perceptions of (in)authenticity were not addressed in depth, as their research gave a broad overview of a variety of informal engagements with the past.

The study reported in this chapter aims to address these gaps in the literature by investigating informal engagements with historical media, through comparatively assessing audience and player perceptions of authenticity across three fictive historical media forms (TV, film, games) and also within each media form. The survey was not intended to assess audience perceptions of non-fiction media, such as TV or film documentaries, or those that are purportedly factual like textbooks. By focusing on fictionalized media, this allowed the media forms to be more explicitly comparable given the fictional nature of almost all historical games.

This study investigated a variety of elements of engagement with historical media, such as researching the historical context, discussing it with others in forums or engaging in other kinds of online activities in reference to all periods of history. However, due to the focus of this volume, only the elements of the research that relate specifically to perceptions of authenticity of the medieval are provided. Despite the survey being inclusive of all historical periods to which the respondents naturally referred, there were nonetheless common trends – regardless of the historical period discussed – when it comes to engaging with fictionalized histories in these informal ways. These trends are thus exemplified in this chapter with data pertaining to receptions of the medieval in fictional TV series, film and games.

As such, the following analysis will add more depth to previous research carried out on this topic and will enhance our understanding of how audiences perceive authenticity as created within contemporary historical visual culture. This chapter presents the results of the study and suggests several apparent trends relating to audience perceptions of authenticity within media addressing the medieval period. Namely: that representations of the Middle Ages in games are typically seen as less authentic than representations in other media formats; that the perceived veracity of material culture has a substantial impact on the perceived authenticity of a piece of media; that the perceived authenticity of media which adapts written work is based substantially on its adherence to the original text; and that media which emphasizes negative aspects of the Middle Ages are more likely to be viewed as authentic.

## Authenticity

Where accuracy is often taken to be the objective, agreed-upon facts of the past, authenticity in the context of this research is subjective: an opinion, perception or 'a sense of the genuine'.[3] The very nature of 'authenticity' is an elusive quality[4] in terms of how history is represented. The definition of 'authenticity' is often contested[5] where 'confusion surrounds the nature and use of the concept'.[6] If considering the nature of authenticity in respect to heritage sites, authenticity is not an absolute to be received but 'a social construction to be negotiated'[7] and 'defined in the tourist's own terms'.[8] Yet, what do these terms mean with reference to historical representations in media? What criteria do audiences use to assess the (in)authenticity of different media *forms* and within particular media texts? As with heritage experiences, authenticity must be defined in the audiences' own terms in relation to historical media. This chapter begins to do this by reporting on this research on audience perceptions of authenticity within their historical media engagements.

## Research aims

The aims of the research were exploratory, and with reference to authenticity the following research questions emerged:

- Which media form (TV, film, games) do audiences think is the most authentic (if any)?

- Which individual texts and titles within those forms produce perceptions of (in)authenticity?
- Which elements within those texts contribute to these perceptions?

The following sections outline the method of how these questions were implemented within an empirical survey and discuss the study findings in relation to audience's perceptions of authenticity.

## Method and instruments

An online survey was created with Bristol Online Surveys (BOS) with the purpose of exploring audiences' perceptions of historical media. The survey consisted of twenty questions, a mix of single- and multiple-choice, Likert-scale questions, and four free text answers. The nature and content of each question will be given in due course. The survey was distributed online via social media and academic mailing lists, adopting a convenience sampling approach. As such, the authors make no claims about the generalizability of the findings to the wider population as no sampling stratification took place. However, over half of respondents were British, and a quarter were from the United States or Canada, so the survey may perhaps provide findings from a particularly Western, Anglo-centric perspective. The survey was active for a period of three weeks, and after this time had accrued 621 respondents.

The gender balance was around 51 per cent female to 49 per cent male, with the breakdown of respondents by age and gender given in Table 5.1. Although females aged fifty and over and men aged between eighteen and thirty-nine who play historical games were over-represented in the data, there were no significant differences in the findings based on the age or gender of the respondents.

The free text data was analysed using a thematic approach,[9] meaning the analysis was not grounded in an existing theoretical framework, allowing themes to be identified from within the data itself. Themes were identified by fundamentality and frequency,[10] that is themes that were considered to be important by the researchers or those that had

**Table 5.1** Demographic of Survey Respondents by Gender and Age

| | What is your age? | | | | | |
|---|---|---|---|---|---|---|
| **What is your gender?** | 18–29 | 30–39 | 40–49 | 50+ | Prefer not to say | Totals |
| Male | 86 | 115 | 57 | 34 | 1 | 293 |
| Female | 75 | 89 | 58 | 96 | 2 | 320 |
| Other | 0 | 0 | 0 | 1 | 1 | 2 |
| Prefer not to say | 2 | 0 | 1 | 0 | 1 | 4 |
| No answer | 1 | 1 | 0 | 0 | 0 | 2 |
| Totals | 164 | 205 | 116 | 131 | 5 | 621 |

| Question | Response count |
|---|---|
| 17 | 621 |
| 17.a | 619 |

a high number of references from the respondents. A colleague outside the research team checked the data for inter-rater reliability, where the discussion from the cross-coding allowed for some themes to be amalgamated on the basis of our joint reflections.

## Approach to assessing authenticity

Respondents were asked for the extent of their agreement with certain statements, in the form of four-point Likert questions. A four-point (as opposed to a five, or seven) Likert was used as Leung[11] found there were no differences between four-, five-, six- and eleven-pointed Likert scales in terms of mean, standard deviation, correlation, reliability or factor analysis. Furthermore, a neutral point also means people with low motivation when completing a survey are more likely to select this option when it does not truly replicate their feeling.[12] For these reasons, a four-point Likert-scale question was implemented for Q13: 'How authentic are the historical representations in each of the media forms, in your opinion?' Respondents were asked to comparatively rate historical film, TV and games on a four-point Likert scale. This was in terms of whether they perceived each form as a whole to be 'Authentic', 'Somewhat authentic', 'Somewhat inauthentic' or 'Inauthentic', though participants were given the option not to answer this question through the use of the phrase 'I don't partake in this media' at the end of the Likert row. All responses for each medium were converted to percentages of the total respondents for that medium in order to make the findings comparable, as different numbers of respondents answered the question relating to historical television ($n = 604$), film ($n = 612$) and games ($n = 402$) respectively.

There were also four free text answers: two asking respondents which historical media they enjoyed and why (Qs 7 and 12) and two asking respondents what media texts, or aspects of media texts, they found to be authentic (Q14) and inauthentic (Q15) correspondingly. These free-text questions were clearly marked as optional, so not all respondents answered these questions. Thus, Q13 gave an overview of the respondents' perceptions of authenticity across media forms, where the aspects within individual media *texts* that produce those perceptions were gathered from the free text responses (Qs 7, 12, 14, 15).

# Findings and discussion

For reasons of clarity and pragmatism, the findings and discussion will be considered together. This is a discussion of general trends found in the data relating to historical TV and film, as the player perceptions of authenticity with reference to historical games, discussed elsewhere,[13] are only included here where productive comparisons can be made between media forms. This section has two parts: the first specifically addresses the elements within the survey relating to perceived authenticity across media forms; the second focuses on aspects within the forms of TV and film, and how these contribute to audiences' perceptions of (in)authenticity. These aspects are material culture, authenticity as fidelity to written texts, sanitized history and negativity bias and the importance of historical authenticity to audiences.

## Perceptions of authenticity across historical media forms

Respondents were asked how authentic they perceived the three media forms (TV, film, game) in terms of how they represented history (Q13) and their responses to each media form were compared (Figure 5.1).

Figure 5.1 highlights that, although no media form was considered definitively to be 'authentic', 59.7 per cent of respondents considered historical TV shows to be 'somewhat authentic'. Where historical film was comparable to historical TV in the 'somewhat authentic' band with 53.6 per cent, only 39 per cent of respondents perceived historical games as 'somewhat authentic'. This trend was inverted in relation to *in*authenticity. 58.6 per cent of the respondents answered that they perceived historical games as inauthentic (24.1 per cent) or somewhat inauthentic (34.5 per cent), compared with only 24.2 per cent (5.3 per cent inauthentic; 28.9 per cent somewhat inauthentic) answering this way in relation to historical TV. Historical film fell between the two at 41.8 per cent (9.6 per cent inauthentic; 32.2 per cent somewhat inauthentic). In terms of perceived inauthenticity, there was a steady increase in terms of degrees of perceived inauthenticity with reference to historical games; with historical TV there was a steady decrease in perceived inauthenticity. The inversion of this was true in relation to perceived authenticity.

These findings indicate that overall, while not considered wholly authentic by any stretch, historical TV was considered the most authentic of the three media forms for representing history. This was followed by film, and games were considered the least authentic media form for historical representation. Some of the reasons that TV and film were considered the more authentic media are discussed in detail in the next sections, though it is worth noting two things here. First, respondents sometimes highlighted in the free text answers that film could be considered inauthentic due to

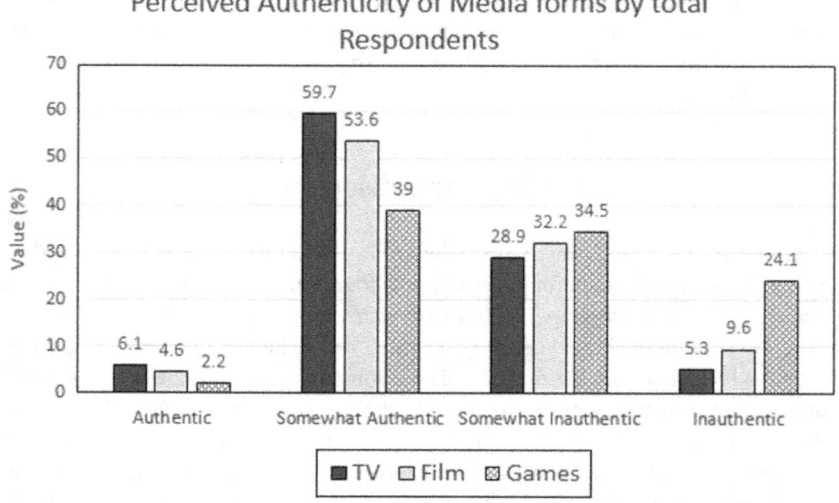

**Figure 5.1** Perceptions of historical authenticity across media forms with % adjustments.

narrative compression, where a story is condensed into a shorter version outlining the fundamental features or events.[14] From this, we can infer that the shorter running time of film in comparison to TV series, and the resulting narrative compression, could account for film being perceived as slightly less authentic than TV. Second, TV far more than film or games is used to relay factual information to viewers in documentaries, live broadcastings or the news. It could be suggested that due to TV's different status as a 'factual' information provider in comparison with the other media forms, perhaps the respondents felt TV drama was more authentic because of this association. These, however, are merely suggestions, and a more comprehensive overview of the qualitative data is covered in subsequent sections.

Broadly speaking, games were considered to be less authentic by the respondents due to the interactive nature of the form. The necessity of having to balance historical authenticity with enjoyable gameplay was seen to distort the historical representation, as the actions taken by the player were not seen to accurately represent the actions available to the historical agent(s). The pressures of the game form, due to the form's interactive nature, was seen to have a greater effect on the authenticity of the historical content represented, in comparison with the associated formal pressures of TV and film.[15]

More in-depth findings relating to historical games have been discussed elsewhere.[16] The next section addresses audience perceptions of authenticity within historical film and television in more detail.

## Perceptions of authenticity within historical film and TV

Understanding why respondents who engaged with historical TV and film answered Q13 in these ways requires analysis and discussion of responses to the free text questions (Qs7, 12, 14, 15). These questions specifically asked participants about their enjoyment of these media (Q7,12), their perceptions of the (in)authenticity of media texts (Q14, 15) and particular aspects within those media texts that contributed to these perceptions.

## Material culture: Authenticity and the 'look' of the past

By far the most prevalent trend in the data was the respondents' focus on the represented material culture. For TV and film, this was in terms of the emphasis upon the tangible artefacts, in particular costumes, props and sets. There were 185 references to authentic representations of material culture within the data from 138 unique respondents, by far the most references to any data theme.[17] Respondents talked about a variety of different media texts representing different historical periods. With specific reference to *Wolf Hall*,[18] a fictionalized historical novel later adapted for television, describing Thomas Cromwell's rise to power between 1500 and 1535 CE, three respondents stated:

> *Wolf Hall* [has] [...] realistic props and costumes. (British female, 50+, Q14)

> *Wolf Hall* [has] [. . .] very accurate costumes and settings (though giving a particular interpretation of their motivations, which may or may not have been accurate). (British female, 18–29, Q14)

> [The] [. . .] interpretations of characters aside, the setting was detailed and accurate. (British female, 18–29, Q14).

While primarily highlighting the focus on material culture when judging authenticity, the latter two pieces of data point to the nuances of audience interpretation of what an 'authentic representation' can be. While costuming, props or sets can be considered authentic, other aspects such as character interpretation might at the same time be seen as inauthentic. This was echoed in more general terms by other respondents:

> I feel that nearly every piece of media that I've seen that's allegedly based on history is inauthentic – though I often find costuming to be good. (Scottish Female, 18–29, Q14)

What the data here implies is that often, even if the media text as a whole is considered to be inauthentic, respondents are still able to pick out individual elements that they consider to be authentic – such as the costumes.

This focus on material culture is also something that has been found in the literature, in that authenticity in visual media is '[m]ost frequently . . . a matter of the "look" of the past, or rather "the period look," "period props," and "period costume"'.[19] This explicitly relates to emphasis on material culture in the findings of this study, both in terms of the increased frequency of references to this theme, as well as the specific types of material culture to which they referred. Indeed, the fact that material culture did seem to be the measure of authenticity in these media for many of the respondents may be unsurprising given that material culture is often used as the 'primary data for developing inferences about cultural, social, and other types of history'.[20] These visual media are a popular form of history, thus these respondents used the representations of material culture to gauge authenticity in a similar way as they would with other histories.

This is also the case if we turn to how authenticity is perceived to be conveyed in real-life historical contexts such as heritage experiences, as it is similarly the material artefacts that visitors are most likely to cite as authentic in empirical studies of visitor perceptions of authenticity.[21] This seems to imply that authenticity is often judged by the same criteria – the authenticity of material culture – regardless of whether the viewer is judging something actually historical at a heritage site, or something that is a reconstruction or representation of something historical, as in film and TV. This echoes other research which states that '[o]fferings can be seen as authentic by referring to other offerings already perceived as real'.[22] In terms of film and TV, this would suggest that if a representation of an artefact (a costume for example) refers earnestly to an artefact that is, or is already seen to be, authentic (genuine period clothing), then it will be considered to be authentic due to this perceived fidelity.

These conceptualizations of authenticity as fidelity and referentiality in relation to material culture were also found in the data relating to other aspects of historical representations in film and TV, with specific reference to written texts.

## Authenticity as fidelity to written texts

Some respondents made explicit comparisons between the historical narratives represented in TV and film with those seen in written texts. Again, with specific reference to *Wolf Hall* some respondents stated:

> *Wolf Hall* [is authentic] – because of the extensive research undertaken by the original author (Hilary Mantel). (Australian female, 50+, Q14)

> *Wolf Hall* [is authentic because it's] – based on a book into which a lot of historical research had gone. (British female, 50+, Q14)

These participants make specific judgements on the authenticity of the *Wolf Hall* television drama, which are based upon the perceived authenticity of the *Wolf Hall* novel.[23] As the respondents perceive the TV show to be a faithful adaptation of the 'authentic' historical novel, the TV show is seen to be authentic due to this perceived fidelity.

This was a recurring theme within the data, where there were ninety-two specific references (from seventy-one unique respondents) to a work of historical film or television being seen as authentic due to its perceived allegiance to a written work that was also seen as authentic. This does not include references from the respondents who talked about plot, storyline or narrative divergences in non-explicit terms. Although in some of the cases where explicit references to specific written texts were evident, the citing of primary or secondary historical sources were in fact a rarity. These seventy-one respondents overwhelmingly referred to historical novels that are fictive works, such as *Wolf Hall* or *The White Queen*[24] (set during the War of the Roses in the fifteenth century), and also non-medieval examples such as *I Claudius*[25] (set in ancient Rome) when they made comparative judgments about the authenticity of visual historical media. With the references to these historical novels, (in this data at least) the respondents did not question the authenticity of the written texts. This could indicate that there was an implicit assumption by the respondents of the novels being authentic and reliable – despite the fictionalized aspects of these works. This was even the case with film and TV adaptations based on written texts that, in terms of historical figures, events or narratives, were entirely fictional, as in this respondent's statement below:

> I would have to pick the Austen or Bronte BBC TV adaptations [as being authentic]. They reach a high level of authenticity and manage to stay close to the original material. (British female, 30–39, Q14)

Although this particular quote does not allude to a representation of medieval culture, it nonetheless demonstrates two important findings relating to this theme. First, it reiterates how authenticity is perceived to be created through the perceived fidelity of visual media to a written text – as evident from the data above. Second, and perhaps crucially, this respondent is referencing a fictional text, yet still perceives that the TV adaptations are authentic due to being seen as faithful adaptations of the fictive source material. Of course, part of this perception could be that respondents felt the media text authentically represented the contemporary society or social setting, rather than actual historical figure or events. Though what does seem to be clear when all the nuanced inferences from respondents are taken into account is that the written word, regardless of how fictional the content is, is seen to possess a historical authority and is thus seen to be the most authentic means by which history can be conveyed.

As Rosenstone suggests, this idea is 'a long time practice which has come to be carved in stone – the notion that a truthful past can only be told in words on the page'.[26] Even when respondents are aware that a written history is a fictionalized account, it appears that its form as a written document is more akin in spirit to the academic study of (written) history, and consequently considered more trustworthy,[27] and thus more authentic. Therefore, using Pine & Gilmore's earlier terminology, as TV and film adaptations of historical fiction refer faithfully to the 'offering' of a written text already perceived as real, they are themselves considered more authentic through this referentiality.

TV versions of historical fiction seem more prevalent than their film counterparts, perhaps in part due to the easier task of adapting the work without having to so drastically compress a book's narrative into two hours. This could be another reason as to why historical TV was considered more authentic than film, and film more so than games, where fidelity to a written work is not a particularly relevant aspect.

## Sanitized histories and negativity bias

The final theme relating to the perceived (in)authenticity of historical representations seen in film and TV is the data that suggests *in*authentic media sanitize, whitewash or 'Hollywoodize' history. Conversely, authentic media are seen to portray the opposite: the negative, upsetting, or even 'dirty' aspects of the past that highlight the difficulties faced by historical agents. In this way, these conceptions form two halves of the same coin: something that is evident within the data outlined in the following. There were eighty-four references to the idea of whitewashing, or the negative opposite, from fifty-seven unique respondents. Some respondents talked in general terms about these aspects of (in)authenticity within historical representations, such as the following respondent:

> I feel that most historical media whitewashes or changes history in order to make it appeal to more people. (Scottish female, 18–29, Q14)

The implicit assumption here is that people are more likely to engage with and enjoy a particular text if the content does not make them uncomfortable or represent any aspect of history that could be challenging to the viewer. Although the previous quote is a broad statement relating to historical media in general, other respondents were more specific about the particular aspects of historical representations that contribute to this perception of an inauthentic, sanitized history. With reference to *The Last Kingdom*,[28] a fictional TV series set in Saxon England in the ninth century, two respondents noted:

[P]eople [are] too healthy and clean in *The Last Kingdom*, the Cornish princess was way too glamourous, riding around in finery and managed to keep her hair and makeup perfect even on the battlefield. (Male, 40–49, Q15)

Films and TV rarely depict just how horrific fighting would have been - *The Last Kingdom* gets an honourable mention as the final battle does show some pretty gruesome fight scenes, but on the whole fights are depicted as being relatively bloodless and painless. (British male, 18–29, Q15)

These respondents make reference to the same text but come to different conclusions about the authenticity of different aspects of the representation. On the one hand, the first respondent considers the particular representation of the Cornish princess *inauthentic*, due to the fact that characters appear 'too healthy and clean', or even too aesthetically presentable given the context (in this case, a battlefield). On the other hand, the second respondent while stating that historical drama rarely shows how 'horrific' fighting would have been (as an indication of their inauthenticity) that *The Last Kingdom* does so, and in this way is more authentic than other media texts. This respondent is not asserting he perceives *The Last Kingdom* to be authentic overall, only that he perceives its depiction of 'gruesome fight scenes' to be an authentic aspect. As well as highlighting how the very nature of authenticity is subjective and nuanced, these pieces of data demonstrate that respondents, generally speaking, viewed inauthentic media as sanitizing or whitewashing history, and authentic media as representing the horror, gore or dirtiness of the past. This was something that was echoed by responses referring to different media titles, such as *Vikings*.[29] This TV series is inspired by the saga of the Viking Ragnar Lothbrok, and begins with the invasion of Lindisfarne at the end of the eighth century CE by Norsemen. In regard to this media, respondents stated:

*Vikings* – not sure about the historical content but they all look historically grubby and smelly! (British female, 30–39, Q12)

The representation of battle in [. . .] [*Vikings*] also brings new realistic realms of horror and gore. (British female, 18–29, Q14)

The first data reflects the respondent's expectation of what the past was like: she imagines the people of the past would have looked dirty and dishevelled, so when the representation in *Vikings* conforms to this conjecture, she considers this authentic as it confirms her existing belief. In addition to emphasizing how the depiction of negative aspects of history produces the perception of authenticity in these representations, this reiterates the authors' view of the nature of authenticity, in that it can be achieved without a viewer having historical context or backing upon which to base assumptions about the (in)authenticity of media texts.

The second piece of data is in some ways similar to that of the previous respondent in relation to *The Last Kingdom* yet offers a different perspective. Where the former respondent stated that media texts do not tend to show the gruesomeness of battle (and thus perceives them as inauthentic), the latter, in relation to *Vikings*, explicitly equates horror and gore with the representation's perceived realism. Although 'realistic' cannot be equated with 'authentic', it appears that this particular respondent is using it in this way given that Q14 asked what historical media was found to be authentic, and why.

In conjunction with the data from the other respondents in relation to this theme, this data as a whole provides empirical evidence for this trend: representations are perceived as authentic if they portray the negative aspects of the past, and they are perceived as inauthentic if they appear to whitewash, or sanitize these histories. While the examples given here relate to visual elements of the historical representations, respondents also cited the types of narratives portrayed as contributing to their perceived (in)authenticity: tragic narratives were considered to be more authentic than the triumphant, 'Hollywoodized' narratives. Blockbuster historical film tends to gravitate towards the latter type of narrative, which implies this could influence the respondent's judging historical film to be less authentic than TV.

This 'negativity bias' is a key finding in relation to the histories represented in popular media and is something that has been seen to occur elsewhere. Negativity bias is the phenomenon 'whereby humans tend to put more emphasis on negative than positive information in their feelings and judgments'.[30] The concept of negativity bias is most often applied in empirical studies relating to perceptions of political broadcasts and media such as the news, in which those eliciting negative emotions (e.g. sadness, disgust, shame) are perceived to be more authentic, or truthful, than those eliciting positive emotions (such as happiness).[31] In light of the findings reported in this chapter, it appears that historical representations in popular media are prone to the same negativity bias in terms of audience judgements of authenticity: not so much '"sad, but true" – as the every-day aphorism implies – but possibly "sad, thus true"'.[32] It is not just perceptions of authenticity that are affected by negative emotions, as studies have found that 'negative affect predicted learning'[33] and that 'negative mood actually induced greater attitude change'.[34] Although the elements of learning investigated by these researchers have not been discussed in this chapter, it is significant to note that there is a thematic correlation between the perceived authenticity of a media representation, its inclusion of negative themes and the learning outcomes occurring through engagement with said media representation. This is an avenue for further exploration, also in relation to a perceived lack of authenticity in digital games, in future research using this dataset.

## Is historical authenticity in visual media important to audiences?

Having outlined some of the ways that historical authenticity is perceived by audiences, it is worth making a final point on the significance placed on authenticity. When the respondents were asked to give an example of media texts, or aspects of media texts, they found to be authentic, eighty-five respondents stated either that they were unable to do so (Q14) or that every media text was entirely, or at least in some way inauthentic (Q15). For example,

> Films and TV series are made to be entertaining [. . .] The verb 'making' already implies that it's constructed . . . . I can't think of a historical film or TV show that is highly authentic. (Dutch male, 18–29, Q14)

Nothing is authentic! And almost everything contains bits and pieces of authenticity. (Finnish male, 30–39, Q15)

Despite the fact that these two representative respondents made blanket declarations about the nature of the authenticity of historical media, they had both previously reported that they nonetheless engaged with them. This was something that was seen elsewhere in the data, where an additional thirty respondents stated explicitly that they didn't feel historical authenticity in media to be that important, for these respondents it seemed more important that the texts be enjoyable or inspiring:

I don't believe inauthenticity is a barrier to being enjoyable. (British male, 18–29, Q14)

I know they're not very historically accurate, but I love the broad strokes of history they paint, and they inspire me to go look to more historically accurate sources for more information. (American female, 30–39, Q12)

These comments from respondents suggest two things. Firstly, they imply that people do not consider authenticity an important aspect of their engagement. These respondents demonstrate that they critically approach these media based on their function as entertainment and question their reliability as a historical source: a historical skill in its own right.[35]

This brings us to the second point. The final respondent suggests that she engages in information seeking behaviour based on the histories she has seen in historical media. Therefore, despite perceiving these media as often inauthentic representations of the past, she enjoys them regardless and turns to perceivably more reliable or credible sources for comparison, thus engaging in learning activities based on this perceived inauthenticity and undertaking a form of historical investigation. This means that perhaps the value of these media texts is not in how authentically they represent the past, but more in how they can engender critical engagement by audiences, providing a foundation for future historical enquiry.

## Conclusion

This chapter has given a broad overview of general trends of audience perceived authenticity in historical film and TV, based on the findings of a self-reported survey. The respondents compared three media forms (TV, film and games) on the basis of perceived authenticity and indicated that TV was considered the most, and historical games were the least authentic media form. The representations of material culture, particularly costumes, props and sets, were demonstrated to contribute to perceptions of authenticity in film and TV. TV and film histories were also perceived to be authentic if they were faithful adaptations or remediations of (even entirely fictional) written works, where TV and the written word were seen as the most authoritative, in that they conveyed the most authentic – or 'truest' – factual information. Historical representations in TV and film appeared to be under the influence of negativity bias, where respondents considered historical media as more authentic if they depicted the negative aspects of the past; conversely representations that were thought to whitewash or sanitize history were seen as inauthentic. Despite these respondents identifying what they felt was (in)authentic and why, these perceptions of (in)authenticity did not seem to obstruct their engagement with or enjoyment of historical media, and they considered historical authenticity to be largely inconsequential.

As a final remark, the findings here have been outlined, where possible, with specific reference to representations of the medieval in media. However, the data as a whole was drawn from references to a much wider range of historical periods. This suggests that it does not appear to matter what specific period of history is represented within a media form, as the audience and player perceptions of these media seem to function in the same way regardless.

## Appendix: Survey questions

1. Are you aged 18 or over? [Yes/No]
2. Do you play Historical Video games? [Yes/No]
3. What genres of historical games do you play? [Select All that apply: Strategy: Real-time; turn based etc.; Action: First Person Shooters, Third-Person games, Action, Action-adventure, etc.; Other: Point and click, Platformer, etc.]
4. When you play historical games, are you **more likely** to play alone or with other people? [Select One: With people face-to-face (co-located); With people online; Alone and with people (face-to-face or online) equally; Don't Know]
5. After you have played historical games, have you ever talked to anyone about the game itself and/or the historical content, either face-to-face or online (i.e. on social media, forums etc.)? [Select One: Yes: I've talked about the game; Yes: I've talked about the historical content; Yes: I've talked about both; No: I haven't talked about either; Don't Know]
6. How much do you agree with the following statements? [Select one: Agree; Somewhat Agree; Somewhat Disagree; Disagree; I do not want to answer]
    6.1. One of the main reasons I play historical games is to learn about history.
    6.2. I have learnt something about history through playing historical games.
    6.3. I have decided to play a historical game because I read a book or story with similar historical content.
    6.4. When I play historical games, I am more likely to engage with other media (e.g. TV, film) with similar historical content.
    6.5. When I play historical games, I will often take part in online activities that relate to the historical content (e.g. post on forums or social media).
7. What specific historical games do you/have you played the most? Why? [Free text]
8. Do you watch historical films or TV shows? (**Fictional**, i.e. **NOT DOCUMENTARIES**) [Yes/No]

9. When you watch historical TV or films (NOT DOCUMENTARIES), are you **more likely** to watch alone or with other people? [Select One: Alone; With people; Alone and with people equally; Don't Know]
10. **After** you have watched an historical film or TV show (NOT DOCUMENTARIES), have you ever talked to anyone about the show/film and/or the historical content, either face to face or online? [Select One: Yes: I've talked about the show/film; Yes: I've talked about the historical content; Yes: I've talked about the show/film AND the historical content; No, I haven't talked about either; Don't Know]
11. How much do you agree with the following statements? [Select one: Agree; Somewhat Agree; Somewhat Disagree; Disagree; I do not want to answer]
    11.1. One of the main reasons I watch historical film/TV is to learn about history
    11.2. I have learnt something about history through watching historical TV/film
    11.3. I have decided to watch a historical film/TV show because I read a book or story with similar historical content
    11.4. When I watch historical film/TV, I am more likely to read books or play video games with similar historical content.
    11.5. When I watch historical TV or films, I will often take part in online activities that relate to the historical content (e.g. post on forums or social media).
12. What specific historical TV shows or films (NOT DOCUMENTARIES) do you/have you watched the most? Why? [Free text]
13. How authentic/realistic are the historical representations in each of the media forms, **in your opinion?** [Select one: Authentic; Somewhat Authentic; Somewhat Inauthentic; Inauthentic; I do not partake in this medium]
    13.1. Video games
    13.2. Feature-length film (not documentaries)
    13.3. TV series (not documentaries)
14. Can you think of a specific historical film (e.g. *Apocalypse Now*, *Gladiator* etc.), TV show (e.g. *The Last Kingdom*, *Vikings*, *Downton Abbey* etc.) or video game (e.g. *Assassin's Creed*, *Total War*, *Wolfenstein* etc.) that is **highly authentic**? Why? [Free Text]
15. Can you think of a specific historical film (e.g. *Apocalypse Now*, *Gladiator* etc.), TV show (e.g. *The Last Kingdom*, *Vikings*, *Downton Abbey* etc.) or video game (e.g. *Assassin's Creed*, *Total War*, *Wolfenstein* etc.) that is **highly inauthentic**? Why? [Free Text]
16. Would you be interested in finding out the results of this survey and how the research develops? If so, please enter your email address. If not, please select 'Next'. [Email addresses will be used **strictly for this research** and not passed on to 3rd parties.] [Free Text]
17. What is your age? [Select One: 18-29; 30-39; 40-49; 50+; Prefer not to say]
    17.1. What is your gender? [Select One: Male; Female; Other; Prefer not to say]
    17.2. What is your nationality? [Drop-down list]

18. What is your occupation? [Select One: Student; Academic; Professional/Other Occupation; Other (Please specify)]
    18.1. What is your academic field/discipline/occupation/occupational area?
19. In an average month, how often do you play digital games of any kind? [Select One: I don't play games; Daily; Several times a week; Weekly; Several times a month; Once a month; Less than once a month; Prefer not to say; Don't Know]
    19.1. How long does an average gaming session last? [Select One: N/A; ½ hour; 1 hour; 2 hours; 3 hours; 4 hours; 5 hours; Over 5 hours; Prefer not to say; Don't Know]
20. In an average month, how often do you watch films or TV **of any kind**? [Select One: I don't watch TV or films; Daily; Several times a week; Weekly; Several times a month; Once a month; Less than once a month; Prefer not to say; Don't Know]
    20.1. How long does an average viewing session last? [Select One: N/A; ½ hour; 1 hour; 2 hours; 3 hours; 4 hours; 5 hours; Over 5 hours; Prefer not to say; Don't Know]
21. In an average month, how often are you online for **any reason**? [Select One: Daily; Several times a week; Weekly; Several times a month; Once a month; Less than once a month; Prefer not to say; Don't Know]
22. On average, how long are you online for? [Select One: N/A; ½ hour; 1 hour; 2 hours; 3 hours; 4 hours; 5 hours; Over 5 hours; Prefer not to say; Don't Know]

## Notes

1 For example: J. Stoddard, 'Film as a Thoughtful Medium for Teaching History', *Learning, Media and Technology* 37, no. 3 (2012): 271–88; Kurt D. Squire, 'Replaying History', PhD thesis (Bloomington: Indiana University, 2004).
2 Roy Rosenzweig and David Thelen, *The Presence of the Past* (New York: Columbia University Press, 1998).
3 Deepak Chhabra, Robert Healy, and Erin Sills, 'Staged Authenticity and Heritage Tourism', *Annals of Tourism Research* 30, no. 3 (2003): 704.
4 Jonathan Stubbs, *Historical Film: A Critical Introduction* (New York and London: Bloomsbury, 2013), 46.
5 Gordon Waitt, 'Consuming Heritage: Perceived Historical Authenticity', *Annals of Tourism Research* 27, no. 4 (2000): 2.
6 K. Andriotis, 'Genres of Heritage Authenticity: Denotations from a Pilgrimage Landscape', *Annals of Tourism Research* 38, no. 4 (2011): 2.
7 Waitt, 'Consuming Heritage', 846.
8 Ibid., 847.
9 Virginia Braun and Victoria Clarke, 'Using Thematic Analysis in Psychology', *Qualitative Research in Psychology* 3, no. 2 (2006): 77–101.
10 Anne Adams, Peter Lunt, and Paul Cairns, 'A Qualititative Approach to HCI Research', in *Research Methods for Human Computer Interaction*, eds Paul Cairns and Anna Cox (Cambridge, UK: Cambridge University Press, 2008), 138–57.
11 Shing-On Leung, 'A Comparison of Psychometric Properties and Normality in 4-, 5-, 6-, and 11-Point Likert Scales', *Journal of Social Service Research* 37, no. 4 (2011): 419.

12 Jon A. Krosnick and Stanley Presser, 'Question and Questionnaire Design', in *Handbook of Survey Research*, eds Peter H. Rossi, James D. Wright and Andy B. Anderson, 2nd edn (Bingley: Emerald Group Publishing Limited, 2010), 269.
13 Sian Beavers and Elizabeth FitzGerald, 'Perceptions, Perspectives and Practices: A Study of the Players of Historical Games', Paper presented at *DiGRA/FDG '16 Conference* (Dundee, 1–6 August 2016); Sian Beavers, 'Medievalism at Play: Audience and Player Receptions of the Medieval in Popular, Digital Media', Paper presented at *The Middle Ages in the Modern World Conference* (Manchester, 28 June–1 July 2017).
14 Michael Toolan, *Narrative: A Critical Linguistic Introduction*, 2nd edn (London: Routledge, 2012), 49.
15 Beavers and FitzGerald, 'Perceptions, Perspectives and Practices'.
16 Ibid.
17 Some respondents talked about multiple media texts in terms of material culture within the same response, the reason why 'references' has been used here.
18 *Wolf Hall* (United Kingdom: BBC Worldwide, 2015).
19 Natalie Zemon Davis, '"Any Resemblance to Persons Living or Dead": Film and the Challenge of Authenticity', *Historical Journal of Film, Radio and Television* 8, no. 3 (1988): 271.
20 Stephen Lubar and David Kingery, *History from Things: Essays on Material Culture*, ed. Stephen Lubar and David Kingery (Washington, DC: Smithsonian Books, 1995): x.
21 Waitt, 'Consuming Heritage'; Chhabra, Healy, and Sills, 'Staged Authenticity and Heritage Tourism'.
22 J. B. Pine and J. H. Gilmore, *Authenticity: What Consumers Really Want?* (Harvard: Harvard Business School Press, 2007), 71.
23 Hilary Mantel, *Wolf Hall* (London: Harper Collins, 2009).
24 Philippa Gregory, *The White Queen* (London: Simon and Schuster, 2009).
25 Robert Graves, *I, Claudius* (London: Penguin, 2006).
26 Robert Rosenstone, *History on Film: Film on History* (Harlow: Pearson, 2006), 5.
27 Robert Rosenstone, 'The Historical Film as Real History', *Film-Historia* 5, no. 1 (1995): 7.
28 *The Last Kingdom* (UK: BBC, 2015–present).
29 *Vikings* (Ireland: MGM Television, History Channel, 2013–present).
30 Chang Sup Park, 'Applying "Negativity Bias" to Twitter: Negative News on Twitter, Emotions, and Political Learning', *Journal of Information Technology & Politics* 12, no. 4 (2015): 342–59.
31 Ibid., 344.
32 Benjamin E. Hilbig, 'Sad, Thus True: Negativity Bias in Judgments of Truth', *Journal of Experimental Social Psychology* 45, no. 4 (2009): 983.
33 '"' Heather L. LaMarre and Kristen D. Landreville, 'When Is Fiction as Good as Fact? Comparing the Influence of Documentary and Historical Reenactment Films on Engagement, Affect, Issue Interest, and Learning', *Mass Communication and Society* 12, no. 4 (2009): 551.
34 Joseph P. Forgas, 'When Sad Is Better than Happy: Negative Affect Can Improve the Quality and Effectiveness of Persuasive Messages and Social Influence Strategies', *Journal of Experimental Social Psychology* 43, no. 4 (2007): 513.
35 Peter Seixas and T Morton, *The Big Six of Historical Thinking* (Toronto: Nelson Education, 2013).

# 6

# *La posta di falcone* and *la porta di ferro*

## Representations and receptions of historical fighting practices in medieval media and contemporary popular culture

Jacob Henry Deacon

## Introduction

In an early scene from *Kingdom of Heaven* (2005), Ridley Scott's adaptation of the events surrounding the 1187 siege of Jerusalem, the blacksmith protagonist Balian is given a brief lesson in swordsmanship by Godfrey, his newfound father.[1] As part of this lesson, Balian is explicitly instructed to 'never use a low guard', and instead strike from what Godfrey calls the *posta di falcone*, the guard of the hawk, holding the sword straight above the head. Such advice runs counter to the teachings of several professional fencing masters of the Middle Ages. An early fifteenth-century manuscript produced by the Italian Fiore dei Liberi, for example, shows multiple ways of approaching an opponent in a low guard. One, which Fiore called the *porta di ferro* (iron gate), involves holding the sword low with the point facing forward: when the opponent strikes, one ought to step in and beat away their sword, leaving them open to a swift counterattack (Figure 6.1). Nevertheless, Godfrey's advice remains with Balian throughout the film, eventually helping him emerge victorious from an impromptu single combat against the disgraced Guy de Lusignan, the (then) former king of Jerusalem.

The dichotomy between representations of historical fighting practices in modern cinema and medieval sources (although it will be shown that even these sources are also only representations themselves) is at the heart of this chapter on the accuracy and authenticity of contemporary understandings of the Middle Ages. This chapter will demonstrate that while it can be difficult to establish links between modern media and pragmatic martial arts literature of the Middle Ages, comparisons to other materials such as romance may be more fruitful. This approach allows one to differentiate between four ways of discerning between violence: real fights as historical practice, fighting as part of a historical martial arts and training culture (i.e. as seen in fight books), medieval representations of real fights/embodied techniques of fighting/

# La Posta di Falcone *and* La Porta di Ferro

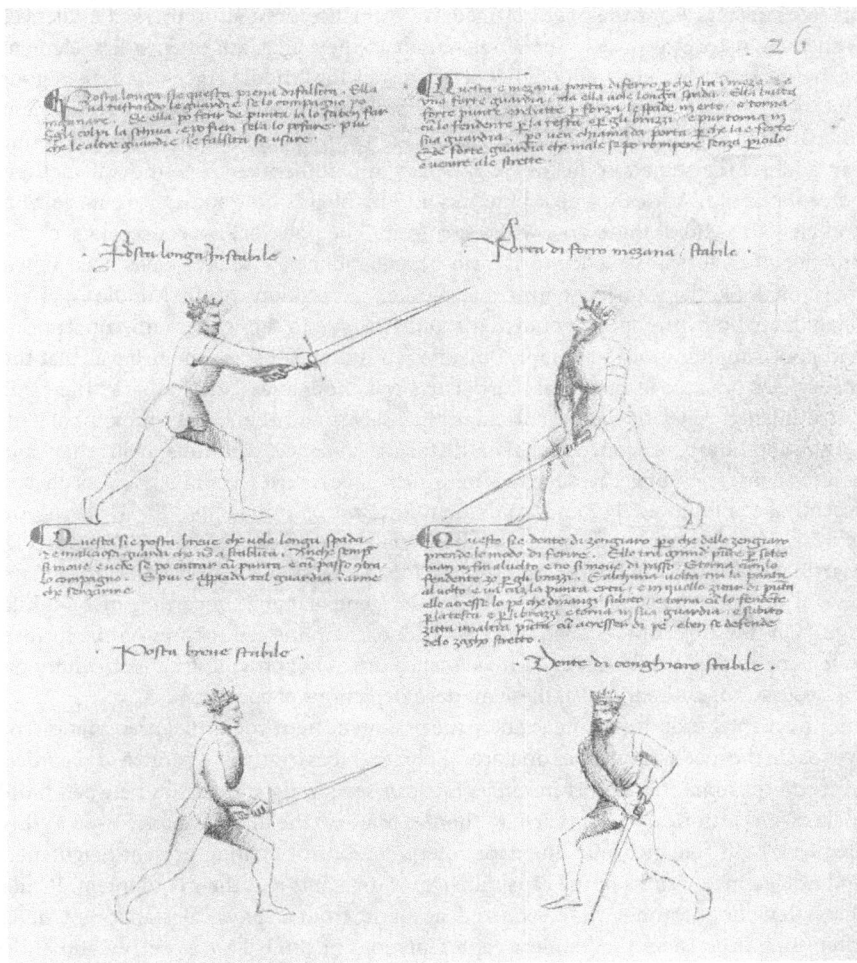

**Figure 6.1** Various low guards from Fiore dei Liberi's fight book. A version of the *porta di ferro* can be seen at the top right. Fiore dei Liberi, *Il Fior di Battaglia*, c. 1410, Los Angeles, J. Paul Getty Museum, MS Ludwig XV 13, fol. 24ʳ. Digital image courtesy of the Getty's Open Content Program.

fictional fights (i.e. chronicles and romance) and modern representations of historical practice and fictional fighting.[2] Central to this is an understanding of the purposes of recording combat in various media. While fight books often fulfil a pragmatic or emotional need, combats in romance and modern media are more alike as they are often designed to entertain audiences.

One of the most memorable ways in which medieval fighting techniques appear on the screen is in single combat. Indeed, even battles tend to be shown as a series of brief single combats fought by the protagonist(s). Heroes like the aforementioned Balian, *Game of Thrones*'s Jon Snow, and a whole Round Table's worth of King Arthurs and other characters from the pages of medieval romance have all impressed audiences with their martial prowess. The single combats they fight are often a key element of the narrative for films and shows set either in the Middle Ages or an analogous fantasy setting. While these combats are certainly opportunities for the development of character and advancement of the plot, they are also a lens through which one can address the subject of historical accuracy and authenticity.[3] A study of modern perceptions of historical combat practices also highlights how audiences engage with and view the Middle Ages on a wider spectrum. The potential for conceptions of the practice of historical violence to inform beliefs about past societies has been noted by Hannah Skoda, who recognizes that modern perceptions of the Middle Ages are often 'haunted by the spectre of extreme violence' due to thoughtless misconceptions and poor simplifications of complex medieval attitudes.[4] If someone believes that the theory and practice of medieval martial arts was thoughtless and barbaric, then this can influence views of the practitioners themselves and the society they inhabited. Correcting these misconceptions of historical violence can thus help challenge assumptions regarding the societies in which it occurred. A similar approach has recently been followed by Ken Mondschein in *Game of Thrones and the Medieval Art of War*. Mondschein's book relies on the overwhelming popularity of George R. R. Martin's *A Song of Ice and Fire* series, and its TV adaptation *Game of Thrones*, to explore several common misconceptions held by the general public regarding the Middle Ages. On the subject of combat, however, Mondschein instead focuses on the history of fencing in the Middle Ages and Renaissance instead of providing a commentary on the accuracy or authenticity of these modern depictions of combat.[5]

This chapter proposes that it is not to the pragmatic fight books that presentations of combat in the media should be compared, but rather to narratives of combat as recorded in medieval romance. In this instance, one can see strong similarities between filmmakers and historical writers such as Thomas Malory (the main romance used in this chapter); both romance and cinematic interpretations of fighting present heightened and exaggerated visions of the capabilities of combatants and their equipment. While these depictions cannot be considered accurate from a physical standpoint, it is interesting to consider that modern representations of combat are, arguably, authentic in creating the same emotional resonance as their romance counterparts. Yet although the effect is similar on these audiences separated by centuries, the subtle difference in the creation of these extreme depictions – for instance the ability of swords to penetrate the strongest parts of armour – should still be taken into account. While some romance writers likely had experience of warfare or were aware of the realities of the use of arms and armour, modern directors' interpretations are often informed by longstanding misconceptions present in popular culture surrounding the Middle Ages.[6]

This chapter also focuses on combat as it is portrayed in films and media, but this is not the only way in which the public interacts with medieval violence: more and more videogames set in the Middle Ages have attempted to incorporate an interpretation of combat influenced by fight books. Given their popularity and potential to inform players' beliefs about the Middle Ages, this line of enquiry could also produce interesting results.[7] Furthermore, although many fight books are illustrated, these are not the only visual depictions we have of medieval combat practices, as they are also seen in manuscript illuminations and other artwork. Aspects of these often present combat, or warfare, in a highly stylized manner, and a comparison between these illustrations and visual depictions of technique in the modern media may make for intriguing similarities.[8] They have, however, not been assessed in this present study due to spatial limitations.

## Representations of combat in fight books and on film

One of the key groups of sources for this study are a heterogeneous corpus of late medieval and early modern texts referred to as fight books (from the German *Fechtbuch*). These materials have increasingly received attention in Anglophone scholarship since the publication of *The Martial Arts of Renaissance Europe* by Sydney Anglo.[9] Fight books are defined by Daniel Jaquet as any text on the theory and practice of (predominantly single) combat, with or without visual depictions.[10] If such a definition seems broad or vague, then it is through necessity. A wide definition is required because of the extensive range of martial content and communication strategies in these sources. Fight books describe the use of a wide curriculum of arms: the medieval material alone depicts combatants fighting unarmed or wielding two-handed swords, swords and bucklers, a variety of staff weapons and even several specialized duelling weapons.[11] The texts, furthermore, address fighting without armour, in harness or on horseback. Nor is their content the only differentiating factor; fight books were also produced for a diverse multitude of purposes and audiences, and often relay their pragmatic contents through complex and varied textual and visual communication strategies.[12] While the limitations of using fight books to assess historical combat will be explored later, it is at this stage important to clarify that they overwhelmingly describe combat between just two individuals, whether in a judicial, sportive or self-defence context, and that many of the techniques shown were likely unsuitable for use in a larger encounter such as on the battlefield.

Studies of historical technique informed by fight books often criticize the depictions of combat offered up by contemporary filmmakers. Rachel Kellett has stressed that the 'complexity and precision' of the fighting system of Johannes Liechtenauer, an itinerant fourteenth-century fencing master whose teachings are central to the German fight books, 'indicates that medieval fencing was very different from the depiction of medieval combat in modern theatre and film as nothing but hacking and slashing'.[13] Stephen Atkinson has also highlighted that there are numerous differences between combat as portrayed in fight books and on the screen.[14] Nor are medievalists the only scholars to show an interest in the subject, as shown by Teresa Ende and Jürgen Müller's study of early modern duelling on film.[15] Such assertions from Kellet and Atkinson are correct; there are remarkably few positive comparisons that can be made between how combat is depicted by the fight book writers and modern directors/choreographers. This is emblematic of the wider treatment of the Middle Ages by filmmakers. Nikolas Haydock argues that films set in the Middle Ages 'flaunt anachronism, designed not to render faithfully their respective sources in Malory or Chaucer, but rather to appeal to a cinematic imaginary about the Middle Ages, composed of bits and pieces drawn from film history and popular culture'.¹⁶ A similar argument can be made regarding combat, in that directors and choreographers are inspired more often by other medieval action films as opposed to historical sources: there is little to separate the physicality of single combat between Arthur and Lancelot in *Excalibur* (1981) from the fights involving the future King Edward II of England and Robert the Bruce in *Outlaw King* (2018).

Modern interpretations of historical combat on the screen also have much in common with longstanding but mistaken opinions originating with Victorian antiquarians that played a significant role in creating the image of the brutal, brawn-over-brains combat of the Middle Ages. Egerton Castle in particular advanced the notion that 'the rough untutored fighting of the Middle Ages represented faithfully the reign of brute force in social life as well as in politics'.¹⁷ According to Castle, a man's 'superiority in action depended on his power of wearing heavier armour and dealing heavier blows than his neighbour, where strength was lauded more than skill', and it was not until the use of armour began to decline that the art of fencing could thrive.¹⁸ Indeed, Castle even lauds those who had to learn how to fight without armour for being more talented, as this was a display of skill, as opposed to simple endurance.¹⁹ This latter point is certainly one echoed throughout modern depictions of medieval combat. A trial by combat in *Game of Thrones* (series 4, episode 8) sees the lithe and relatively unarmoured Oberyn Martell fight against Gregor Clegane, known as The Mountain due to his extraordinary height, who takes to the arena clad head to toe in armour. The armoured Gregor is clumsy and uncoordinated, relying on his brute strength as opposed to Oberyn's dexterous strikes. Eventually it is Oberyn's hubris that costs him his life, but the choreography still serves to illustrate prevailing notions regarding the mobility of armoured combatants. Rather, the late medieval knight was able to perform all sorts of athletic feats in his harness seemingly unhindered by the weight of his armour.²⁰ The anonymous biographer of the French knight, Jean II le Maingre, known as Boucicaut, wrote in the early fifteenth century how his master could leap on to a horse, perform a somersault, or even 'climb right to the top of the underside of a scaling ladder leaning against a wall, simply from swinging from rung to rung by his two hands', all while wearing his harness.²¹

This trope is just one of several to be found in films depicting the use of medieval arms and armour. Weapons themselves are often treated not like swords, but lightsabres capable of cutting through anything before them. Even the epitome of late medieval protection for the body, plate armour, is regularly overcome by cuts and slashes, even though such armour was designed to withstand these assaults. A striking instance of the exaggerated capabilities of weapons can be seen in *Ironclad* (2011), a story centred on a drastically altered interpretation of the 1215 siege of Rochester Castle. Defender of the castle and reluctant Templar Thomas Marshall at one point cleaves an opponent from clavicle to pelvis with a single stroke of his anachronistic two-handed sword.²² Neither the haft of his opponent's axe, his gambeson, nor even skeletal structure is enough to prevent the horrific injury from completely destroying him. Such strikes do not appear in the corpus of late medieval and early modern fight books. Admittedly, some fight books censor the violent consequences of success, but even the most graphic do not depict swords causing such destructive wounds.²³ The 1459 fight book of the

German master Hans Talhoffer can be regarded as one of the most violent of the genre: combatants decapitate opponents and dismember limbs, but nothing as destructive as Marshall's strike is depicted.[24] When such strikes are parried in modern film, these are often little more than static blocks, with actors often stood at a distance to make parrying unnecessary. Combatants swing their weapons back, signalling their intent, before striking another blow.[25] This manner of fighting runs directly against what is often described in German fight books: strikes that threaten the opponent while countering their attack. Talhoffer, in his recital of the mnemonic *Zettel* of Johannes Liechtenauer, suggests that '*wer dier Oberhowt, zorn how ortt dem trowt*', that if one's opponent cuts from above with an *oberhow*, then one should throw one's own strike, a *zornhow*, to counter this and swivel the point towards him.[26]

There are occasionally, however, aspects of fight books that do appear on film. The aforementioned scene involving Marshall also shows him using a technique called half-swording, placing the left hand on the blade of the sword. This gives greater control over the sword's point, allowing for more accurate thrusts aimed at the weaker parts of an opponent's armour. It also results in more powerful thrusts and makes it easier to use the sword as a lever and control the opponent's body in close-quarter grappling. Cinematic protagonists are sometimes aware of similar principles: in the fencing lesson between Balian and Godfrey, Balian is swiftly taught that 'the blade isn't the only part of a sword' when he finds his father's pommel threatening to pummel his face. Marshall also wields his sword with both hands on the blade to execute a *Morttschlag*, or murder-strike, a blow aimed at an opponent's head with the quillons or pommel of a sword. It is important to bear in mind, however, that the inclusion of techniques is, by far, the exception to the rule in cinema.

With that said, the fight books provide, at best, a highly flawed framework for researching historical technique. On an epistemological level, a close reading of them encourages scholars to thus distinguish between real fights as historical practice and fighting as part of a martial arts and training culture: the second of these is what is depicted in the fight books. Eric Burkart has noted several problems inherent in using the fight books as a record of historical embodied technique, the most significant of these being how the act of interpretation is informed by modern rather than historical cultures of movement.[27] Drawing on the work of Ben Spatz and his discussion of technique and practice (technique is defined as bodily knowledge which can inform practice, while practice is a singular, unrepeatable moment of utilizing technique), Burkart has shown that a historical culture of fighting informed by cultural techniques, real practices and a didactic concept of technique has been replaced by a modern culture of fighting informed by different cultural techniques, modern fighting practices, and thus only a possible concept of what individual techniques may have been.[28] This distinction further creates a divide between the record of combat in fight books and in modern film (indeed, the former can be categorized as a modern image of real fights as historical practice), but also between such sources and the ability of the historian to fully comprehend them.

Another issue relates to how well the fight books represent the totality of fighting knowledge from the Middle Ages. Only one fight book manuscript, describing the use of sword and buckler, can be dated to the fourteenth century with any certainty, and it is only from the fifteenth century onwards that these texts began to appear regularly.[29] Fencing masters and professional instructors were certainly active long before this. There are, for instance, examples of individuals training students for judicial combat in England from the twelfth century onwards, but no trace of their teachings remain.[30] Given the evolution of arms and armour over the Middle Ages, however, and the impact of technology on the way in which people fought, it is readily apparent that these later works cannot fully represent the practices of earlier centuries.[31]

A further important consideration is how representative the fight books are of medieval practices, not only from an epistemological perspective but one pertaining to their actual content and audiences. Writers were keen to stress that their contents should remain secret. Fiore dei Liberi claimed that a close relative of his pupil would only be admitted to observe the class after swearing to secrecy.[32] The writer of a later fight book heavily influenced by one of Fiore's works, Filippo Vadi, went as far as espousing what sorts of people he believed should be allowed to learn the contents of his manuscript: 'never, by any means, [should] this art and doctrine fall into the hands of unrefined and low born men. Because Heaven did not generate these men, unrefined and without wit or skill, and without any agility, but they were rather generated as unreasonable animals, only able to bear burdens and to do vile and unrefined works.'[33] Rather, Vadi argued that only those of 'perspicacious talent and lovely limbs', that is to say courtiers, scholars, barons, princes, dukes and kings were among those who should learn how to fight.[34] Given the privileged audiences of many of the fight books, one wonders how well the genre represents general martial practices of the Middle Ages. Jeffrey Forgeng has taken this argument further, questioning how much the skills of already experienced practitioners would have been influenced by the possession of such books.[35]

Yet despite these limitations, fight books remain among the least problematic materials for engaging with the subject of historical combat. One potential source of information regarding the conduct of combatants in combat is the extensive corpus of chronicles, some of which contain detailed accounts of hand-to-hand fighting in different contexts, whether during war, trial by battle, or tournament. Sydney Anglo, however, has illustrated the caution that must be exercised in dealing with narrative sources that face the difficulty of trying to record technical and subtle movements in written text, and which often directly contradict each other when recorded by multiple eyewitnesses. To illustrate this point Anglo gives the example of a series of single combats held in 1467 between Antoine de Bourgogne, Bastard of Burgundy, and Anthony Woodville, Earl Rivers.[36] Even though there were four eyewitnesses to the combat they all disagree on how the action unfolded. They are unable to establish a consensus as to how or when the Bastard's horse died, let alone which combatant came out on top in the subsequent pollaxe combat. Chris Given-Wilson has explored similar themes for a joust that occurred while King Edward III was campaigning in France. According to Walsingham's chronicle, one Thomas Colville rode across the River Somme to joust with a French knight who had insulted the king and consequently slew him. The *Eulogium historiarum*, however, and the *Anonimalle Chronicle*, offer alternative interpretations: in the former neither party is injured, and in the latter they even departed as friends.[37] As such, even though chronicles can contain detailed accounts of how combats were fought, they should be used only with utmost caution in assessing the physicality of medieval combats, and more, in a manner similar to romance, an idealized depiction of the way writers believed that combats should be fought. Indeed, Joanna Bellis and Megan G. Leitch have shown how romance, *chansons de geste*, and historical chronicles alike draw on similar chivalric themes, especially in how they 'reflected, and reflected on, their society and its ideals'.[38] Key to this understanding is that 'what was important about stories focusing on the wars and quests of kings and knights was not always their factual truth-value, but the moral or instrumental truth they conveyed'.[39]

## Representations of combat in Middle English romance

In turning from fight books towards late medieval romance the similarities between historical and modern representations of combat become more frequent. One such example is the aforementioned theme of protagonists dealing blows capable of rending and sundering armour and wearer alike. Perhaps the most visceral example of this is to be seen in the mortal duel between Arthur and Mordred at the climax of Malory's *Morte Darthur*.

> And there Kyng Arthur smote Sir Mordred undir the shylde, with a foyne of hys speare, thorowoute the body more than a fadom. And whan Sir Mordred felte that he had hys dethys wounde he threste hymselff with the myght that he had up to the burre of Kynge Arthurs speare, and ryght so he smote his fadir, Kynge Arthure, with hys swerde holdynge in both hys hondys, uppon the syde of the hede, that the swerde perced the helmet and the tay of the brayne. And therewith Mordred daysshed downe starke dede to the erthe.[40]

Both Arthur and Mordred deal blows that render their armour superfluous for anything but indicating their noble status. Arthur's spear pierces through Mordred's harness front and back, while a cut from Mordred's sword cleaves through Arthur's helmet.[41] This is far from an unusual theme in the text, as several of the most memorable strikes in the *Morte Darthur* are devastating cuts. Indeed, it could be claimed that they are so memorable because they are so impossible.[42] Arthur performs similar deeds in his earlier combat with the Emperor Lucius, striking him so that 'frome the creste of his helme unto the bare pappys hit wente adoune, and so ended the emperour'.[43] Atkinson has commented how 'slashing cuts are virtually unknown' in Malory, yet they emerge as some of the most memorable strikes in the whole text.[44] Other knights perform similar feats. Gareth cleaves one knight from helmet to shoulders, splitting his head open in the process, while the brothers Balyn and Balan unknowingly duel one another until stripped entirely of their harnesses.[45] Robert Maslen has also considered the implications of 'armour that doesn't work' in Middle English literature and how the failings of harness serve to create suspense when it either breaks or a combatant must do without.[46] The ease with which armour can be destroyed in romance and on screen is thus another way in which one can demonstrate the emotional authenticity of medieval representations of combat. The performers of such deeds are transformed by their annihilation of armours into 'medieval supermen' capable of performing feats of arms unobtainable by, but aspirational for real knights.[47] Whilst it has been argued that 'readers (or listeners) would not envision [. . .] great slashing wounds but a refined, deft set of techniques, their own raised to an extraordinary level of expertise', I would argue that it is not increased expertise but instead exaggerated physical capabilities which have been bestowed upon the protagonists, allowing them to perform techniques impossible for other fighters, and create a more entertaining narrative.[48] Similar conclusions are shared by Abels in that the exaggeration of violence in manuscript illustrations likely 'added to the enjoyment' of its audience.[49]

Nor is this an uncommon trope in films depicting the Middle Ages and medieval-inspired worlds. In a judicial combat between Sandor Clegane and Berric Dondarrion in *Game of Thrones*, the former delivers a blow comparable to that of Arthur's in his combat with Lucius. Clegane strikes at his opponent with a descending cut that first cleaves through Dondarrion's raised sword, and then through his steel pauldrons, becoming embedded in his chest before Dondarrion keels over. Examples such as this demonstrate how a comparison of modern media with romance is far more apt than one with the seemingly didactic fight books. That is not to say, however, that romance are completely analogous with historical combat practices. At the very least, there is occasionally an overlap of the terminology for certain techniques, but this often refers to basic techniques. In the fight between Tristram and Nabone, Malory describes how the two knights 'fought longe on foote, trasynge and transversynge, smytynge and foynynge longe withoute ony reste'.[50] Foining (Malory's 'foynynge') appears frequently in Middle English fight books to describe thrusts.[51] The appearance of this terminology in the *Morte Darthur* is, however, more limited than the propensity for combatants' blows to cave in helmets and cause other exaggerated wounds, and must be considered an exception in the genre. Malory is thus arguably conceiving of combat in his work not as a record of a real fight as historical practice but simply as a representation of a fictional fight. Such a distinction would limit what can be gained by seeking to compare fight books and romance to gain a more complete understanding of historical technique.[52]

Another observable trope in both romance and film is the popularity of depicting protagonists as engaging in single combat during battles and sieges, occasionally to decide the outcome of the encounter and thus acting as a form of judicial combat.[53] This trope has previously been commented on by Lynch, who noted that 'Malory's ideal of a perfectly informed and universally acceptable fighting narrative is a patent fantasy, if one thinks of the babble of conflicting accounts succeeding a real late-medieval battle', and that he tends to treat all fights as a series of single combats.[54] Other romances also employ single combat in the form of a judicial duel as a means of resolving political conflict. The anonymous fourteenth-century romance *Sir Tryamour* has the eponymous protagonist duel with the emperor's champion, the giant Moradas, in a bid to prevent further bloodshed between the armies of King Ardus of Aragon, and the Holy Roman Emperor.[55] The reasoning behind the propensity for engagements to be decided by single combat has been commented upon by Lee Ramsey, who notes that audiences were 'less interested in armies fighting armies than in one man sallying out against the world and subduing it by force'.⁵⁶ One could even argue that the same principal is the reason why fight books so overwhelmingly focus on combat between only two individuals. The desire of audiences, both medieval and modern, to engage with the arc of a single protagonist may also be why combat in romance and films rarely ends with the medieval practice of ransom, which Michele Poellinger notes is almost unheard of in the genre: the request of one knight to be ransomed in *Kingdom of Heaven*, for example, is met with a swift strike to the back of the head with a warhammer.⁵⁷

Lynch's assessment that single combat represents an ideal form of fighting for the writers of romance can certainly be seen on a much wider scale as something that real knights and men-at-arms often aspired to. Although there is no record of a war in the late Middle Ages being resolved by single combat, several chronicles record them taking place before battle.⁵⁸ The fourteenth-century English chronicler Geoffrey le Baker gives two such instances. The first of these is a single combat fought before the battle of Halidon Hill in 1333. Le Baker records how an enormous Scottish champion called Turnbull, 'a second Goliath', stood between the English and Scottish armies and challenged any Englishman to fight with him.⁵⁹ The challenge was answered by Robert Benhale, who first dispatched Turnbull's dog before cutting off his left hand, and then his head.⁶⁰ The second relates to how, at the battle of Poitiers in 1356, the French army was preceded by jousters 'as was the custom', who were in turn met by English knights from the vanguard who were 'especially chosen' to take part in the jousts.⁶¹ Opportunities to compete like this were not to be missed: Robert Jones argues that brave deeds not only had to be done but also needed to be 'seen to be done' in order to satisfy the performative nature of chivalry.⁶² Due to the strong streak of individualism in this chivalric ethos, single combat provided participants a good chance to distinguish and make a name for themselves.⁶³ Despite single combat featuring as a common literary trope in romance, historical narratives show that knights and men-at-arms never actually crossed blades in order to settle the fate of a battle or a siege. That is not to say that such challenges were not issued. Both King Edward III and King Henry V of England are recorded as having sent challenges to single combat to King Philippe VI and Prince Louis of France.⁶⁴ These challenges, however, appear to have been issued as clever pieces of propaganda which their issuers knew would go unanswered, allowing them to claim the moral high ground by submitting themselves to the judgement of God and acting to prevent further unnecessary death.

The occurrence of single combat to resolve conflict is, however, a frequent narrative device in films depicting the Middle Ages. At the end of *Ironclad*, Thomas Marshall and the leader of the Danish mercenaries engage in single combat. The defeat of the Danish captain is the final nail in the coffin for King John's siege. Likewise, as the battle for Camelot rages around them in *First Knight* (1995), Lancelot and Maleagant lock eyes and cross swords. It is only once Lancelot reclaims Excalibur that he defeats Maleagant and the scene cuts to the warlord's army fleeing the city after his demise. Ramsey's comments about the preferment of romance audiences to focus on the actions of the individual as opposed to the narrative of a battle as a whole can again be seen here.⁶⁵ Indeed, even in large battles the emphasis often remains on one or a few protagonists as opposed to the deeds of the numerous warriors surrounding them. For example, *Game of Thrones*'s Jon

Snow remains the focal point of the climactic Battle of the Bastards around which all the action is centred until the arrival of an allied army (series 6, episode 9).

The similarities between medieval romance and modern visual media are thus clear to see. In addressing questions of accuracy and authenticity, this comparison is certainly an interesting one to make, and arguably more fruitful than a comparison to fight books. Unlike the fight books, which often fulfil a pragmatic function, combat in both romance and modern visual media are present primarily to entertain an audience.[66] It should be noted, however, that the overall function of romance was not solely to delight audiences: Catherine Nall, for example, has shown how Malory's rhetoric of war, particularly in relation to Arthur's conflict with Rome, can be read as an argument for expansionism.[67] Martha Driver suggests that to a modern audience, film 'provides immediacy and simultaneously appeals to the imagination, engaging the viewer in the past and involving him emotionally and imaginatively in the action on screen'.[68] To modern audiences, such combats do not have to look accurate, but rather only need to feel authentic.

## Conclusion

Medieval arms and armour are often depicted and used in ways that bear little resemblance to what is depicted in fight books, or what can be learned today from wearing armour, as combatants weighed down by their harnesses hack and slash at each other using largely ineffectual strikes. This chapter has demonstrated, however, that the issue is not as black and white as it may first appear. Fight books are not the sole body of literature to which modern interpretations of historical technique can be compared; moreover, the fight books themselves offer only an imperfect record of these historical techniques. At the same time, scholars such as Kellet and Atkinson are not wrong to suggest that the physicality of combat representations in film is lacking. In this regard there is much room for improvement, as presenting combatants and their martial arts as barbaric can create a damaging portrayal of the Middle Ages.

Popular culture relating to the Middle Ages, however, is rarely designed to be an accurate reflection of the medieval past, but rather is meant to entertain. As such, it is more fitting to compare these modern interpretations to other historical materials that are also designed to entertain, such as romance. When this comparison is made far more similarities become apparent, especially in comparison to the exaggerated wounds and destruction of armour. Similar contexts for these conflicts can also be established given the popularity of the trope of single combat to determine the outcome of an engagement in both romance and film. Interacting with such forms of popular culture offers scholars the chance to critique and challenge modern interpretations of the Middle Ages, and also to reassess their own notions of accuracy and authenticity.

## Notes

1   The author would like to offer his thanks to the kind improvements offered by the anonymous reviewer, Eric Burkart, Trevor Russell Smith and Karen Watts.

2   A similar typology of violences has been proposed in Eric Burkart, 'Zweikampfpraktiken zwischen sozialer Normierung, medialer Präsentation und wissenschaftlicher Einordnung', in *Agon und Distinktion: Soziale Räume des Zweikampfs zwischen Mittelalter und Neuzeit*, ed. Uwe Israel and Christian Jaser (Berlin: Lit Verlag, 2016), 4–14.
3   The subject of accuracy and authenticity in popular presentations of medieval combat and warfare is one which has attracted increasing attention outside of academia. Key scholars of medieval military history such as Kelly DeVries have given interviews commenting on the historicity of warfare in the popular *Game of Thrones* series. Tom Barnes, '"Game of Thrones": We Talked to Historians and a Military Expert about Who Will Win the Iron Throne', *Mic*, 21 July 2017, https://mic.com/articles/182474/game-of-thrones-we-talked-to-historians-and-a-military-expert-about-who-will-win-the-iron-throne, accessed 9 September 2019.
4   Hannah Skoda, *Medieval Violence: Physical Brutality in Northern France, 1270–1330* (Oxford: Oxford University Press, 2013), 1.
5   Ken Mondschein, *Game of Thrones and the Medieval Art of War* (Jefferson, NC: McFarland, 2018), 75–104.
6   P. J. C. Field, *Malory: Texts and Sources* (Cambridge: D. S. Brewer, 1998), 65.
7   A similar framework was recently adopted by Victoria Cooper, who explores attitudes to race and identity play in the game *The Elder Scrolls V: Skyrim* (2011). Victoria Elizabeth Cooper, 'Fantasies of the North: Medievalism and Identity in Skyrim', Unpublished doctoral thesis, University of Leeds, 2016. While at first glance, it might seem that because video games are designed primarily to entertain consumers and thus depictions of medieval combat serve the same purposes, there are differences in the purposes of including it and representing it in different ways. In a video game the aim of the developers is not just to show the fight, add tension, and advance the narrative, but also to make the player feel as if they are the protagonist (or antagonist!) and as if they belong in that world. For this reason, developers have in recent years become more interested in attempting to use fight books and other sources in order to create a more 'realistic' interpretation of combat. *Kingdom Come: Deliverance* (2018), a game set in fifteenth-century Bohemia, even released a documentary about the influence of fight books on their creation of the game: *Fechtbuch: The Real Swordfighting behind Kingdom Come* (2019).
8   For some approaches to the presentation of war in medieval artwork, see the following: Richard Abels, 'Cultural Representations of Warfare in the High Middle Ages: The Morgan Picture Bible', in *Crusading and Warfare in the Middle Ages: Realities and Representations. Essays in Honour of John France*, ed. Simon John and Nicholas Morton (Farnham: Ashgate, 2014), 13–35; John R. Hale, *Artists and Warfare in the Renaissance* (New Haven, CT: Yale University Press, 1990); Pamela Porter, *Medieval Warfare in Manuscripts* (London: British Library, 2000).
9   Sydney Anglo, *The Martial Arts of Renaissance Europe* (New Haven and London: Yale University Press, 2000).
10  Daniel Jaquet, 'Combattre en armure à la fin du Moyen Âge et au début de la Renaissance d'après les livres du combat', unpublished doctoral thesis, Université de Genève, 2013, 18–20.
11  For a recent study of duelling weapons in the fight books, see Ariella Elema, 'Tradition, Innovation, Re-enactment: Hans Talhoffer's Unusual Weapons', *Acta Periodica Duellatorum* 7, no. 1 (2019): 3–25.

12  Jacob Henry Deacon, 'Prologues, Poetry, Prose and Portrayals: The Purposes of Fifteenth-Century Fight Books According to the Diplomatic Evidence', *Acta Periodica Duellatorum* 4, no. 2 (2016): 69–90; Jeffrey L. Forgeng, 'Owning the Art: The German *Fechtbuch* Tradition', in *The Noble Art of the Sword: Fashion and Fencing in Renaissance Europe*, ed. Tobias Capwell (London: Wallace Collection, 2012), 164–75; Jens Peter Kleinau, 'Visualised Motion: Iconography of Medieval and Renaissance Fencing Books', in *Late Medieval and Early Modern Fight Books: Transmission and Tradition of Martial Arts in Europe (14<sup>th</sup>–17<sup>th</sup> Centuries)*, ed. Daniel Jaquet, Karin Verelst, and Timothy Dawson (Leiden: Brill, 2016), 88–116.
13  Rachel E. Kellett, '". . . Vnnd schüß im vnder dem schwert den ort lang ein zů der brust": The Placement and Consequences of Sword-blows in Sigmund Ringeck's Fifteenth-Century Fencing Manual', in *Wounds and Wound Repair in Medieval Culture*, ed. Larissa Tracy and Kelly DeVries (Leiden: Brill, 2015), 130.
14  Stephen Atkinson, '"They . . . toke their shyldys before them and drew oute their swerdys . . .": Inflicting and Healing Wounds in Malory's *Morte Darthur*', in *Wounds and Wound Repair*, 529.
15  Teresa Ende and Jürgen Müller, 'En Garde! Duelldarstellungen in der bildenden Kunst und im Film', in *Das Duell. Ehrenkämpfe vom Mittelalter bis zur Moderne*, ed. Ulrike Ludwig, Barbara Krug-Richter, and Gerd Schwerhoff (Konstanz: UVK Verlaggesellschaft, 2010), 325–47.
16  Nickolas A Haydock, 'Arthurian Melodrama, Chaucerian Spectacle, and the Waywardness of Cinematic Pastiche in *First Knight* and *A Knight's Tale*', *Studies in Medievalism XII: Film and Fiction, Reviewing the Middle Ages*, ed. Tom Shippey (Woodbridge: Boydell, 2003), 5.
17  Egerton Castle, *Schools and Masters of Fence, from the Middle Ages to the Eighteenth Century* (London: Bell, 1885), 5.
18  Ibid., 13.
19  Ibid., 14.
20  Daniel Jaquet and Vincent Deluz, 'Moving in Late Medieval Harness: Exploration of a Lost Embodied Knowledge', *Journal of Embodied Research* 1, no. 1 (2018). Available online: https://jer.openlibhums.org/article/10.16995/jer.7/, accessed 18 October 19.
21  *The Chivalric Biography of Boucicaut, Jean II Le Meingre*, trans. Craig Taylor and Jane H. M. Taylor (Woodbridge: Boydell, 2016), 31.
22  Such weapons would not become widespread until over a century later.
23  Kleinau, 'Visualised Motion', 111–13.
24  Ibid., 112.
25  This is of course done for reasons of safety. It would be unreasonable to expect actors to put themselves at unnecessary risk.
26  Hans Talhoffer, 1459, Kopenhagen, Det Koneglige Bibliothek, MS Thott.290.2°, fol. 2<sup>v</sup>.
27  Eric Burkart, 'Limits of Understanding in the Study of Lost Martial Arts: Epistemological Reflections on the Mediality of Historical Records of Technique and the Status of Modern (Re-)Constructions', *Acta Periodica Duellatorum* 4, no. 2 (2016): 24.
28  Burkart, 'Limits of Understanding', 11–21; For Spatz's discussion of technique and practice, see Ben Spatz, *What a Body Can Do: Technique as Knowledge, Practice as Research* (London: Routledge, 2015), 40–41.
29  The first of these is Leeds, Royal Armouries, MS FECHT 1, often dated to the turn of the fourteenth century. The second is Nürnberg, Germanisches Nationalmuseum, Cod. Hs. 3227a, the dating of which has proven more problematic. For the dating

of the latter 3227a, see Eric Burkart, 'The Autograph of an Erudite Martial Artist: A Close Reading of Nuremberg, Germanisches Nationalmuseum, Hs. 3227a', in *Late Medieval and Early Modern Fight Books*, 451.
30  Anglo, *The Martial Arts of Renaissance Europe*, 7.
31  For an overview of the evolution of arms and armour in the Middle Ages, see Kelly DeVries and Robert Douglas Smith, *Medieval Military Technology*, 2nd edn (North York: University of Toronto Press, 2012).
32  Fiore dei Liberi, *Il Fior di Battaglia*, fol. 1$^v$.
33  Filippo Vadi, *Arte Gladiatoria Dimicandi: 15$^{th}$-Century Swordsmanship of Master Filippo Vadi*, trans. Luca Porzio and Gregory Mele (Union City, CA: Chivalry Bookshelf, 2003), 33–4.
34  Ibid.
35  Forgeng, 'Owning the Art', 171.
36  Anglo, *The Martial Arts of Renaissance Europe*, 18–19.
37  Chris Given-Wilson, *Chronicles: The Writing of History in Medieval England* (London: Hambledon, 2004), 106.
38  Joanna Bellis and Megan G. Leitch, 'Chivalric Literature', in *A Companion to Chivalry*, ed. Robert W. Jones and Peter Coss (Woodbridge: Boydell, 2019), 251.
39  Ibid., 252.
40  Thomas Malory, *Le Morte Darthur*, ed. P. J. C. Field (Cambridge: Brewer, 2017), 923–24.
41  For the social importance attached to armour, see Shelagh Mitchell, 'The Armour of Sir Robert Salle: An Indication of Social Status?', in *Fourteenth-Century England VIII*, ed. J. S. Hamilton (Woodbridge: Boydell, 2014), 83–94.
42  Similar conclusions have been reached by Richard Abels. In his work on depictions of warfare in the Morgan Picture Bible, Abels highlights that despite the improvements to armour in the twelfth and thirteenth centuries, which are carefully recorded in the illustrations, none of it offers any protection from the weapons wielded by warriors shown in the manuscript. Abels, 'Cultural Representations of Warfare in the High Middle Ages', 23.
43  Malory, *Le Morte Darthur*, 173.
44  Atkinson, 'They . . . toke their shyldys before them and drew oute their swerdys', 529.
45  Malory, *Le Morte Darthur*, 231; Ibid., 72.
46  R. W. Maslen, 'Armour That Doesn't Work: An Anti-meme in Medieval and Renaissance Romance', in *Medieval into Renaissance: Essays for Helen Cooper*, ed. Andy King and Matthew Woodcock (Cambridge: D. S. Brewer, 2016), 35–54.
47  Lee C. Ramsey, *Chivalric Romances: Popular Literature in Medieval England* (Bloomington, IN: Indiana University Press, 1983), 45.
48  Atkinson, 'They ... toke their shyldys before them and drew oute their swerdys', 543.
49  Abels, 'Cultural Representation of Warfare in the Middle Ages', 30.
50  Malory, *Le Morte Darthur*, 353.
51  London, British Library, MS Harley 3542, fols 82$^r$–85$^r$; London, British Library, MS Additional 39564. For an introduction to the terminology, see James Hester, 'The Terminology of Medieval English Fight Texts: A Brief Overview', in *'Can these Bones Come to Life?': Insights from Reconstruction, Reenactment, and Re-creation, Volume 1: Historical European Martial Arts*, ed. Ken Mondschein (Wheaton, IL: Freelance Academy Press, 2014), 70–9. As indicated by Hester's title, this chapter is only a brief introduction to the issue of terminology in these sources, and several important terms are left untreated.

52 This approach has recently been adopted by Brian Price, 'Yron & Steele: Chivalric Ethos, Martial Pedagogy, Equipment, and Combat Technique in the Early Fourteenth-Century Middle English Version of *Guy of Warwick*', *Journal of Medieval Military History* 16 (2018): 159–88.
53 For the origins of trial by battle, see Ariella Elema, 'Trial by Battle in France and England', unpublished doctoral thesis, University of Toronto, 2012, 23–56.
54 Andrew Lynch, *Malory's Book of Arms: The Narrative of Combat in 'Le Morte Darthur'* (Cambridge: Brewer, 1997), 32, 48.
55 *Four Middle English Romances: Sir Isumbras, Octavian, Sir Eglamour of Artois, Sir Tryamour*, ed. Harriet Hudson (Kalamazoo, MI: Medieval Institute Publications, 2006), 212–13.
56 Ramsey, *Chivalric Romances*, 52.
57 Michele Poellinger, 'Violence in Later Middle English Arthurian Romance', Unpublished doctoral thesis, University of Leeds, 2013, 16.
58 Matthew Strickland, 'Provoking or Avoiding Battle? Challenge, Judicial Duel, and Single Combat in Eleventh- and Twelfth-Century Warfare', in *Armies, Chivalry and Warfare in Medieval Britain and France. Proceedings of the 1995 Harlaxton Symposium*, ed. Matthew Strickland (Stamford: Watkins, 1988), 317–43.
59 Geoffrey le Baker, *Chronicle*, trans. David Preest (Woodbridge: Boydell, 2012), 46.
60 Ibid.
61 Ibid., 126.
62 Robert W. Jones, *Bloodied Banners: Martial Display on the Medieval Battlefield* (Woodbridge: Boydell, 2010), 19.
63 Maurice Keen, *Chivalry* (New Haven, CT: Yale University Press, 1984), 224.
64 *Chronicon de Lanercost, MCCI–MCCCXLVI*, ed. Joseph Stevenson (Edinburgh: Edinburgh Printing Company, 1839), 286; *Gesta Henrici Quinti: The Deeds of Henry the Fifth*, ed. and trans. Frank Taylor and John S. Roskell (Oxford: Clarendon Press, 1975), 57–8.
65 Ramsey, *Chivalric Romances*, 52.
66 Burkart, 'Autograph of an Erudite Martial Artist', 455.
67 Catherine Nall, *Reading and War in Fifteenth-Century England, from Lydgate to Malory* (Woodbridge: Brewer, 2012), 139–58.
68 Martha W. Driver, 'Historicity and Authenticity in Medieval Film', in *The Medieval Hero on Screen: Representations from Beowulf to Buffy*, ed. Martha W. Driver and Sid Ray (Jefferson, NC: McFarland, 2004), 19.

# 7

# Malevolent and marginal

## The feminized 'Dark Ages' in modern card game cultures

Daisy Black

Since the early 1980s, things medieval have provided a fertile source of narrative concept, artwork and play in popular board and card game culture. These tabletop games have produced detailed, often surprisingly nuanced models of medieval societies, with game-plays demonstrating a strong awareness of the ways in which medieval lay, civic, religious and literary communities operated.[1] As well as creating an attractive aesthetic, these often form part of strategy and are able to teach the games' participants something about the mechanisms of medieval narratives as well as the histories of commerce, combat strategy or land management and expansion. However, a heavy focus on warfare, civic politics, knightly activity and monasticism frequently has the effect of rendering the medieval female a marginal, spectral figure – that is, a figure re-produced for a variety of purposes, but very rarely employed as a historical figure or to signify (her)self. In this, I am adapting Stephen Kruger's definition of spectrality in another fantasy figure: the medieval Jew:

> The Jews we encounter in medieval Christian texts [. . .] are constructions that do not correspond in any easy way to the lived experiences of Jews, or even of Christians who elaborated and made use of these constructions.[2]

The complex male hierarchies in medievalist games are rarely matched by those of female characters, who, if they are present, rarely 'correspond in any easy way to the lived experiences' of medieval women. This chapter highlights how often overlooked tabletop games provide just as a rich a resource of study into ludic and narrative medievalism as digital gaming has, while opening a discussion about the games' lack of engagement with diverse medieval female roles. Giving attention to the prefatory narratives accompanying two card-based games, the artwork of cards featuring human characters and the mechanics of gameplay, this chapter analyses the ways their representations of 'medieval' men and women are constructed, performed and valued. It also contends that the medieval female is often figured as a point of dark origin, which gives us insight into the ways these games interact with notions of 'past' and history.

This chapter examines two recent card games employing medieval aesthetic and narrative in their play: *Dominion* (2008) and the less complex micro-game *Love Letter* (2012). Neither of these games claims to be 'historical' or 'authentic' and, while they engage with elements of medieval culture, they also contain aspects from later eras. For example, *Dominion*'s 'Seaside' expansion pack (2009) includes pirates and characters wearing eighteenth-century wigs, while the clothing shown in the artwork of *Love Letter* admit trends from the eleventh to the sixteenth centuries. This kind of temporal playfulness is captured in David Matthews' claim that 'one of the enabling conditions of medievalism is unending play with the instability of temporal boundaries'.[3] While these games also tend to merge the aesthetics of medievalism, fantasy and romance, they also present a Middle Ages that is both recognizable and sufficiently 'other' to generate interest in the game play and narrative as being of a time unlike ours. In this, both games might be more properly considered neomedievalist, as they mingle referents from a number of periods.[4] While, as will be shown, female figures are often marginal, misrepresented or absent in the mechanics of *Dominion*'s game play and artwork, female figures in both games do appear in the narratives with which games introduce their medievalist fantasies. These kinds of narrative appear as contextualizing literature within games' rulebooks or publicity material and create a sense of context or 'history' for the game. Both games align the 'time before' the medieval context of the game with ambitious, morally dubious or malignant female figures. These depictions often concur with a game's (either deliberate or unconscious) presentation of pre-medieval society as 'backward', regressive or simplistic, thus playing into the mid-sixteenth-century dialectics figuring the (Catholic) past as 'middle' or 'dark'.[5] This centring of the woman in establishing these 'Dark Ages' simultaneously provides foundation and inspiration for the gameplay whilst simultaneously articulating a warning – constituting a less civilized, unruly and feminine past to which the players might revert if they are unsuccessful.

## Dominion

*Dominion* is a deck-building card game. It was created in 2008 by Donald X. Vaccarino and has sold over a million copies, winning, among other awards, the prestigious *Spiel des Jahres*. It has been translated into several languages and has spawned eleven expansion packs and one standalone pack. In character, the game reflects the kinds of medievalism trope identified by M. J. Toswell:

> The tropes of medievalism, of which there are a congeries (knights; heroes; swords; vast landscapes with castles and forests and mountains; handmade artefacts; treasure hunting; questions; witches and warlocks; various representations of the Other [. . .] offer ways in which someone engaged in recreating the Middle Ages can do so with a kind of useful shorthand.[6]

As the speed of the gameplay and rapid discarding of cards means players might have cards in their hand for less than five minutes, this rapid accretion of tropes temporarily suggests a kind of coherent 'authenticity' where coherency does not, on more leisurely inspection, exist. While the original *Dominion* base set had an early medieval theme, with elements referencing pre-industrial social structures, the expansion packs *Dark Ages* and *Empires* extended the game's time period backwards. *Guilds* extends it forwards to fifteenth century civic guild cultures, while *Hinterlands* extends the game geographically to engage with the medieval outside Europe. In 2016, a second edition of the game's base-set was released, which removed some cards, introduced others and, as will be shown later, slightly changed the artwork and gender representation on the cards.[7] While this chapter will primarily focus on the 2008's original base game, which was current at the time of this research and to date has sold the most copies, the game's principles have remained the same across all expansions and editions. The object is to gain the highest number of victory points which, in the base set, are cards representing land (Estates, Duchies and Provinces).[8] Players must gain enough money to buy these 'land' victory points by purchasing and using action cards, which helps them build machines within their deck that increase their purchasing power. These action cards represent certain roles, trades or spaces within the medieval world.

The base game's world-building is first established in the rule book, which sets *Dominion* within a non-specific feudal era of 'fiefs, freeholds and *feodums*':

> You are a monarch, like your parents before you, a ruler of a small pleasant kingdom of rivers and evergreens. Unlike your parents, however, you have hopes and dreams! You want a bigger and more pleasant kingdom, with more rivers and a wider variety of trees. You want a Dominion! In all directions lie fiefs, freeholds, and feodums. All are small bits of land, controlled by petty lords and verging on anarchy. You will bring civilization to these people, uniting them under your banner. But wait! It must be something in the air; several other monarchs have had the exact same idea. You must race to get as much of the unclaimed land as possible, fending them off along the way. To do this you will hire minions, construct buildings, spruce up your castle, and fill your treasury. Your parents wouldn't be proud, but your grandparents, on your mother's side, would be delighted.[9]

While the game refers to its players as ungendered 'monarchs', the actions the player is asked to perform are those which have conventionally been gendered male. The rulebook sets up a colonialist fantasy: the player will subdue the 'petty lords verging on anarchy', with conquest and warfare being framed as positive forces of 'civilization' and the assertion of order. In this, *Dominion* follows the alignment of the medieval world with warfare and conquest, which has been long-established in digital gaming as well as in the medieval fantasy aesthetic of *Dungeons and Dragons*.[10] However, it is curious that *Dominion* suggests that this drive to expand comes from the maternal line: 'your grandparents, on your mother's side, would be delighted.' This claim, appearing at the end of the passage in which the game introduces its medievalist fantasy, does two things. First, it aligns conquest with an ambitious and less content past – that is, with the violent, land-based ambitions of a 'Dark Ages'.

Second, this final sentence genders this ambition female by making it the desire of the maternal grandparents. While, of course, the mention of grandparents suggests a male and a female desire for conquest and order, the fact that this drive comes from the player's imagined maternal line complicates the earlier narrative of conquest as a fully masculine occupation. While the *actions* of the game play are historically often aligned with the masculine, the source of the *desire* for expansion is therefore located in the maternal line which experienced 'anarchy' but longed for order – a feminized Dark Ages.

Origin myths of this kind, in which chaotic, feminine dominion is superseded by a more 'civilized' masculine order, have long been part of European medieval narratives of nation. In the late thirteenth to fourteenth centuries, a new myth was added to the foundation histories of Britain and preceded the myth of Trojan exile Brutus.[11] This origin myth appeared in several versions, including in Geoffrey of Monmouth's *Historia Regum Britanniae*. It began in Syria or Greece, where a king had many daughters, whom he married off to his subject kings. The daughters resented this and the oldest daughter, Albina, suggested they kill their husbands. When the plan was revealed, the sisters were exiled in a leaky boat. They landed on an island, which Albina named 'Albion', after herself. After a while, the island's native devils begot a race of giants with the sisters. The giants ruled until Brutus and his company arrived. They expelled or killed the giants and renamed the island 'Britain'.[12] There are several similarities between the way this myth functions and the way *Dominion* fashions its medievalist mythology. First, they both create myths of national identity and history which pre-empt the narratives of martial dominion which follow. Through the figures of the maternal grandparents, *Dominion*'s gameplay forms its own network of communal associations by establishing a familiar foundation 'past'.[13] Albina is ambitious: resisting her father's splintering of his daughters and kingdom between 'small bits of land, controlled by petty lords', she claims ownership over her new land through giving it her own name. Yet in both stories, these ambitious ancestors left the civilizing process incomplete. While the bloodthirsty Albina and her sisters demonstrate a desire for power and risk anarchy through murdering their husbands, when they arrive on the island they express no desire to conquer or build on it; they instead live peaceably and cultivate the land. It is not until Brutus arrives that Albion is subjected to the 'civilizing' forces of warfare, building and trade. While Albina's giant descendants are easily overcome by the Greco-Roman 'civilization' of Brutus, *Dominion* tasks its players with carrying out the same work. *Dominion*'s opening narrative also marks a similar movement from an arable, subsistence farmed landscape – 'a small pleasant kingdom of rivers and evergreens' – to one open to conquering, building and commerce. This becomes particularly evident in the game's expansions, which suggest the further expansion of territory, trade and industry. The players thus perform the role of Brutus. Like Albina, whose name is superseded by Brutus' in Britain's re-naming, the maternal line provides both the origin of the drive to dominate and a warning against reversion to a prior, less civilized time.

The tension this opening establishes between male and female gendered activities and their implied moral statuses is continued through *Dominion*'s gameplay. The game's several expansion packs treat both the medieval and gender slightly differently. In early

2016, when the research for this paper was undertaken, *Dominion* and its expansion packs had between them:

**108 cards featuring male figures** (of which 5% are 'fantasy' or romance roles, that is, roles that are inspired by medieval legend or literature but could not have historically existed e.g. giant, golem, cultist). The majority of these benefit the player.

**27 cards featuring female figures** (of which 56% are 'fantasy' roles, for example, witches and female knights). The majority of these benefit the player but are malignant towards other players.

**74 cards featuring scenes or spaces with men in them**

**24 cards featuring scenes or spaces with women in them**.

While several cards show multiple figures in one environment, there is a significant lack of cards showing men and women occupying the same spaces. In those that do, these spaces are chiefly celebratory or carnivalesque environments (as opposed to, say, commercial, craft or domestic environments). This gives the impression of a medieval era in which men and women lived separate lives and women were generally excluded from commercial life. As Angela Jane Weisl observes, this creates a simpler, if historically unrealistic, game world: 'by conforming to older genres, modern stories continue ideas and assumptions – such as those about race and gender – that can no longer be intellectually articulated.'[14] While recent historical work attests to the complexity of female commercial production and trade in the Middle Ages, in the world of *Dominion* these roles are marginalized or absent.

In contrast, the 2008 base game features a complex variety of male occupations and trades. The male figures making up the action cards may be placed into five categories:

**Fighting Men:** Militia
**Exploring Men:** Adventurer
**Criminal Men:** Spy, Thief
**Working Men:** Mine, Smithy, Woodcutter
**Bureaucratic Men:** Chancellor, Bureaucrat, Moneylender

Although *Dominion*'s expansion packs add more male figures and roles to the game, these categories remain constant. I have not included the category 'religious men' here as, while the game's expansions contain roles hinting at a kind of pre-Christian faith (such as Soothsayer and Cultist – both of which are represented as being of ambiguous sex in the artwork), the only recognizably medieval religious figure is that of the hermit. Likewise, knights are missing from the base game, though they do appear (anachronistically) in the *Dark Ages* expansion pack and in a single foreground figure on the Village card. In the base set, the Militia card provides a distinctly un-chivalric (and perhaps, more realistic) portrayal of military force, giving its player two gold coins while forcing other players to discard cards to their disadvantage. This suits the conquest-driven nature of the game's narrative. Again, times are collapsed in the artwork of the Militia card. The two soldiers wear a mixture of Viking, Saxon and Norman armour, including the kind of leather tunic worn by Guy of Ponthieu in the Bayeux Tapestry.[15] This hotchpotch of military gear marks the militia out as having apparently pillaged across history, thus making them timeless and stateless representations of fighting men and diminishing any potential chivalry associated with their role. Two further depictions of disreputable masculinity appear in the attack cards of Spy and Thief. These loosely resemble the most famous outlaw, Robin Hood – a figure whose film representations, Andrew Higson has noted, frequently blur the boundaries between different periods.[16] Depictions of working men also have something of Robin Hood about their costuming, while the long-bearded man working in the Smithy draws on the aesthetic legacy of Tolkien's dwarves. Meanwhile, the dress of the second figure in the Smithy, with his double-bladed axe, braided beards and leather fetish-wear, appears to emphasize the most threatening aspect of the labouring craftsman's skills.

The bureaucratic men represented in the *Dominion* base set, however, reflect an economically 'civilized' Middle Ages in which the mechanisms of state are seen at work. However, their representation and costuming in the game's artwork places them towards the very end of the 'medieval' period, with their early Tudor garb contrasting with the medievalist fantasies of warfare seen in the other male images. The Chancellor, for example, is an elderly Henry VII lookalike and grants his player gold. Meanwhile, the Bureaucrat and Moneylender perform more morally complex transactions, as they each temporarily increase their player's money while sabotaging the next turn of the other players. The occupations of these male figures, who are engaged in political and economic, rather than military functions, is communicated through their presentation in the game's artwork. The Moneylender card shows a pale, thin bespectacled, young figure wearing an early Tudor man's bonnet, seemingly in velvet. While his clothing is ambiguous on this small card, it appear to be a loose white robe. The Bureaucrat, meanwhile, appears in a wide-sleeved pink shirt, a neatly-trimmed, well cared-for beard and small early Tudor hat. Noting the beard's preponderance in early Renaissance portraiture, Will Fisher has argued that 'Renaissance facial hair often conferred masculinity: the beard made the man'.[17] Both the Bureaucrat and the Moneylender are surrounded by books and both wear a jewelled ring on their right hands. While the pink and white colours of their costumes are expensive, their clothes do not have the layered, hotchpotch nature of the clothing associated with warfare in the game. In playing these cards, the player engages with an age in which there is a perceived introduction of bureaucracy and more complex monetary systems.

These cards, alongside the Chancellor's nod to early Tudor portraiture, therefore not only align more 'civilized' economic structures with a later, Tudor age but also indicate difference from the game's (medieval) military masculine identities, locating the violence involved in conquest in a 'medieval' past. While creating a game world sophisticated enough to contain bureaucrats, chancellors and libraries, *Dominion* creates a 'middle' ages which is, as Pat Clements has suggested, 'filtered through a variety of eras, cultures, zeitgeists'.[18] The 'filtering' effect of *Dominion*'s asynchronous medievalism aligns its male figures with a variety of time periods and features Saxon, Norman, Viking and Tudor elements in its imagining of masculinity.[19] As Daniel T. Kline's discussion of the 'virtual medieval' in digital games attests, this palimpsest of temporal signifiers 'reveal[s] a constellation of related ideas that influence a game player's understanding of the Middle Ages'.[20] It also, however, maintains the idea of a Middle Ages of warfare and primitive administration, which did not develop into something more complex until the Tudor period.

Yet while the artwork of *Dominion*'s cards show an attempt to reflect diversity in its depictions of medieval and early modern masculinities, its temporal inconsistency indicates that the game is not so much concerned about reflecting historical research as it is in reproducing extant medievalist cultural productions already made familiar through film and digital gaming cultures. Male figures also appear in the artwork for the Festival, Mine, Library, Village and Laboratory cards. Between them, these place/space cards give the impression of a Middle Ages that is simultaneously chivalric, industrious, learned and scientifically advanced. Yet these are solely masculine spaces. The lack of inclusion of female and non-white bodies in game play is an issue much discussed in digital game criticism as something which 'privileges the ethics of simulation' over plurality or inclusivity.[21] As Aaron Trammel has noted:

> Pursuits of authentic recreations and representations of past histories (such as in historical re-enactments) can be problematic for the ways in which they offer an airtight alibi for the reproduction of predominantly white, male, historical vignettes.[22]

This game, like many other medievalist products, presents histories that are ultimately outdated – that is, histories compiled before feminist historical and literary enquiries began to take notice of the ways in which women *were* present in medieval spaces. The game's depiction of a Middle Ages of binary exclusion consequently leaves no space to acknowledge figures such as the nuns of Syon Abbey, who held one of the biggest libraries in fifteenth-century England, women engaging in trade and craft, the women who worked in smelting and sorting ore in mines, or the many female thinkers whose writings covered a variety of theological and scientific subjects.[23] The game's chief problem is not, therefore, so much a question of its 'authenticity', but a question about what we view as 'past history' and whose past histories we choose to reproduce.

The original *Dominion* base game represents the medieval female in a single card: the Witch. Unlike the game's male figures, the figure of the Witch straddles the limen between medievalism and fantasy. Accounts of witchcraft are more a feature of the sixteenth century than the Middle Ages, though the conception of a 'medieval era' which burnt and tortured witches is firmly entrenched in modern popular culture.[24] Furthermore, the witch depicted in *Dominion*'s gameplay and artwork feeds more into modern fantasy than medievalist tropes. The Witch does not look like an elderly woman, midwife, herbalist or any of the other female groups who fell victim to witchcraft accusations during the late fifteenth and sixteenth centuries.[25] Her body is cloaked and her long fingernails twist between them a spell, suggesting that she is really able to conduct supernatural activity, rather than merely being accused of it. This card is unambiguously malicious. While there are four male cards (Bureaucrat, Militia, Spy and Thief) whose actions are beneficial towards their player while acting malignantly towards others, the Witch card is the only one whose sole feature is to devalue other player's cards. The other players gain a curse card, losing some of their victory points. The game's sole female figure therefore poses a threat to the players' land-based economies.

The Witch's spectrality is based on the fact she is the only character in the base set to occupy a fantasy status. In moving the game's medievalism to medievalist fantasy, the card effectively removes all medieval female bodies from the game's playing space. It also suggests the absence of the female body from the *medieval* social space. The Witch, unlike the Miner, Smith, Chancellor or Moneylender, is not part of an economic community, but outside it: the ultimate 'other'. Witches are found at the edges, not the centers, of civilizations. In medieval romance, they are also almost always distinguished by their malignant opposition to masculine progress and rule.[26] This dynamic is also reflected in the Arthurian board game *Shadows Over Camelot* (2005), where the Guinevere cards disrupt the quest-play of the gamers, while Morgan le Fay is figured as the chief enemy, watching malevolently from the margins: 'The forces of evil are gathering around Camelot – the Black Knight was sighted atop a desolate ridge; a scheming Morgan plots her revenge.'[27] Like the spectral maternal ancestors featured at the opening of the game, *Dominion*'s Witch constitutes a figure of malevolence whose power temporarily interrupts the masculine narratives of dominion, conquest and bureaucratic order: much as Albina in the English foundation myths disrupted her father's attempt to consolidate territories through marriage. Yet the power of these women is always limited. Depending on play, there is usually a point at which *Dominion*'s Witch ceases to function as a useful card – something widely criticized in forum discussions.[28] As with the Albina myth, the neutralization or 'death' of this card allows players to strive towards the (masculine) 'civilization' outlined as the game's object. This casting of female figures as outside society and crossing into the realm of fantasy is replicated throughout all but the most recent expansion packs. Of the twenty-seven action cards featuring women throughout these expansions, fifteen can be classed as 'fantasy' roles. These include a Sea Hag, Swamp Hag, Mystic, Soothsayer and Young Witch. Meanwhile, the *Dark Ages* expansion contains some of the more interesting female action cards through its five male and five female knights. However, unlike the cross-dressing knights of medieval romance, whose chivalric action relies on maintaining their disguise, these figures exist in a fantasy world in which women are apparently allowed to *be* knights.[29] As with the Witch, the knight cards all benefit their player at the expense of the game's other participants. Even some of the more historically plausible roles performed by women in the expansions, such as Herbalist and Peddler, are associated with social and economic liminality. Women are very much marginalized in this medievalist world-building.

In 2016, Vaccarino released a second edition of the *Dominion* base set of cards. In a forum post for *Board Game Geek*, he outlined his reasons for this, which included improving the artwork, rulebooks and card wordings as well as replacing 'some cards with better ones'.[30] This involved dropping six cards from the original set and the addition of seven new cards. These new cards suggests a commitment to increasing the representation of women in the game, with the artwork Harbinger, Merchant, Poacher, Bandit, Sentry and Artisan featuring female figures. As these cards are intended to form the base set for other expansions, this significantly increases female presence within the game, while the fact that four of the cut cards depict men or male roles means the game has far more balanced gender representation. Apart from the Sentry and the mystical role of Harbinger, these new cards are not solely confined to fantasy world-building and represent roles that a medieval woman might have performed. Moreover, several of these are action cards that do not undermine the other players. While Vaccarino does not draw attention to this in outlining his reasons for the changes in artwork and role, he does suggest that gender was a consideration in changing the wording, both of these cards and on future prints of all expansion packs prior to *Empires*: 'we now use "they" instead of "he."'[31] While this does not change the game play or the medievalist theme of the game, this small change in language does acknowledge the implicit gender bias of earlier editions, and the more inclusive 'they' allows women to exist in the game beyond a shadowy, malevolent mythical past.

## Love Letter

While the makers and artists of *Dominion* are doubly rewriting the past through their first and second edition of their base cards, gender is not (and is not intended to be) an integral part of the game's mechanics. Later card games, however, do give us examples of the ways in which medieval gender roles might productively be engaged in a game's mechanics as well as its narrative concept. Unlike the complex 2008 *Dominion* base set, Seiji Kanai's micro-game *Love Letter* (2012) is comprised of just sixteen cards. Unlike *Dominion*, it takes between ten and fifteen minutes to play and the game mechanics operate via a romance-like courtly love narrative. The player performs as a suitor trying to get a love letter to a Princess by passing it through a hierarchy of other characters. As with *Dominion*, the game's framing narrative features a shadowy, morally dubious female character. The rulebook says:

> In the wake if the arrest of Queen Marianna for high treason, none was more heartbroken than her daughter, Princess Annette. Suitors throughout the City-State of Tempest sought to ease Annette's sorrow by courting her to bring some joy into her life.[32]

Although she does not make an appearance in the game, the arrest of Queen Mariana themes and frames the gameplay, while her daughter's sorrow becomes the focus of the players' actions. Again, this is consistent with the kinds of foundation myth established both at the beginning of *Dominion* and in medieval traditions. Patrick Geary has noted that:

> Prominent women [in myths of origin] are often distinguished by their wickedness. [. . .] If present, women at the beginning tend to die violently so that proper, male civilization could develop.[33]

This arrest therefore leaves the players with a number of questions concerning the nature of this 'high treason', which they might draw on their own medievalist knowledge to answer. Perhaps she, like Albina, plotted to kill the King or perhaps her treason was reminiscent of Guinevere and Lancelot's story. The Queen's unspecified treason at the game's opening enables the player to invest in an already familiar world, while the players themselves become cast members in this story: performing as a lover trying to get their letter to Princess Annette.

By giving balanced attention to its male and female figures, *Love Letter*'s gameplay performs a series of gendered and hierarchical negotiations. Characters are ranked in a hierarchy which indicates their proximity to the Princess. The highest card is the Princess (8 points), followed by the Countess (7); King (6); Prince (5); Handmaid (4); Baron (3); Priest (2) and Guard (1). Within the micro-world of *Love Letter*, the cards gendered female in the game hold as powerful, if not more powerful, positions as those gendered male. This ranking implicates that the spectre of the absent queen might plausibly have filled the empty space above the Princess. With her out of the gameplay, the Princess becomes the highest-scoring, most desirable card – if you can keep hold of her. The rule book characterizes the Princess as rather naïve and easily influenced: 'When she reads enough letters from one suitor, she becomes enamored and grants that suitor permission to court her. [. . .] However, she is self-conscious about matters of the heart, and, if confronted, will toss your letter in the fire and deny ever seeing it.'[34] Unlike *Dominion*, which is more invested in mechanics than the character of its cards, this game creates back stories and motives, for each of its figures.

The highest card below the Princess is the Countess. This suggests that, when it comes to narratives of love, the Princess and the Countess form a female hierarchy which circumvents the patriarchal hierarchies of the King and Prince: '[Countess] Wilhelmina's age and blood make her one of Princess Annette's friends.'[35] Even the Handmaid is worth more points than the Baron and Priest. This is consistent with the romance narrative tropes which act as the conceit for the game. Weisl argues:

> In the medieval romance, women are given a great deal of freedom and authority because of their power in love, and within the liminal worlds these texts construct, women on the narrative periphery may still occupy important positions, ranging from confidants and go-betweens to judges and doctors.[36]

As the game already inhabits a 'liminal world', women perform more complex functions. The romance theme therefore brings female characters in from the narrative margins occupied by the imprisoned Queen to place them at the operating centre of the game's mechanics. This suggests that the game has a good knowledge of the ways in which medieval courtly narrative operates, with female allies helping lovers to communicate and eventually meet.[37] It also reflects medieval accounts in which men express their anxieties concerning their wives' and daughters' networks of female friends and the ability of these relationships to threaten their own authority.[38] This fear of female treachery is likewise reflected in the rule book's description of Handmaid Susannah:

> Few would trust a handmaid with a letter of importance. Fewer still understand Susannah's cleverness, or her skilled ability at playing the foolish handmaid. That the queen's confidante and loyal servant escaped any attention after the queen's arrest is testament to her clever mind.[39]

In fashioning the Handmaid as a go-between for both the Princess and her absent, treacherous mother, *Love Letter* reflects the female servant's role both in romance and in comic literature.

As in medieval romance, however, the go-between does not always come out well in *Love Letter*'s game play. The Countess's power is limited when placed in proximity to either the King or the Prince. The female hierarchy is limited when the Countess card is subject to a sexually suggestive discard if caught in the company of either of these male cards. Women are also sexualized in the artwork, the Countess being shown in flirtatious positions and wearing a dress which emphasizes her breasts. Moreover, despite her high value, the Princess fulfils the popular medievalist trope of fragile love object. In mourning and, like many romance heroines, without a mother-figure, she is figured as a prize and is vulnerable to male pursuit. More tellingly, she is unable to act except by being discarded and thus losing her player the game. If, as Kevin and Brent Moberly have argued in relation to the functions of medievalism, '[medievalism in] play . . . is one of the primary means through which the inequalities of late capitalism are constructed as inevitable and unassailable', it seems that female characters in this game retain their unequal role as sexualized currency.[40] Where the game's narrative therefore acknowledges and mechanizes a medieval literary tradition of female agency within the courtly love narrative, the artwork and play remain invested in more limiting medievalist tropes.

## Token women

While this chapter has explored only two of a vast and growing number of popular games employing medievalism, it is clear that diverse medieval constructions of women are frequently overlooked in modern game culture. Veronica Ortenberg West-Harling has noted that one of the attractions of medievalism is that it offers participation in a world involving 'returning to a traditionally-gendered role, of women doing women's things and men fighting'.[41] In certain games, however, the women represented are not even 'doing women's things'. This trend is worrying. Studies into gender representation in digital gaming have shown that the marginalized (or sexualized) representations of women in games have led to real-life consequences (often expressed via misogynist trolling and the exclusion of female gamers).[42] As Adrienne Shaw's work on digital gaming has recognized, this lack of representation not only denies women's right to be present in game-spaces, they can also lead to behaviours which 'flat out rejec[t] *anyone's* right to critique games as cultural texts'.[43] Yet as this chapter has demonstrated, critical analyses of games as modern cultural texts (and, in the case of *Love Letter*'s storytelling rulebook, *as* texts) can tell us a great deal both about how modern game-makers and players understand medieval gender roles, but also hints at how such games might themselves creatively engage with medieval cultural texts concerning notions of origin, agency and identity.

Recent years have produced a number of works on medievalism in digital gaming, roleplay and 'living history' groups. However, there remains a great need for more consideration of medievalist functions in tabletop game cultures, which offer material, as well as ludic engagements with ideas of the medieval. As small successes in diversifying gender representation in the digital game industry have shown, there is an ongoing need to acknowledge the gender biases written into the games we play.[44] We, as medievalists, need to consider how we might use our work to expand popular knowledge and enrich gameplay opportunities, world building and designs.

## Notes

1. Earlier games, such as Klaus Teuber's *Settlers of Catan* (Kosmos, 1995), Klaus-Jürgen Wrede's *Carcassonne* (Rio Grande Games, 2000) and Bruno Faidutti's *Citadels* (MultiSim, 2000) used an indeterminate 'medieval' era as a setting but didn't engage with medieval culture beyond that. More recent games are increasingly using aspects of medieval social and literary history as gameplay mechanisms. For example, in Sébastien Dujardin, Xavier Georges and Alain Orban's *Tournay* (Pearl Games, 2011) the players aim to rebuild the city's military, religious and mercantile districts after the Norman invasion of 881. Bruno Cathala and Serge Laget's *Shadows Over Camelot* (Days of Wonder, 2005) uses Arthurian romance, especially the works of Malory, to drive the game mechanics and narrative, while, in the short card and dice game *Biblios* (IELLO, 2016), you compete with other monasteries to build the greatest library of rare and illuminated books.
2. Steven F. Kruger, *The Spectral Jew: Conversion and Embodiment in Medieval Europe* (Minneapolis, MN: University of Minnesota Press, 2006), xvii–xx. The link between medieval depictions of both Jews and women as spectral, malignant symbols of regression into an uncivilized 'prior' has also been outlined in Joan Young Gregg, *Devils, Women, and Jews: Reflections of the Other in Medieval Sermon Stories* (New York, NY: SUNY Press, 1997).
3. David Matthews, *Medievalism: A Critical History* (Cambridge: D. S. Brewer Editions, 2015), 49.
4. See Pat Clements, 'Authenticity', in *Medievalism: Key Critical Terms*, eds Elizabeth Emery and Richard Utz (Cambridge: D.S. Brewer Editions, 2014), 25: 'One definition of neomedievalism considers postmodern works that abandon any attempt at historical coherence in favour of a playful intermingling of themes, tropes, images, and referents from numerous time periods, thus revelling in historical inaccuracy'.
5. See David Matthews, 'Middle', in *Medievalism: Key Critical Terms*, eds Elizabeth Emery and Richard Utz (Cambridge: D.S. Brewer Editions, 2014).
6. M. J. Toswell, 'The Tropes of Medievalism', in *Defining Medievalism(s)*, ed. Karl Fugelso (Cambridge: Boydell and Brewer, 2009), 69–70.
7. On the creator's changes and the reasons for them, see Donald X. Vaccarino, 'The Secret History of the Dominion 2 Editions', *Board Game Geek*. Available online: https://boardgamegeek.com/thread/1648227/secret-history-dominion-2nd-editions, accessed 10 September 2019.
8. Later editions also feature Victory points as metal tokens, which do not follow the 'land' theme, but which also sit outside the player's deck and do not therefore clutter up their hands with points that will have no use until the end of the game.
9. Donald X. Vaccarino, *Dominion Rulebook* (Rio Grande Games, 2008).

10  See David W. Marshall, 'A World Unto Itself: Autopoetic Systems and Secondary Worlds in *Dungeons and Dragons*', in *Mass Market Medieval: Essays in the Middle Ages in Popular Culture*, ed. David W. Marshall (Jefferson, NC: McFarland and Co., 2007).
11  Anke Bernau, 'Albina: Remembering the Nation', *Exemplaria* 21.3 (2009), 248.
12  On the giants of Britain, see Ruth Evans, 'Gigantic Origins: An Annotated Translation of *De origine gigantum*', *Arthurian Literature* 16 (1998): 191–211; Jeffrey Jerome Cohen, *Of Giants: Sex, Monsters and the Middle Ages* (Minneapolis, MN: University of Minnesota Press, 1999).
13  See Bernau, 'Albina: Remembering the Nation', 249: 'The story of Albina allows us to think about the processes involved in the construction of a communal web of associations that have to do specifically with national history and which acts of remembrance'.
14  Angela Jane Weisl, *The Persistence of Medievalism: Narrative Adventures in Contemporary Culture* (New York, NY: Palgrave Macmillan, 2003), 19.
15  See Michael John Lewis, 'Identity and Status in the Bayeux Tapestry: The Iconographic and Artefactual Evidence', *Anglo-Norman Studies* 29 (2007): 105.
16  Andrew Higson, '"Medievalism", the Period Film and the British Past in Contemporary Cinema', in *Medieval Film*, eds Anke Bernau and Bettina Bildhauer (Manchester: Manchester University Press, 2009). On the legacy of Robin Hood as a medievalist trope, see Stephen Knight, 'Parody and Archery: Re-generating the Robin Hood Tradition', in *Robin Hood in Outlawed Spaces: Media, Performance, and Other New Directions*, ed. Lesley Coote and Valerie B. Johnson (Abingdon: Routledge, 2017).
17  On the rise of the beard and its importance in Early Modern artwork and politics, see Will Fisher, 'The Renaissance Beard: Masculinity in Early Modern England', *Renaissance Quarterly* 54, no. 1 (2001): 156, 158.
18  Clements, 'Authenticity', 20.
19  'Asynchronous medievalism' is examined in Matthews, *Medievalism: A Critical History*, 45–64.
20  Daniel T. Kline, 'Virtually Medieval: *The Age of Kings* Interprets the Middle Ages', in *Mass Market Medieval: Essays on the Middle Ages in Popular Culture*, ed. David W. Marshall (Jefferson, NC: McFarland, 2007), 154–5.
21  Aaron Tramell, 'Misogyny and the Female Body in *Dungeons and Dragons*', *Analog Game Studies* 2, no. 4 (2014). Available online: http://analoggamestudies.org/2014/10/constructing-the-female-body-in-role-playing-games/, accessed 3 March 2018.
22  Ibid.
23  See the diverse essays on work contained in Barbara A. Hanawalt, *Women and Work in Preindustrial Europe* (Bloomington, IN: Indiana University Press, 1986); Liz Herbert McAvoy and Diane Watt, eds, *The History of British Women's Writing, 700-1500* (New York, NY: Palgrave Macmillan, 2011); and Veronica O'Mara's extensive work on literacy and writing at Syon Abbey, including her *Nuns' Literacies in Medieval Europe* series and her article 'A Middle English Text Written by a Female Scribe', *Notes and Queries* 37, no. 3 (1990): 397. On medieval women and mining, see Paweł Cembrzyński, 'The Ecology of Mining. Human–Environmental Relations in the Medieval and Early Modern Mining in Central Europe', *Kwartalnik Historii Kultury Materialnej* 67, no. 1 (2019): 26.
24  Matthews, *Medievalism: A Critical History*, 13.
25  Alison Rowlands, 'Witchcraft and Gender in Early Modern Europe', in *The Oxford Handbook of Witchcraft in Early Modern Europe and Colonial America*, ed. Brian P. Levack (Oxford: Oxford University Press, 2013), 449–51.

26　See for example, the role of Morgan le Fay in Thomas Malory, *Le Morte D'Arthur* (1485).
27　Cathala and Laget, *Shadows Over Camelot Rulebook*.
28　On the various strategies and limitations of the Witch card, see 'Witch', *Dominion Strategy*. Available online: http://wiki.dominionstrategy.com/index.php/Witch, accessed 10 March 2018.
29　See Michele Perret, 'Travesties et Transsexuelles: *Yde, Silence, Grisandole, Blanchandine*', *Romance Notes* 25 (1985): 328–40 at 329.
30　Vaccarino, 'The Secret History of the Dominion 2 Editions'.
31　Ibid.
32　Seiji Kanai, *Love Letter Rulebook* (Alderac Entertainment Group, 2012), 5.
33　Patrick Geary, *Women at the Beginning: Origin Myths from the Amazons to the Virgin Mary* (Princeton, NJ: Princeton University Press, 2006), 3–4.
34　Kanai, *Love Letter Rulebook*, 10, 17.
35　Ibid., 16.
36　Weisl, *The Persistence of Medievalism*, 26.
37　See for example, the Duenna's speech in the thirteenth-century *Le Roman de la Rose*. Guillaume de Lorris and Jean de Meun, *The Romance of the Rose*, trans. Charles Dahlberg (Princeton, NJ: Princeton University Press, 1971), ll. 13434–5248.
38　See Sandy Bardsley, *Venomous Tongues: Speech and Gender in Late Medieval England* (Philadelphia, PA: University of Pennsylvania Press, 2006), 1–13.
39　Kanai, *Love Letter Rulebook*, 20.
40　Kevin Moberly and Brent Moberly, 'Play', in *Medievalism: Key Critical Terms*, eds Elizabeth Emery and Richard Utz (Cambridge: D. S. Brewer Editions, 2014), 175.
41　Veronica Ortenberg West-Harling, 'Medievalism as Fun and Games', *Studies in Medievalism* XVIII (2009): 9.
42　Patricia G. Lange, 'Learning Real-Life Lessons from Online Games', *Games and Culture* 6, no. 1 (2011): 17–37.
43　Adrienne Shaw, *Gaming at the Edge: Sexuality and Gender at the Margins of Gamer Culture* (Minneapolis, MN: University of Minnesota, 2014), 4.
44　Ibid., 207–32.

Part III

# Creating authenticity

8

# The tourist gaze and the 'medieval' landscape

Megan Arnott

If asked to identify a medieval landscape, no one's first thought would be Toronto, Ontario. But if you are a day visitor to the city, there are at least two attractions which will try to sell you a 'medieval' experience.[1] Visitors could take in some sightseeing at Casa Loma, Sir Henry Pellatt's early twentieth-century creation, 'Toronto's Camelot'. Constructed 'with soaring battlements and secret passageways', it 'paid homage to the castles and knights of days gone by'.[2] After a day spent at the castle, attention turns to Medieval Times Dinner and Tournament, where patrons enjoy a joust, some falconry and eating their meal with their hands. This venue promises a journey through time:

> Travel through the mists of time to a forgotten age and a tale of devotion, courage and love – at Medieval Times Dinner and Tournament. Imagine the pageantry and excitement that would have been yours as a guest of the royal court ten centuries ago. That's exactly what you will experience at North America's most popular dinner attraction.[3]

While neither attraction refers to actual medieval artefacts or history (they don't commemorate a well-known historic event or necessarily house any medieval artefacts), they create two enclaves of the 'medieval' right in the middle of Canada's largest city. Both Casa Loma and Medieval Times offer visitors a chance to see and engage with commonly accepted signifiers of the 'Middle Ages', like jousting or castle crenellations. The average North American, who lives nowhere near the abbeys, cathedrals or geographic locations traditionally associated with the Middle Ages, can still often find a 'medieval' landscape close by – a space that has been coded for the tourist as a 'medieval' space. Through the tourist gaze, a 'medieval landscape' takes shape. Ongoing popular interest in the Western European Middle Ages (despite the inconstancy of that concept), particularly from the second half of the twentieth century onwards, has resulted in a plethora of locations where one could go to meet the 'medieval'.

Ewa Skowronek et al. have recently worked to determine what is meant by a 'tourist landscape', acknowledging that academics use the term amorphously, depending on the aims of their research.[4] Part of the difficulty is there are many definitions for even the concept of a 'landscape'.[5] Ewa Skowronek et al. come to the conclusion that a tourist landscape is a significant type of landscape, functionally related to tourists and tourism activity. It's an integrated and complementary whole meeting the needs of tourists and tourism through its operationalising of natural and cultural elements. Tourist landscape is not uniform (there are different types and variations thereof). It is characterized by subjective evaluation and a confrontation by tourists, in connection with their perceptions and expectations, which affect its continuous transformation.[6]

Tourist landscapes are created when cultural representations that signify tourism are applied to places and interpreted by the tourist.[7] And, as Theano Terkenli shows, those signs which indicate 'tourist space' are subject to change:

> The development of new types of landscapes with the advent of new forms of tourism catering to new social needs, cultural preferences, and economic contingencies has certainly been an ongoing practice since the appearance of the phenomenon of tourism [. . .] the segregation, for instance, of leisure from home life that modernization instilled becomes more and more tentative and irrelevant in the postmodern Western world.[8]

In this chapter, I will look at different kinds of 'tourist landscapes' – landscapes shaped by and for tourists, that, in various ways and for various reasons, take the shape of 'medieval landscapes'.

There are several kinds of 'medieval' spaces created by and for tourists. The first, most obvious, example is the one attached to actual medieval artefacts or architecture. Despite their seemingly obvious medieval status, the way the structures have been preserved and interpreted reflects the tourist gaze. This tourist gaze creates a specifically 'medieval' space, since preservation is in part due to tourism, and since, despite ongoing use of the structures, for the tourist seeking a 'medieval' experience, these places have been coded as a place where the past, and specifically the medieval past, endures. A second kind of medieval space is that which has been recreated by historians and tourist boards in order to make objects for the tourists to gaze upon, attempting to draw attention to real history that would otherwise go unseen. This includes local attempts at commemoration, as well as signs or maps which help interpret landscape in light of the medieval history that has occurred there. A third kind of 'medieval' landscape is created as a site that temporarily houses the medieval. A 'medieval' themed event, whether bringing medieval enthusiasts together to celebrate objects or spaces dedicated to commemoration of the medieval period or bringing together medieval and fantasy enthusiasts with commonly acknowledged 'medieval' referents like dragons, creates medieval landscapes where they may not previously have existed. A fourth kind of 'medieval' landscape includes these 'medieval' inventions, which range from extensions of existing medieval sites to surrounding landscapes, like what has occurred on Newfoundland's Northern Peninsula, to nearly complete fabrications like Medieval Times. These are also spaces for the tourist to engage in the 'medieval'.

Authenticity is an important factor in the way that 'medieval' experiences are marketed to tourists, but what authenticity means is flexible. No one would really think that Medieval Times is historical, but its use of signifiers that tourists have learned to associate with the medieval might be deemed, by some definitions, authentic. The tourist gaze, including those who participate in the gaze and those who construct for the gaze of others, has created many different kinds of 'medieval' landscapes and will continue to do so as long as 'medieval' as a concept has meaning for the target audience of tourism boards.

## The tourist gaze and the landscape

Because tourism and the tourism industry are such complex phenomena, it is not easy to pin down the meaning of the terminology. According to Russell Staiff et al., '"travel" to "special places" is one of the enduring legacies and characteristics of people of many cultures throughout history.'[9] Social practices like medieval pilgrimages are forerunners of our modern concept of tourism. Tourism as Western society experiences it has been traced to the nineteenth century, out of which emerged packaged tourism companies like Thomas Cook, which sanitized the travelling experience for patrons who could afford it.[10] I will use the word tourist in the same way that Staiff et al. do, as meaning 'people performing tourism in performative contexts'.[11] It is an active intention on the part of the visitor, who has come to visit a specific locality.

John Urry's book *The Tourist Gaze* was originally published in 1995, but, with the help of Jonas Larsen, it is now in its third edition. In it, Urry and Larsen build on the theoretical framework of the gaze: 'people gaze upon the world through a particular filter of ideas, skills, desires and expectations, framed by social class, gender, nationality, age and education. Gazing is a performance that orders, shapes and classifies, rather than reflects the world.'[12] The tourist gaze shapes spaces into certain forms because tourists' expectations shape their experience of place and catering to those expectations further shapes a landscape. The tourist gaze is often associated with a hegemonic, white, middle class or male perspective, but it is not limited to this. The visual nature of the tourist experience is used here as an organizing principal, although the concept of the tourist gaze is not meant to exclude the other ways – like social interaction or touching – that tourists can experience a place.[13] In this chapter, the idea of the tourist gaze will stand for the ways tourists expect to (or do) interact with a space, especially by sight, but also by sound, touch or feel. For example, in the discussion of the imagined 'medieval spaces' it will be clear that tourists come to gaze on a fabricated 'Middle Ages', but this doesn't exclude the expectation that they will smell it, taste it or otherwise experience it.

'Tourism' takes many shapes and has many definitions. As Steve Watson points out, 'tourism [. . .] depends to a large extent on the perception of distinctions of various kinds, most obviously between work and leisure, but more significantly, perhaps, between home and destination.'[14] In this chapter, it is imagined as activities and practices associated with the tourist gaze: for one thing, the tourist gaze creates spaces coded for other kinds of behaviour into tourist spaces; for another, places are created or altered to attract or hold the tourist gaze. These processes, where tourists form spaces and spaces are made for tourists, inform each other.

Scholarship and the tourist industry have identified several different categories of tourism, including 'eco-tourism' or 'adventure tourism'. 'Heritage tourism', as a subset of 'tourism', proves as hard to define as tourism itself. For Yaniv Poria et al., it is the personal connection to heritage – the active connection with the place visited — that is the core of heritage tourism, rather than any performance of 'history' on the part of the tourism location. Adding to this, Wiendu Nuryanti points out that 'the word *heritage* in its broader meaning is generally associated with the word *inheritance*; that is, something transferred from one generation to another'.[15] Tourist locations that perform history are marketing a personal connection, but common associations of the term with different places means that 'heritage in this sense has been described as a commodified version of the received past that depends upon natural, built and artefactual resources in order to market tourist destinations for economic gain'.[16] When discussing 'medieval' tourist sites, one is inevitably discussing 'heritage' tourist sites.

In the following analysis, the emphasis is on the self-conscious performativity of 'heritage' on the part of the tourist location, keeping in mind that the personal connection of the tourist is both manipulated by the marketing and feeds/creates the marketing. Not all tourists who travel to heritage tourism sites are there as 'heritage tourists' according to Poria et al., that is, tourists who come with a specific view of engaging with signifiers of 'the past' or 'history'. Some come to engage with a local outdoor spot that happens to involve castles. Yet, the site's performance as a site of 'history' or 'heritage' is often part of its existence, and the reason the outdoor space exists where it does, so that vicariously, the other kinds of tourists are participating in heritage tourism.

Dean MacCannell's 1973 theory that tourist spaces were organized around a kind of 'staged authenticity' has been very important for the development of heritage tourism, since from the perspective of those constructing a space, their concept of authenticity and its importance dictates the structure of these kinds of tourist landscapes.[17] Likewise, tourists' concepts of authenticity help develop the character of heritage sites. 'Authenticity is [. . .] often consciously invoked as an actual marketing strategy', for heritage sites, like the Viking sites investigated by Chris Halewood and Kevin Hannam.[18] In addition, tourists' perception of a site's 'authenticity' can influence the way they interact with it. 'Authenticity' is as amorphous as any of the other terms; it is very subjective. Thomas W. Paradis states that, while trying to nail down this term, 'more recent authors have tackled this conundrum by treating authenticity "as a social construction the meaning of which varies with different people, at different times, and in different places"'.[19] The concept of authenticity is further complicated by the postmodern tourist. One of the criticisms of MacCannell's theory was that all cultures are invented, remade and reorganized, so what made the tourist experience that different from other cultural practices?[20] Some tourists, sometimes called 'post-tourists', deliberately engage in the inauthenticity of their experience, acknowledging that there is no 'authentic' experience, or at least acknowledging that the definition is important, but subjective.[21] For instance, Leavenworth, Washington was rebranded as 'Bavarian', an '*authentic* alpine village' despite the absence of any local German heritage.²² The authenticity lay in the creation, not its origins. Authenticity is a moving target in a 'medieval' space aimed at tourists, but an important one for drawing the tourist gaze.

## Built heritage and the medieval

The most obvious 'medieval' landscape is one populated with the remnants of things built in Europe between 400 and 1500 CE. This kind of landscape could be said to exist outside of the tourist gaze; still, it is most often the focus of heritage tourism. Emma Waterton notes that most often 'heritage is equated with the sum total of museums, galleries, cathedrals, castles, stately homes, ruins, industrial sites, palaces and cathedrals'.²³ Yet, as Nuryanti observes:

> Heritage tourism, as a production or reproduction of the past, is particularly problematic in the case of built heritage. Interpretation of built heritage not only involves issues such as ascribing meaning to past events, cross-cultural sensitivity, professionalization and education or training [...] but also is influenced by a series of other interrelated activities including conservation planning, architectural design and reconstruction techniques.²⁴

Differing interpretations of the meaning of built heritage affect the way that a site is preserved. For instance, in England in the nineteenth century, preservation practices involved making alterations to churches to correct perceived imperfections. Those making the changes thought they were achieving a higher degree of authenticity. In 1877, William Morris founded the Society for the Preservation of Ancient Buildings, which challenged church authorities, insisting that these restorations undertaken by the Church of England and their lead architect, George Gilbert Scott, were damaging these ancient structures.²⁵ Since the Middle Ages, the built heritage has had a history which has involved intentional destruction, neglect, restoration, repurposing or additions. To see a structure with origins in the Middle Ages as 'medieval' is not necessarily to forget the ongoing history of that structure, but it is to focus on its origin. In marketing these sights/sites to tourists, 'medieval' is very deliberately invoked.

The United Kingdom has an enduring legacy of medieval structures. According to Steve Watson, the 'stock of abbeys and monasteries made picturesquely and conveniently ruinous by Henry VIII's commissioners after the dissolution in 1538', mean that 'it is hardly surprising that touring the medieval has long been a national pastime'.²⁶ In Britain, legislation such as the Ancient Monuments Protection Act of 1882 and 1900, or the Ancient Monuments Consolidation and Amendment Act of 1913, have had an impact on what has been preserved and to whom it belongs.²⁷ These enduring structures became the basis for much of the tourist draw in the UK. With globalization, certain spaces or countries were coded for certain 'kinds' of tourism, with Britain specializing in history and heritage.²⁸ From 1975 to 1994, there was a 23 per cent growth in visits to historic properties.²⁹ Watson argues that, since 1980, the past is fashionable in a way the future used to be and that 'the period since 1980 has seen a particularly vigorous increase in public interest'.[30] According to English Heritage, in 2010 heritage tourism was worth £12.4 million.[31] This tourist interest in the past means it is worthwhile for tourist boards to market the 'medieval' abroad, drawing attention to the origins of their built heritage.

The medieval wall surrounding the downtown core of the City of York actually marks out the majority of the city's tourist space. As in places like Leicester, circumstances have allowed many of the medieval structures to remain in the city, making the medieval a potent marketing tool for York. York Minster, the thirteenth-century cathedral, attracts more than 2 million visitors a year, 'second only to Westminster Abbey on the national scale'.[32] In 2018, www.visityork.org invited the world to see Clifford's Tower, 'a proud symbol of England's medieval kings', to make yourself at home at Barley Hall, 'a stunning medieval townhouse', or to discover Bedern Hall, 'York's hidden medieval hall.' There is a deliberate nature to the theming; as Thomas Paradis notes, 'the proliferation of themed environments is central to the success of urban tourism, focused as they are on the consumption of products and places'.[33] 'Medieval' is the city of York's main brand, the theme of much of its downtown core.

This kind of urban branding is not limited to England. Paradis argues that 'large cities worldwide are responding to an emerging post-industrial economy by rooting their economic base less in traditional secondary manufacturing and more in the realm of tertiary tourism, sports, culture, and entertainment', which has had an effect on the way urban centres are themed.[34] Visitestonia.com, in 2018, invited visitors to Tallinn Old Town, 'the best preserved medieval city in Northern Europe boasting Gothic spires, winding cobblestone streets and enchanting architecture'. The website encourages the visitor to 'spend a day in an authentic medieval milieu and you will soon realise why so many visitors described Tallinn Old Town as mystical, mesmerizing and addictive'. The tourist board asks us to imagine the city as a moment in time, despite the ongoing presence of its citizens since the Middle Ages. Similar landscapes are created in places like Visby, Sweden or Dubrovnik, Croatia. All three of these cities are UNESCO World Heritage Sites because of the built heritage preserved there. Arguably, there is a medieval space that might exist outside of the tourist gaze at all these cities, but the tourist gaze helps shape these landscapes through promotion of preservation and by imposing an interpretation on these places.

There are three kinds of built heritage. 'Fixed' elements, such as buildings, town or ruins, make excellent bases for heritage tourism. Semi-fixed elements, like furniture and plants, or non-fixed elements, like attributes of the human occupants of the setting, must be gathered together to be gazed upon or interpreted.[35] Places where they are gathered are still coded as 'medieval' spaces, but instead of having medieval architecture or ruins, there are medieval artefacts. Some semi- or non-fixed artefacts are associated with fixed architectural elements if the building has been repurposed into a museum or there is a museum on the grounds, like at the Tower of London. But it is museums (in an ancient building or not) where tourists go to engage with the artefacts. Some examples include the boat museums in Scandinavia, such as the Viking Ship Museum in Roskilde, Denmark (a Michelin 3-star attraction) or the Viking Ship Museum in Oslo.[36] Tourists must travel to these spaces to engage with the medieval.

This is not to discount museums as research sites, but their function as spaces for public education and objects of the tourist gaze governs their organization.

Museums are all a mixture of artefacts and interpretations. The Viking Ship Museums have a greater focus on artefacts, presenting the reconstructed remains of several different boat burials: The Viking Ship Museum in Oslo features the ships found at Oseberg, Gokstad and Tune; The Viking Ship Museum in Roskilde displays the remains of the five Viking Ships found at Skuldelev. Yet, at the Roskilde location there are also several reconstructed boats:

> Newly constructed replicas of fully equipped Viking ships invite tourists to step on board as fully clad Vikings. While intended for children and young families with the objects appearing as 'second-rate copies', many adults spend much time and take many pictures in this Viking experience. Almost everyone inspects the wood and the sails, sits in and walks around boats, hold objects in their hands and play with the various weapons. Many adults dress up in Viking costumes.[37]

The interpretive element, including the seeing and playing in history, are an important attribute of this museum.[38] These museums create 'medieval' spaces by being sites where the medieval can be visited, but also by creating a site where the 'medieval' can be played at.

Even in places where there is less built heritage or material remains to work with, it is still possible to construct a 'medieval' landscape around the tourist gaze through reconstruction and interpretation. 'Medieval' York includes not only the architecture of the city centre, remnants of the High Middle Ages, but also 'Jorvik', Viking York, a medieval history which predates the Minster and city walls. The Jorvik Viking Centre, arguably, takes the creation of a 'medieval' landscape even further than the earlier examples, because it must create more, do more interpretation, to satisfy the tourist gaze. The Jorvik Viking Centre, a mix between theme park and museum, brings the Viking history of the city to life by taking visitors on automated cars around a reconstruction complete with the sights, sounds and smells of Jorvik. It then deposits visitors into an area that, while resembling a more 'traditional' museum, still has more of an emphasis on interpretation than on artefacts.[39]

Louise D'Arcens argues that the Museum plays on visitors preconceived notions to signify 'medieval':

> In particular, during a visit to the Centre in October 2009 (I have since returned three times) I was intrigued by how the headgear worn by the desk- and guide staff opted for the register of irony discussed earlier to negotiate the difficulties of embodying Vikingness in a way that was historicist and postmodern in equal parts. This was especially striking in the case of one young man who had been employed as a guide not only because he was clearly conversant with Viking England but also because of his stalwart build and impressive red-blond beard which evoked the popular modern signifiers of the Scandinavian warrior.[40]

The museum brings varying concepts of authenticity to visitors, though authenticity is always at the forefront. Watson argues that the Jorvik Viking Centre, and other open air museums, attempt to duplicate the reality of the past, 'but in the process they create their own reality, which is then re-represented elsewhere as tenth-century York'.[41] The tourist gaze has perceived a 'medieval' space and one has been deliberately created for them in a more dramatic way than when there is already something for the tourist to gaze on.

Even Jorvik takes as its basis 'medieval' artefacts, though more of the space has been carefully created than in other examples. Built heritage, fixed, semi-fixed and non-fixed, are easy signifiers of the medieval, but the tourist gaze is very active in taking these medieval artefacts, architectural and otherwise, and making 'medieval' landscapes by coding a building as 'medieval' or creating a space where the 'medieval' can be gazed upon.

## 'Medieval' landscapes

The medieval can be transmitted in many ways besides through built heritage: it can be found 'preserved in place names, field and parish boundaries, patterns of land holding as well as oral traditions, local myths and legends and even the way that people speak'.[42] Translating this into something the tourist can gaze on involves the creation of a 'medieval' tourist landscape. 'Medieval' maps of Europe have allowed tourists to see the 'medieval' around them. In the nineteenth century, 'medieval' maps of England allowed a certain class of tourist to view, analyse and catalogue the 'medieval':

> Architectural and historical accounts are accurate and encyclopaedic, and lists are appended of all the medieval churches with their dedication and predominant architectural styles according to the Rickman taxonomy . . . the principal castles and towers, ruined churches and chapels and the remains of monastic houses. This was medievalism for the tourist (the principal hotels and inns are also listed), and the medievalist buildings of the nineteenth century are also included as objects of the tour.[43]

These maps took built heritage as their starting point and re-imagined a landscape associated with a time and place (a landscape that very much reflected their own period, including their wants and needs as 'heritage tourists').

The Icelandic Saga and Heritage Association, formerly the Icelandic Saga Trail Association, has developed a vision of the whole country of Iceland as a place full of Viking, or at least Icelandic saga, specific cultural heritage. Iceland is 103,000 km², and is characterized 'by a varied rugged, volcanic topography, glaciated mountains, an uninhabited high-plateau desert interior and fjord coastal landscapes to the east and west'.[44] Since the global financial crisis of the 2000s, tourism has been one of the main tools identified for economic or regional development.[45] On www.sagatrail.is/en, it is possible to reimagine Iceland as a series of places mentioned in the medieval sagas, including places where that history is specifically interpreted. The saga trail requires tourists to reinterpret existing landscape, which could be tied to any age in its existence, in light of their understanding of the Viking Age. Only in a few places has the landscape been actually changed.

Starting from the harbour in Stockholm, Sweden, right beside city hall, you can take a ferry through the archipelago to the modern island of Björko, site of the Viking market Birka. Today, you will find a museum, Vikingastaden Birka, several reconstructed city blocks and, if you come on the right day, a Viking market with local re-enactors. And, in fact, who would go there save for the few families who continue to farm certain portions of the island, if it weren't for the museum? There are over 1,000 islands in the archipelago, but Birka is a significant destination. Ansgar's cross, a relic from a previous generation of public historians, reminds us of the changing tastes of the tourist or historian and of the changing signifiers of the 'medieval' that tourists respond to. Today, most tourists who come to Birka have been drawn by the promise of the Viking market town, but earlier historians and travelers were drawn here because it is where St. Ansgar carried out his missionary work. At Björko, the landscape of the island is altered by the physical presence of the museum and tourists to reflect a more medieval space, but the space is also reconceived to be 'medieval', like Iceland or York is, except that here the 'medieval' is the dominant interpretation.

Halewood and Hannam trace the rise of Viking tourism to the development of the heritage tourism industry broadly in Europe.[46] Iceland is not the only option if you want to tour Viking places. The tour company, 50° North Nordic, in 2018, offered a Viking Trail tour of Denmark. In 2004, you could take the guided Viking Land Tour:

> The 'Viking Land Tour'! This is an awful tour; it is a terrible tour. You won't see anything but tombs and graves and so on. But don't worry. At the end you'll love it. [. . .] We're taking you out in the beautiful Danish countryside showing you a bit around. Then we are going to the renowned Viking Ship Museum. That'll make you specialists in the Vikings. On the way to a 5000 years old dusky old passage-grave we're again taking you on a picturesque crosscutting tour through the countryside. [. . .] Before we're having a typical Danish buffet at an old charming inn we are visiting the stunning cathedral of Roskilde.[47]

And you would not be limited to Scandinavia if you wish to take a Viking tour. Outside of Rouen, France, there are also signs which let visitors know that they are 'sur le trace des Vikings'.[48] Whole regions are themed according to a perception of the medieval to shape a tourist experience. These are new spacial divisions of the landscape, new ways (hearkening back to old ways) of conceiving of the space.[49]

The Vikings are particularly popular subjects for tours, just as they are for living history museums, because their material remains are less dramatic than the castles and cathedrals left by other cultures. The proliferation of Viking sites is in part because there is a sense that this history is connected to the people who live there; the proliferation is tied to identity politics and Europeans' sense of their own history. But these sites are building on a demonstrable history. They can make claims to 'authenticity', despite the wide variety of these 'medieval' landscapes. Halewood and Hannam show that 'degrees of authenticity are often consciously invoked at all the Viking tourism sites'.[50] Sites and maps that explore a 'medieval' heritage are constructed by and for the tourist gaze; the tourist gaze is more actively *creating* the medieval, as well as perceiving it.

## 'Medieval' events

Some subjects of the tourist gaze are located less in space than they are in time. As Chhabra et al. explain:

> Built environments (such as historical homes, castles, and industrial sites) are perhaps the most obvious manifestations of heritage and the most popular destinations of heritage tourism. But in terms of cultural production (recreation and display of culture), some of the largest and most visited destinations are cultural heritage festivals.[51]

Events are popular since, even if they are repetitions of previous events, each one is different, so they appeal to tourists searching for novelty.[52] Events are part of the collective tourist gaze. Urry and Larsen argue that this involves 'conviviality': 'other people also viewing the site are necessary to give liveliness or a sense of carnival or movement. Large numbers of people indicate that this is the place to be.'[53] 'Medieval' events temporarily code landscapes as places to enjoy the past, bringing many people together to participate.

An event, however, more than built heritage, or even medieval themed re-imaginings of the landscape, creates its own Middle Ages. No longer is it just to be gazed at, but it is to be participated in. As Chhabra et al. argue, 'the authenticity targeted today by heritage festival tourism is a blend [. . .] first, an attempt is made to copy the original; then the copy is modified to meet the needs of the modern community.'[54] They add:

> According to Fine and Speer (1997), an authentic experience involves participation in a collective ritual, where strangers get together in a cultural production to share a feeling of closeness or solidarity. This cultural production is not a total re-creation of the past. In fact, nostalgic collective memory selectively reconstructs the past to serve needs of the present.[55]

Many of these events are associated with places that already use 'medieval' to promote tourism. 'Medieval' cities often have 'medieval' events which try to concentrate those people interested in a 'medieval' experience, to capitalize the most on their pre-existing resources and maximize tourist revenues. These festivals have become very popular, so much so that it seems nearly possible to spend your year travelling from festival to festival: in June, there is the Provins Medieval Festival in Provins, France; in July you could visit Medieval Days in Tallinn, Estonia, followed by Medieval Week in Visby, Sweden; if you are around in February, why not check out the Jorvik Viking Festival in York. York had declared 2018 to be 'the year of the Viking'.

These events are drawing on their local 'medieval' resources, built heritage and re-creations, to give them their theme.[56] All of these examples are located in cities with great medieval walls around certain portions of the city, which give these festivals atmosphere. According to Chhabra et al., 'satisfaction with a heritage event depends not on its authenticity in the literal sense of whether or not it is an accurate re-creation of some past condition, but rather on its perceived authenticity (consistency with nostalgia for some real or imagined past).'[57]

Some kinds of medieval events do not derive authenticity from the built heritage but by their association with certain peoples or events. One example includes the proliferation of Viking trading fairs or markets.[58] The first market was organized at Moesgård in Denmark in 1977. The idea came from the director and curator of the local museum, who organized a Viking ship show, a craft fair and a horse demonstration put on by the local Icelandic Horse Society.[59] In 2017, Blogger www.thevikingqueen.com counted twenty-one Viking/medieval markets in Norway alone. Halewood and Hannam argue about the Viking fairs:

> Viking markets can be viewed as an attempt to replicate all the fun of medieval fairs; and, while they are not true carnivals, they are carnivalesque performances which emphasize the body and bodily processes, the community, and their relationship with their environment (Bakhtin 1984). The Viking markets are transgressive spaces where people can come to play and where the conventions of retailing are modified.[60]

These kinds of events more obviously create a 'medieval' landscape because they create 'medieval' objects for the tourist gaze, where nothing was necessarily readily available.

Comparing the event landscapes here to those created by built heritage or re-interpretations of the pre-existing landscape, these are most obviously creations of the tourist gaze. The tourists or potential of tourists have made something, sometimes where there was nothing before. Rather than seeing this as less authentic than the gazing of the previous instances of 'medieval' landscapes, this instead draws attention to the way that our perceptions of a space impact its character. Instead of pointing to an object and saying 'that is medieval', or to a space where an event happened and saying 'that is medieval', people are engaging in practices that they have associated with the term 'medieval'.

## Inventing a 'medieval' landscape

This chapter conceives of four different kinds of 'medieval landscapes', but it should be clear that there is significant overlap between all of these spaces. Even when a 'medieval' landscape is created using artefacts or built heritage which arguably have a medieval existence outside of the tourist gaze, it has been shown that the tourist gaze has still helped invent, or at least preserve, the 'medieval' space. If there isn't a medieval artefact to celebrate, an often intangible cultural heritage can be brought in to fill in the gap (weaving, woodworking, storytelling etc.), which is no less medieval than the physical object. Destinations which create a 'sight' or experience for the tourist gaze often have a comedic element, drawing attention to elements of artificiality while at the same time marketing authenticity. Interpretive sites vary in how seriously they take themselves or, alternately, how self-reflexively postmodern they are. Another example would be the Canterbury Tales attraction in Canterbury England, which recreates a literary scene (which would obviously have no specific built heritage to draw on) for tourists to gaze on. King Arthur's Labyrinth in Machynlleth, Wales, positions itself as 'authentic' by offering a more Welsh version of the legend (as opposed to an anglicized one), despite a lack of Arthurian literature associated with the site.[61] Viking Land, a subsection of the theme park Tusenfryd in Vinterbro, Norway, makes few pretensions about the history represented at the site, except that Viking is a word with resonances for the local population, so that heritage is still being used as one of the marketing tools here.[62]

Whether it is a ruined castle, a Viking tour or the annual celebration of 'Medieval Days', all of these things create 'medieval' landscapes by focusing the tourist gaze. All of them draw on different ideas of authenticity to market the 'medieval' to tourists. As Chabbra et al say, 'Authenticity – or more accurately, the perception of it – generates revenue and its preservation is considered important by the tourist.'[63] There are some landscapes, however, which have less to work with and so do more work than others to create something to be the object of the tourist gaze. North American 'medieval' sites engage in a lot of invention that is more obvious to the tourist than it would be in European locations. European commemoration of the 'medieval' is going to be different from North American. Coming back to Poria et al.'s point about how personal connection is at the heart of heritage tourism, in Europe explorations of the 'medieval' are easily marketable as local heritage, while in North America this heritage is linked primarily with North Americans' identity as a settler/invader people. The Norse, who landed on North American shores around the year 1000, are of course not actually connected to the large-scale immigration of European settlers/invaders; however, they are perceived as the first Europeans, with first implying a link to the others that will follow.

Parks Canada is not inventing the Norse landing site at L'Anse aux Meadows in Newfoundland, Canada. Like other open-air museums mentioned earlier, it does build things for the tourist to gaze upon and hosts different interpretive guides to help 'bring the history alive' for the visitors; so in this way it creates a 'medieval' landscape similar to the recreations of Eirikr the Red's home in Garða, Greenland. Norstead Viking village, the open-air museum beside the Parks Canada site, is a replica of a Viking port of trade. It's relationship with invention is different than the Parks Canada site. Norstead does not claim that there was such a thing as a Viking port of trade at that location, but the authenticity of the archaeology just two kilometres away and the effort taken in reproducing an authentic Viking Age port in both look and feel are part of the marketing to the tourists.

Wayne Fife argues that the primary method for creating authority for the site 'seems to be to create an association between the new tourist site and the older archaeological site of L'Anse aux Meadows through a symbolic process that emphasizes both the physical and verbal proximity of the two sites.'[64] Fife calls this authenticity by association 'semantic slippage', which is 'a process by which an original artifact or sign justifies the authenticity of a "similar" reproduction. Successful slippage occurs when what is taken to be the "original" meaning of an object (or event) largely collapses into the contemporary meaning of an object of enactment.'[65] In fact, in the last forty years the whole Northern Peninsula of Newfoundland has been reshaped to accommodate the Viking tourism that now drives much of the economy in that area. The road along the northern peninsula has been rebranded 'The Viking Trail'. Despite the inability to definitively pin down the locations mentioned in the Vinland sagas, a large sign saying, 'Welcome to Vinland' has been placed on the road leading to L'Anse aux Meadows and St. Anthony (Figure 8.1).

As in Iceland, the whole area has been re-imagined in terms of Norse history, particularly in relation to saga literature. Applying a new map to the area makes it a 'medieval' landscape. Unlike Iceland, however, it is more of a stretch for the tourist to re-imagine that whole area in the light of the Viking Age. It is similar to Björko, where Viking tourism has literally altered the landscape and dominated other possible interpretations of the space, except that it is harder for the tourist to imagine, outside of the confines of the Parks Canada site, that all the land that is under their feet that is part of this 'medieval' landscape, was once walked on by Vikings. A small kernel has grown into a much larger area under the tourist gaze. In many ways, this is very similar to European sites, but the process of invention is made more explicit by placing it in a North American context, where the link to the history is more tenuous.

The Runestone museum in Alexandria, Minnesota, emphasizes again the tenuous link between history/heritage and tourism. As a site of Norse history, the link is dubious at best, which is confirmed by the Runestone Museum website. The museum celebrates Norse history, but as a local historical institution, it also hosts Fort Alexandria, which gives presentations about more credible local American (including Native American) history. But even though the history is tenuous, the impact of Viking tourism can be felt throughout the town. In 2018, you could attend the Vikingland Band Festival

**Figure 8.1** A sign along Hwy 430 leading into St. Anthony and L'Anse aux Meadows, Newfoundland, Canada.

and Viking Plaza Crazy Days. You could visit the Scandinavian gift shop, take a turn around the Viking Speedway or go to Viking Pawn. As Paradis says,

> culturally-based aspects of authenticity, trends in popular culture, and social status must also contribute to how and why theming occurs in certain places. Individual perception of authenticity engenders local discussions regarding the appropriateness of specific themes for representing their own collective identity.[66]

Viking tourism has shaped the construction of the town in profound ways, despite the probable lack of actual Vikings. Alexandria plays with the signifiers of the medieval, despite no verifiable claim to medieval history, creating a 'medieval' landscape.

The postmodern playing with the symbols of the medieval is inherent in any 'medieval' event. A quick perusal of the Provins Medieval Festival website's pictures of previous events shows as many fantasy costumes as those going for a sense of historic realism. Participants at these kinds of events regularly (and many intentionally) play with the signifiers of the Middle Ages, creating a new sense of the 'medieval'. Without the backdrop of medieval architecture, North American medieval festivals cannot even make the claim that they are, as Halewood and Hannam argued the Viking markets were, creating a sense of local identity or culture – at least, not in the same way that they can in Europe. There is the link to the history of the settler/invader culture, but these are as often transgressive spaces as they are hegemonic ones. Rachel Rubin calls the American Faires a 'functional paradox'.[67] According to Rubin, the festivals were born out of the counter culture of the 1960s in Laurel Canyon, California and originally imagined as a transgressive space.[68] Many of these festivals do still market an authenticity, relating their event back to an event or tradition that occurred in a medieval or renaissance time period, or claiming authenticity through references to medieval ballads or literature. The first fair in Laurel Canyon set itself in the Old Woodbury Hill Fair in Dorset, England.[69] As Rubin says, 'there has not been a year when the word "authentic" has not found its way into discourse about the faire: in marketing, praise or criticism, or insider debate. In the fifth decade of [. . .] faires, historical authenticity characterizes them, and their participants, unevenly.'[70] There is also a sense of authenticity in a North American medieval or renaissance festival, since many of the events in Europe, like Medieval Week in Visby, became traditions only after it was a popular pastime in the United States.

Rubin points out 'it is worth remembering in the twenty-first century that for every educated stickler, there are others who genuinely feel that the faire has enriched them by encouraging an interest in another time and place.'[71] Daniel Kline agrees that 'the love of the medieval as remediated by amateur role-players and gamers is everywhere evident in the time and attention they devote to their characters and to their games in festivals and basements across the globe.'[72] Authenticity is a conversation; it is a highly flexible term, while at the same time, conveying specific meanings to certain communities. These 'medieval' fairs do create a 'medieval' landscape since attendees agree that that is what they are participating in.

Just as the research function of museums should not be discounted, likewise the performative aspect of a 'medieval' faire is an important part of its raison d'etre. Yet the 'coming to see', the tourist aspect, is a major part of their organization and existence. Arguably, since many of the fairs across the United States were corporatized, the focus on tourism (as opposed to performing in a transgressive space) has grown.[73] More performative events include LARPing or conventions of the SCA (Society for Creative Anachronism). The distinction between these kinds of events is blurry when investigated closely; however, fairs and events hosted by towns have more of an economic motive. They are created more for, and cater more to, tourists. The concept of the gaze is complicated here if we do not remember that the idea of a 'tourist gaze' was never meant to encompass just the looking; the looking was just the organizing principle. Indeed, many come to these fairs to participate, so it is a combination of a 'heritage tourism' with a 'performance tourism'.

In North America, and in places all over the globe where performance blurs the lines between 'medieval' and 'neomedieval' (often fantastic reinterpretations of medieval subjects, aesthetics and themes into new material, a kin to Tolkien's work), the invention of a 'medieval' landscape is more explicit and easier to see.

## Conclusion

'Medieval' as a brand changes with different times and different places. What a society imagines to be 'medieval' depends on the time, geography and experiences of an individual. At Björko, one group of travellers themed the land with a cross of St. Ansgar, putting their interpretation of the 'medieval' up to be gazed upon. Later generations would build a Viking Age market, more in tune with their interpretation of the significant medieval history there. Neither group meant to exclude the other interpretations available of the island, including the interpretation of the island as a family farm, but the tourist gaze left different marks at different times, constructing different kinds of 'medieval' landscapes.

Built heritage is an obvious signifier of the 'medieval' that can be exploited (or explored if exploited has too many negative connotations) for tourism, but even there the interpretive work to get a tourist to experience built heritage as 'medieval' has often already been done for them, making 'medieval' a dominant theme. Without built heritage, things can be added to the landscape for tourists to see. If you link the built and re-created heritage together, you have reimagined the landscape, which could belong to any age, as specifically 'medieval' for tourist purposes. Different interpretive tools can be used to help the tourists create a 'medieval' in their mind, even when there is nothing already there to be gazed upon.

Some 'medieval' landscapes are more explicitly and purposefully created for tourists. These same processes are more clearly seen when there is not an immediate medieval signifier, which can be exploited (or explored). It may be true, as Watson laments, that

> if postmodernity is accepted as the prevailing social and cultural condition (and this is by no means necessary) then the medieval is reduced in status to one of many depthless forms which may be consumed without significance. Touring the medieval is a meaningless activity for *touring* is the essential thing, it matters not what.[74]

But medieval as an aesthetic is always subject to our interpretation; embracing the interpretations that shade more toward the postmodern may be to further acknowledge this. Nor is research and representation of different aspects of the Middle Ages likely to go away, as authenticity will always be part of the marketing strategy of selling the 'medieval' to the tourist.

## Notes

1. In this chapter, I will use quotation marks around medieval when there is some question about how much the adjective is an accurate representation of what it is describing. Because this chapter argues that the tourist gaze creates 'medieval' spaces, these qualifiers will be used often.
2. Liberty Entertainment Group, 'The Early Days: Toronto's Camelot', *Casa Loma: Toronto's Majestic Castle*. Available at http://casaloma.ca/camelot.html, accessed February 26, 2018.
3. Medieval Times Dinner and Tournament, *Medieval Times Dinner and Tournament* (2018). Available at https://www.medievaltimes.com/about-medieval-times/index.html, accessed 26 February 2018.
4. Ewa Skowronek et al., 'What Is the Tourist Landscape? Aspects and Features of the Concept', *Acta Geographica Slovenica* 58, no. 2 (2018): 77.
5. Ibid.
6. Skowronek et al. have further defined some of the variable aspects of 'tourist landscape', which is relevant to this chapter since the 'medieval' landscapes created by and for tourists take on such different shapes:

    Genetic aspect – in this approach 'tourist landscape' is a form of cultural landscape. It is a consequence of landscape changes resulting from the development of tourist functions. It is a consecutive 'layer of cultural landscape, which can be homogenous or heterogenous (coexistence of different types of landscapes attractive for tourism in a given destination). It can be featured with different levels of authenticity.

    Physiognomic aspect – tourist landscape reflects tourism development which is aimed at meeting tourists' expectations and the requirements of the tourist economy. It is a particularly physiognomy of tourist space, which links natural and cultural elements with the effects of tourism activity, which differs fundamentally from other types of landscape.

    Functional aspect – tourist landscape has a potential (not necessarily used) to have tourist functions. It is an area where tourism can have, at least temporarily, a predominant role. Each stage of development of tourist function is accompanied by different stages of development whereby tourist and para-tourist facilities are built.

    Interrelated network aspect – tourist landscape is composed of various network connections (internal and external), characterising internal coherence which consists of complementary facilities and services.

    Social aspect – tourist landscape is closely connected with the presence of tourists, it is the object of tourists' interest and can potentially generate tourist movement. It is made to meet tourists' expectations and build a tourist economy. It is selected and used by tourists according to the preferred form of action. Tourist landscape is the object of subjective evaluation and confrontation by tourists having their expectations. It is taken into considerations in plans and implementation schedules. Skowronek, 'What is the Tourist Landscape', 80–1.

7   Theano S. Terkenli, 'Tourism and Landscape', *A Companion to Tourism*, eds Alan A. Lew, Michael Hall and Allen Williams (Massachusetts: Blackwell Publishing Ltd., 2004), 340; As Terkenli argues:

> Tourism marketing reproduces images and discourses about landscapes through representations of cultural signs, on the basis of which the tourist, through processes of experiential reinterpretation of the sign, may assess the sight and validate the meanings of the visited landscape within the predominant discourse. Iconographical methods of construction, signification, decodification, and deconstruction are central to the making of tourist landscapes (Norton 1996; Stefanou 2000). Terkenli, 'Tourism and Landscape', 340.

8   Terkenli, 'Tourism and Landscape', 347.
9   Russell Staiff et al., 'Introduction – Place, Encounter, Engagement: Context and Themes', in *Heritage and Tourism: Place, Encounter, Engagement*, eds Russell Staiff, Robyn Bushell and Steve Watson (New York: Routledge, 2013), 3.
10  Steve Watson, 'Touring the Medieval: Tourism, Heritage and Medievalism in Northumbria', in *Appropriating the Middle Ages: Scholarship, Politics, Fraud*, eds T. A. Shippey and Martin Arnold (Cambridge: Boydell and Brewer, 2001), 251; Louis D'Arcens, 'Laughing in the Face of the Past: Satire and Nostalgia in Medieval Heritage Tourism', *Postmedieval: A Journal of Medieval Cultural Studies* 2 (2011): 156; John Urry and Jonas Larsen, *The Tourist Gaze 3.0* (London: SAGE Publications, 2012), 6.
11  Staiff, 'Introduction', 6.
12  Urry, *The Tourist Gaze*, 2.
13  Ibid., 195; Poria et al. researched 'heritage tourism' and discovered that their 'research . . . challenges the perception that all those who visit a place come only to 'gaze', be educated or to enjoy themselves. For some, it is argued this is an emotional experience, that people come to 'feel' rather than to 'gaze'.
    Yaniv Poria et al., 'The Core of Heritage Tourism', *Annals of Tourism Research* 30, no. 1 (2003): 239.
14  Watson, 'Touring the Medieval: Tourism, Heritage and Medievalism in Northumbria', 241.
15  Windu Nuryanti, 'Heritage and Postmodern Tourism', *Annals of Tourism Research* 23, no. 2 (1996): 249.
16  Watson, 'Touring the Medieval', 241; Deepak Chhabra et al., 'Staged Authenticity and Heritage Tourism', *Annals of Tourism Research* 30, no. 2 (2003): 703; In addition, 'Zeppal and Hall also Emphasize Motivation, and View Heritage Tourism, as "Based on Nostalgia for the Past and the Desire to Experience Diverse Cultural Landscapes and Forms" (1991:49)', Chhabra, 'Staged Authenticity', 703.
17  Urry, *The Tourist Gaze*, 10–11.
18  Chris Halewood and Kevin Hannam, 'Viking Heritage Tourism: Authenticity and Commodification', *Annals of Tourism Research* 28, no. 3 (2001): 567.
19  Thomas W. Paradis, 'Theming, Tourism, and Fantasy City', in *A Companion to Tourism*, eds Alan A. Lew, Michael Hall and Allen Williams (Massachusetts: Blackwell Publishing Ltd., 2004), 198.
20  Urry, *The Tourist Gaze*, 11; Chhabra, 'Staged Authenticity', 706.
21  Urry, *The Tourist Gaze*, 13.
22  Paradis, 'Theming, Tourism, and Fantasy City', 202.
23  Emma Waterton, 'Heritage Tourism and Its Representations', *Heritage and Tourism: Place, Encounter, Engagement*, eds Russell Staiff, Robyn Bushell and Steve Watson (New York: Routledge, 2013), 70.

24 Nuryanti, 'Heritage and Postmodern Tourism', 252.
25 Watson, 'Touring the Medieval', 247.
26 Steve Watson, 'Country Matters: The Rural-Historic as an Authorised Heritage Discourse in England', in *Heritage and Tourism: Place, Encounter, Engagement*, eds Russell Staiff, Robyn Bushell and Steve Watson (New York: Routledge, 2013), 110.
27 Watson, 'Touring the Medieval', 248.
28 Urry, *The Tourist Gaze*, 54.
29 Watson, 'Touring the Medieval', 253.
30 Ibid.
31 Waterton, 'Heritage Tourism', 69.
32 Watson, 'Touring the Medieval', 253.
33 Paradis, 'Theming, Tourism and Fantasy City', 197.
34 Ibid., 195.
35 Staiff, 'Introduction', 252.
36 Urry, *The Tourist Gaze*, 151.
37 Ibid.
38 Bærenholdt argues, 'Debates on heritage tourism in general and Viking heritage in particular have revolved around the concepts of "authenticity" and "commoditization" [. . .] Much of this debate has falsely presented the question as one of either/or, presenting museums as necessarily being either serious or entertaining, thus neglecting the ways in which visitors ascribe meaning to and inscribe their own practices within heritage sites.' Jørgen Ole Bærenholdt and Michael Haldrup, 'On the Track of the Vikings', in *Tourism Mobilities: Places to Play, Places in Play*, eds Mimi Sheller and John Urry (London: Routledge, 2004), 79.
39 D'Arcens shows that for 'comic medieval tourism . . . is a form of tourism in which odor is in fact vital to its aims, playing a central role in this niche-industry's production of what historian Linda Austin has described as a powerful non-cerebral or embodied nostalgia (Austin, 2007, 14–23)', D'Arcens, 'Laughing in the Face of the Past', 161.
40 Louise D'Arcens, *Comic Medievalism* (New York: Boydell and Brewer, 2014), 167.
41 Watson, 'Touring the Medieval', 255.
42 Ibid., 241; Skrowonek et al. argue that 'social awareness of the importance and function of landscape has been increasing in recent years. It is commonly considered as the primary element of European heritage, and as an important factor affecting the quality of life of people'. Skrowonek, 'What Is the Tourist Landscape?', 75.
43 Watson, 'Touring the Medieval', 251.
44 Gunnar Thór Jóhanesson et al., 'Icelandic Tourism: Past Directions – Future Challenges', *Tourism Geographies* 12, no. 2 (May 2010): 281.
45 Jóhannesson, 'Icelandic Tourism', 285.
46 Halewood, 'Viking Heritage Tourism', 568.
47 Larsen 148–9 qtd. In Urry, *The Tourist Gaze*, 202–3.
48 Bærenholdt, 'On the Track of the Vikings', 87.
49 Urry, *The Tourist Gaze*, 125.
50 Halewood, 'Viking Heritage Tourism', 574.
51 Chhabra, 'Staged Authenticity', 704.
52 Donald Getz, 'Geographic Perspectives on Event Tourism', in *A Companion to Tourism*, eds Alan A. Lew, Michael Hall and Allen Williams (Massachusetts: Blackwell Publishing Ltd., 2004), 412.
53 Urry, *The Tourist Gaze*, 19.

54  Chhabra, 'Staged Authenticity', 704.
55  Ibid., 705.
56  Getz, 'Geographic Perspectives', 414.
57  Chhabra, 'Staged Authenticity', 705.
58  Halewood, 'Viking Heritage Tourism', 573.
59  Ibid.
60  Ibid., 579.
61  Benjamin Earl, 'Places Don't Have to Be True to Be True: The Appropriation of KING Arthur and the Cultural', in *Mass Market Medieval: Essays on the Middle Ages in Popular Culture,* ed. David Marshall (Jefferson, NC: McFarland, 2007), 108.
62  Halewood, 'Viking Heritage Tourism', 571; 'At Viking Land, for instance, the mark of authenticity is provided by two of Norway's most renowned archaeologists, Helge and Anne Ingstad, who were consultants during the construction of the site. However, at Viking Land there is no archaeological site in the locality to provide a basis for the recreation nor even any finds from the period'. Halewood, 'Viking Heritage Tourism', 575.
63  Chhabra, 'Stages Authenticity', 716.
64  Wayne Fife, 'Semantic Slippage as a New Aspect of Authenticity: Viking Tourism on the Northern Peninsula of Newfoundland', *Journal of Folklore Research* 41, no. 1 (2004): 72.
65  Ibid., 63–4.
66  Paradis, 'Theming, Tourism and Fantasy City', 202.
67  Rachel Rubin, *Well Met: Renaissance Faires and the American Counterculture* (New York: New York University Press, 2012), 2.
68  Ibid., 4.
69  Ibid., 33.
70  Ibid., 36.
71  Ibid., 70.
72  Daniel T. Kline, 'Participatory Medievalism, Role-Playing, and Digital Gaming', in *The Cambridge Companion to Medievalism,* ed. Louise D'Arcens (Cambridge: Cambridge University Press, 2016), 75.
73  'The first of these, Renaissance Entertainment Corporation (later Renaissance Entertainment Productions), a for-profit publicly traded entity, acquired its first faire in 1989: King Richard's Faire in Bristol, Wisconsin, which it renamed Bristol Renaissance Faire. This traceable network of business deals on the part of motivated individuals, with their own artistic vision and, later on, aggressive corporations methodically consolidating their holdings, is as important to the story of the faires' expansion across the country as is the spread of countercultural values or theatrical innovation'; Rubin, *Well Met,* 66–7.
74  Watson, 'Touring the Medieval', 256.

9

# Playing at the crossroads of religion and law

## Historical milieu, context and curriculum hooks in *Lost & Found*

Owen Gottlieb

### Introduction: Creating a game series for learning

In this chapter, I use design case studies to demonstrate how collaborating designer-researchers and I approached questions of historical accuracy and notions of authenticity in the creation of games designed to teach about religious legal systems of North Africa in the twelfth century. I intend for these cases to share the processes and considerations of the team during the creation of these games. The decisions spanned a number of fields, as the games for learning cover history, law, art history and comparative religion. By providing such a record, this text also serves as a supplementary text to the games themselves, for those educators using the games in formal and informal learning environments and for those examining design considerations regarding representations of history in games. This work is an account of philosophy in action as we created artefacts addressing a variety of problems in teaching history, law and comparative religion.

The *Lost & Found* game series is set in Fustat (Old Cairo) at the time when the great legal scholar, philosopher, rabbi and physician, Moses Maimonides was writing his fourteen-volume law code, the *Mishneh Torah* (1170–1180 CE). Maimonides was seeking to write a Jewish law code that could provide his contemporaries with a more concise approach to the hundreds of years of accrued debates following the first post-biblical law code, the Mishna (redacted circa 250 CE) and the legal debates and story literature of the Talmud (Babylonian Talmud redacted circa 600 or 650 CE) as well as all the various debates, glosses and commentaries that followed the Talmud. He sought to provide a more clarified legal code that could be followed in daily life. Maimonides was also influenced by great Islamic jurists and scholars including Averroes and Al-Ghazli, and Fustat at this time was a crossroads moment for Jews, Muslims and Christians. The period and locale is one that is rich with opportunity for study and exploration and, unlike Spain during *La Convivencia*, has received, in my estimation, less popular attention that twelfth-century Fustat.

The *Lost & Found* series currently consists of two published tabletop (board/card) games concerned with the law around lost and found objects. The first game is *Lost & Found*,[1] a strategy game about balancing trade-off decisions between communal and family needs in the face of legal cases. The second is *Lost & Found: Order in the Court – the Party Game*,[2] which is a storytelling and legal reasoning game. The design team has also developed a digital mobile prototype of the strategy game for the National Endowment for the Humanities,[3] and the team is currently developing an expansion module of the tabletop strategy game addressing Islamic laws of the period and locale. For purposes of clarity in the remainder of the chapter, the original strategy game is referred to as *Lost & Found*, while the party game is referred to as *Order in the Court*. The mobile version of the strategy game will be referred to as 'the digital prototype'.

The first two tabletop games took over four years to develop. I led the interdisciplinary teams, which included twelve scholars and twenty-eight graduate and undergraduate students. Scholars on the team included those covering the fields of medieval Jewish and Islamic studies, religious literacy and comparative religion, as well as game design and development, illustration and graphic design. Students worked with faculty on aspects of the games including game design, illustration, sound design (for the digital prototype), knowledge management, project management, software development and more.

The impetus for the creation of the series was twofold. First, the series seeks to expand the discourse around religious legal systems. Today, the study of religious legal systems is often relegated to graduate courses at universities which provide the deep context to those who pursue advanced studies. On the other hand, the broader public may only hear of religious legal systems through sensationalized clips on cable news. All too often, these clips, without context or research, lead to incitement by fear. For example, contemporary discourse is influenced by mentions of 'Sharia law' as a modern legal system to fear, as opposed to a set of historically grounded, specifically contextualized ideas to understand. The second driver beyond the development of the *Lost & Found* series is a desire to explore the boundaries of the discipline of games and learning[4] by investigating how historically contextualized legal systems might be modelled by game systems. Both games and legal systems are rule-based, and so this intersection appeared an important parallel to explore for the field of games and learning.

The central purpose of the *Lost & Found* series is to serve as a learning artefact to use in formal and informal learning environments. The goal of the use of these artefacts is to expand the discourse around religious legal systems, including promoting the understanding of the historical prosocial aspects of these systems, namely collaboration, cooperation, governance and community sustainability. Team member Diane Moore writes of the importance of setting religion in its context of time and place in her text *Overcoming Religious Illiteracy*.[5] The team went to great lengths to design historically accurate reproductions in the games, with illustrations of architectural patterns, coinage and other artefacts of the period including various vessels. When considering questions of authenticity, the series takes into account a number of possible interpretive stances educators and learners may take while playing, exploring and reflecting on the games.

## The structure of the games

Prior to moving onto notions of accuracy and authenticity, and in order to provide a window in the games themselves, this section will describe an overview of gameplay of the two games. This is not an in-depth description of play, given the purpose of this particular chapter, but rather is intended to provide enough context to appreciate the design work concerned with issues of historical accuracy and authenticity. For an extended discussion of the game systems, see Gottlieb, 2017; Gottlieb & Schreiber, 2018; Gottlieb and Schreiber, forthcoming. Detailed manuals/rulebooks for the games are available at www.lostandfoundthegame.com.

The first game, *Lost & Found*, is a strategy game combining mid-weight Euro-style competitive mechanics with cooperative mechanics from American games such as *Pandemic* (Leacock, 2008). This competitive-cooperative game[6] is targeted to high school students. The game is for three to five players, comprising six turns through thirty-three game events. Play lasts between forty-five minutes and seventy minutes depending on players' familiarity with the rules. In the game, players take on roles representing families in twelfth-century Fustat. Over the course of the game, players must resolve Events, such as losing or finding animals or other belongings. The Events are mostly drawn from cases in the *Mishneh Torah*. Players must address the events with limited resources. For example, they may need to decide whether to follow the law, break the law, or go above and beyond the law to help their neighbours. If a neighbour's cow has wandered away, what will they decide? Meanwhile the path to winning requires contributing resources (in the form of the in-game currency, *dinarim*) to both family and communal responsibilities. Family responsibilities include, for example, teaching one's children a trade, or teaching them how to swim. Communal responsibilities include building a bathhouse and training a doctor. Family responsibilities are incentives specific to the player while communal responsibilities must be achieved cooperatively. Additional cooperative actions include working together to solve Crises and Disasters such as fires, windstorms, and plagues.

Any or all players can win. If any player 'goes destitute', the term for a player unable to cover basic resource requirements, then all players immediately loose. In order to be eligible to win, the group must collectively complete at least six communal responsibilities prior to the end of the game. If by end of game, the 'communals' are completed, then those players who have also completed three family responsibilities win. If players decide during the game to either break the law (for example, in using property owned by another for their own gain) or go above and beyond the law to help a neighbour, then the number of required family responsibilities may be altered in the end game turns. The uncertainty of whether law breakers are caught and whether those who go above and beyond the law are managed through a late-in-game card draw from the *heshbon*, or accounting, deck. The core mechanic of the game is weighing trade-off decisions as players navigate the events and their responsibilities to family and community while under resource constraints. If all players win (one of the possible, yet challenging, outcomes), it is considered to be a 'thriving community'.

*Order in the Court* is a very different type of game, based on the same underlying material. Designed for faster play and particularly concerned with encouraging conversations about legal reasoning, this game can be played by three to five or more players (we have had games with up to eight players). It is targeted for learners in junior high and up, and a three- to five-player game takes about thirty minutes. Larger groups may increase the time of play. In the game, players take turns as judge as the other players use Story Cards with people and objects referenced in the chapter of *Mishneh Torah*. The goal of their stories is to explain how an arcane law the judge reads might have gone to a court in the first place. The Ruling Card has the arcane ruling on one side. Players compete for the judge's favour, often through humour, crafting and then presenting their stories using at least three of the cards in their hands in the story. Once the judge decides on a winner for the round, the players can hear the actual historical context for the ruling, which is on the back of the Ruling Card. The judge role rotates among players. The game's core mechanic of developing legal stories focuses on legal reasoning, and the tone of the game is humorous. With this overview of gameplay and mechanics as foundation, I now turn to design approaches and concerns regarding historical accuracy in the design of these games.

## The pursuit of historical accuracy

I pursued accuracy in representations of material culture by working closely with experts in medieval Jewish and Islamic North Africa, most often Phillip Ackerman-Lieberman at Vanderbilt University. We sought source images that were period and locale-accurate and that would help us develop illustrations of various social scenes of the period. Ackerman-Lieberman and I then worked with student illustrators including lead illustrators Mimi Ace, Tori Bonagura and Annie Wong, who created original illustrations of the artefacts, architectural patterns and social tableaus, taking care to always adapt the reference imagery in order to create original illustrations. This often meant imagining the objects from different angles and views than portrayed in photography in order to avoid any potential copyright infringement of the photographs we studied. No artefact appears in the game as it does in a particular photograph, yet we worked to honour the original object while shifting angles, sometimes colours, sometimes 'restoring' artefacts through our illustrations.

In *Lost & Found*, the original strategy game, there are various types of cards in the game, each serving different purposes, including resources, goal cards (responsibilities), roles, event cards and other card classes. Each unique set of cards has a card *back*, and each card back features a pattern that Annie Wong located from photography of buildings from Fatimid architecture in Fustat (referencing texts such as Bloom, 2007). She enlarged detail patterns to create the card backs and image frames on the cards. Each card *face* also has an architectural pattern framing the main card illustration (Figures 9.1, 9.2 and 9.3).

Each artefact or situation the team rendered went through an initial discussion between a scholar or scholars of the period, illustrators and designers, and then through a further discussion among illustrators and designers regarding various approaches

**Figure 9.1** Card back showing architectural patterns from Fatimid Fustat in *Lost & Found*. © Rochester Institute of Technology. (Illustrated by Annie Wong.)

for representing that research through illustration. When working on various scenes, Ackerman-Lieberman helped us find reference images – what would the following scenes look like: a court room, a study circle, a bathhouse, a bathroom or a scale from the period? Along with reference images and discussions, the illustrators created a consistent style, which they described as 'inviting', a pleasant warm style. They also created a style guide and a video tutorial for other student illustrators who would later join the team.

Our research covered a wide range of subjects beyond architecture. We researched information about garb of the period, for example, people in the game wear turbans. When depicting a scale from the period, we worked to find representative scales from which to design. We illustrated an inkwell and reed pens as well as a box in which to keep pens. See Figure 9.5. These are just a few examples of the many period images rendered in the game (Figures 9.4 and 9.5).

In *Lost & Found*, event cards include game events involving the loss and discovery of objects and animals as well as other events. Players then must contend with choices

**Figure 9.2** Card back showing architectural patterns from Fatimid Fustat in *Lost & Found*. © Rochester Institute of Technology. (Illustrated by Annie Wong.)

as to how to behave regarding the event. Will they work to return the lost object? Will they break the law? When not required to return something, will they preserve their family resources, or consider going above and beyond the law to assist their neighbours or strangers at a cost to themselves? In addition, there are other event card types including Crises and Disasters. Crises and Disasters require players to work together, either immediately in the case of disasters, or over the course of the next round of play with Crises cards. When illustrating event cards, we spoke with scholars about details of the event, whether it was regarding the loss of an animal, typical crops of the region, or what a 'plague' might have meant in Fatimid North Africa. We learned, for example, that plague usually referred to disease carried by flies that flew into people's eyes and that there were monsoons in the region. We learned about key crops of the period, such as flax, sugar cane and rendered them in illustration (see Figures 9.6, 9.7 and 9.8).

**Figure 9.3** Card back showing architectural patterns from Fatimid Fustat in *Lost & Found*. © Rochester Institute of Technology. (Illustrated by Annie Wong.)

Our mode of evoking the period and locale focused on developing 'accurate' imagery through the collaboration with scholarly experts and illustrators. Illustrators worked to translate ideas and references shared by the expert, and then illustrators applied a consistent style in consultation with the executive producer (Gottlieb) and the game design team. We developed a system of communication, discussion, references and illustration that we applied to each image. I found approaching ideas of historical authenticity far more slippery.

## Defining and pursuing historical authenticity

What do I mean by historical 'authenticity'? In considering authenticity, I have found the literature on this topic in the field of heritage tourism particularly helpful.

**Figure 9.4** Card from *Lost & Found* illustrating objects, garments and milieu. © Rochester Institute of Technology. (Illustrated by Mimi Ace, Tori Bonagura, and Annie Wong.)

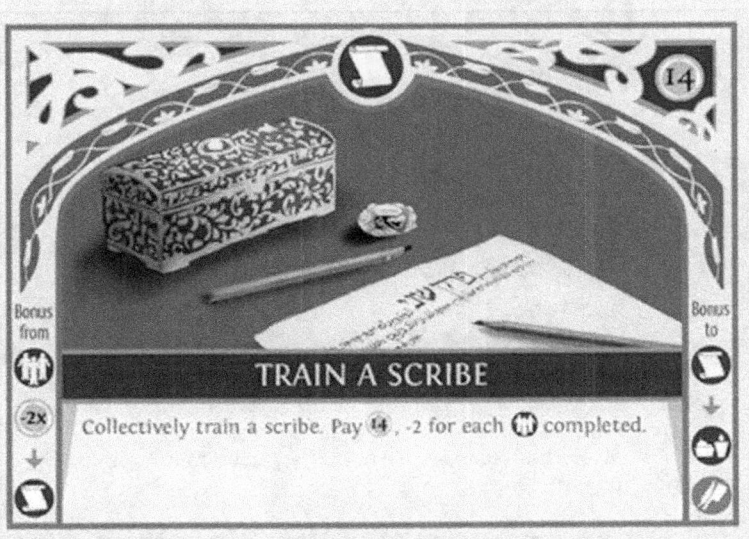

**Figure 9.5** Card from *Lost & Found* illustrating objects and milieu. © Rochester Institute of Technology. (Illustrated by Mimi Ace, Tori Bonagura, and Annie Wong.)

**Figure 9.6** Events Card: Plague. © Rochester Institute of Technology. (Illustrated by Mimi Ace, Tori Bonagura, and Annie Wong.)

**Figure 9.7** Events Card: Monsoon. © Rochester Institute of Technology. (Illustrated by Mimi Ace, Tori Bonagura, and Annie Wong.)

**Figure 9.8** Events Cards: Bumper Crop. © Rochester Institute of Technology. (Illustrated by Annie Wong.)

Heritage studies and tourism studies are fields which have had to wrestle with ideas of authenticity in a variety of contexts including restoration of historical sites.

Gordon Waitt, in his examination of perception of historical authenticity of The Rocks in Sydney Australia draws from a number of scholars to articulate a post-structuralist understanding of authenticity.[7] Waitt identifies various competing interests and perspectives through which a place's past is interpreted such as those of academics, government institutions, tour operators, residents and tourists. He notes that each group has its own agendas and viewpoints.[8] Waitt explains a means to understand authenticity as the product of a process of a negotiation:

> [A] post-structuralist critique of how place is assimilated into the tourism production system rejects the dichotomies of true/false, real/invented, and staged authenticity/back regions. Instead, authenticity is regarded as a process of negotiation between various competing interpretations of past events in a particular place. The version of authenticity that is socially constructed for consumption is conceived of as a manifestation of a negotiation process between the various stakeholders in that place.[9]

I understood that any attempt at authenticity in the game would be both constructed as well as contrived and considered how I might include this understanding within the design of the game itself. I hypothesized about how I might foreground the particularly constructed nature of authenticity and settled on an approach I refer to as 'Maimonides' Dream'. 'Maimonides' Dream' would situate the game during the time and in the place Maimonides was writing. This would be as close as we could emulate Maimonides perspective as he studies and considers texts from different periods, such as the Mishna and the Talmud, and creates the new text of the *Mishneh Torah*. All the while, we understood our emulation would be a far approximation. The 'authenticity' would come from picking this particular perspective as a grounding position and a reference point. If the stakeholders were those concerned with material culture, we would clearly date certain periods relative to twelfth-century Fustat (coins would appear from twelfth-century Fustat, but also the times Maimonides was reading about in the Mishna and the Talmud). If the stakeholders were those concerned about the interpretation of the law, we would fall back on Maimonides time period. If the stake holders were concerned about gender portrayals, we would allow for players to play male or female roles, yet depict in our tableaus when we believed men would likely have a role (such as a 'judge' or 'teacher') during the time of Maimonides' life and the times he considers in the texts he is reading. Each stakeholder would be situated relative to Maimonides' imagined position. I will provide more detailed examples later of how the team rendered this idea of 'Maimonides' Dream'.

## Imagining 'Maimonides' Dream'

I had previously used a science-fiction wrapper narrative in my mobile augmented reality history game *Jewish Time Jump: New York*.[10] Players took on the roles of time travelling reporters, who go back in time to recover a story 'lost to time'. In visiting the past, they encounter historical characters and events including primary source material. In this way, I worked to emphasize the constructed nature of the narratives – both the historical narrative, which is always constructed, and the game narrative, which was an interweaving of historical drama and primary source material.[11] Given the goal of the *Lost & Found* games, I had decided early in the process that the history would be one I might articulate for the design team as well as educators as 'Maimonides' Dream' of the Mishnah Torah. This required that a number of different ideas had to be combined. First, that we might communicate a flavour of the material culture of the period, imagining Maimonides walking the streets of Fustat during the years he was writing the *Mishneh Torah*. What would the streets and buildings look like? How would people dress? What might a visit to a doctor's 'office', or a marriage contract (*ketubah*) look like? (see Figure 9.9).

The dream also meant asking the question of how Maimonides might imagine something like a *dinar*. The *dinar* (plural in Hebrew, *dinarim*[12]) is a coin of the period. The *dinar* is also referred to in the Mishna as well as the Talmud, which interprets and comments on the Mishna. So, what might Maimonides be thinking about when he writes 'dinar' in the *Mishneh Torah*? Perhaps he thought about the *dinarim* that he himself used in transactions. Perhaps he was thinking of the dinar of the Mishna; perhaps after considering a Talmud passage interpreting the Mishnah, he would consider a dinar of the Talmud. When we decided on the illustrations for the *dinarim* cards, we decided to render *dinarim* of *all three periods*. This was to provide a sense

*Playing at the Crossroads of Religion and Law* 151

**Figure 9.9** A *ketubah*, or marriage contract, from *Lost & Found*. © Rochester Institute of Technology. (Illustrated by Mimi Ace, Tori Bonagura and Annie Wong.)

that 'dinar' could have multiple interpretations, and that the *Mishneh Torah* was built upon earlier texts, interpretations and debates. This was also an example of one of the numerous curricular 'hooks' we embedded in the game. An educator, working with a pre-written curriculum or educators developing curricula with our team, could use this as a teachable moment, exploring the questions of a moment in time, the literary work or works, and the different meanings and values over time of a concept such as a 'dinar'. I imagined a question prompt such as 'Why do you think there are different *dinarim* with different periods on the cards?' (Figures 9.10 and 9.11).

We also had to render social scenes. This was less about material culture and more about the social milieu: how might we depict a judge making a decision, or a teacher with a circle of students. Out of discussions with Ackerman-Lieberman, we determined position of people and items such as the wand or stick that a teacher might hold, how

**Figure 9.10** Dinarim cards marked with dates and locales of different dinarim from *Lost & Found*. © Rochester Institute of Technology. (Illustrated by Mimi Ace, Tori Bonagura and Annie Wong.)

a judge would be on a raised platform and how the judge or teacher would most likely be a man during this period (Figures 9.12 and 9.13).

Beyond material culture and aspects of social scenes, we also had to come to an understanding of questions raised by the law. What did certain obscure or decontextualized phrases or passages in the law mean, or why was the law this way? For example, in order to understand the *halacha* (law), around negotiating a price for assistance with a broken vessel, we had to understand that honey, made from dates was more valuable than wine.[13] The law revolves around pre-negotiating dumping out one's wine to assist someone losing their honey: one cannot, after the fact, without having asked in advance, charge the person being helped for the loss of the wine (Figure 9.14).

Another example of understanding of the laws can be seen in how Maimonides makes a distinction between a cow that a neighbour neglectfully abandons – neither

**Figure 9.11** Dinarim cards marked with dates and locales of different dinarim from *Lost & Found*. © Rochester Institute of Technology. (Illustrated by Mimi Ace, Tori Bonagura and Annie Wong.)

keeping the door to the enclosure closed nor tying the animal down. In this case (*Mishneh Torah*, Gezelah Va'Aevdah 11:11), the statement of the *halacha* does not obligate the neighbour finding the cow to intervene. Other jurists disagree, but in this instance, we can see the balancing of two principles – the obligation to return a neighbour's belonging, often at great expense to the finder (feeding, keeping, trying to return at intervals, not making a profit for at least a year, hiring it out to not benefit from it). At the same time, by accounting for neglect, Maimonides places boundaries and balance on the requirement to intervene. We would call this dealing with 'undue burden'.

And so, in this case, *accuracy* was in rendering the meaning of the law to the best of our ability and translating that into the game (in this case with three possible decisions for the player – follow the law (do the minimum), or go above and beyond the law and

**Figure 9.12** Train a Judge and Train a Teacher cards from *Lost & Found*. © Rochester Institute of Technology. (Illustrated by Mimi Ace, Tori Bonagura, and Annie Wong.)

**Figure 9.13** Train a Judge and Train a Teacher cards from *Lost & Found*. © Rochester Institute of Technology. (Illustrated by Mimi Ace, Tori Bonagura, and Annie Wong.)

*Playing at the Crossroads of Religion and Law* 155

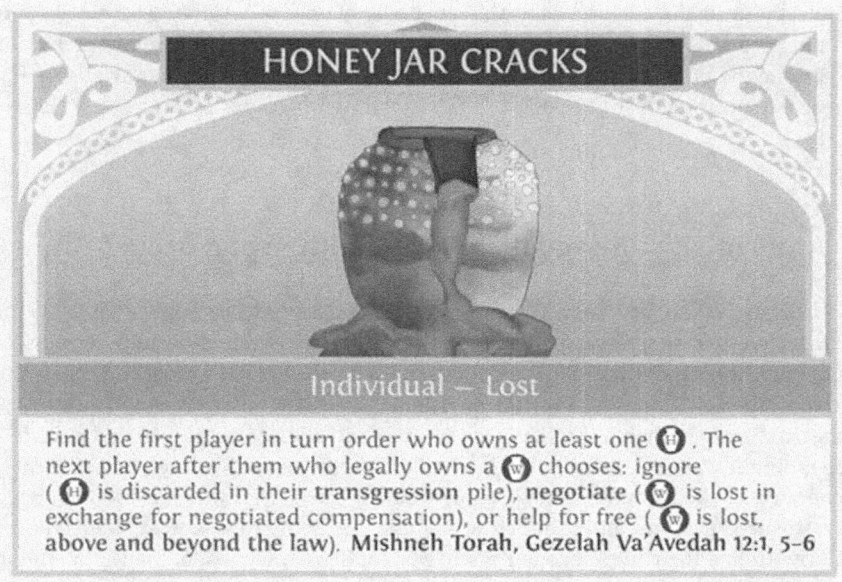

**Figure 9.14** Honey Jar Cracks event card from *Lost & Found*. © Rochester Institute of Technology. (Illustrated by Tori Bonagura and Annie Wong.)

**Figure 9.15** Abandoned Cow event card in *Lost & Found*. © Rochester Institute of Technology. (Illustrated by Mimi Ace and Annie Wong.)

return the animal while sacrificing the remainder of one's own turn). Here *authenticity* would need to be drawn out during reflection or discussion – to come to a reckoning regarding the potential implications of the law within society/community and to add those perspectives to the seeking of understanding of the period and locale (Figure 9.15).

## Authenticity through dialogue, reflection and deeper study

As I illustrated in the examples earlier, I made a design decision to work from the perspective that the games should approach authenticity by allowing educators to encourage learners to ask questions about the game. In this way, those learners could delve deeper into sources, and this questioning and delving itself would add to the construction of authenticity. The more learners and educators engaged and reflected, the more the dimensionality of the law and the period might be developed. The cases generated by events in the strategy game would create stories which could be further investigated. If Maimonides hoped to help people come to a better understanding of how to live their lives through his newly condensed law code, then in a similar way,[14] I wished to provide cases that could allow the law to be understood as a system that could hold neighbours responsible to one another in prosocial ways. As the design team spent months playing through various cases in this particular section of *Mishneh Torah* in the process of designing the game systems, from objectives through to events, we came to understand, at deeper and deeper levels, the purpose and power behind the law. In fact, in searching for objectives in the game, we attempted to look at underlying principles in the law, which we concluded, balances the needs of the community with the needs of the individual, providing various incentives and boundaries.

Could players/learners examine the various laws and come to a deeper understanding of the underlying principles of the system? The curriculum, currently in development, seeks to illicit such observations and questions, working in concert with the game artefacts. The second game in the series, *Order in the Court*, also arose out of our desire to experiment centring play around meta-questions about the law: Why is the law constructed this way? How might it have been constructed originally? By using the storytelling suppositional structure of *Order in the Court*, Ian Schreiber and I worked to move those meta-questions to the centre of play. I theorized that if both the strategy game and party game are played together, we could have both generated cases to dissect through curricular reflection (from the strategy game), and a game system to play with the concepts of the purpose of the laws and their possible origin in the second game. Together we could cover different types of reflection and widen our designed construction of the period. Further research on the games in classrooms will tell us more about how the games function separately, on their own, and in concert with curriculum (Figures 9.16 and 9.17).

Though my mobile AR history game *Jewish Time Jump: New York* used a science-fiction tale inspired by primary and secondary sources, the game was replete with

*Playing at the Crossroads of Religion and Law* 157

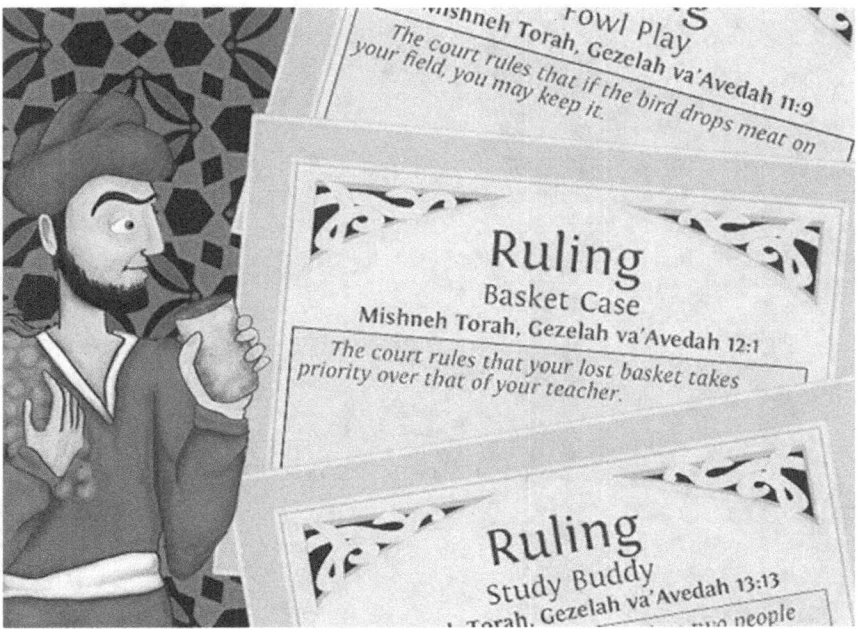

**Figure 9.16** Rulings and Explanations cards in *Lost & Found: Order in the Court – the Party Game*. © Rochester Institute of Technology. (Illustrated by Mimi Ace and Annie Wong.)

primary source material (digitizing of ephemera for example) and is informed by secondary source material. *Lost & Found* is also a construction of history drawing on primary and secondary source material. For this game series, the negotiations between the stakeholders could be understood as those between the educators, the learners, the scholars, the players and the designers. The illustrations are clearly constructed (painted or drawn), yet they are drawing on actual artefacts and images. The laws are from the actual text written in the period, yet the cases of origin pre-date the period considerably. Would the cases represent actual cases of the time period, or rather act as illustrations of principles that would be applied in the twelfth century, yet drawing from much earlier concerns?

My goal was to raise the opportunity to discuss these questions with adequate texture to encourage and engender further exploration, but not to answer them directly. There could be space for competing interpretations and that would be the ideal place for an educator and/or curriculum guide to engage learners. If free-floating without curriculum, then the strategy game could evoke a sense of a rich material culture and ideally, a mysterious and different time and a place inviting further exploration. We also would be leaving a player with scenarios embedded with legal cases as well as cases of play emulating the push and pull of the family, the community and the role of the law in moderating and circumscribing behaviour. By having players consider whether or not to break the law and, in some cases, having players make the decision to break the law, such play experiences could allow for cases of transgressive play that could

**Figure 9.17** Rulings and Explanations card in *Lost & Found: Order in the Court – the Party Game*. © Rochester Institute of Technology. (Illustrated by Mimi Ace and Annie Wong.)

be used by educators to examine motives and position with regards to the law. Here learners would have opportunity to discuss choices and examine how the law relates to those choices. Sometimes the game rules will come in conflict with the law, but the strategy game was designed that way purposefully. I imagined questions such as 'how did it feel when she did not return your cow?' or 'What was the decision like when you decided to transgress the law?'

## Methods and future curriculum design: Building authenticity through negotiation and dialogue over time

I have approached research and design on the *Lost & Found* game system through two sets of methods. The design team uses a 'playcentric' design approach, Fullerton's articulation of iterating on a game design to improve its player engagement and reduce 'fun killers'.[15] This kind of design research is not generalizable, but rather is used to improve the designed artefact. It may lead to design cases studies. We conducted several dozen playtests while designing the games. We conducted internal design reviews both among the team members and also external playtests, bringing the games to players outside the team. Over much of the course of the school year and during some summer months for more than three and half years, we were conducting these playtests weekly.

We also conducted a small number of social science research investigations under the rubric of methods known as Design-Based Research (DBR).[16] As we move into curricular development working with educators and learners, we are expanding these studies. Design-based research's target outcome is design-relevant social science. Design-based research is suited for any 'rich contextualized setting in which people have agency'.[17] Design-based research is an iterative, proto-theory-testing approach to developing learning theory and design knowledge. Designer-researchers prototype a learning environment or intervention (such as a game or curriculum) over the course of a number of iterative cycles comprising design, field trial, data gathering, analysis and return to design. Learning theory is used as a starting point for design, and that theory is held suspect (a learning sciences term meaning 'held in doubt') during investigation. Our data gathering involves a number of diverse and mixed methods approaches, including participant observation with video and audio, pre-and post-tests and semi-structured interviews. Using DBR, we can work to develop new knowledge about learning while focusing the games and the curriculum towards improved formal and informal learning environments.

*Lost & Found* and *Lost & Found: Order in the Court – the Party Game* are both for sale to the public now. We are gathering data and expanding our research further. For example, the games are currently in use in a high school on the east coast of the United States and the teacher has joined our research project. As the *Lost & Found* team moves forward working on the forthcoming Islamic law module, we are also turning towards curriculum, which is critical for any learning game and which we eventually hope to make available to the wider public. The reflective moments – the questions, discussion and the delving – are key for building out the learning environment. I argue that pursuing historical authenticity also requires the kind of dialogue generated by a carefully design curriculum, whether in a classroom or a less formal learning environment. If, the heart of authenticity, as Waitt teaches us, is the social construction that is manifested by a negotiation process between many and varied stakeholders, then perhaps we can consider an authentic approach to history learning games as one that engenders thoughtful multi-vocal negotiations and reflections about time and place, guided by well-researched curriculum designed with teachers. Perhaps authenticity in games can only be understood in that searching and negotiation process.

## Notes

1 *Lost & Found* (Gottlieb, Schreiber, Murdoch-Kitt, 2017).
2 *Lost & Found: Order in the Court – The Party Game* (Gottlieb and Schreiber, 2017).
3 This work is supported by the GCCIS, Office of the Vice President for Research, and the MAGIC Center at RIT. This work is also supported and funded by the National Endowment for the Humanities. Any views, findings, conclusions or recommendations expressed in this chapter do not necessarily represent those of the National Endowment for the Humanities.
4 In Game and Learning, or Games for Learning, scholars and designers looking to the affordances of games systems to enhance learning environments. See: Owen

Gottlieb, 'Jewish Games for Learning: Renewing Heritage Traditions in the Digital Age', in *Digital Judaism: Jewish Negotiations with Digital Media and Culture*, ed. Heidi Campbell, Routledge Studies in Religion and Digital Culture (New York, NY: Routledge, 2015).

5   Diane Moore, *Overcoming Religious Illiteracy: A Cultural Studies Approach to the Study of Religion in Secondary Education* (New York, NY: Palgrave Macmillan, 2007).

6   While cooperative games have become more popular since *Pandemic's* debut in 2008, this combination of competition and cooperation is rare and is discussed in greater length in: Owen Gottlieb, 'Design-Based Research: Mobile Gaming for Learning Jewish History, Tikkun Olam, and Civics', in *Methods for Studying Video Games and Religion*, eds Vít Šisler, Kerstin Radde-Antweiler and Xenia Zeiler (New York, NY: Routledge, 2017); Owen Gottlieb, and I. Schreiber, 'Designing Analog Learning Games: Genre Affordances, Limitations, and Multi-Game Approaches', in *Rerolling Boardgames*, eds E. MacCallum-Steward and D. Brown (Jeferson, NC: McFarland Press, Forthcoming).

7   Gordon Waitt, 'Consuming Heritage: Perceived Historical Authenticity', *Annals of Tourism Research* 27, no. 4 (1 October 2000): 835–62.

8   Ibid., 848.

9   Ibid.

10  *Jewish Time Jump: New York* (Owen Gottlieb and Jennifer Ash, 2013).

11  Owen Gottlieb, 'Who Really Said What? Mobile Historical Situated Documentary as Liminal Learning Space', *Gamevironments*, no. 5 (December 2016): 237–57.

12  The *Mishneh Torah* (1170–1180 CE) was written in Hebrew in the style of the Mishnah (the first post-Biblical Jewish law code, written circa 250 CE) as opposed to Maimonides' Guide for the Perplexed (circa 1185), which was written in Judeo-Arabic.

13  While there is evidence that the Fatimid court had bee honey, Maimonides is referring to date honey, which would have been far more plentiful in twelfth-century Egypt, as there were date orchards. During the Talmudic period, bee honey would have been even more rare (Phillip Ackerman-Lieberman, personal conversation).

14  Holo notes the parallel between the goal of the *Mishneh Torah* and our goal with *Lost & Found*: making the laws accessible to a contemporary audience. Joshua Holo, 'Rabbi Owen Gottlieb: Playing with Judaism in the Digital Age', *Bully Pulpit Podcast: Torah with a Point of View*. Available online: https://collegecommons.huc.edu/bully_pulpit/judaism-in-digital-age/, accessed 22 April 2020.

15  Tracy Fullerton, *Game Design Workshop: A Playcentric Approach to Creating Innovative Games* (Boca Raton, FL: A K Peters/CRC Press, 2014).

16  See: The Design-Based Research Collective, 'Design-Based Research: An Emerging Paradigm for Educational Inquiry', *Educational Researcher* 32, no. 1 (January 2003): 5–8; Gottlieb, 'Design-Based Research'; Christopher Hoadley, 'Methodological Alignment in Design-Based Research', *Educational Psychologist* 39 (December 2004): 203–12; Christopher Hoadley, 'Fostering Productive Collaboration Offline and Online: Learning from Each Other', in *Internet Environments for Science Education*, eds Marcia Linn, Elizabeth A. Davis, and Philip Bell (Mahway, NJ: Lawrence Erlbaum Associates, Inc., 2004), 145–74.

17  Christopher Hoadley, 'Design-Based Research', Presented at the ECT PhD Colloquium (New York University, 2013).

10

# Modding and authentic, gritty medievalism in *Skyrim*

Victoria Cooper

## Introduction

When discussing a historical or pseudo-historical game's setting, we, both players and scholars, will regularly use the words 'realistic' and 'authentic' when appraising that game world's representation of its historical setting. These words are used interchangeably but cover at least two distinct concepts: first, we might be referring to the extent to which a game reflects an academic, source-led understanding of the past. Second, we might be referring to how well the game conjures the spirit of its setting, or how well it conforms to its time period in the popular imagination. I imagine that in discussing a game's historical authenticity we likely refer to both at the same time, but there is use in delineating the two ideas in order to gain a fuller understanding of how the past is conceptualized in the popular imagination.

I use realism to describe a game's attempt to portray the real world as objectively as possible. This might mean its graphical fidelity and how closely the rules and natural laws that govern the virtual world map onto our own. I also use the term to refer to the accurate representation of the past as we would understand it through scholarly study as well as the likelihood of a game's historical narrative. As Houghton argued in discussing factual accuracy in Crusader Kings, while historically inaccurate, Harold defeating William at Hastings is a realistic historical possibility.[1] Providing space for alternate historical scenarios might make a game less historically accurate but does not necessarily render the game unrealistic.

Authenticity, on the other hand, is a term I am using to cover the affective elements of medievalism. Salvati and Bullinger term this affective quality 'selective authenticity', where historical games are 'more concerned more with creating a "feel" and "experience" than with strict factual fidelity'.[2] When something is authentic, it doesn't necessarily mimic an accurate or scholarly understanding of the past. It is rather that it 'feels right'. When something is authentic it cognitively fits, even if it is not accurate or even realistic. Authenticity is the characteristic of conforming to the audience's expectations of space, time, genre and culture. Following this definition, I argue that authenticity is more critical for creating enjoyable and immersive pseudo-historical spaces than accuracy or even realism. When a game creates an authentic portrayal of the Middle Ages, the narrative and temporal cohesion and coherence in the game world can be maintained even through instances of wild inaccuracy, anachronism or unrealism.

What feels medieval, what seems right and proper and authentic for a medieval world, stands to tell us a great deal about how the Middle Ages are perceived in the modern world, as well as which elements of the medieval are currently resonant and relevant. Furthermore, as I explored in my doctoral thesis, deconstructing authentic medievalisms is key to understanding how the Middle Ages, as a popular concept, is important in conceptualizing the modern world and the ideologies, desires and anxieties of the modern self.[3] Typically, traditional textual analysis of games and direct work with consumers are the means of understanding how medieval authenticity is created and perceived. These are both important, but I argue that this type of audience reception and engagement data might be gathered productively through additional means.

Outside of, but in addition to, the formally published game lie the 'mods'. The term 'mod' (short for modification) can refer to any type of alteration made to a game outside its proprietary development. Scacchi describes mods as 'a leading form of user-led innovation in game design and game play experience', with 'user-led' being a key part of the definition for this chapter.[4] Modders, those who create mods, are typically players looking to make some desired adjustment to an existing game. These adjustments can range from tweaking code to fix glitches, to major aesthetic or functional changes to the game. Mods might add new content, such as new zones or quests, or change the aesthetics of the game's world and its characters. They might modify or add new mechanics in order to alter the gameplay, such as removing a respawn function in order to raise difficulty and increase a player's sense of tension. Some mods are so comprehensive that they can change the nature of the original game, creating entirely new worlds and fundamentally altering the playful experience and potential for meaning from the source. A few mods have become fully fledged, standalone games, released from dependence on their source game.[5]

Mods are a form of audience response to games. While games, especially role-playing games, are inherently interactive and place the player in a collaborative role, modding is an activity through which the player-modder more directly becomes a co-author. As well as providing bug fixes and new ways to play an existing game, mods can be seen as a mode of reflexive communication within player communities. They engage with current events and popular culture in a myriad of ways: sometimes in pure parody or as absurdism played for laughs, as in the case of the niche but well-reported subgenre of mods for *The Elder Scrolls V: Skyrim* (henceforth, *Skyrim*), which replace dragons with whimsical things, such as *Thomas the Tank Engine* or *My Little Pony*.[6] At other times, this takes the form of more serious socio-political engagement: one feature of a popular mod increased the racial diversity of *Skyrim*'s armies, with the modder noting in their description: 'See, in order to join the imperials or the [S]tormcloaks, apparently, you have to be a white male. THAT'S DISCRIMINATION AND WE DON'T HAVE TO STAND FOR IT.'[7] The same modder later removed their work from *Nexus Mods* in response to Donald Trump's presidential campaign, and in support of Hillary Clinton's candidacy, leaving the following note:

In a time where hatred screams loud from the dark recesses of the internet and my country, I will use my soapbox for something. For more information on what you can do to help, I suggest you visit Amnesty International. #BlackLivesMatter #LGBTRights #TransIsBeautiful #RefugeesWelcome #OccupyWallStreet #YesAllWomen and... #ImWithHer.[8]

As mods 'speak back' to the original game, they provide a useful pool of data for investigating where players perceive faults in a game and how they could be corrected or improved, and they also provide a new avenue of exploration to understand the interactions of gaming communities and culture. They demonstrate creative responses to the original material, showing what is of significance to players by way of their additions, alterations, and omissions.

Mods are typically shared with other players for free and are usually hosted in online repositories, such as *Nexus Mods*, *Game Modding* and *CurseForge*.[9] These hosted mods are usually well-packaged with marketing materials to outline their purpose and encourage downloads, often including detailed descriptions of the software, screenshots, videos, artwork and changelogs. These marketing materials, alongside user comments and download statistics provided by the repositories, provide further resources for the productive exploration of mods.

Though it would be difficult, if not impossible, to establish exactly how many players use mods and to what extent, large mod repositories provide some public data that gives us a means of quantifying the types of mods that are popular. Mod repositories will often provide statistics on the number of times a mod has been downloaded, including unique downloads, and how many people have added it to their list of favourites or advocated for it, usually by means of upvotes or recommendations on the site.

Dey, Massengill and Mockus' recent preliminary study used this type of data in an effort to establish a data-driven methodology for researching mods. Their work investigated which types of mods were most popular for certain games in order to draw links between genre and content.[10] On a smaller scale, this chapter combines the quantitative data from mods with qualitative analysis of their content and marketing as a means of exploring audience response to medievalist themes and ideas in games. Looking specifically at the medieval fantasy genre, mods give us an insight into what players perceive as fitting inside the medievalist space. Additions and alterations to virtual medieval environments give a player-led (as opposed to a developer-led) perspective on what will be read as coherent in historical fantasy, which is always paradoxically fantastical and grounded in perceptions of the past. These perceptions change over time and are matched by changes in popular media.

This chapter engages with a broad study of user modifications of Skyrim to consider popular perceptions of authenticity within medieval fantasy fiction. It argues three core points:

1) That, as is the case within other media, 'gritty' visions of the Middle Ages are typically accepted as more authentic within modding community around Skyrim.

2) That this characterization of the medieval is not accurate, but nevertheless provides a sense of authenticity within the mods and is coherent with the medieval fantasy within the game and elsewhere.
3) That authenticity within these mods ultimately rests on the cohesion of the worlds they provide to the contemporary trend towards 'gritty' medievalism within visual and literary media, and that the representations within these mods perpetuate this trend among audiences and creators.

## Methodology

This chapter acts as a case study to demonstrate how ideas of realism and historical authenticity can be explored through game mods, using a single game and mod repository as its examples. As the rest of this book demonstrates, the construction and reception of historical accuracy can be interpreted and unpacked in a variety of media. I propose that game mods provide a fruitful, largely untapped source of material with which to explore the popular perception of the Middle Ages.

*Skyrim* is a roleplaying game set in a pseudo-medieval fantasy world. Though *The Elder Scrolls* series is long-running and well-regarded, *Skyrim*, in the six years since its release, has come to be genre-defining.[11] It has been praised by fans and critics for the size and depth of its world, and the immersive feeling engendered by its narrative and its use of new technologies. *Skyrim*'s *medieval fantasy space* has become a benchmark, with new games set in medieval worlds now measuring themselves against it and often using these comparisons as a selling point.[12]

*Skyrim* has an active and prolific modding community. One of the largest mod repositories online, *Nexus Mods*, hosts over a quarter of a million mods for various games and has almost 15 million members. Of these mods, 53,350 have been developed for *Skyrim*. My own manual investigation of the most-downloaded mods on *Nexus Mods* confirms Dey, Massengill and Mockus' findings that Look-and-Feel mods, those which seek to alter and/or improve the game's aesthetics, rank most highly. Not all explicitly mark historical accuracy as their aim, but the ways in which they add, extend or correct the aesthetics of the base game provide the scholar with a direct perspective on players' preferences and expectations of a medieval fantasy world.

In order to limit the sample to a reasonable size for the scope of the chapter, I will primarily examine those items which appear in the top forty most-downloaded mods for *Skyrim*. I have also provided the total number of unique downloads (i.e. the number of unique member accounts which have downloaded the mod) to provide a measure of its popularity.[13] To explore some of these mods in more detail, I have broadly classified them into three categories based on what they aim to modify: environment, material culture and the body. This model uses three categories encompass the three layers of *Skyrim* as I see them: the world itself, the assets and objects that fill the world and the characters that populate the world.

## Environment

*Skyrim* is an open-world roleplaying game that makes use of environmental storytelling. In line with this, many of the most-downloaded mods work to improve visual detail and alter the world around the player. The game is set in a fantasy medieval locale with a distinctly northern flavour and the mods typically follow the base game's lead in its Eurocentric medievalism. At least ten of the top forty mods alter the graphics and textures, typically increasing the graphical fidelity of the world to bring it closer to photorealism. The most-downloaded mod by a significant margin is '*Skyrim* HD – 2K Textures' with over 3 million unique downloads.[14]

Beyond the mods that provide purely aesthetic improvements to textures and higher resolutions, there are mods which change gameplay elements, namely in the way that the player interacts with the environment. Of particular note are 'Frostfall' (1 million unique downloads) and 'Wet and Cold' (1.23 million unique downloads), which alter the way that the environment affects the player character.[15] They add effects such as visible moisture when exhaling, movement reductions in high winds, temporary blindness in blizzards and heavy rain, and penalties for exposure which can result in the player-character losing consciousness. They are both categorized and described as immersion mods: immersion might be thought of as a player's deep absorption within the game world, a feeling which is engendered by the world's plausibility. A game world does not need to be believable in order to be immersive; immersion is usually linked to a game's internal consistency and the extent to which the player can be encouraged to suspend their disbelief and see the fantasy world as 'real'. This is a term regularly used by players and developers, and is generally regarded as a positive and sought-after characteristic of a video game.

In keeping with the gritty, unsanitized theme of *Skyrim*'s most popular environmental mods, 'Enhanced Blood Textures' (2.6 million unique downloads) provides higher resolution textures, increased blood spatter, spurting and pooling.[16] In the forum for the mod, users praise the 'realism' of the added gore, and one specifically points to the game feeling 'more medieval' with the addition of more blood.[17]

In contrast with nineteenth-century romantic medievalisms – which typically portray medieval life as being in harmony with the natural world – modern, gritty fantasy focuses more on the challenge to survive in pre-modern environments. Indeed, Young defines Gritty Fantasy as 'a sub-genre created in the late twentieth and early twenty-first centuries [. . .] marked by low-levels of magic, high-levels of violence, in-depth character development, and medievalist worlds that are "if not realistic, at least have pretensions to realism" in their depictions of rain, blood, and mud'.[18] The popularity of mods which increase the hostility of the environment to create a more immersive and, by their own definition, authentic experience demonstrates the trend away from a romantic, agrarian view of pre-industrialization and towards a gritter vision of the past in which the hero must master their environment as well as conquer more traditional enemies.

While the scope of this chapter is limited to the top forty mods, it is worth a short digression to briefly touch upon the many combat mods that saturate the database.

Though not among the top forty at the time of writing, these mods are still relatively popular and remain so over time, with the number of downloads in the hundreds of thousands. As with 'Enhanced Blood Textures', combat mods typically serve to increase violence and gore. For example, the creator of 'Warzones 2015: Civil Unrest' explained that *Skyrim*, as a land in the midst of a civil war, did not feature enough violent warfare.[19] The mod adds new battles and combat encounters, enraged non-player characters keen to do the player harm, and many battlefield corpses. These battles take place on a much larger scale, involving many more combatants than in the default version of the game. The mod operates on the implication that grand battles and gory bloodshed provide an additional level of authenticity to a story of a pre-modern war. The spectacle of combat and the visual melee becomes much more reminiscent of cinematic medieval battles, hinting at the way popular medievalisms across different media are in dialogue with one another, demonstrating how a sense of genre authenticity is developed, and feeding a desire for coherent visuals across games and television.

## Material culture

Unsurprisingly for a pseudo-medieval fantasy game, weapons and armour feature heavily in *Skyrim*'s array of material assets. The base game includes over thirty complete sets of armour – not counting clothing and apparel which do not have armour values – and around one hundred different weapons. 'Immersive Armors' and 'Immersive Weapons' feature in the top twenty *Skyrim* mods, with 2.8 million and 2.4 million unique downloads respectively.[20] They add hundreds of new weapons and over sixty new armour sets. The majority of the pieces reimagine and redevelop existing armour styles, adding new looks that fit consistently with the pre-established lore. The marketing of both mods emphasizes the way that they seek to enhance the game world in a way that does not disturb its original lore and aesthetic, with the key word being 'immersive', as used in the titles and descriptions.

Again, the use of the term demonstrates the connection between immersion and believability. In this case, there is specific reference to the way this immersive mod will not 'break . . . the natural feel of the game', implying that it seeks to provide an authentic experience that will not be disturbed by the jarring use of incoherent assets. Within this mod, the image of authentic and believable medieval fantasy is the recognizable patchwork of history, nostalgia, fantasy conceits and modern cultural norms dressed in medieval-esque costume. 'Immersive Armors' hints at its patchwork of inspiration for fantasy medievalism: historically-themed 'Viking', 'hedge knight', and even 'Samurai' sets sit comfortably alongside the more fantasy-aligned 'paladin' and 'barbarian' outfits. It is telling that the juxtaposition of historically inspired armour with traditional fantasy designs does not disturb the medievalist coherence of the world. Indeed, in some cases adherence to the visual conventions of the genre is privileged above the environmental realism that is clearly so highly prized to modders and mod users in *Skyrim*.

In line with the game's frigid, medieval North aesthetic, the new outfits primarily comprise of leather or mail accented with fur. Unlike most of the clothing in 'Immersive Armors', the barbarian sets abandon adherence to the realities of exposure to a cold climate in favour of appealing to the more familiar tropes of the barbarian as popularized by the literary and subsequent visual depictions, of Robert E. Howard's *Conan the Barbarian*.[21] As such, these sets comprise of scant leather underwear accessorized with wrist-wraps and occasional fur trim. Here, the aesthetic of the medievalist archetype is valued more highly than the potential conflict with environmental realism. Authenticity in a medieval fantasy world, then, is linked more closely with popular convention and the perception of a particular kind of Middle Ages, rather than a sense of historical, or even physical, accuracy.

Similarly, a mod which alters the in-game map also creates a more realistic medievalist experience by working within the traditional conventions of fantasy. The default map in *Skyrim* is an aerial, topographic view, much like a satellite image. 'A Quality World Map' provides an upgrade to the standard map by improving the textures and adding roads, but also adds the option to use a flat, paper map instead. A similar, parchment-style map can be found adorning walls and planning tables in *Skyrim*, but this mod adds a high-resolution, hand-drawn copy that can serve as the player's own primary map. 'The result is something any adventurer would be proud to have tucked away in their pack' as it provides what appears to be the desired balance between functionality in the game world and an authentic medievalist aesthetic.[22]

A key element in medievalist fantasy across media is world building. Readers and players expect to find themselves in plausible secondary worlds: places of fantasy that reflect enough of their audience's perceptions of the real world, history, and ideology that they retain a sense of believability. Reflecting upon the sense of the real in *The Lord of the Rings*, G. R. R. Martin notes that 'it was not a picture of Frodo that Tolkien's readers taped to the walls of their dorm rooms, it was a map. A map of a place that never was.'[23] Tolkien, Martin, and Le Guin's work is often visually associated with maps, and this key marker of a well-developed fantasy world exists in parallel in digital worlds. Maps in games can serve as medieval set-dressing, evoking the pre-modern and creating a sense of temporal depth, but with their practical use they also transplant modern sensibilities onto the past.

Medieval cartography was usually associated with understanding one's place in the world in a religious and historical mode rather than geographic one, especially when considering maps of the world.[24] Medieval *mappa mundi* are explicitly constructed to demonstrate the order of the world, directly inspired by religious belief, culture and history. This is in opposition to the way in which maps function or are perceived in the modern world: as navigable representations of the space around us with a specifically geographic function. Although it might feel more authentic and congruent to players, the parchment map is clearly set in the modern mode which emphasizes the geographic functionality of a map over its other potential uses. The paper map, hand-drawn in brushed ink, is typical of medieval fantasy. The yellowed, uneven colouring of the parchment might imply use, but it also directly appeals to the common representation of medieval texts in the way that a modern audience is accustomed to seeing them: historical artefacts that are worn and discoloured by age. It also imitates the style of medieval maps in its hand-drawn appearance, less specific cartography, and its marking locations with crests signifying dominion. This imitation is quite superficial, of course, in that it primarily conforms to our expectations of a medieval map – tempered by fantasy world-building over the last century – and does not really bear much similarity to surviving medieval *mappa mundi*. It lacks cultural images or aesthetic details that might place the locations or peoples in context with their understanding of the world. This being said, the image still serves to generate a sense of historical authenticity in appealing to the popular imagining of medieval maps and, more broadly, to the imagery with which the Middle Ages are popularly represented.

Although 'A Quality World Map' is the most popular mod of this kind, with around three million unique downloads, there are several similar paper map mods in the *Nexus Mods* repository which appeal to more traditional fantasy sensibilities. In the forum for one such mod, players compliment the paper map as being more 'realistic' and 'immersive', and express disappointment in the incoherence of what one player calls the 'cell phone GPS' satellite map designed by Bethesda.[25] In this instance, modders have implemented medievalisms in order to fix a perceived incongruence, replacing the jarringly modern satellite view with a map that invokes a pre-modern, if inaccurate, aesthetic.

Here we see that authenticity in material culture is generated in a way that appeals to the sensibilities and conventions of the medieval fantasy genre. As such, medieval*ism* can feel more authentic than references to evidence-based history.

## The body

Where the environmental and asset-based mods typically work to increase immersion by creating an authentic, ostensibly more realistic game world, the vast array of mods related to the body are almost entirely grounded in unrealistic physical ideals. Of the top forty mods, almost half relate to modifying physical aesthetics and body physics for both the player and non-player characters.

Wysocki notes that in many games, nudity mods typically map onto the existing character bodies 'revealing the traditional stereotypical gender portrayals of most existing female video game characters'.[26] *Nexus Mods* holds many of these basic nudity mods, but the most downloaded are those which alter the character mesh and add new textures, allowing significant changes in the shape, size and general appearance of body parts. These further reveal the prevalence of gender stereotyping in the creation of fantasy characters, with mods that specifically adjust female bodies (e.g., 'Caliente's Beautiful Bodies', 2.8 million unique downloads, 'Better Females by Bella', 1.2 million unique downloads) or add a prostitution mechanic that is limited to female characters ('Animated Prostitution', 1.2 million unique downloads).[27]

Even where mods are not designed to alter female bodies exclusively, the marketing appeals directly to their use in enhancing feminine aesthetics. For example, 'Apachii Sky Hair' (2.7 million unique downloads), 'The Eyes of Beauty' (1.6 million unique downloads), and 'Race Menu' (2.2 million unique downloads) add new customization options for male and female characters, but the preview images for all three mods overwhelmingly feature female characters made exaggeratedly glamorous or attractive according to the typical Western construction of beauty. For women, this often entails smoother skin and hair, the use of modern makeup and hairstyles, and hugely emphasized lips, eyes, breasts and buttocks.

Beyond the ability to create glamorous, airbrushed characters that could be plucked from a modern fashion magazine, many mods add full nudity, animated sex, and the ability to adjust a character's genitals as one would any other feature. Titillating sexual scenes and nudity are a common element of historical-themed television and games, particularly those in the gritty medieval category, and are often characterized as being more realistic in their presentation of a more carnal, and violent, past.[28] Elements of explicit, sometimes inexplicable, sexuality are so common that the first season of *The Last Kingdom* added a small but humorous parody of the 'sexposition' trope, whereby Brida suddenly devises a plot-driving plan during sexual intercourse with Uhtred, much to the latter's confusion.[29]

Notably, the unmodified *Skyrim* doesn't include any of this by default. While there is dirt, mud and blood, nudity and sex are absent. Some of the most long-lived and most-downloaded files on the repository are those which address this perceived lack.

The beauty standards of the modified bodies are distinctly modern, but rather than detract from a feeling of authenticity and narrative cohesion in a world so firmly rooted in the medieval past, this adherence to modern standards with medieval costume is in keeping with medievalist visuals across different visual media. Alongside the many aesthetic mods, there are numerous online discussions which lament the ugliness and grubby appearance of *Skyrim*'s default character options. Where players opt for extra dirt, suffering and conflict in their medieval environments, there is a distinct desire for characters' bodies, especially female bodies, to conform to contemporary, Western standards of beauty. Again, this impression is coherent across games, film and television in the gritty medievalist mode. Thus, the audience's expectations of hostile, distinctly pre-modern environments populated by violent warriors and highly sexualized women in medievalist media can be measured by how those expectations are modded into virtual spaces.

## Unpopular realism

From even this brief examination of *Skyrim*'s most popular mods, we get a strong impression of what seems to work for many players to create an immersive, authentic-feeling environment in a medieval fantasy world. In the world of *Skyrim*'s mods, authenticity and immersion are tied together to create mods that keep the world in a state of perceived coherence: what 'feels' right. What operates with perceived consistency in the realm of fantasy medievalism adheres to the trend of the dirty, sexy and violent Middle Ages. Although this style of medievalism is currently the most popular across games and television, it is not the only type of medievalism in which modders and players are engaging.

There are several mods that add medieval armour based on reference images from historical study, archaeological finds, reconstructions and so on, that work to implement more 'realistic' medieval armour, weapons and symbols. 'Credo – Medieval *Skyrim* Overhaul' (10k unique downloads), which adds medieval clothing and armour adorned with *Skyrim*'s own heraldry, is particularly praised by users for adding a more realistic feel to *Skyrim* while maintaining elements of its own worldliness, suggesting that some players are invested in a level of historical accuracy that is not considered important by the creators and users of more popular mods.[30] Rather than forsaking scholarly accuracy for the affective appeal of authenticity, these mods offer a replacement for the more fantastical elements of *Skyrim*'s armour, replacing them with assets that are based in real-world European history.

This commitment to a level of historical accuracy is particularly evident in 'True Medieval Economy' (4662 unique downloads), a mod which aims to 'make *Skyrim*'s economy as close to the real Middle Ages Europe as possible'.[31] The goals of the author, DanielUA, are to 'add even more realism and immersion to the world of *Skyrim*'. Where more popular mods increase immersion by appealing to the themes of gritty medievalism as seen across media – blood, sex, conflict – these mods are based on adding details that, ostensibly, come directly from historical study. DanielUA even lists his sources in the mod description area, appealing to scholarship rather than affect in his construction of realism: a 2003 doctoral thesis on Technology and Military Policy, a 1993 Berkley newsgroup archive of medieval price lists with its own scholarly bibliography, a 1984 article on the cost of grain storage from the American Economic Review, and an independent translation of the *Lex Francorum Chamavorum*, a ninth-century legal text.[32] The limited mixture of popular and traditional scholarly sources from a wide range of dates is not what we would typically consider rigorous scholarship, but it is clear that this modder, and those like him, are endeavouring to operate in an evidence-based mode rather than the aesthetic mode seen in the more popular mods.

'Historically accurate' mods appeal to a different kind of medievalism than the gritty, visceral medieval fantasy seen earlier. While there is some interest in source-based historical modding, the popularity of this style is vastly lower than the fantasy mods discussed earlier, with the number of unique downloads, and even total downloads, typically only in the thousands. It would require further investigation to understand the causes of this disparity, though it should be noted that what is *un*popular stands to tell us much about how historically immersive mods function within their communities as those that are more well-used.

## Conclusion

Taking the most popular mods for *Skyrim* as a group points to the predominance of a particular kind of gritty medievalism. As Young has pointed out across her work, 'the idea that Gritty Fantasy represents "the real Middle Ages" in ways that earlier medievalist texts do not is central to its existence as a sub-genre.'[33] Much has been made of the supposed historical realism of the gory, carnal world of *Game of Thrones* and similar texts, and this certainly links with the way that games, and their players as co-authors, construct immersive medieval environments. The authentic, gritty medievalism of games is inextricably connected to the genre as it appears outside of the medium. As well as examining the genre through its appearance in film and games, we can see new levels of audience development and reception of this style of medievalism through popular mods.

The pattern that has emerged in the style of medievalism favoured by mod users is unlikely to surprise medievalists or medievalism enthusiasts. The most popular mods subscribe to a gritty, sexy, dark and difficult Middle Ages that is simultaneously sublime and aesthetically pleasing, much like what is contemporarily portrayed in popular film and television. These portrayals characterize an authentic Middle Ages if not an accurate one; they add to the flavour of medieval fantasy in a way that is coherent and that feels right in spite of its conflict with accuracy or even plausibility.

When something is authentic, it doesn't necessarily mimic an accurate or objective understanding of the past, but it 'feels right'. It conforms to expectations of space, time and genre, and maintains the narrative and temporal cohesion of the game world. What feels medieval, what seems right, proper and authentic for a medieval world, stands to tell us more about how people popularly perceive the Middle Ages.

This authentically dark, medieval world is built by, and continues to feed into, the current trend for grim, more carnal historical worlds as seen across medievalist media including film and literature. The dialogue between transmedia medievalisms builds up a set of expectations for darker medieval fantasy worlds: as Elliott has pointed out with regards to film, 'modern audiences are perhaps less concerned about accuracy to the dusty and remote Middle Ages of traditional scholarship, but are already conditioned by previous medieval-themed films to know what to expect from a cinematic Middle Ages, thanks to conventions established by other films making up the genre'.[34] Within games, the element of interactive co-authoring adds an extra layer to the way that we can analyse audience reception: where these expectations are not met by the source material, modders can fill the gaps and give us a new lens through which to explore how authentic historical worlds are constructed. They provide us with an avenue through which to explore the 'subtle shifts in trends of representing the past that affect a viewer's "horizon of expectations"'.[35]

From here, there is scope to dig deeper into the functions of medievalism through studying player response: taking our emphasis away from historical accuracy, as the most successful modders already have, and examining trends in authenticity stands to offer us more information about the way players adapt genres across media and construct historical settings for a multitude of purposes.

## Notes

1 Robert Houghton, 'It's What You Do with It That Counts: Factual Accuracy and Mechanical Accuracy in Crusader Kings II', *The Public Medievalist*, 30 September 2014. Available online: https://www.publicmedievalist.com/ckii-houghton, accessed 22 April 2020. I have combined historical accuracy with realism for simplicity's sake, but Houghton argues convincingly how historical games can separate these last two concepts to create playful experiences which are inaccurate but not unrealistic.
2 Andrew J. Salvati and Jonathan M. Bullinger, 'Selective Authenticity and the Playable Past', in *Playing with the Past*, eds Matthew Wilhelm Kapell and Andrew B. R. Elliott (London: Bloomsbury, 2013).
3 Victoria Cooper, 'Fantasies of the North: Medievalism and Identity in *Skyrim*', PhD diss., University of Leeds, 2016.

4   Walt Scacchi, 'Computer Game Mods, Modders, Modding, and the Mod Scene', *First Monday* 15, no. 5 (May 2010).
5   Some of the most commercially and critically successful games of the 2000s originated as player-created mods. For example, *Team Fortress* series (Valve Corporation, 1999 – 2007); *Counter Strike* (Valve Corporation, 2000); *Dota 2* (Valve Corporation, 2013).
6   Tom Phillips, '*Skyrim* Mod Replaces Dragons with *My Little Pony*', *Eurogamer*, 19 January 2012. Available online: https://www.eurogamer.net/articles/2012-01-19-skyrim-mod-replaces-dragons-with-my-little-pony (accessed 22 April 2020); John Funk, "*Skyrim* Mod Turns Dragons into *Thomas the Tank Engine*," *Polygon*, 9 December 2013. Available online: https://www.polygon.com/2013/12/9/5192710/skyrim-mod-turns-dragons-into-thomas-the-tank-engine, accessed 22 April 2020.
7   Apollodown, 'Civil War Overhaul', *Nexus Mods*, last updated 9 November 2016, https://web.archive.org/web/20161109184105/http://www.nexusmods.com/skyrim/mods/37216.
8   Ibid. Note that these pages are currently hidden by the author and are now only visible via the Web Archive.
9   *Nexus Mods*, https://www.nexusmods.com; *Game Modding*, https://gamemodding.com; CurseForge, *curseforge.com*.
10  Tapajit Dey, Jacob Logan Massengill, and Audris Mockus, 'Analysis of Popularity of Game Mods: A Case Study', in *Proceedings of the 2016 Annual Symposium on Computer-Human Interaction in Play Companion* (New York: ACM, 2016).
11  The first title in *The Elder Scrolls* series was released in 1994, and up to 2017 there have been twenty releases in the series, with further games forthcoming.
12  For example, *Kingdom Come: Deliverance (Warhorse Studioes, 2018)* was widely described and praised as being just like *Skyrim* but without supernatural elements: Kevin Dunsmore, 'E3 2015: *Kingdom Come: Deliverance* Is *Skyrim* without Magic', *Hardcore Gamer*, 26 June 2015. Available online: https://www.hardcoregamer.com/2015/06/26/e3-2015-kingdom-come-deliverance-is-skyrim-without-magic/155984, accessed 22 April 2020; Lorenzo Veloria, '*Kingdom Come: Deliverance* Is a Historically Accurate *Skyrim*', *GamesRadar*, 7 March 2016. Available online: http://www.gamesradar.com/kingdom-come-deliverance-historically-accurate-skyrim, accessed 22 April 2020.
13  Data is accurate as of May, 2018. Note that *Nexus Mods*' catalogue is still in regular use.
14  NebuLa1, 'Skyrim HD - 2K Textures', *Nexus Mods*, last updated 27 September 2015, https://www.nexusmods.com/skyrim/mods/607.
15  Chesko, 'Frostfall', *Nexus Mods*, last updated 22 December 2016, https://www.nexusmods.com/skyrim/mods/11163; Isoku, 'Wet and Cold', *Nexus Mods*, last updated 28 October 2016, https://www.nexusmods.com/skyrim/mods/27563.
16  dDefinder1, 'Enhanced Blood Textures', *Nexus Mods*, last updated 26 October 2015, https://www.nexusmods.com/skyrim/mods/60.
17  Karasu24, 'Enhanced Blood Textures', *Nexus Mods Forums*, last modified 27 December 2011, https://forums.nexusmods.com/index.php?/topic/457817-enhanced-blood-textures/page-36#entry4157769
18  Helen Young, *Race and Popular Fantasy Literature: Habits of Whiteness* (London: Routledge, 2015), 63.
19  MGE, 'WARZONES 2015 - Civil Unrest', *Nexus Mods*, last updated 24 April 2015, https://www.nexusmods.com/skyrim/mods/9494.

20  hothtrooper44, 'Immersive Armors', *Nexus Mods*, last updated 4 November 2015, https://www.nexusmods.com/skyrim/mods/19733; Hothtrooper44, Ironman500, Eckss, 'Immersive Weapons', *Nexus Mods*, last updated 8 April 2013, https://www.nexusmods.com/skyrim/mods/27644.
21  For a detailed analysis of Conan the Barbarian's influence on media and pop culture, see Jonas Prida, ed., *Conan Meets the Academy: Multidisciplinary Essays on the Enduring Barbarian* (London: McFarland, 2013).
22  IcePenguin, 'A Quality World Map and Solstheim Map - With Roads', *Nexus Mods*, last updated 11 December 2016, https://www.nexusmods.com/skyrim/mods/4929.
23  G. R. R. Martin, 'Introduction', in *Mediations on Middle-Earth*, ed. Karen Haber (New York: St Martin's, 2001), 1–5.
24  David Woodward, 'Reality, Symbolism, Time, and Space in Medieval World Maps', *Annals of the Association of American Geographers* 75, no. 4 (1985): 510–21.
25  See the discussions on realism in 'Detailed Paper World Map', *Nexus Mods Forums*, last updated 15 July 2018, https://forums.nexusmods.com/index.php?/topic/806594-detailed-paper-world-map/?p=6997514.
26  Matthew Wysocki, 'It's Not Just the Coffee That's Hot: Modding Sexual Content in Video Games', in *Rated M for Mature: Sex and Sexuality in Video Games*, ed. Matthew Wysocki and Evan W. Lauteria (London: Bloomsbury, 2015), 203.
27  BellaGail, 'Better Females by Bella', *Nexus Mods*, last updated 12 December, 2011, https://www.nexusmods.com/skyrim/mods/2812; Caliente, 'Caliente's Beautiful Bodies Edition -CBBE-', *Nexus Mods*, last updated 31 December, 2015, https://www.nexusmods.com/skyrim/mods/2666; JoshNZ, "Animated Prostitution - *Skyrim* – WIP," *Nexus Mods*, last updated 28 February 2014, https://www.nexusmods.com/skyrim/mods/10748.
28  See, for example, Shiloh Carroll, 'Rewriting the Fantasy Archetype: George R. R. Martin, Neomedievalist Fantasy, and the Quest for Realism', in *Fantasy and Science Fiction Medievalisms: from Isaac Asimov to a Game of Thrones*, ed. Helen Young (New York: Cambria, 2015), 59–76.
29  *The Last Kingdom*, 2, 'Episode 2', (BBC Two, October 17 2015).
30  See the forum discussions in 'Credo', *Nexus Mods Forums*, last updated 20 July 2018, https://forums.nexusmods.com/index.php?showtopic=1287972.
31  DanielUA, 'True Medieval Economy', *Nexus Mods*, last updated 16 January 2018, https://www.nexusmods.com/skyrim/mods/72896.
32  DanielUA's full bibliography, along with links to the texts, is available in the description section for 'True Medieval Economy'.
33  Young, *Race and Popular Fantasy*, 83.
34  Andrew B. R. Elliott, *Remaking the Middle Ages: The Methods of Cinema and History in Portraying the Medieval World* (London: McFarland, 2010), 182.
35  Andrew B. R. Elliott, 'Our Minds Are in the Gutter, But Some of Us Are Watching Starz: Sex, Violence and Dirty Medievalism', in *Fantasy and Science Fiction Medievalisms: From Isaac Asimov to a Game of Thrones*, ed. Helen Young (New York: Cambria, 2015), 105.

# Playing with taskscapes

## Representing medieval life through video games technologies

Juan Hiriart

## Introduction

The understanding of the world around us, along with the comprehension of our position within it, has always been a key cultural concern manifested in a myriad of representational forms that focus on the landscape as their main subject. The 'landscape idea', as Cosgrove calls it, conforms 'a characteristically modern way of encountering and representing the external world: in its pictorial and graphic qualities, in its spatiality and ways of connecting the individual to the community'.[1] Within this wide spectrum of representational forms, video games are undoubtedly a newcomer. Even though they inherit and follow the conventions and representational traditions of previous media forms, video games also come with new and distinct ways to encode and communicate the meanings of landscapes.

In contrast to previous forms of representation, which can only offer the illusion of entering alternate reality spaces without providing the means to walk through and interact with them, video games for the first time give visitors the power not just to navigate game worlds but also to become a participatory agency in their procedural structuring, which is manifested through the social and cultural processes involved in their production. As Longan argues, '[b]ecause they are interactive, video games have the potential to directly involve players in the production of virtual landscapes and therefore [. . .] to imagine and recognise the labor required to produce the concrete landscapes they see when they go outside'.[2] In other words, whereas our relationship with the landscape in previous non-interactive media was restricted to that of an external observer, in video games it can potentially be extended to that of an *inhabitant* – a form of engagement that opens the door to understanding historical processes in ways that were not possible before.

In this chapter, my purpose is to explore the new affordances of video games as mediations of historical landscapes; therefore, I will base the discussion on the analysis of Timothy Ingold's ideas on inhabitation as presented in his influential paper 'The

Temporality of the Landscape'.[3] To steer the analysis towards the context of video games, I will discuss the ways in which Ingold's arguments, explained through his analysis of Bruegel the Elder's painting *The Harvesters*,[4] were translated into an experimental historical game based on the Anglo-Saxon period of British history. In the discussion that follows, I will describe the multiple systems implemented in the game prototype, focusing on the design solutions devised to embed social and cultural meanings into the game's objects and environment.

## Taskscapes

In 'The Temporality of the Landscape', Ingold proposed a new conceptual framework to study inhabited environments by analysing them in terms of the processes and changes occurring from human intervention. More than anything, with this framework Ingold made an attempt to bring together two aspects traditionally understood as separate: 'the naturalistic view of the landscape as a neutral, external backdrop to human activities, and the culturalistic view that every landscape is a particular cognitive or symbolic ordering of space'.[5] For Ingold, both dimensions need to be integrated, and should not be seen in isolation from each other. As an entity in constant change, the landscape predisposes and affects the lives of people living within its boundaries and, in turn, it is affected by them as they go along with their 'business of life'. Citing Heidegger, Ingold defines this view as the 'dwelling perspective' – an approach where the actions and tasks carried out by inhabitants, whether performed in the imagination or in the physical substrate of their world, become intertwined with 'the specific relational contexts of their practical engagement with their environment'.[6]

In an attempt to make this complex web of human interventions visible, Ingold proposed to map them in a new conceptual layer – the taskscape – to be laid out over the physical surface of the landscape. This new layer constitutes of a way to make visible 'the practices of work in their concrete particulars',[7] bringing to the fore the relationships and interdependencies between inhabitants and the environment. In the same way that the landscape can be described as an array of related features, by analogy, the taskscape can be seen as an array of related activities or tasks ('the constitutive acts of dwelling'[8]) that allow us to decipher the processes of human inhabitation.

Seen as a form of representation, the idea of the taskscape has a profound impact on the ways we have traditionally communicated the meanings of landscapes. For centuries, our understanding of the places where we live has been mediated by different forms of representation, which have determined the way we think about our surroundings. Far from remaining static, the landscape as a term, idea or 'way of seeing' the external world has evolved to reflect the dominant ideologies of their historical period. However, as Cosgrove indicates, throughout all these changes the idea of the landscape has remained a visual term, one that arose initially during the renaissance and redefined the way we represent concepts of space. So, how the ideas contained in the taskscape fit into this history of landscape representation? How can they be meaningfully expressed using contemporary means of representation?

Ingold explicitly states that only by 'recognising the fundamental temporality of the landscape itself',[9] we are able to access the meanings of taskscapes. Arguably, for this to happen, we need a medium capable of dealing with the dimension of time. This requisite can be observed in Ingold's efforts to explain his ideas about the landscape as an entity in constant change. As he writes:

> Imagine a film of the landscape, shot over years, centuries, even millennia. Slightly speeded up, plants appear to engage in very animal-like movements, trees flex their limbs without any prompting from the winds. Speeded up rather more, glaciers flow like rivers and even the earth begins to move. At yet greater speeds solid rock bends, buckles and flows like molten metal. The world itself begins to breathe.[10]

In this exercise of imagination, the medium that Ingold first identifies as a film becomes an interactive simulation, where the observer can effectively 'play' with the scales and cycles that determine the passing of time.

Continuing with his exposition, Ingold later references the painting *The Harvesters*. Originally part of a series of six pieces representing different times of the year and from which only five survived to present day, the painting represents the agricultural life of a rural community from the Netherlands during the month of August. Using this painting pedagogically as an entry point to understand landscapes, Ingold invites the reader not to look at the picture as an external reality hanging on the wall, but to become immersed in the representation. In his words, he asks the reader 'to regard this painting by Bruegel as though it were its own world, into which you have been magically transported. Imagine yourself, then, set down in the very landscape depicted, on a sultry August day in 1565.'[11] Although this exercise can only be achieved through the use of imagination, it illustrates an important point: the understanding of the landscape from a 'dwelling perspective' requires us to become, at least in imagination, dwellers ourselves, in order to establish a connection with a world that can only be gained by being part of it. This connection cannot be made from an external point of view and certainly cannot be established in only one direction. As Ingold explains:

> Whereas both the landscape and the taskscape presuppose the presence of an agent who watches and listens, the taskscape must be populated with beings who are themselves agents, and who reciprocally 'act back' in the process of their own dwelling. In other words, the taskscape exists not just as activity but as interactivity.[12]

In spite of the mastery of their author, traditional non-interactive means of representation (e.g. books) appear limited to achieve this, but interactive technologies, computer games in particular, are uniquely equipped to fulfil the requirements of immersion, participation and interactivity within representations. In what follows, my goal is to explore this argument by contextualizing Ingold's ideas in the concrete example of a historical video game.

# Bringing taskscapes to life

## The Anglo-Saxon game

With the aim of investigating video games as representations of historical landscapes, I set myself the project of designing and producing an educational game prototype situated in the early Anglo-Saxon period of England, around the fifth century. As it is possible to discern from historical and archaeological sources, this was a time of great change in Britain as the physical characteristics of the people, language, social and cultural institutions were radically transformed by the mass migration of Germanic tribes who arrived and settled in this land after the departure of the Romans, around AD 410. Due to the lack of primary historical sources documenting this period, it is still unclear how this process, in which a significant part of the Celtic British population was replaced by Germanic incomers, took place. In line with the accounts from the venerable Bede,[13] it was assumed for the most part of the twentieth century that this was a violent process during which great hordes of Germanic invaders arrived and pushed the native population out of their lands, but this account has been called into question in light of more recent historical and archaeological interpretations. In particular, Härke[14] challenges the 'maximalist' narrative of a mass migration, conceiving it as a process rather than an event, where geographically diverse groups with differing origins, composition and sizes arrived at different times to British shores. According to this author, these different migration patterns can be broadly grouped into two phases: a first 'conquest' period during the fifth and sixth centuries where immigrants and their descendants practiced a form of apartheid with the native population in order to establish and preserve their dominance, followed by a phase on the seventh and eighth centuries with an increasing acculturation and assimilation between both groups.

In line with these interpretations, an important goal of the game was to represent the drastic social and cultural changes of the time and communicate the different patterns of integration and culturally distinct 'ways of life' of Roman-British and Anglo-Saxons. To emphasize these processes, I decided to centre the game on the representation of everyday life during this time of drastic change and to avoid the excessive focus on the representation of violent conflict. In this sense, the game prototype is in contrast to most historical games based around this period, in which combat mechanics are designed to be the most important form of interaction. The reasons for this are not difficult to comprehend; Salen and Zimmerman[15] and Crawford[16] stated that games are primarily systems of conflict, naturally inclined to represent any determined situation as a clash between opposing forces. In this respect, Stuart warns that 'in games, violence is often the core feedback loop, the defining mechanism. Everything gets swallowed up into this dysfunctional vortex.'[17] To avoid this, the game prototype purposely avoided the implementation of combat mechanics, focusing instead on translating everyday tasks and environmental dynamics to gameplay form. As such, the prototype's leading design concept was to implement a 'playable taskscape', a form of gameplay where the player, embodying the identity of an Anglo-Saxon free peasant, has to find the means to settle in the new land. For this, the player has to spend much of his or her time performing the everyday tasks and routines representative of this period. In-game tasks, thus, were conceptualized as multi-layered clusters of meaning, which had to be enacted to be fully understood by the player. At its most basic, these tasks could be interpreted as the means to survive in a challenging environment, but in a more in-depth reading, they could be seen as carriers of cultural meanings, driving players to 'inhabit' the identity of a historical agent to interact with a rich and complex historical environment.

## Inhabiting game worlds

Ingold begins his analysis of *The Harvesters* painting by examining the spatial composition, structured by a juxtaposition of perspectival planes describing representative activities from agricultural life. A clear visual path is connecting all these planes, established by the many tracks carved by the movements of the community over the years, providing evidence of the continuity of their productive work. For Ingold, these tracks are 'the taskscape made visible'[18] – a representation that not only describes the movements of the people but it does so by inviting the observer to be part of it. As a master in the art of landscape representation, Bruegel created the illusion of a world not just to be 'seen' but to be 'felt', compelling the viewer to follow in their imagination the paths and tracks throughout the undulations of the landscape. The painting is constructed to be 'directly incorporated into our bodily experience'.[19]

Even though Bruegel's artistic skill makes the best of the medium to create the illusion of 'being there', this representational goal remains as 'an aesthetic entrance, not an active engagement with nature or space that has its own life'.[20] In contrast, video games are the first medium to allow observers to navigate the represented world by changing their point of view and spatial relation with the objects of the landscape, while becoming also a participatory agency in the procedural structuring of the world. This ability is augmented by the technological prowess of the medium, which is now capable of rendering in real-time highly detailed worlds, almost indistinguishable from their real referents. With these new affordances, we could be tempted to think that the illusion is complete as the observer can now be magically transferred inside the representation, as Ingold asked readers to do at the beginning of his paper. I would argue, however, that this is not the case. Even with the added power of navigating the scene through the virtual embodiment of an avatar, a critical distance between the player and the virtual world persists, preventing them to gain a meaningful connection with the landscape. To close this gap, it is necessary to convert players from external navigating observers to inhabitants of the game world.

Nevertheless, can game worlds be inhabited? To answer this question, I would like to invite the reader to first consider the observation that Ingold makes about the tree – a prominent detail in *The Harvesters* painting:

> In its present form, the tree embodies the entire history of its development from the moment it first took root. And that history consists in the unfolding of its relations with manifold components of its environment, including the people who have nurtured it, tilled the soil around it, pruned its branches, picked its fruit, and – as at present – use it as something to lean against. The people, in other

words, are as much bound up in the life of the tree as is the tree in the lives of the people.[21]

In other words, the space where the tree stands has become a *place*, clearly distinguishable from the space and other objects around, imprinted in the personal and collective memories of the people that have decided to rest under its shadow. This distinction is important; Kalay and Marx asserted that '[p]eople inhabit places, not spaces'.[22] Arguably, a game world devoid of meaningful places will remain at an abstract level, detached from the player and failing to bring the subtle layers of meaning of historical worlds.

According to Tuan, a place has history and meaning, and incarnates the experiences and aspirations of its inhabitants. Virtual places, therefore, cannot be produced within game worlds by merely reconstructing historical landscapes through high-resolution geometry and beautifully crafted textures, no matter how realistic they look when put together in the virtual world. Rather, virtual places need to somehow incorporate the historical and relational meanings that we find in real places, which are composed of memories and feelings as much as rational thoughts. Tuan stated:

> [t]o know a place fully means both to understand it in an abstract way and to know it as one person knows another. At a high theoretical level, places are points in a spatial system. At the opposite extreme, they are strong visceral feelings.[23]

To create a sense of inhabitation in historical game worlds, a connection needs to be established between the player in the form of knowledge that is both personal and social, and manifests itself in a juxtaposition of narratives created from lived experiences. Game worlds devoid of these narratives are condemned to feel empty and soulless[24] – spaces that cannot be defined as relational, historical or concerned with identity (what Auge describes as 'non-places'[25]). Any mediation – through video games, films or any other media – with the aspiration of conveying a sense of place needs to create this primary feeling of inhabitation that rises from the reading and writing of the continuous flow of experiences that bring meaning to a place.

In this Anglo-Saxon game prototype, the important design decision to bring an otherwise inert world into life was accomplished by making every object of the world something to be 'learned' from. The guiding principle behind this was to construct a responsive, meaning-rich world, in which every object could be appreciated as something more than just visual graphics and collision geometry. By directing the player's attention to the surrounding objects (i.e., by highlighting them upon their proximity), as well as simulating real-world interactions through computer metaphors such as 'rolling-over' and 'clicking', the medium became tuned to a way of accessing the meanings of the environment that Ingold, citing Gibson, identifies as an 'education of attention'.[26] Described as a way of knowing and guided discovery, this process operates by directing the attention of the novice to salient features of the environment, letting them construct their knowledge without mediation, through a fine-tuning of their perceptual skills. Following this idea, a combination of diegetic and non-diegetic systems were implemented in the game prototype to make every object accessible, guiding the player to perceive the world, not only as the manifestation of a quantitative rule-based model but also as a collection of narratives and situated understandings connecting the people and the place.

### Representing everyday tasks

Continuing with his analysis of Bruegel's painting, Ingold's attention turns to the agricultural tasks that form the central motif of the representation. Ingold describes how the painter, instead of registering the scene as a cameraman would do by taking a snapshot of what is happening at a particular moment in time, he offers a series of passages, which, although presented synchronically in the static pictorial space, are meant to represent the entire process of agricultural production. Accordingly, narrative appreciation of the painting by looking at the different characters busily working on different tasks yields a general reading where the 'cycle of production and consumption ends where it began, with the producers'.[27] In essence, Bruegel's painting appears as an early attempt to generate a procedural representation of reality: a snapshot of what could have been an agent-based simulation if that technology was available in the sixteenth century. If Ingold was to push his initial invitation even further, he would encourage the reader not only to immerse themselves into Bruegel's world but to become one of the harvesters and access the meanings of medieval rural life by taking an active part in the cycle of production and consumption.

This form of engagement, even though impossible to be implemented in non-interactive forms of representation, is precisely what defines the medium of video games. As Aarseth argued, video games are not objects but processes, which do not materialize without the active involvement of players playing them.[28] How can taskscapes be translated into video game form? Given the ability of modern game technology to produce hyper-realistic worlds, it would be tempting to aim for the maximum level of realism that the medium is able to achieve and produce a direct depiction of the real world into the video game. This aim seems to have been achieved by the second wave of VR technology, with a proliferation of heritage and archaeological projects attempting to create a complete sense of immersion. However, this achievement in development can be misleading. We should not miss the point that video games, despite their level of realism, are always simulations of reality and to this extent the translation of any real-world semantics always implies a degree of simplification.[29] Hence, a key part of this translation depends on determining what aspects will be included in the simulation, and what level of fidelity will be incorporated in their representation.

In the context of the Anglo-Saxon prototype game, its emphasis on everyday life is expressed primarily by actions linked to the exploration of the affordances provided by the objects available in the environment. This process is implemented in four stages. In the first stage (object selection), the player selects a specific object from the space near their avatar. This selection, made simply by mouse-clicking on the object, exposes a list with the object's affordances (an enumeration of what the player can do with or through the selected object). Once one of the available affordances is selected the game opens the interface of a new task, where the player is asked to decide its allocation, defining who (player or family member) will perform the task. While deciding the task allocation, the interface displays the duration of the task as one of the most important factors to consider. In fact, if the task is allocated to a family member the player is free to move and occupy themselves with another activity but, if the task is assigned to the player its execution demands the player to wait until the task is finished. With this mechanic, the design of the game recognizes the duration of the task as its 'cost' or what Ingold defines as 'the currency of labour'.[30]

## Simulating people

In the final part of his article, Ingold focuses on the social dynamics of the taskscape, which in the painting are suggested by multiple characters busily working on different tasks. He argues that the taskscape's very existence depends on the presence of these working agents:

> Far off in the distance, wafted on the light wind, can be heard the sounds of people conversing and playing on a green, behind which, on the other side of the stream, lies a cluster of cottages. What you hear is a taskscape.[31]

In other words, the taskscape is essentially a social reality. Although single individuals can carry on with their tasks in relative isolation from each other, it is in the intricate web of relations and interdependencies between them that the taskscape becomes alive.

Even though the representation of social environments has been the focus of many game titles it is also true that, in most of them, non-player characters (NPCs) exist only as support of gameplay or as mere decorations put together to create the illusion of an inhabited reality. In virtual heritage projects, virtual characters are primarily used as guides programmed with limited conversational capabilities.[32] Both in games and virtual heritage environments, sooner rather than later it becomes apparent to users that the simulation of social life is reduced to theatrical props barely holding the illusion of a more meaningful social and cultural interactions. Some titles, however, have implemented more complex social behaviours, by including NPCs with their own individual routines and goals, carrying on with their lives even when they are not in the player's field of view.[33] Games of this type bring gaming worlds close to Agent Based Modelling (ABM) simulations, used in social and natural sciences research. In these scientific applications, complex phenomena can be explored by adjusting sets of variables to control micro-behaviours of individual agents, which in turn affect the macro-behavioural patterns of the system as a whole. As Graham[34] asserts, an ABM simulation 'can be thought of as a game that plays itself'. Indeed, by allowing researchers to tinker with the data and the procedures embedded in the simulation, many of these systems look and feel like a game and it is not uncommon to find efforts made by researchers to 'gamify' ABM models with the goal of converting them into full playable games.[35] In my view, however, these initiatives find themselves missing a crucial point: video game mechanics and aesthetics can and should do more than just simulate social environments, no matter how realistic and historically accurate their implementation may be.

The main potential of games does not reside on their capacity to accurately simulate past realities in the intricate detail of 'how things worked' but to engage players in a dramatic experience that drives them to 'care' about the way things worked in the past. As Heidegger famously argued, the attitude of care or concern (Sorge) lies at the very basis of our existential relationship with the world. There is no such thing as a human being completely indifferent of the happenings in their surroundings and the consequences of their decisions. This primordial attitude of care, however, is distorted in worlds devoid of any 'moral physics'.[36] Although this makes digital games and simulations ideal platforms for testing hypotheses that would be unthinkable to perform in the real-world, by the same token it converts them into environments where anything can be done and nothing really matters. Any game that aspires to foster a meaningful understanding of the past requires altering this practice in order to urge players to reflect on the effect of their decisions with an elevated sense of choice and responsibility.[37]

Fortunately, there are gaming instances that can be used as referents to build this type of worlds. The intriguing gadgets known as *Tamagotchis* certainly are noteworthy; invented by Akihito Yokoi (Wiz Co. Ltda.) and Aki Maita (Bandai Co. Ltda.), they were first sold in Japan in 1996 and consisted of virtual pets designed to replicate the bond that real-world owners have with their real-world pets. In these minimalistic simulations, the representation of a pet was reduced to a few pixels on the screen and the way to interact with it depended almost entirely on the fulfilment of the incessant flow of virtual needs, symbolized as quantitative scales varying from 'full' to zero. If neglected, the consequences were severe. In fact, a pet not properly looked after could effectively 'die' (a condition set to be irreversible in the first versions of the toy). As the philosopher Žižek notes:

> the uncanny enigma of the *Tamagotchi* resides on its power to drive the owner/player to feel the appropriate emotions – responsibility, affective attachment, loss and so on – in spite of the complete awareness that there is nothing beyond the screen and that the representation is a radical reduction of imaginary resemblance to the symbolic level.[38]

After their appearance and success, *Tamagotchis* became an influential reference for later simulation games. Will Wright's *The Sims* appears particularly relevant in this analysis. This game, described as 'a cross between a doll house, a Tamagotchi and the television programme Big Brother'[39] simulates an idealized modern suburban environment in which players interact with a group of semi-autonomous agents from a 'god-like' perspective. As with *Tamagotchis*, the player is responsible for satisfying the characters' needs, expressed as a series of bars covering basic and social parameters. Notably, in *The Sims* the single-entity engagement from the classic *Tamagotchi* is extended to a group of characters, generating situations much more difficult to predict and resolve. While with *Tamagotchis*, the player is required to keep the flow of needs in check with simple timely performed operations, in *The Sims* the needs and subsequent player actions may vary depending on the relationship of agents between each other and with their environment.

Using these examples as references, a series of NPCs were implemented in the Anglo-Saxon game. These characters had no virtual representation in the three-dimensional game world, but interacted with the player through text-based conversation systems accessible through the game's Graphical User Interface. While most of the characters have no blood relationship with the player-character, two of them – a small son and teenage daughter – were presented as 'family members', who could take care of everyday tasks as long as they were provided with the basic means of subsistence. Although the conversations and narrative events with these characters were completely fictional, they were constructed under the assumption that children in the Anglo-Saxon period were considered psychologically different from adults and, in general, were loved by their parents, which are notions supported by historical evidence.[40]

## Conclusion

In this chapter, I have explored how the ideas about the landscape that Ingold synthesizes as the 'dwelling perspective' can be expressed through video game technology, using the immersive and interactive properties of the medium to 'bring the player in' a virtual historical world. Through this analysis, I have raised the argument that, compared with previous non-interactive media, video games are better suited to communicate the defining concepts and relationships from human inhabitation that Ingold deconstructs in his analysis of Bruegel's painting *The Harvesters*. Video games have the ability to generate worlds able to be influenced by the actions of players, non-player agents and environmental forces, and hence they can 'bring to life' taskscapes, allowing players to become virtual inhabitants of the simulated world. In spite of these undeniable advantages, the quantitative bias of the medium renders its use problematic for communicating meanings that cannot be expressed only in numerical form. A sense of place also depends on establishing an affective connection with the environment, people and objects, which can be problematic to encode and communicate through procedural algorithms. Arguably, the recognition of this fundamental part of our relationship with landscapes requires the integration of systems capable of conveying meanings in the form of stories, designed to make the player 'care' about the world and what happens in it.

The perspectives discussed in this chapter can be of special interest to historians and archaeologists exploring ways to translate historical knowledge or data into games worlds and virtual heritage environments. As argued, this is not simple nor a direct process; the meaningful communication of historical content in a video game demands a thorough understanding of the conventions and affordances of this medium, beyond the simplistic translation to conflict mechanics. In this sense, the ideas outlined here can be helpful to researchers from the disciplines studying the past to work with game designers, or to become game designers themselves in the effort of creating historical game environments.

## Notes

1 Denis Cosgrove, 'Modernity, Community and the Landscape Idea', *Journal of Material Culture* 11, no. 1–2 (2006): 49–66.

2   Michael Longan, 'Playing with Landscape: Social Process and Spatial Form in Video Games', *Aether: The Journal of Media Geography* 2 (2008): 23–40.
3   Tim Ingold, *The Perception of the Environment* (London: Routledge, 2000).
4   The painting was finished in 1565 DC.
5   Ingold, *The Perception of the Environment*, 152.
6   Ibid., 186.
7   Ibid., 195.
8   Ibid.
9   Ibid., 201.
10  Ibid.
11  Ibid., 202.
12  Ibid., 199.
13  Bede, *The Old English version of Bede's Ecclesiastical History of the English People*, trans. Thomas Miller (London: N. Trübner, 1898). Available online: https://archive.org/detai ls/oldenglishversio04bede/page/n5/mode/2up, accessed 28 March 2018.
14  Heinrich Härke, 'Anglo-Saxon Immigration and Ethnogenesis', *Medieval Archaeology* 55 (2011).
15  Eric Zimmerman and Katie Salen, *Rules of Play: Game Design Fundamentals* (Cambridge, MA: MIT Press, 2004).
16  Chris Crawford, *Chris Crawford on Game Design* (Thousand Oaks, CA: Peachpit, 2003).
17  Keith Stuart, 'The Last of Us, Bioshock: Infinite and Why All Video Game Dystopias Work the Same Way', *The Guardian*, 1 July 2013. Available online: https://www.the guardian.com/technology/gamesblog/2013/jul/01/last-of-us-bioshock-infinite-male-view%5Cnhttp://www.guardian.co.uk/technology/gamesblog/2013/jul/01/last-of-us -bioshock-infinite-male-view?CMP=twt_gu, accessed 28 March 2018.
18  Ingold, *The Perception of the Environment*, 204.
19  Ibid., 203.
20  Denis Cosgrove, 'Prospect, Perspective and the Evolution of the Landscape Idea', *Transactions of the Institute of British Geographers* 10, no. 1 (1985): 55.
21  Ingold, *The Perception of the Environment*, 204.
22  Yehuda Kalay and John Marx, 'Architecture and the Internet: Designing Places in Cyberspace', *First Monday* Special Issue 5 (2005). Available online: http://firstmonday .org/ojs/index.php/fm/article/view/1563, accessed 28 March 2018.
23  Yi-Fu Tuan, 'Place: An Experiential Perspective', *Geographical Review* 65, no. 2 (1975): 152.
24  Matt Burdette in a blog post describes this lack of presence in virtual environments as 'Swayze effect', in reference to the 1990's film 'Ghost'. The term describes the sensation of not having a meaningful tangible relationship with the represented social and physical surroundings, despite being immersed in the virtual world. Matt Burdette, 'The Swayze Effect', *Story Studio*, 18 November 2015. Available online: https://www.ocu lus.com/story-studio/blog/the-swayze-effect/?locale=en_GB, accessed 21 April 2020.
25  Marc Augé, *Non-Places: Introduction to an Anthropology of Supermodernity* (London and New York, NY: Verso, 1995).
26  James Gibson, *The Ecological Approach Visual to Perception* (Boston, MA: Houghton Mifflin, 1979), 254.
27  Ingold, *The Perception of the Environment*, 205.
28  Espen Aarseth, 'Playing Research: Methodological Approaches to Game Analysis', in *Proceedings of the Digital Arts and Culture Conference* (Melbourne: MIT School of Applied Communication, 2003), 2.

29. Gonzalo Frasca, 'Simulation versus Narrative: Introduction to Ludology', in *The Video Game Theory Reader*, eds Mark Wolf and Bernard Perron (New York, NY: Routledge, 2003).
30. Ingold, *The Perception of the Environment*, 195.
31. Ibid., 207.
32. Erik Champion, 'Defining Cultural Agents for Virtual Heritage Environments', *Presence* 24, no. 3 (2015): 179–86.
33. *S.T.A.L.K.E.R.: Clear Sky* (GSC Game World, 2008) implemented characters with complex A-Life systems, which enabled them to carry on with their simulated lives at all times during the game.
34. Shawn Graham, 'Review of Evolving Planet [game]', *Internet Archaeology* 42 (2016). Available online: https://doi.org/10.11141/ia.42.4, accessed 28 March 2018.
35. For example, the game prototype 'Farm It Right', part of a project lead by Dr Armin Schmidt, from the University of Bradford. The project consists in a web-based computer game designed to explore the relationship between environmental factors and human decision-making in early Viking settlements from Iceland. The game is a good example of a learning game developed from a scientific simulation.
36. This concept was introduced by Janet Murray, *Hamlet on the Holodeck: The Future of Narrative in Cyberspace* (New York, NY: The Free Press, 1997). The argument is that in the same way that physic engines deal objects movement, gravity and so on, game stories have to have systems in place to deal with the consequences of player actions.
37. Robert Farrow and Ioanna Iacovides, 'Gaming and the Limit of Digital Embodiment', *Philosophy & Technology* 27 (2013): 221–33.
38. Slavoj Žižek, *The Žižek Reader*, eds Elizabeth Wright and Edmond Wright (Malden, MA and Oxford: Wiley, 1999), 107.
39. Celia Pearce, 'Towards a Game Theory of Game', in *First Person: New Media as Story, Performance, and Game*, eds Noah Wardrip-Fruin and Pat Harrigan (Cambridge, MA: MIT Press, 2004), 150.
40. Matthew S. Kuefler, '"A Wyred Existence": Attitudes towards Children in Anglo-Saxon England', *Journal of Social History* 24, no. 4 (1991): 823–34.

12

# If you're going to be the king, you'd better damn well act like the king

## Setting authentic objectives to support learning in grand strategy computer games

Robert Houghton

This chapter addresses the impact of play objectives on player interaction with grand strategy games set in the Middle Ages and the impressions of history they acquire from these games. To this end, this chapter will first suggest a framework for the classification of game objectives and consider the differing ways in which different objectives can influence the player. On this basis, the chapter will then address the impact of the objectives of Grand Strategy Games on the behaviour of their players, and argue that the deviation of these objectives from the medieval reality has a distorting effect on players' perceptions of the Middle Ages and a negative impact on their experience of the game. Finally, the chapter will use a case study of the medieval grand strategy game *Crusader Kings II*[1] to consider the effect of the removal of game objectives on player behaviour in game.

Historical computer games in general can be immensely powerful tools for the portrayal and communication of information and ideas. Their potency in this regard has been demonstrated by numerous studies,[2] and has led to the use of historical games as teaching tools at several levels of education.[3] The communicative importance of historical game worlds or aesthetics has been acknowledged: games can present not just literature but audio and visual environments.[4] The detailed reconstructions of medieval and early modern cityscapes in the *Assassin's Creed*[5] series or the meticulous recreation of vast and obscure aristocratic family trees in *Crusader Kings II* can serve as useful introductions to the worlds they present. Indeed, the 'Discovery Tour' downloadable content for *Assassin's Creed: Origins*[6] is designed specifically with educational intent and acts as a pseudo interactive museum exhibit (a 'living museum').[7] De Groot has criticized games for a perceived inability to move beyond this representation of data,[8] but the potential of game rules and mechanics to convey historical ideas and theories has been discussed by a growing range of authors.[9] The *Civilization*[10] series provides a potent and interactive explanation of many driving forces within human history,[11] even if its representations of the past are sometimes two dimensional or socially or intellectually problematic.[12] Although players may retain some distinction between history as presented in game and actual history,[13] there is overwhelming evidence for the influence of games on players' perceptions of the past.[14]

However, while the impact of game worlds and mechanics on their players' formative understanding of a period have been considered in some depth, the influence of game objectives (ranging from victory conditions, to subquests, to Steam achievements) on players' perceptions of the past has not been considered in any great depth. Elliott and Kapell have highlighted the connection between ahistorical rules and ahistorical outcomes: players will typically play to win, so unrealistic objectives will lead to unrealistic behaviour.[15] This is an important concept which needs to be investigated further in relation to the formative impact of digital games on their audience: game objectives have a massive potential to change the way players act and hence how they think about the subject matter of the game.

Game objectives are important in historical games as they form one of the principle means by which a game may influence player behaviour and hence can play a major role in structuring the player's perceptions of the past.[16] Whether the completion of objectives is required to progress through the game to receive some mechanical advantage or simply to gain a purely cosmetic reward or acknowledgement, game objectives form an easily recognized framework for the player and encourage them to act in a particular manner. Within historical games this can encourage the player to act in a manner befitting their character and period, or to embrace a different and alien set of ideals. Used poorly, they can encourage erratic and inconsistent play or rob the player of agency by restricting their choices and input thus reducing the impact of the game.

This influence over player agency ties objectives strongly to the most potent influencing element of digital games: their interactive nature.[17] This interactivity demands the engagement of the player with the environments and rules of the presented world in order to progress and ultimately complete the game.[18] Requiring attention in this manner ensures a deeper learning experience for the player than that provided by more passive literary or visual media,[19] strengthening the power of the game to influence its audience.[20] Their interactive nature also demands that games present coherent and complete, if abstract, worlds.[21] They must provide an environment which can be fully explored and manipulated by the player, one which is visibly consistent and holistic and hence apparently authoritative. This can easily cement the image of periods, characters and events presented by the game as the foundation of a player's knowledge. As so much of a game's educational impact is based on the interactive nature of the medium, it is of fundamental importance for the game's objectives to encourage exploration of the game world in a constructive manner.

Furthermore, game objectives can influence roleplay which emerges through the game. The interactive nature of games gives the player an unrivalled audience-centric experience of their world. The player is the driver of the game's story, and to a certain extent they come to embody the character or force they control.[22] The player can develop an almost personal connection with the game world. Objectives can influence roleplay by encouraging specific player actions through rewards (providing mechanical advantages, granting cosmetic options, or changing narratives) or through coercion (demanding actions be completed to progress or win the game). They can hence change how players perceive their characters and their behaviours, goals or morality.

This roleplaying element is particularly important when considering the learning impact of historical games. As McLaughlan and Kirkpatrick have demonstrated, roleplay encourages a deeper engagement with the subject matter of the game and can hence play a substantial influencing role on the player's understanding of this material.[23] Roles assigned to players can also strongly influence player behaviour.[24] Players of historical games are encouraged by the nature of the medium to roleplay as figures from the actual, fictional or mythological past. This may be concrete and defined, as in Western RPGs such as *Baldur's Gate*[25] or *The Witcher*,[26] where gameplay and mechanics revolve around roleplay. The roleplay may be looser and more incidental, as in *Thief: The Dark Project*[27] or *Assassin's Creed*, where the player takes control of a specific character, but has limited agency in their actions. Roleplay can be abstract, as in *Civilization*, where a player acts as a totemic and immortal force driving their people's destiny, but nevertheless has opportunity to play to a particular ideal or worldview. In each of these cases, the player can occupy the complex bimodal relationship with their Avatar as identified by Burn: sometimes the player plays as their Avatar, and sometimes they observe the Avatar's story.[28] In any event, this element of play demands that the player engage with the game world in a deep manner which is unique to this medium. Furthermore, their own actions and decisions will inform a player's understanding of the period presented. Roleplay and the player agency it represents can therefore greatly reinforce the impact of a game.

As a result, if a game is to provide an image of the past which is useful for historical study or even research, it is beneficial for that game to make use of objectives which guide the player towards gameplay which is consistent with the carefully prepared game world and game rules. In short, the game objectives must be realistic. They must encourage the player to act in a manner in keeping with the character they assume. They must encourage roleplay without restricting player agency.

Accuracy, authenticity and realism in historical computer games are remarkably slippery terms and often mean different things to designers, players and scholars with marked divisions within each of these groups.[29] It is important to emphasize that games, like all media, can never be truly 'accurate' recreations of past events nor should they be designed to be this way. As is the case with all popular media and academic texts, historical accuracy is an unachievable phantom: we can never know the exact details of events and all history is theoretical to a substantial extent. The nature of games exacerbates the issue. No matter how meticulously a game world (whether for a digital or board game) is designed, any pretext of accuracy is shattered as soon as play begins.[30] As the player takes actions and the game reacts to these actions, divergences from history occur and multiply exponentially. For a game to be truly 'accurate', any elements of interactivity and play must be removed, undermining the core nature of the game and turning it into a documentary: a valuable item, but nevertheless a very different form of media from a game. Games cannot be historically accurate in the traditional sense.

As has been addressed in several chapters within this volume, 'historical authenticity' is increasingly understood to refer to whether or not an item of media conforms to audience expectations of a period, whether or not these expectations relate to the reality of the era. Historical authenticity is a potent tool for developing a sense of emersion within a game but, as has been noted elsewhere, this frequently leads to the prioritization of an inaccurate, gritty, white and male vision of the Middle Ages, which perpetuates harmful stereotypes and assumptions in the modern world. Beyond these important issues, conforming to inaccurate popular perceptions of the medieval period for the sake of authenticity undermines the educational utility of these games.

Games may nevertheless contain historically realistic components,[31] and in the case of historical games such realism is often a desirable trait. Through the world they present, they can display information and images of the past. Through their rules and mechanics, they can show functioning historical models and theories.[32] Through their play and dynamics, they are able to encourage players to engage with the past in innovative ways.[33] This is beneficial for academic purposes, but is also desirable for an improved game experience through greater immersion – as players of some genres of historical game demonstrate a concern for accuracy which moves beyond the authentic – and for commercial purposes – as these demands for accuracy and depth can readily translate into improved sales.

Discussion of accuracy, authenticity and realism in games generally focuses on reconstruction of aesthetic game elements: outfits, locations and weaponry are frequent themes. While authenticity in these areas is desirable for the sake of immersion, and accuracy or realism here is useful for teaching about material culture or as an introduction to a period or region, this is a rather superficial educational use of games. While games can be, and are, used as means to communicate historical data and imagery, this is a capacity which they share with other media.[34] A more important, but less frequently discussed, issue is that of mechanical realism: the presentation of working abstract models of the historical world which can be used to introduce players to historical theories.[35] There are often limitations here, but these models can act as influential and valuable learning tools. Realistic gameplay – having players behave in a manner befitting their characters – has barely been considered within pedagogical literature but, as outlined earlier, this element has great potential as a tool for learning and viewing the past.

Grand Strategy Games are particularly relevant when discussing the impact of objectives as they have a substantial capacity to influence their players' perceptions of the medieval period (or indeed any other period of history). These games give the player control over a kingdom, empire or other polity, often in the form of an immortal and unseen influencing power. The player is typically granted near total control over the political, diplomatic, economic, social, cultural and (above all) military aspects of their faction and competes against rival powers for supremacy. Games of this genre require the player to interact extensively with vast and complex interlocking models of every element of their chosen polity: the player must become intimately familiar with the presented workings of their empire to ensure victory.[36] Furthermore, the complexity of these games contributes to their appearance as authoritative sources, a pretence supported by pseudo-academic elements within games (such as in game encyclopaedias and hyperlinks to external websites) and by declarations of historical veracity by their creators. Through their complexity and typically free roaming nature, these games also provide their players with a great deal of agency, allowing them near infinite meaningful pathways through the game. For these reasons, games such as those of the *Civilization* series can strongly influence players' perceptions of the past and can be very effective in the classroom.[37] However, the very factors which can make these games so effective as learning tools can equally lead to the propagation of inconsistent or otherwise problematic views of the past.

## Classifying objectives

A substantial variety of objectives exist within digital games. Andersen et al. highlight a distinction between primary objectives (those which are required to complete the game) and secondary objectives ('optional challenges that reward the player upon completion or simply exist for their own sake').[38] This distinction between mandatory and additional goals is important, but does not quite encapsulate the full spectrum of game objectives. Therefore, this framework may be fruitfully expanded and elaborated to consider the following four types of objective:

1) Core or Victory Objectives – the end goal of the game which must be completed to win.
2) Primary or Progression Objectives – which must be fulfilled in order to advance through the game.
3) Secondary or Beneficial Objectives – which are not required to complete the game, but nevertheless provide some narrative or mechanical advantage or change.
4) Tertiary or Challenge Objectives – which provide no substantive in game change and which exist solely as achievements for the player.

This framework is not encyclopaedic and within these categories there is substantial variation. Objectives may be established through in-game narrative, additional materials or through indications outside the game, from the games' creators or its players. They may be established at the start of the game, revealed as the game progresses or hidden until they are accomplished. Objectives may be prescriptive, dictating player actions at the expense of freedom of exploration. They may be less stringent, allowing greater player agency. However, whatever their form, they share the ability to steer player action to varying degrees and in several ways.

The most fundamental objectives are victory conditions: the circumstances which must be met to complete the game. Grand strategy games tend to present these goals at the outset. *Medieval II: Total War*[39] informs the player of their objectives (conquering a set number of provinces or defeating a specific rival or rivals) through its 'Faction Selection' screen at the start of each new game. Roleplaying games more typically present victory conditions through narrative over the course of the game. *Baldur's Gate* introduces the ultimate goal of the game gradually and alongside the plot over seven chapters.

Victory objectives guide the actions of any player attempting to complete the game.[40] To win a game of *Medieval II: Total War*, the player must defeat particular rivals and control a certain amount of territory: England must defeat Scotland and France and hold at least fifteen regions. While it is technically possible to eliminate rivals through extensive campaigns of assassination and to acquire the requisite number of regions through purchase or bribery, the impracticality of these methods and the pretext of the game dictate that warfare and conquest form the central activity throughout the game. In order to complete this ultimate victory objective the player is led to concentrate on military matters and the management of an empire necessary to support them.

Many games present the player with a choice of victory objectives. *Civilization VI*,[41] a grand strategy game which gives the player control of a civilization from 4000 BC to the near future can be won in five ways. The 'Domination' victory condition requires the player to conquer the capital cities of all the other civilizations. 'Science' requires the establishment of a colony on Mars, 'Religious' demands that at least half of the cities in each civilization follow the religion controlled by the player, and 'Culture' necessitates the creation of a tourist industry strong enough to dominate the world. The final victory type, 'Score', simply requires the player to survive until the end of the game (the year 2050 by default) and gain the highest score based on the size and achievements of their civilization.

The various victory objectives presented by *Civilization VI* and other games can dictate player behaviour to a significant extent, especially when playing on the higher difficulty levels of the game when computer-controlled rivals receive numerous advantages over the player or are designed to conduct near perfect play. To win the game on these higher difficulty levels, the player is almost required to plan their path to victory from the very first turn. Early settlements must be established where they will be effective immediately, but also where they will best be able to make use of resources in the late game sometimes relying on developments which will not occur for hundreds of turns. For example, Mountains and Rainforests are initially of little agricultural or economic use but can be harnessed to support scientific research in the later stages of the game. This long-term planning can extend to the choice of civilization for a particular game as the unique advantages afforded to each civilization dictates that some are better able to achieve certain victory conditions than others. For example, Arabia receives bonuses to scientific research for each religious building within its empire and for each city which follows the civilization's religion globally. Arabia is therefore at an advantage over many other civilizations in securing a scientific victory.

Beyond these overarching victory objectives, many games incorporate intermediate or incremental progression objectives. These goals do not end the game, but must be completed before victory conditions can be met. A common format of such progression objectives are game levels which must be completed sequentially. The campaign mode of the real-time strategy game *Age of Empires II: The Age of Kings*[42] is a paragon of this model. The game presents several campaigns to the player allowing them to explore the game's presentation of the achievements of various historical figures such as William Wallace, Frederick Barbarossa or Genghis Khan. These campaigns consist of a series of scenarios which must be completed in order to complete the William Wallace campaign: the player must progress through seven scenarios going through the raising of forces, forming alliances, fighting the Battle of Stirling and culminating in the Battle of Falkirk. Each of these scenarios consist of several further progression objectives, which must be completed in sequence to complete the scenario.

These progression objectives micromanage the actions of the player – enforcing particular behaviour while reducing player agency. A player working their way through the William Wallace campaign in *Age of Empires II* has their route to victory set out in some detail through the scenarios and progression objectives within each of these scenarios. The player has control over their military and civilian units, the construction of buildings and the development of their society, but this is constrained by the requirements of the progression objectives. The player follows the designers' script quite closely and has little meaningful freedom to dictate the development of the narrative.

Beneficial objectives change the game in some, usually positive, manner but are not required to complete the game. These often take the form of optional missions or side quests. For example, over the course of a game of *Medieval II: Total War*, the player will receive missions, such as conquering a particular settlement or securing peace with a rival, assigned by the pope, council of nobles or various guilds. If the player completes these missions, they receive rewards including additional troops or funds. *Baldur's Gate* presents the player with numerous optional subquests ranging from clearing a basement of rats to storming an enemy stronghold. In exchange, the player receives mechanical advantages: they are rewarded with funds, more powerful weapons, experience points to strengthen their characters or access to new characters. These objectives are not compulsory – the player may ignore them and still complete the game. However, the rewards received for their completion can aid the fulfilment of progression objectives and victory objectives through their provision of mechanical benefits to the player.

These beneficial objectives influence player actions in a different manner from victory or progression objectives. Where progression objectives dictate player actions, or at least demand that they must complete some of a range of possible actions, beneficial objectives exert softer influence. The player is drawn to behave in a certain manner because it will provide an in-game advantage. The potential receipt of powerful military units in *Medieval II: Total War* draws the player to attempt faction missions as these units can provide an immediate and often significant tactical advantage. The rewards for completing side quests in *Baldur's Gate II: Shadows of Amn*[43] are even more lucrative: many unique and powerful items, such as the sword *Carsomyr* (arguably the best weapon in the game), are available only through the completion of these beneficial objectives.

Like beneficial objectives, challenge objectives are wholly optional and are not required to progress through the game. However, challenge objectives are distinguished by the nature of their rewards which provide no in-game advantage and typically do not alter the game in any substantial way. Many first-person games like *Assassin's Creed* encourage the collection of items or tokens from obscure or hard to reach locations encouraging thorough exploration of the game world. However, any rewards received from completing these objectives are purely cosmetic. Many challenge objectives are only recognized outside the game through Steam Achievements, Playstation Trophies or other similar methods.

Despite the superficial nature of the rewards, these challenge objectives can strongly influence play, as demonstrated by the substantial completion rates listed on Steam. These objectives often encourage the player to act in an unintuitive manner but nevertheless provide a motivation and direction for play. Anderson and his co-authors have demonstrated the influence of these challenge objectives in practice: unless they align closely with the progression objectives, they can easily draw players into different behaviour.[44]

Game objectives are therefore hugely varied, but all have the potential to influence the actions of their players. On the macro scale, victory objectives encourage particular behaviour of their players throughout the game. Progression objectives steer players through the game with some limited options, restricting player agency to control their behaviour. Beneficial and challenge objectives drive players in a different way, presenting them with tangible or intangible rewards for actions which are not required for the game. In combination, these various objectives provide game designers with a substantial variety of means to manipulate how their players play and hence how they experience and think about the game's content.

Within historical games, whose content focuses on history by definition, this process plays a leading role in influencing the player's perceptions of the past. The player undertakes the role of their in-game character and consciously or unconsciously associates their in-game behaviour with the actions and goals of their avatar. As game objectives can influence this behaviour, they have substantial potential in guiding learning through play, but can also be hugely detrimental if employed carelessly.

## Influential objectives in grand strategy games

Grand strategy games have perhaps the greatest potential to influence their players' understanding of the past through their detailed mechanics and apparent authority, but this is almost universally limited or undermined through actual gameplay within this genre. Players typically revert to certain common patterns of behaviour: classified by Emrich in 1993 in relation to *Master of Orion*[45] as exploring their environment, expanding their territory, exploiting resources and exterminating rivals.[46] This '4X' system of gameplay emerged organically and unintentionally from early grand strategy games such as *Civilization* and *Master of Orion*,[47] but the system is now almost universal within grand strategy games as a genre. Players are encouraged and expected to expand their power and territory rapidly, aggressively and violently.[48]

This is problematic from a historical perspective as the geo-political behaviour represented by this form of play very often diverges considerably from the attitudes and actions of the rulers and groups represented in game. '4X' games represent hugely aggressive, combative and expansionist forms of rule, which only reflect a very narrow and extreme section of polities throughout human history. This disconnect has been raised most visibly through a series of public controversies such as the representation of the Cree in *Civilization VI*, which was condemned for its imposition of imperialist values and goals on the indigenous nation.[49] More generally, these games tend towards a eurocentric and colonialist perspective and hence provide a rather skewed vision of history and the marginalization of 'barbarian' or 'native' peoples.[50] They present a Whiggish vision of deterministic progress.[51] Many players of these games have noted the absurdity and historical implausibility of such continuous expansion.[52]

The representation of the rulers and polities of the Middle Ages through the dynamics of these games is particularly problematic. Players are encouraged or required to expand their kingdoms to implausible borders and to do so primarily through military force, but this places them firmly at odds with the aims and behaviour of most medieval rulers. There were obviously substantial variations across the geographical and chronological scope of the period, but medieval rulers nevertheless had very different motivations and objectives from their modern counterparts.[53] Centralization of power into the hands of an absolute ruler was impractical (if not impossible); instead rulership was generally accomplished through the construction and manipulation by the king of systems of alliances among the magnates of a kingdom.[54] Although warfare was undeniably a key role of medieval monarchs,[55] this formed only one part of their portfolio. These rulers were also administrators,[56] creators and enforcers of laws,[57] and representatives of their faith.[58] The emphasis placed on military expansion in these grand strategy games is largely divergent from the actions, capabilities and goals of medieval kings: unrealistic play is encouraged undermining the utility of these games as presentations and discussions of history.

These extreme, almost megalomaniac, dynamics of '4X' games are driven in large part by their objectives. As noted previously, the victory conditions of *Medieval II: Total War* demand the conquest of a vast portion of medieval Europe almost inevitably driving the player towards military expansion. Even when other victory conditions are available, conquest is typically the most straightforward way to win. Of the range of objectives presented by *Civilization VI*, 'Domination' requires the conquest of every rival capital city (the first city constructed by each civilization). This can be a difficult and lengthy task, but the overarching objective is clear and concrete from the very start of the game. By comparison, the 'Cultural' and 'Religious' victory conditions rely on the accumulation of 'tourism' and 'faith' respectively, abstract concepts given numerical value, in order to complete equally abstract and shifting goals. Conquest-orientated victory conditions are typically more intuitive if not necessarily easier than other options drawing a substantial proportion of players to this style of play.

This focus on conquest as the main victory condition is particularly pronounced when these games deal with the Middle Ages. Of the five victory conditions presented by *Civilization VI*, only 'Domination' and 'Religious' are achievable during the medieval portion of the game. 'Cultural' and 'Science' require technologies from more modern periods while 'Score' requires the play to the end of the game's timeframe. The image presented through the game's victory conditions corresponds with typical popular perceptions of the Middle Ages as violent and religious, devoid of culture and scientifically backwards.

Beneficial objectives in grand strategy games also tend to focus on warfare and their rewards are often military in nature. The missions presented by the 'Noble Council' of *Medieval II: Total War* often revolve around conquest. Most notably, the player can receive missions to take a settlement of an existing enemy or to annex a settlement of a currently neutral neighbouring power. Through these objectives, the player is encouraged to continue an ongoing conflict to gain territory or to initiate a war for the same purpose. The rewards for the 'Noble Council' missions are semi-randomized but always include a strong probability of receiving additional military units, often the best units currently available to the player. The player is guided towards expansionism through these objectives and granted the means to expand further through their completion.

Beyond this problematic focus on expansionism, the lack of intermediate progression objectives within grand strategy games emphasize planning in the extreme long term. *Civilization VI* with its 6,000-year time span is a clear example of this, but even games set wholly within the Middle Ages such as *Medieval II: Total War* require the player to develop strategies over centuries of game time. While medieval rulers (and indeed ancient and modern rulers) evidently did think to the future to a certain extent, looking to secure the succession for example, these games tend to place too great an emphasis on multi-generational planning over the consideration of concerns within the ruler's own lifespan. Through gameplay, generation after generation of kings or emperors strive for the same, typically extremely expansionist, objectives.

The omission of intermediate progression objectives also tends to distance the player from the world presented in grand strategy games. Play of these games, particularly at the higher levels of difficulty or multiplayer competition, often focuses on the intricate balancing of the various abstract values within the game to gain marginal benefits over opponents. A plethora of strategy guides and forum threads are devoted to establishing optimal play. Because of this trend, players often engage with these games as puzzle solving exercises rather than roleplaying opportunities or explorations of historical periods.[59]

The absence of distinct progression and beneficial objectives for different factions and rulers within grand strategy games presents a very flat image of the Middle Ages and the different polities which existed during this period. The victory conditions for *Medieval II: Total War* are fundamentally similar for each faction: defeat a predefined rival faction or factions and conquer a certain number of provinces. While different rivals and numbers of provinces are required, the essence of the objective does not change. The goal is conquest whether the player takes the role of a king of France, England or Scotland; the Emperor of Byzantium; the Fatimid Caliph or the Seljuk Sultan; or the Doge of Venice or Consul of Milan. Each of the rulers of these various polities held fundamentally different ideologies and goals, of which military expansion was only a small factor. By reducing these factions to two dimensional facsimiles, the creators of the game have undermined any historical nuance in the period.

The objectives present in medieval grand strategy games therefore tend to restrict play and induce players to act in an ahistorical manner. Most notably, victory conditions and beneficial objectives often encourage the prioritization of aggressive expansion over all other activities thereby simplifying and undermining the representation of medieval rulership within these games. The nature and distribution of these and other objectives also encourage an emphasis on excessively long-term strategies and a distancing of the player from the subject matter of the game, further reducing the ability of the games to usefully portray the role of medieval kings and other rulers. A lack of diversity in objectives for very different factions and individuals cements these issues and presents a further challenge in the representation of ideologies and practicalities of rulership in this period. For a genre otherwise well placed to communicate information and ideas about the medieval world, these shortcomings in objectives are particularly damaging to the games' ability to present and discuss history.

## Historical and ahistorical play in *Crusader Kings II*

*Crusader Kings II* represents an important, substantial and positive step away from the typical focus on conquest through game objectives in medieval grand strategy games.[60] The game is designed to represent historical systems and societies in a deep and considered manner. Game mechanics are complex and constructed to encourage historically feasible outcomes. Furthermore, these mechanics place substantial emphasis on non-military activities ranging from diplomacy and family politics, through economic management, to maintenance of personal piety and prestige. The effectiveness of military conquest is muted through various mechanics, which limit the speed at which territory can be acquired and even whether the player is able to initiate a war.[61]

Several simple but fundamental differences in game mechanics further distinguish *Crusader Kings II* from most other games of the genre and further reduce the prominence of aggressive expansion within gameplay. The player takes the role of the head of a medieval dynasty rather than the leader of a medieval polity, and while this family does rule lands, they are distinct from them. It is perfectly possible to gain or lose control of different counties, duchies, kingdoms and empires over the course of the game or to install independent dynasty members in positions of power across the map. This encourages a historically realistic focus on succession and the maintenance and management of different sections of the family tree. Military action can play an important part in the development of family power, but it is not the only or even most important element here.

This focus on dynastic leadership is tied to well-considered interpersonal mechanics surrounding character development and roleplay.[62] Unlike the totemic and abstract rulers of the *Civilization* series, players of *Crusader Kings II* are cast in the role of distinct individuals with complex and evolving strengths and weaknesses. A character may be an able steward, but naïve to the world of intrigue. They may be a poor soldier but a learned scholar. Many of these qualities are driven by personality traits: 'Paranoid' characters make better spies while 'Gregarious' individuals are stronger diplomats. This is all relayed through a character sheet, similar to those found in roleplaying games, and the presence of different traits and abilities allows different reactions to in-game events. As a result of this complex system, it is often beneficial to play to a character's strengths rather than invariably focusing on all out warfare, potentially encouraging the development of roleplay or emergence of narratives.[63]

Aggressive expansion is further marginalized as the game does not restrict play to the highest tiers of society. While the player may choose to play as an independent king or emperor, they can also play as vassals or even sub-vassals of these powerful figures. Gameplay typically focuses on the politics and intrigue within medieval polities, often over and above relationships with external powers. A great deal of gameplay is devoted to activities within the player's kingdom rather than external expansion.

Most importantly, *Crusader Kings II* is a game with very few objectives. Victory objectives have never been a focus for the designers or for the majority of players. The only nod to a victory condition is in the form of a dynasty score awarded at the end of the game or when the player quits. With no victory conditions, there are likewise no progression objectives to direct the player. Beneficial objectives do exist in the form of character 'ambitions' such as 'amass wealth' or 'become paragon of virtue', which require the player to accumulate set amounts of money and piety respectively in exchange for mechanical rewards. However, the majority of these objectives and rewards are unrelated or only tangentially connected to warfare. There are a more substantial range of challenge objectives presented through Steam achievements (136 at the time of writing), but the majority of these are also unrelated to warfare. The players are largely left to set their own objectives which provides a substantial and positive opportunity to move away from the narrow warfare orientated goals of most of this genre.

To gauge the impact of this near total absence of objectives, a brief, informal and open survey was conducted on the *Crusader Kings II* reddit. A single question was asked: 'What goals do you set yourself when you start a game?' A total of 121 comments were received in response. Participants were self-selecting and anonymous, answers were reflexive, and there was no attempt to verify their relationship to actual playstyles. However, while the survey is of limited use in quantitative terms, the qualitative nature of the results provides a basic but significant illumination of the impact of the limited objectives within *Crusader Kings II* on player behaviour.

None of the respondents reported that their chosen goals were influenced by the victory conditions or 'ambitions' (the victory objectives and beneficial objectives respectively) provided by the game. This is perhaps unsurprising given the low-key role of these elements within the game design, but it is still noteworthy as it underlines the almost objective-free nature of the game. Players overwhelmingly chose their own objectives in the absence of any strong steer from the designers.

While none of the respondents reported being influenced by progression or beneficial objectives, several indicated play led by challenge objectives in the form of Steam achievements.[64] This small group of responses highlight the impact which purely cosmetic official goals can have on player behaviour. Challenge objectives have the potential to steer players towards realistic (or unrealistic) play.

Most respondents, however, reported setting their own goals. These included a vast and varied range of objectives, many of which were non-military or non-expansionist in nature. Several looked to extend their family's influence over multiple independent realms rather than conquering and consolidating a single polity.[65] Many of these players specifically emphasized that their goal was to achieve this dynastic hegemony through non-military means, most typically through strategic marriages and intrigue.[66] Other players set objectives which completely ignored expansion, looking instead to create a dynasty which dominated science and medicine,[67] trade and economics,[68] or culture.[69] One reported focusing on the manipulation of other realms and funding proxy wars without engaging in conflict themselves.[70] Another simply sought to produce a large dynasty.[71] Simply surviving was a core goal for some players,[72] some of whom deliberately selected precarious positions to increase the challenge.[73] This substantial range of objectives matches the diverse mechanics within the game. Players are able to engage extensively with *Crusader Kings II* without making substantial use of the military mechanics and are hence able to set an array of objectives in several fields.

Numerous other respondents reported setting roleplaying objectives for each character they played.[74] In many cases, this roleplay was led by the ability statistics and traits of the character.[75] This focus on roleplay among a substantial minority of the player base reflects the mechanical design of the game and the corresponding focus on individuals and dynasties rather than faceless polities. Furthermore, by following the relatively realistic (if abstract) models of characters' personalities presented within the game, players tend towards behaviours which are appropriate to their characters. Through these roleplay-led objectives, players can gain a more informative experience of the world presented in *Crusader Kings II*.

Many players reported deliberately limiting the expansion of their realm.[76] These limits were often arbitrary and self-imposed, but some players used game mechanics to limit the size of their kingdom in a more organic manner allowing them to retain an expansionist bent but ensuring they could never retain substantial conquests.[77] Some players restricted their expansion even further, avoiding independent rulership and instead seeking influence within their Lord's realm as important vassals.[78] The motivations behind this approach varied: some players attempted to create artificial semi-historical boundaries around and within their realm;[79] others limited expansion to enhance the challenge posed by the game and their enjoyment of play;[80] some sought to create and maintain an 'aesthetically pleasing empire'.[81]

It is important to note, however, that despite this range of goals conquest remained the core objective for most respondents. In a substantial minority of these cases this violent expansion was fairly restrained and tended towards historical or semi-historical goals. Several players sought to match or exceed the achievements of actual medieval dynasties or polities.[82] Notably, this focus on great dynasties was far from universal: around the same number of respondents reported a preference for more obscure historical families and characters.[83] A likewise substantial range of players sought to re-establish empires of the ancient world.[84] These groups of players reverted to the typical expansionist goals of grand strategy games, although they justified this expansion to an extent through their understanding of history.

Most players who set conquest goals for themselves placed no limitations on their planned expansion,[85] often specifically aiming for the conquest of the entire game world.[86] There is nothing inherently wrong with this type of play, and indeed it can be immensely entertaining. However, the popularity of unabashed conquest displayed here suggests that even the complex and varied game world created by the designers of *Crusader Kings II* with its open-ended play and objectives has not overcome the tendency towards expansionist goals propagated within the grand strategy genre as a whole.

The deliberate sparsity of formal objectives in *Crusader Kings II* seems therefore to have encouraged a greater range of play. A small group of players looked to the challenge objectives to guide their play, but the majority set their own goals. These goals were varied and often incorporated non-military and non-expansionist objectives and several players demonstrated reflexive roleplay based on the characteristics of their characters. While conquest was the dominant objective for the majority of players, the conquest was often driven by perceived historical goals. By reducing the visibility and impact of progression, beneficial and challenge objectives, the creators of *Crusader Kings II* created a play environment which allowed players to pursue their own goals. These goals, possibly because of the historical credentials and mechanics of the game and possibly because of the typical audience for historical grand strategy games, tended to have a historical bent.

The impact of this approach towards objectives should not be overstated. Conquest remained the primary objective for most respondents, and threads on the *Crusader Kings* reddit and forums demonstrate the appeal of world conquest to many players of the game. This is quite possibly a consequence of the broader trends within grand strategy games which encourage military domination. Despite its differences from other games in its genre, *Crusader Kings II* shares many aesthetic and mechanical qualities with other grand strategy games: on a superficial level the game is similar to *Civilization* and, especially, *Medieval: Total War*. These similarities may well invite player assumptions, whether conscious or unconscious, about the nature and objectives of the game. Conquest objectives have been removed or downplayed in *Crusader Kings II*, but in the absence of a distinct goal most players continue to use these expansionist objectives on an informal basis.

More generally, the lack of objectives within the game leaves players without guidance. As demonstrated earlier, play often focuses on reconstructing historical goals, but with very limited direction within the game the player is responsible for establishing the nature of these goals. If, as was the case with many respondents to the survey, the player is relatively well informed with regards to the period of the game, then this agency can provide a great deal of scope for constructive and informative play. If, however, the player has little knowledge of the period, this freedom of action does nothing to inform them of the goals and attitudes of medieval rulers.

## Conclusion

The objectives of historical computer games can influence gameplay and the player learning experience in several ways. In the case of grand strategy games set in the Middle Ages, game objectives generally encourage violent expansion in a manner and on a scale very much at odds with the goals and actions of actual medieval rulers. As a result, the dynamics of these games provide a misleading representation of the medieval period and feed into a narrative of the Middle Ages as an overwhelmingly violent and war-torn era. By removing and limiting these conquest-orientated objectives, the creators of *Crusader Kings II* have influenced the playstyles of many of their players encouraging a move away from territorial expansion and facilitating play based in other sociopolitical areas and on roleplay. In doing so, the developers have created a very different game from most within the genre, which allows for different and experimental playstyles, provides new opportunities for teaching, and has contributed to the great commercial and critical success of the game. However, this influence has been limited by player preconceptions regarding the medieval period and by the military focus of most other games of this genre. Furthermore, while the removal of victory conditions and progression objectives grants the player immense freedom in exploring and enjoying the world created within the game, it also denies the player fundamental guidance with regards to how their character should behave. Removing troublesome objectives is insufficient to fully overcome their legacy. To facilitate realistic play, it is necessary to create realistic objectives.

The simplest way to achieve this is to establish player-defined goals around a game. Objectives can be set informally without incorporating them into game mechanics. This approach was used successfully by several players within this study and there is little reason why it could not be transferred to the classroom. After familiarizing themselves with the game, a class could consider the goals of a particular historical figure, compile a list of these goals and then set out to achieve these goals through play. The level of detail, focus on roleplay mechanics and open-ended objectives of *Crusader Kings II* make this game a strong candidate for such an educational approach.

Beyond the classroom, there are several ways in which the objectives of grand strategy games could be adjusted to better present the medieval world and its rulers and to encourage more 'realistic' play. *Crusader Kings II* is certainly a strong example of a game which can easily facilitate historical play and which does so to a substantially greater extent than many of its contemporaries. However, this could be taken further. The introduction of victory conditions which are not focused solely on warfare would be an important first step in this regard. A more meaningful development of the score system employed within *Crusader Kings II* is a possible solution. Rewarding players with points for actions in keeping with their role as ruler is an abstract and blunt method of changing behaviours, but can be an effective one. Such a system was implemented within the original *Medieval: Total War*.[87] In this case, the majority of points were awarded for holding particular territories, but with some alteration this could easily form the basis of a broader system of scoring encouraging more balanced and realistic play.

Such a points system could also encourage more diverse play and greater player agency than the rigid victory conditions of most grand strategy games. Games with a single victory condition coerce their player towards a playstyle which will achieve that victory. Games with multiple victory conditions provide some variation, but as it is usually still necessary to focus on a single overarching goal, often from very early on in the game, play is often restricted to one of a very finite number of core pathways. Receiving points for actions and achievements in a variety of socio-economic areas would provide a stronger basis for hybrid playstyles and support changes of approach within a campaign.

Another potential approach would use progression and beneficial objectives to guide player behaviour on a smaller scale. Players could choose from a small range of objectives based on their ruler, polity and situation within the game and would gain points or mechanical advantages for achieving these goals. Examples of similar systems exist within the grand strategy genre such as the mission system of *Europa Universalis IV*,[88] but these often focus on military objectives and can be overly prescriptive encouraging nations to expand their interests in the same directions as their historical counterparts with limited regard for the geopolitical situation within the current game. The 'wishes' system employed within *The Sims 3*[89] provides the player with a selection of short-term goals for their characters based on their current situation which serves as an effective guide to player behaviour within that sandbox game and a similar system could provide a more useful model with a stronger focus on the personal qualities of a medieval ruler. Such a model for game objectives would allow for easy variation of goals across different characters and polities and create a deeper experience. It could also encourage an emphasis on shorter term goals better reflecting medieval attitudes and realities.

Indeed, a similar and deeper system has emerged in the ongoing development of *Crusader Kings III*.[90] At its release in September 2020, the game builds on the roleplaying depth of *Crusader Kings II* to provide a number of important developments around the use of objectives to promote realistic behaviour. The developers provide the player with a choice of fifteen 'lifestyles' for each of their characters, each representing a medieval paragon from Family Hierarch through military Strategist to devout Theologian. These lifestyles provide substantial benefits within the relevant areas of the game and, through a series of tailored events and choices, encourage the player to engage with their chosen role and fulfil appropriate objectives. Beyond this, the 'Stress' mechanic penalizes players for taking actions which do not conform to the traits and beliefs of their characters: conscientious characters are penalized for making arbitrary decisions while cynical figures struggle to express their faith.[91] Through these mechanics, players are steered towards appropriate behaviour and objectives for their characters and the period. There are some limitations to these mechanics – the game encourages planning in the extreme long term and the focus of most gameplay remains on military affairs – and the game is very much a developing entity, but these are incredibly promising signs of the integration of realistic objectives within a commercially and critically successful games. As a result, *Crusader Kings III* has huge potential within the classroom and its ongoing development will have substantial importance for this area of pedagogy.

Moving beyond these beneficial objectives, a more drastic measure towards increasing player focus on the short term would be to base objectives and even victory conditions on the lifespan of individual rulers. Play could be limited to a single king with victory determined by achieving certain objectives or by accruing sufficient points over their reign. Such systems exist informally in 'succession games' where a string of players take control of a faction in turn, passing control on to the next player when the protagonist dies. Formal implementation of such succession games raises some design issues, but these are far from insurmountable.

These methods all rely on an increased emphasis on roleplay within grand strategy games. They require rulers to be viewed as distinct and unique individuals with varied and changeable motivations. This demands a move away from the totemic rulers of traditional grand strategy games such as *Civilization* in favour of the more personal and useful models presented by *Crusader Kings II* and emerging within *Crusader Kings III*. There are various ways in which this could be accomplished but this will inevitably require a more careful consideration of the nature of the grand strategy genre.

More careful curation of game objectives would also aid the expression of history in other periods and in other genres of game. Megalomaniac conquerors were very much in the minority throughout the course of history and a more careful consideration of the aims of Roman emperors or American presidents would facilitate the development of a stronger understanding of history among the players of games set in the ancient or modern periods. Outside the grand strategy genre, roleplaying games could look more closely at medieval moral systems when constructing their own alignment systems. Combat simulators could base their victory conditions more heavily on the goals of medieval combatants.

This move towards more realistic objectives has applications beyond the educational and academic spheres. Various designers are looking to objectives as a means to reinvigorate this genre, changing game dynamics to produce a more interesting experience (particularly in the often repetitive end-game) and greater replayability.[92] As indicated earlier, a substantial section of the playerbase places emphasis on the historical realism of these games and is willing and able to move beyond the tropes associated with authenticity within popular perspectives of the Middle Ages. In some cases, this extends to demands for more realistic objectives and gameplay, such as facilitating the meaningful play of an empire in decline.[93] Realistic play can be beneficial from commercial and recreational standpoints.

There are of course limits to this approach. The creation of realistic objectives relies on an understanding of the goals of the player character. Discerning these motivations is subjective and often controversial. This issue can be mitigated to a certain extent by basing objectives on paragon models of the period: while it is very hard to establish the motivations of individual kings, models of ideal rulership are readily available throughout most of the medieval period. Numerous works such as the *Administrando Imperii*,[94] *Gesta Chuonradi II Imperatoris*[95] and *Vita Ludovici regis*[96] were written primarily to provide a guide for young rulers while an even more substantial pieces of literature went to great lengths to present their protagonists acting as paragon models of rulership (and their antagonists as imperfect foils). Games can reproduce these models of rulership even if they cannot depict the exact goals of specific rulers.

Ultimately, for a historical game to retain its utility as a learning and research tool its objectives must not be so prescriptive as to remove, or greatly reduce, player agency. The interactive and player driven nature of computer games are vital and unique elements of this medium and form the basis for much of their learning potential. Zealous implementation of objectives may corral players into unrealistic behaviour, but this could easily destroy the player's free will undermining their ability and desire to explore their environments and experiment with game mechanics. Realistic objectives have great capacity to enhance the learning experience provided by computer games, but great care must be taken to ensure that the end product remains a dynamic experience: that it can still be considered a game.

## Notes

1 *Crusader Kings II* (Paradox Interactive, 2012).
2 Johannes Fromme, 'Computer Games as a Part of Children's Culture', *Game Studies* 3, no. 2 (2003); Marc Prensky, *'Don't Bother Me Mom, I'm Learning!'*: *How Computer and Video Games Are Preparing Your Kids for Twenty-First Century Success and How You Can Help!* (St. Paul, MN: Paragon House, 2006); Hakan Tüzün, Meryem Yılmaz-Soylu, Türkan Karakuş, Yavuz İnal and Gonca Kızılkaya, 'The Effects of Computer Games on Primary School Students' Achievement and Motivation in Geography Learning', *Computers & Education* 52, no. 1 (2009): 68–77; Robert Houghton, 'Where Did You Learn That? The Self-Perceived Educational Impact of Historical Computer Games on Undergraduates', *Gamevironments* 5 (2016).
3 Andrew McMichael, 'PC Games and the Teaching of History', *The History Teacher* 40, no. 2 (2007): 203–18; William R. Watson, Christopher J. Mong, and Constance A. Harris, 'A Case Study of the In-Class Use of a Video Game for Teaching High School History', *Computers & Education* 56, no. 2 (2011):466–74; Jeremiah McCall, 'Teaching History With Digital Historical Games: An Introduction to the Field and Best Practices', *Simulation & Gaming* 47, no. 4 (2016): 517–42.
4 Laura Zucconi, Ethan Watrall, Hannah Ueno and Lisa Rosner, 'Pox and the City: Challenges in Writing a Digital History Game', in *Writing History in the Digital Age*, eds Jack Dougherty and Kristen Nawrotzki (Ann Arbor, MI: University of Michigan Press, 2013).
5 *Assassin's Creed* (Ubisoft, 2007).
6 *Assassin's Creed Origins* (Ubisoft, 2017).
7 Dominic Tarason, 'Assassin's Creed Origins becomes Edutainment Feb 20th', *Rock, Paper, Shotgun*, 13 February 2018. Available online: https://www.rockpapershotgun.com/2018/02/13/assassins-creed-origins-becomes-edutainment-feb-20th/, accessed 5 April 2018; Ubisoft, 'Discovery Tour by Assassin's Creed: Ancient Egypt', *Assassin's Creed*. Available online: https://assassinscreed.ubisoft.com/game/en-gb/news/detail.aspx?c=tcm:154-319359-16&ct=tcm:154-76770-32, accessed 5 July 2018.
8 Jerome De Groot, *Consuming History: Historians and Heritage in Contemporary Popular Culture* (New York, NY: Routledge, 2016), 7–8.
9 Harry J. Brown, *Videogames and Education* (Armonk, NY: M. E. Sharpe, 2008), 118; Adam Chapman, 'Privileging Form Over Content: Analysing Historical Videogames', *Journal of Digital Humanities* 1, no. 2 (2012): 42–6; Daniel Floyd and James Portnow, 'Historical Games – Why Mechanics Must Be Both Good and Accurate', *Extra Credits* 9, no. 6 (10 September 2014). Available online: https://www.youtube.com/watch?v=l8yl09GcI48, accessed 10 May 2018; Robert Houghton, 'It's What You Do With It That Counts: Factual Accuracy and Mechanical Accuracy in Crusader Kings II', *The Public Medievalist*, 30 September 2014. Available online: https://www.publicmedievalist.com/ckii-houghton/, accessed 10 May 2018.
10 *Civilization* (MicroProse, 1991).
11 Adam Chapman, 'Affording History: Civilization and the Ecological Approach', in *Playing with the Past: Digital Games and the Simulation of History*, eds Matthew Kapell and Andrew B. R. Elliott (New York, NY: Bloomsbury, 2013); Adam Chapman, 'Is Sid Meier's Civilization History?', *Rethinking History* 17, no. 3 (2013): 312–32; Rolfe Daus Peterson, Andrew Justin Miller and Sean Joseph Fedorko, 'The Same River Twice: Exploring Historical Representation and the Value of Simulation in the Total War,

Civilization and Patrician Franchises', in *Playing with the Past: Digital Games and the Simulation of History*, eds Matthew Kapell and Andrew B. R. Elliott (New York, NY: Bloomsbury, 2013).

12  Emily Joy Bembeneck, 'Phantasms of Rome: Video Games and Cultural Identity', in *Playing with the Past: Digital Games and the Simulation of History*, eds Matthew Kapell and Andrew B. R. Elliott (New York, NY: Bloomsbury, 2013); Rebecca Mir and Trevor Owens, 'Modeling Indigenous Peoples: Unpacking Ideology in Sid Meier's Colonization', in *Playing with the Past: Digital Games and the Simulation of History*, eds Matthew Kapell and Andrew B. R. Elliott (New York, NY: Bloomsbury, 2013); Dom Ford, '"eXplore, eXpand, eXploit, eXterminate": Affective Writing of Postcolonial History and Education in Civilization V', *Game Studies* 16, no. 2 (2017): 33–55.

13  Katie Salen Tekinbaş and Eric Zimmerman, *Rules of Play: Game Design Fundamentals* (Cambridge, MA: MIT Press, 2003), 92–9; Diane Carr, 'The Trouble with Civilization', in *Videogame, Player, Text*, eds Barry Atkins and Tanya Krzywinska (Manchester: Manchester University Press, 2007), esp. 222–5.

14  Adam Chapman, *Digital Games as History: How Videogames Represent the Past and Offer Access to Historical Practice* (New York, NY: Routledge, 2016); Houghton, 'Where Did You Learn That?'; Ford, '"eXplore, eXpand, eXploit, eXterminate"'.

15  Andrew B. R. Elliott and Matthew Kapell, 'Introduction: To Build a Past That Will "Stand the Test of Time"- Discovering Historical Facts, Assembling Historical Narratives', in Sid Meier's Colonization', in *Playing with the Past: Digital Games and the Simulation of History*, eds Matthew Kapell and Andrew B. R. Elliott (New York, NY: Bloomsbury, 2013), 12.

16  Adam Smith and Soren Johnson, 'Soren Johnson on Challenging the Norms of 4X Games', *Rock, Paper, Shotgun*, 6 April 2018. Available online: https://www.rockpapershotgun.com/2018/04/06/soren-johnson-4x-strategy-interview/, accessed 5 May 2018.

17  G. Frasca, 'Simulation versus Narrative', in *The Video Game Theory Reader*, eds M. Wolf and B. Perron (New York, NY: Routledge, 2003); Espen Aarseth, 'Playing Research: Methodological Approaches to Game Analysis', *Game Approaches/SPil-veje. Papers from Spilforskning.dk Conference* (2004); Jesper Juul, *Half-Real: Video Games between Real Rules and Fictional Worlds* (Cambridge, MA: MIT Press, 2005): i–1123; Chapman, 'Privileging Form Over Content'; Jeremy Antley, 'Going Beyond the Textual in History', *Journal of Digital Humanities* 1, no. 2 (2012).

18  Christopher Douglas, '"You Have Unleashed a Horde of Barbarians!": Fighting Indians, Playing Games, Forming Disciplines', *Postmodern Culture* 13, no. 1 (2002); James Paul Gee, *What Video Games Have to Teach Us about Learning and Literacy* (New York, NY: Palgrave Macmillan, 2003); Juul, *Half-real*; Claudio Fogu, 'Digitizing Historical Consciousness', *History and Theory* 48, no. 2 (2009): 118; Elliott and Kapell, 'Introduction: To Build a Past That Will "Stand the Test of Time"'; Bernard Suits, Thomas Hurka and Frank Newfeld, *The Grasshopper: Games, Life, and Utopia* (Peterborough, ON: Broadview Press, 2014).

19  Andrew B. R. Elliott, *Remaking the Middle Ages: The Methods of Cinema and History in Portraying the Medieval World* (Jefferson, NC: McFarland, 2011); Mirjam Vosmeer and Ben Schouten, 'Interactive Cinema: Engagement and Interaction', in *Interactive Storytelling*, eds Alex Mitchell, Clara Fernández-Vara and David Thue (Cham: Springer, 2014); Melvin G. Hill, 'Tale of Two Fathers: Authenticating Fatherhood in Quantic Dream's Heavy Rain: The Origami Killer and Naughty Dog's The Last of Us', in *Pops in Pop Culture*, ed. Elizabeth Podnieks (New York, NY: Palgrave, 2016).

20  Steven Johnson, *Everything Bad Is Good for You: How Today's Popular Culture Is Actually Making Us Smarter* (New York, NY: Riverhead, 2006).
21  Ian Bogost, 'The Rhetoric of Video Games', in *The Ecology of Games: Connecting Youth, Games, and Learning*, ed. Katie Salen Tekinbaş (Cambridge, MA: MIT Press, 2008); Jeremiah McCall, 'Historical Simulations as Problem Spaces: Criticism and Classroom Use', *Journal of Digital Humanities* 1, no. 2 (2012); Tracy Fullerton, *Game Design Workshop: A Playcentric Approach to Creating Innovative Games* (Boca Raton, FL: CRC Press, 2014).
22  Richard M. Ryan, C. Scott Rigby, and Andrew Przybylski, 'The Motivational Pull of Video Games: A Self-Determination Theory Approach', *Motivation and Emotion* 30, no. 4 (2006): 344–60; Barbaros Bostan, 'Player Motivations: A Psychological Perspective', *Computers in Entertainment* 7, no. 2 (2009): 1; Wolmet Barendregt and Tilde M. Bekker, 'The Influence of the Level of Free-Choice Learning Activities on the Use of an Educational Computer Game', *Computers & Education* 56, no. 1 (2011): 80–90; Hill, 'Tale of Two Fathers'.
23  R. G. McLaughlan and D. Kirkpatrick, 'Online Roleplay: Design for Active Learning', *European Journal of Engineering Education* 29, no. 4 (2004): 477–90; Robert McLaughlan and Denise Kirkpatrick, 'Peer Learning using Computer Supported Roleplay Simulations', in *Peer Learning in Higher Education: Learning from and with Each Other*, eds David Boud, Ruth Cohen, and Jane Sampson (Hoboken, NJ: Taylor and Francis, 2014); Paul Sturtevant, 'Playing with the Middle Ages', *The Public Medievalist*, 9 November 2014. Available online: https://www.publicmedievalist.com/playing-middle-ages/, accessed 10 May 2018.
24  Ignacio X. Domínguez, Rogelio E. Cardona-Rivera, James K. Vance and David L. Roberts, 'The Mimesis Effect: The Effect of Roles on Player Choice in Interactive Narrative Role-Playing Games', *CHI '16: Proceedings of the 2016 CHI Conference on Human Factors in Computing Systems* (New York, NY: ACM, 2016).
25  *Baldur's Gate* (Interplay Entertainment, 1998).
26  *The Witcher* (CD Projekt, 2007).
27  *Thief: The Dark Project* (Eidos Interactive, 1998).
28  Andrew Burn, 'Playing Roles', in *Computer Games: Text, Narrative, and Play*, ed. Diane Carr (Cambridge: Polity Press, 2006), esp. 87.
29  Tara Jane Copplestone, 'But That's Not Accurate: The Differing Perceptions of Accuracy in Cultural-Heritage Videogames Between Creators, Consumers and Critics', *Rethinking History* 21, no. 3 (2017); Jeremiah McCall and Adam Chapman, 'Discussion: Historical Accuracy and Historical Video Games (Part 1)', *Gaming the Past*, 26 December 2017. Available online: https://gamingthepast.net/2017/12/26/discussion-what-is-historical-accuracy-in-an-historical-video-game-part-1/, accessed 13 February 2018.
30  Floyd and Portnow, 'Historical Games'; McCall and Chapman, 'Discussion: Historical Accuracy and Historical Video Games (Part 1)'; Jeremy Antley, 'Period Piece: Board Games Can Manipulate Players by Manipulating History', *Real Life*, 11 December 2017. Available online: http://reallifemag.com/period-piece/, accessed 8 May 2018.
31  Jeremiah McCall and Adam Chapman, 'Discussion: Historical Accuracy and Historical Video Games (Part 2)', *Gaming the Past*, 8 April 2018. Available at https://gamingthepast.net/2018/04/08/discussion-authenticity-the-characteristics-of-a-historical-game/, accessed 13 April 2018.
32  Floyd and Portnow, 'Historical Games'; Sturtevant, 'Playing with the Middle Ages'; Houghton, 'It's What You Do with It That Counts'.

33  Zucconi, Watrall, Ueno and Rosner, 'Pox and the City'; Stephen Ortega, 'Representing the Past: Video Games Challenge to the Historical Narrative', *Syllabus* 4, no. 1 (2015): 1–2.
34  Juan Francisco Jiménez Alcázar, 'The Other Possible Past: Simulation of the Middle Ages in Video Games', *Imago Temporis* 5 (2011): 311.
35  Chapman, 'Privileging Form Over Content', 42; Floyd and Portnow, 'Historical Games'.
36  A. Martin Wainwright, 'Teaching Historical Theory through Video Games', *The History Teacher* 47, no. 4 (2014): 579–612.
37  John K. Lee and Jeffrey Probert, 'Civilization III and Whole-Class Play', *The Journal of Social Studies Research* 34, no. 1 (2010): 1–28; John Pagnotti and William B. Russell, 'Using Civilization IV to Engage Students in World History Content', *The Social Studies* 103, no. 1 (2012): 39–48.
38  Erik Andersen, Yun-En Liu, Richard Snider, Roy Szeto, Seth Cooper and Zoran Popović, 'On the Harmfulness of Secondary Game Objectives', *FDG '11: Proceedings of the 6th International Conference on Foundations of Digital Games* (New York, NY: ACM Press, 2011), 30.
39  *Medieval II: Total War* (Sega, 2006).
40  Smith and Johnson, 'Soren Johnson on Challenging the Norms of 4X Games'.
41  *Civilization VI* (2K Games, 2016).
42  *Age of Empires II: The Age of Kings* (Microsoft, 1999).
43  *Baldur's Gate II: Shadows of Amn* (Black Isle Studios, 2000).
44  Andersen, Liu, Snider, Szeto, Cooper, and Popović, 'On the Harmfulness of Secondary Game Objectives', 33–4.
45  *Master of Orion* (MicroProse, 1993).
46  Alan Emrich, "MicroProse' Strategic Space Opera Is Rated XXXX!', *Computer Gaming World* 110 (September 1993): 92–3.
47  Smith and Johnson, 'Soren Johnson on Challenging the Norms of 4X Games'.
48  McMichael, 'PC Games and the Teaching of History', 214; Ernest Adams, *Fundamentals of Game Design* (Berkeley, CA: New Riders, 2014), 423; Ortega, 'Representing the Past', 2.
49  Adam Smith, 'Cree Concerns Hammer Home Why Civ Needs to Reject Its Own Traditions', *Rock, Paper, Shotgun*, 5 January 2018. Available online: https://www.rockpapershotgun.com/2018/01/05/civilization-vi-cree-nation-cultural-representation/, accessed 5 May 2018.
50  Douglas, '"You Have Unleashed a Horde of Barbarians!"'; Mir and Owens, 'Modeling Indigenous Peoples'; Ortega, 'Representing the Past', 3; Bembeneck, 'Phantasms of Rome'; Ford, '"eXplore, eXpand, eXploit, eXterminate"'.
51  Alex Whelchel, 'Using Civilization Simulation Video Games in the World History Classroom', *World History Connected* 4, no. 2 (2007); Fogu, 'Digitizing Historical Consciousness', 117.
52  Ortega, 'Representing the Past', 2.
53  Hagen Keller, 'Grundlagen ottonischer Königsherrschaft', in *Reich und Kirche vor dem Investiturstreit: Vorträge beim wissenschaftlichen Kolloquium aus Anlass des achtzigsten Geburtstags von Gerd Tellenbach*, ed. Karl Schmid (Sigmaringen: J. Thorbecke, 1985); Janet L. Nelson, *Charles the Bald* (London: Longman, 1992), 1–9; I. N. Wood, *The Merovingian kingdoms, 450-751* (London; Longman, 1994).
54  Karl Ferdinand Werner, 'Untersuchungen zur Frühzeit des französischen Fürstentums (9.-10. Jahrhundert)', *Die Welt als Geschichte* 18 (1958); Barbara H. Rosenwein,

'Friends and Family, Politics and Privilege in the Kingship of Berengar I', in *Portraits of Medieval and Renaissance Living: Essays in Memory of David Herlihy*, eds Samuel Kline Cohn and Steven A. Epstein (Ann Arbor, MI: University of Michigan Press, 1996); Barbara H. Rosenwein, *Negotiating Space: Power, Restraint, and Privileges of Immunity in Early Medieval Europe* (Ithaca, NY: Cornell University Press, 1999), 3–19.

55  Karl Leyser, *Rule and Conflict in an Early Medieval Society: Ottonian Saxony* (Oxford: Blackwell, 1989), 1–7.

56  François Louis Ganshof, *Frankish Institutions under Charlemagne* (New York, NY: W.W. Norton, 1970), 46–55; Karl Ferdinand Werner, 'Missus-marchio-comes: Entre l'administration centrale et l'administration locale de l'empire carolingien', in *Histoire comparee de l'administration (IVe-XVIIIe siècles): actes du XIVe Colloque historique franco-allemand, Tours, 27 mars–1er avril 1977*, eds Werner Paravicini and Karl Ferdinand Werner (München: Artemis Verlag, 1980), 191–4.

57  François Bougard, *La justice dans le royaume d'Italie: de la fin du VIIIe siècle au début du XIe siècle* (Rome: Ecole française de Rome, 1995), 146–76; Matthew Innes, 'Charlemagne's Government', in *Charlemagne: Empire and Society*, ed. Joanna Story (Manchester: Manchester University Press, 2005), 76–9; Simon MacLean, 'Legislation and Politics in Late Carolingian Italy: The Ravenna Constitutions', *Early Medieval Europe* 8, no. 4 (2010): 394–8; John Watts, *The Making of Polities: Europe, 1300-1500* (Cambridge: Cambridge University Press, 2009), 207–18.

58  Jon N. Sutherland, *Liudprand of Cremona, Bishop, Diplomat, Historian: Studies of the Man and His Age* (Spoleto: Fondazione CISAM, 1988), 29; Geoffrey Koziol, 'Is Robert I in Hell?: The Diploma for Saint-Denis and the Mind of a Rebel King (25 January 923)', *Early Medieval Europe* 14, no. 3 (2006): 256–61.

59  Daniel Floyd and James Portnow, 'Strategic Uncertainty - Keeping Strategy Games Fresh', *Extra Credits* 8, no. 18, 18 January 2017. Available online: https://www.youtube.com/watch?v=PJKTDz1zYzs, accessed 10 May 2018.

60  Smith and Johnson, 'Soren Johnson on Challenging the Norms of 4X Games'.

61  Ibid.

62  Houghton, 'It's What You Do With It That Counts'; Alex Wiltshire, 'How Crusader Kings 2 Makes People Out Of Opinions', *Rock, Paper, Shotgun*, 11 November 2016. Available online: https://www.rockpapershotgun.com/2016/11/11/crusader-kings-2-characters/, accessed 10 May 2018.

63  Bertrand Lucat and Mads Haahr, 'What Makes a Successful Emergent Narrative: The Case of Crusader Kings II', in *Interactive Storytelling*, eds Henrik Schoenau-Fog, Luis Emilio Bruni, Sandy Louchart and Sarune Baceviciute (Cham: Springer, 2015).

64  'I usually play for achievements' (Ignis92); 'I mostly just find an achievement I haven't done and work on that' (DOLamba); '[I] try a[n] achiev[e]ment' (Dzharek); 'every new campaign I start is to get 3 - 5 new achievements' (Colonel_Chow); 'Achievement hunting' (Creative_Username_44).

65  'I try to spread my dynasty to as many kingdoms as possible' (capt_pessimist); 'I try to play as a kingdom and spread my lineage around the map without making my own realm too big' (wrongbuton); 'I try to get my dynasty on as many thrones as possible!' (sabersquirl); 'My primary goal is to give the Dynasty as much land as possible' (NorthAndEastTexan); 'Sometimes I'll play, not to rule the most land myself, but have my family be in a position of power, with every major kingdom and empire ruled by my dynasty' (Pixel871).

66 '[I expand] without wars. Just your ability to plot and play the game of thrones' (Lord Hawkman); 'I like to play long game marriage/intrigue' (bloodofkorne); 'I try to use unorthodox methods such as expanding purely through marriage' (Mage13lade).
67 'I keep myself as small vassal in HRE, honing my knowledge skill to the max so I can be the Court Physician of my liege - basically creating the dynasty of doctors and scientists' (The_Heichou); 'I like the fact that you can do some preliminary science' (Sansophia).
68 '[I] play Merchant [R]epublic, and my goal is to have all sea trade posts on a map' (andrewwewwka); '[I conduct] land reforms within the realm for stability, and [spend] money on building cities for additional income and infrastructure' (Mage13lade).
69 'One of my goals is always to be the new cultural centre of the world' (Peanutcat4).
70 'I love shaping/influencing the world outside my realm. I usually build my empire so that I have very high income. Then I use the money to fund other realms' wars, support underdogs, depose foreign rulers, install claimants etc . . .' (__october__).
71 'I like to [. . .] Have heaps of kids' (dunnymunch).
72 'Survival is the main goal' (ElagabalusRex).
73 'My jam lately is limiting myself to a single kingdom [. . .] and trying to hold out against larger neighbors' (mister_accismus).
74 'my favorite way to play the game is by playing to my character's personality as much as possible to create personal plot arcs' (TheMeatiestRocket); 'I would have side objectives for each character and try to make an interesting story for each character while going towards the ultimate goal' (SentientHAL); 'I play a lot more around the role playing aspect of the game' (Big-Island); 'The most fun for me is to make an interesting story and personality for each ruler' (5firtrees).
75 'I'll usually do what my character's traits tell me to do. Rulers who are masters of intrigue try to assassinate their way to the top. Diplomats through marriage. Marshals through bigger army diplomacy' (medokady); ' I [. . .] roleplay the situations according to the character's traits' (itssofluffie); 'sometimes I will do a roleplay game, where every decision is based on my character stats and traits' (Pixel871); 'I play Crusader Kings II for the "Role-Playing" [. . .] The traits within the game help a lot with this' (X_Clint_Beastwood_X).
76 'My main objective usually ends up being to set myself up for a solid but not overpowered realm by the end of the game' (HijabiKathy); 'After getting to a place of power I'm content with, I just strive to keep the dynasty in power' (itssofluffie); 'I've really tried to avoid forcing as rapid expansion as I can and instead see what happens when I dedicate prolonged periods of time to peace' (TurrPhennirPhan).
77 '[I'm] forcing myself to stay gavelkind [an early form of succession which divides the father's lands between his sons], so every time my character dies the realm shatters, and [I] have to choose where [t]o expand next' (lokhrohk).
78 'I like to play as a count and ascend to be a regional power in a Kingdom or Empire' (Blasoon); 'Started at the beginning as Count Loup in southern France. Never declared war, worked my way up in the Benedictine order, gave money, built churches' (NotGoodAtCleverNames); 'I'm trying to do a full game from 769 to the end without going any higher than duke rank' (SeeEmmDee).
79 'I usually try to make my realm as de jure as possible, in the sense of making sure all of my vassals control the land that people think they are entitled to control without making any one of them too powerful' (medokady); 'I always try to keep my vassals cleanly inside their de jure dutchies/kingdoms using any means' (Dark__Pearl).

80  'I try to avoid blobbing [expanding excessively] because there's a point where that becomes too repetitive for entertainment value' (OctoberNoir).
81  'I try to make the most aesthetically pleasing empire/kingdom while also remaining a world power' (Admiral_Aenoth).
82  'I also like to recreate historic empires but better' (TheEpicCorvix); 'Like starting as Count Robert Capet of Liege in 769 start and get Capet to the top of the list. Or the last Karling [Carolingian] in the 1066 start' (DOLamba); 'I try and follow the historical rise of a dynasty, then avert their fall' (NoctisRex); 'I've also played through most of the neat historical figures like Charlemagne, Rurik, and Ragnar' (FloridaMan_69); 'I'll more often than not have kind of a "phase", usually started by gorging on wiki page after wiki page of a certain country or ethnic group' (PM_ME_YOUR_EMRAKUL).
83  'I like to play historical underdogs or also-rans and elevate them out of obscurity' (PlanetOfHats); 'I like to play some random irrelevant character, try to do something very ahistorical and see how it plays out' (Kosinski33); 'I enjoy winning with the historical "loser" [. . .] I also like starting with dynasties when they are insignificant or weak (NoctisRex); 'I like to play as those who historically died out' (ziggymister); 'I like taking historical losers and underdogs and making them into superpowers'(The_Vulture1).
84  'the restoration of Persia, two restorations of Rome [. . .] and I'm currently trying to restore Alexanders empire starting as the count of Philippopolis' (CMGA99); '[a] reformed Rome complete with re-unification of the Catholic and Orthodox Church, and also a Persian Empire that worships the sun' (Simmons_M8); 'to restore the Achaemenid Empire' (Senza32); 'reforming Rome and uniting the Arab and European worlds under Roman (Catholic) rule' (OranjePatriot); 'Become the emperor of the Roman Empire as a Catholic' (EastGuardian); 'Either restore Rome or make Alexander proud and invade India' (Renegard); 'restore Carthaginian control of the Mediterranean' (Hatlessspider); '[as the Byzantine Empire] do reconquests that would make Justinian proud' (Peanutcat4); 'restoring the Kingdom of Israel' (The_Vulture1); 'restore the Roman Empire' (Norse_Emperor).
85  'see how large I can get' (Sparkyninja); 'conquest, trying to get as much land as possible' (The_Heichou); 'try to form Empires. Mainly through conquest and military might' (vtheawesome); 'amass as much power as I can' (miauw62); 'Blob' (Deflatriot), 'climb the ladder and become the most powerful warlord on the block' (FloridaMan_69); 'go from count to emperor, and spread the dynasty wherever possible' (LostThyme); 'conquer as much as I can' (wstudholme); 'Conquer land and kill people' (aaragax); 'get as much territory as possible' (LosEagle); 'Crush my enemies' (SotiCoto); 'I just like the typical start-as-a-count-then-become-an-emperor scheme' (ARADPLAUG); 'try to conquer something' (skadefryd).
86  'Usually world conquest' (Ganduin); 'I've done the whole paint the world my colour thing' (ehkodiak); '[I] make a bid for the world' (JakobTykesson); 'destroying everything' (lkmertgurcan); 'aim for world conquest' (HSTEHSTE); 'conque[r] the world [. . .] with murder and gold' (mrMalloc); 'to conquer the world' (Cathsaigh).
87  *Medieval: Total War* (Activision, 2002).
88  *Europa Universalis IV* (Paradox Interactive, 2013).
89  *The Sims 3* (Electronic Arts, 2009).
90  *Crusader Kings III* (Paradox Interactive, 2020).
91  Paradox Interactive, 'Dev Diary #9: Lifestyles', *Crusader Kings III*, 14 January 2020. Available online: https://www.crusaderkings.com/news/dev-diary-9-lifestyles, accessed on 22 April 2020.

92 Floyd and Portnow, 'Strategic Uncertainty'; Smith and Johnson, 'Soren Johnson on Challenging the Norms of 4X Games'.
93 Ortega, 'Representing the Past', 4.
94 Constantine Porphyrogenitus, *De administrando imperio*, ed. Gyula Moravcsik, trans. R. J. H. Jenkins (Washington, DC: Dumbarton Oaks, 1967).
95 Wipo, 'The Deeds of Conrad II', in *Imperial Lives and Letters of the Eleventh Century*, trans. T. E. Mommsen and K. F. Morrison (New York, NY: Columbia University Press, 1962).
96 Suger, *The Deeds of Louis the Fat*, eds Richard Cusimano and John Moorhead (Washington, DC: Catholic University of America Press, 1992).

# Bibliography

@medievalpoc. 'Hi! I've Been Looking at a Kickstarter for a "Realistic" Medieval-Era Game Called 'Kingdom Come: Deliverance' and Realized It Looked Rather… White'. *People of Colour in European Art History*, 2014. http://medievalpoc.tumblr.com/post/75252294049/hi-ive-been-looking-at-a-kickstarter-for-a.

@medievalpoc. 'On Telling the Truth'. *People of Colour in European Art History*, 2014. http://medievalpoc.tumblr.com/post/88796194073/on-telling-the-truth.

50° North Nordic. 'Denmark's Viking Trail Tour'. *50 Degrees North*. Available at https://us.fiftydegreesnorth.com/tour/denmarks-viking-trail-tour (accessed 26 February 2018).

Aarseth, Espen. 'Playing Research: Methodological Approaches to Game Analysis'. In *Proceedings of the Digital Arts and Culture Conference*, 1–7. Melbourne: MIT School of Applied Communication, 2003.

Aarseth, Espen. 'Playing Research: Methodological Approaches to Game Analysis'. *Game Approaches/SPil-Veje. Papers from Spilforskning.dk Conference* (2004): 1–7.

Abels, Richard. 'Cultural Representations of Warfare in the High Middle Ages: The Morgan Picture Bible'. In *Crusading and Warfare in the Middle Ages: Realities and Representations. Essays in Honour of John France*, edited by Simon John and Nicholas Morton, 13–35. Farnham: Ashgate, 2014.

Aberth, John. *A Knight at the Movies: Medieval History on Film*. New York, NY: Routledge, 2003.

Adams, Ernest. *Fundamentals of Game Design*. Berkeley, CA: New Riders, 2014.

Alcázar, Juan Francisco Jiménez. 'The Other Possible Past: Simulation of the Middle Ages in Video Games'. *Imago Temporis* 5 (2011): 299–340.

Alexandria Tourism. Explore Alexandria Minnesota (2015). Available at https://explorealex.com/ (accessed 26 February 2018).

Álvarez, Pablo, Paulí Dávila, and Luis M. Naya. 'Education Museums: Historical Educational Discourse, Typology and Characteristics. The Case of Spain'. *Paedagogica Historica* 53, no. 6 (2 November 2017): 827–45.

Ambroise. *Estoire de la Guerre Sainte – Histoire en Vers de la Troisieme Croisade (1190–1192)*, edited by G. Paris. Paris: Imprimerie nationale, 1897.

Andersen, Erik, Yun-En Liu, Richard Snider, Roy Szeto, Seth Cooper, and Zoran Popović. 'On the Harmfulness of Secondary Game Objectives'. *FDG '11: Proceedings of the 6th International Conference on Foundations of Digital Games*, 30–7. New York, NY: ACM Press, 2011.

Andriotis, Konstantinos. 'Genres of Heritage Authenticity: Denotations from a Pilgrimage Landscape'. *Annals of Tourism Research* 38, no. 4 (October 2011): 1,613–33.

Anglo, Sydney. *The Martial Arts of Renaissance Europe*. New Haven and London: Yale University Press, 2000.

Antley, Jeremy. 'Going Beyond the Textual in History'. *Journal of Digital Humanities* 1, no. 2 (2012).

Antley, Jeremy. 'Period Piece: Board Games Can Manipulate Players by Manipulating History'. *Real Life*, 11 December 2017. Available online: http://reallifemag.com/period-piece/ (accessed 8 May 2018).

Ariella Elema. 'Tradition, Innovation, Re-enactment: Hans Talhoffer's Unusual Weapons'. *Acta Periodica Duellatorum* 7, no. 1 (2019): 3–25.

Arif, Shabana. 'Kingdom Come: Deliverance's Player Base Has Dropped by 95% on Steam'. *IGN India*, 2018. https://in.ign.com/kingdom-come-deliverance/122081/news/kingdom-come-deliverances-player-base-has-dropped-by-95-on-s.

Atkinson, Stephen. '"They ... toke their shyldys before them and drew oute their swerdys ...": Inflicting and Healing Wounds in Malory's *Morte Darthur*'. In *Wounds and Wound Repair in Medieval Culture*, edited by Larissa Tracy and Kelly DeVries, 519–43. Leiden: Brill, 2015.

Augé, Marc. *Non-Places: Introduction to an Anthropology of Supermodernity*. London and New York, NY: Verso, 1995.

Author unknown. 'Competitive Designs for the Wallace Statue in Aberdeen'. *Aberdeen Weekly Journal*, 5 July 1884.

Author unknown. 'Glasgow International Exhibition'. *Glasgow Herald*, 29 August 1888.

Author unknown. *Popular Ballads and Songs, from Tradition Manuscripts, and Scarce Editions*. Paris, 1825.

Author unknown. 'Royal Dunfermline: King Robert the Bruce'. *Royal Dunfermline* website, accessed 3 December 2016. http://www.royaldunfermline.com/Resources/DUNFERMLINE_AND_ROBERT_THE_BRUCE.pdf.

Author unknown. 'Wallace Memorial at Elderslie'. *Aberdeen Daily Journal*, 25 September 1912.

Bærenholdt, Jørgen Ole and Michael Haldrup. 'On the Track of the Vikings'. In *Tourism Mobilities: Places to Play, Places in Play*, edited by Mimi Sheller and John Urry, 78–89. London: Routledge, 2004.

Baerg, Andrew. 'Governmentality, Neoliberalism, and the Digital Game'. *Symploke* 17, no. 1–2 (2009): 115–27.

Baker, Geoffrey le. *Chronicle*, translated by David Preest. Woodbridge: Boydell, 2012.

Baker-Whitelaw, Gavia. 'Is a Medieval Video Game Historically Accurate without People of Color?' *The Daily Dot*, 2014. http://www.dailydot.com/gaming/reddit-tumblr-medieval-video-game-poc/.

Baldwin Brown, G. 'Letters from Readers'. *The Scotsman*, 12 January 1912.

Barber, R. 'Edward, Prince of Wales and of Aquitane'. Oxford Dictionary of National Biography. http://www.oxforddnb.com/view/10.1093/ref:odnb/9780198614128.001.0001/odnb-9780198614128-e-8523.

Bardsley, Sandy. *Venomous Tongues: Speech and Gender in Late Medieval England*. Philadelphia, PA: University of Pennsylvania Press, 2006.

Barendregt, Wolmet and Tilde M. Bekker. 'The Influence of the Level of Free-Choice Learning Activities on the Use of an Educational Computer Game'. *Computers & Education* 56, no. 1 (2011): 80–90.

Barnes, Tom. '"Game of Thrones": We Talked to Historians and a Military Expert about Who Will Win the Iron Throne'. *Mic*, 21 July 2017. https://mic.com/articles/182474/game-of-thrones-we-talked-to-historians-and-a-military-expert-about-who-will-win-the-iron-throne (accessed 9 September 2019).

Barnett, T. *Sacred Relics: Pieces of the Past in Nineteenth-Century America*. Chicago: University of Chicago Press, 2013.

Beavers, Sian, and Elizabeth FitzGerald. 'Perceptions, Perspectives and Practices: A Study of the Players of Historical Games'. *DiGRA/FDG '16* Conference, 1–5 August. Dundee, 2016.

Beavers, Sian. 'Medievalism at Play: Audience and Player Receptions of the Medieval in Popular, Digital Media'. In *The Middle Ages in the Modern World Conference*. Manchester, n.d.

Bede. *The Old English Version of Bede's Ecclesiastical History of the English People*. Translated by Thomas Miller. London: N. Trübner, 1898. Available online: https://archive.org/details/oldenglishversio04bede/page/n5/mode/2up (accessed 28 March 2018).

Bell, Alice. 'The 5 Most Extremely Historically Accurate Things in Kingdom Come: Deliverance – VideoGamer.Com'. *VideoGamer*, 2018. https://www.videogamer.com/features/the-5-most-extremely-historically-accurate-things-in-kingdom-come-deliverance.

Bellis, Joanna, Leitch, Megan G. 'Chivalric Literature'. In *A Companion to Chivalry*, edited by Robert W. Jones and Peter Coss, 241–62. Woodbridge: Boydell, 2019.

Bembeneck, Emily Joy. 'Phantasms of Rome: Video Games and Cultural Identity'. In *Playing with the Past: Digital Games and the Simulation of History*, edited by Matthew Kapell and Andrew B. R. Elliott, 77–90. New York, NY: Bloomsbury, 2013.

Bernau, Anke. 'Albina: Remembering the Nation'. *Exemplaria* 21, no. 3 (2009): 247–73.

Bildhauer, Bettina. *Filming the Middle Ages*. London: Reaktion Books, 2011.

Bildhauer, Bettina. 'Medievalism and Cinema'. In *The Cambridge Companion to Medievalism*, edited by Louise D'Arcens, 45–59. Cambridge: Cambridge University Press, 2016.

Bildhauer, Bettina, and Chris Jones, eds *The Middle Ages in the Modern World: Twenty-First Century Perspectives*. Proceedings of the British Academy 208. Oxford: Oxford University Press, 2017.

Billcliffe, James. 'Kingdom Come Deliverance Guide'. *VG24/7*, 2018. https://www.vg247.com/2018/03/01/kingdom-come-deliverance-guide-tips-walkthrough/.

Blakemore, Erin. 'This Nasty Medieval Remedy Kills MRSA'. *Smithsonian*. https://www.smithsonianmag.com/smart-news/nasty-medieval-remedy-kills-mrsa-180954808/.

Bloom, J. M. *Arts of the City Victorious: Islamic Art and Architecture in Fatimid North Africa and Egypt*. New Haven, CN: Yale University Press, 2007.

Blumenfeld-Kosinski, Renate. *Not of Woman Born: Representations of Caesarean Birth in Medieval and Renaissance Culture*. Ithaca: Cornell University Press, 1991.

Bogost, Ian. 'The Rhetoric of Video Games'. In *The Ecology of Games: Connecting Youth, Games, and Learning*, edited by Katie Salen Tekinbaş, 117–40. Cambridge, MA: MIT Press, 2008.

Bonilla-Silva, Eduardo, and Tukufu Zuberi. 'Toward a Definition of White Logic and White Methods'. In *White Logic, White Methods: Racism and Methodology*, edited by Eduardo Bonilla-Silva and Tukufu Zuberi, 1–27. New York: Rowman & Littlefield, 2008.

Bonilla-Silva, Eduardo. 'Rethinking Racism: Toward a Structural Interpretation'. *American Sociological Review* 62, no. 3 (1997): 465–80.

Boothby, Richard. *Sex on the Couch*. London: Routledge, 2005.

Boss, Jeffrey. 'The Antiquity of Caesarean Section with Maternal Survival: The Jewish Tradition'. *Medical History* 5, no. 2 (1961): 117–31.

Bostan, Barbaros. 'Player Motivations: A Psychological Perspective'. *Computers in Entertainment* 7, no. 2 (2009): 1–26.

Bougard, François. *La justice dans le royaume d'Italie: de la fin du VIIIe siècle au début du XIe siècle*. Rome: Ecole française de Rome, 1995.
Bower, Walter. *A History Book for Scots: Selections from Scotichronicon*, edited by D. E. R. Watt. Edinburgh: Mercat Press, 1998.
Braun, Virginia, and Victoria Clarke. 'Using Thematic Analysis in Psychology'. *Qualitative Research in Psychology* 3, no. 2 (2006): 77–101.
Brown, Harry J. *Videogames and Education*. Armonk, NY: M. E. Sharpe, 2008.
Burdette, Matt. 'The Swayze Effect'. *Story Studio*, 18 November 2015. Available online: https://www.oculus.com/story-studio/blog/the-swayze-effect/?locale=en_GB (accessed 21 April 2020).
Burkart, Eric. 'Limits of Understanding in the Study of Lost Martial Arts: Epistemological Reflections on the Mediality of Historical Records of Technique and the Status of Modern (Re-)Constructions'. *Acta Periodica Duellatorum* 4, no. 2 (2016): 5–30.
Burkart, Eric. 'The Autograph of an Erudite Martial Artist: A Close Reading of Nuremberg, Germanisches Nationalmuseum, Hs. 3227a'. In *Late Medieval and Early Modern Fight Books: Transmission and Tradition of Martial Arts in Europe (14th–17th Centuries)*, edited by Daniel Jaquet, Karin Verelst, and Timothy Dawson, 451–80. Leiden: Brill, 2016.
Burkart, Eric. 'Zweikampfpraktiken zwischen sozialer Normierung, medialer Präsentation und wissenschaftlicher Einordnung'. In *Agon und Distinktion: Soziale Räume des Zweikampfs zwischen Mittelalter und Neuzeit*, edited by Uwe Israel and Christian Jaser, 4–14. Berlin: Lit Verlag, 2016.
Burn, Andrew. 'Playing Roles'. In *Computer Games: Text, Narrative, and Play*, edited by Diane Carr, 72–87. Cambridge: Polity, 2006.
Butler, R., ed. 'Annalium Hibernae Chronicon'. Irish Archaeological Society. 1849. 35–7. In *The Black Death*, edited by Rosemary Horrox, 84. Manchester: Manchester University Press, 1994.
Caldwell, David. 'The Wallace Sword'. In *The Wallace Book*, edited by E. J. Cowan. Edinburgh: Birlinn Limited, 2007.
Cameron, M. L. *Anglo Saxon Medicine*. Cambridge: University of Cambridge Press, 1993.
Cannadine, David, ed. *History and the Media: Conference Held in London in December 2002*. Basingstoke: Palgrave Macmillan, 2007.
Carr, Diane. 'The Trouble with Civilization'. In *Videogame, Player, Text*, edited by Barry Atkins and Tanya Krzywinska, 222–36. Manchester: Manchester University Press, 2007.
Carr, Edward Hallett. *What Is History?* New York: Vintage, 1961.
Carroll, Shiloh. 'Rewriting the Fantasy Archetype: George R. R. Martin, Neomedievalist Fantasy, and the Quest for Realism'. In *Fantasy and Science Fiction Medievalisms: From Isaac Asimov to a Game of Thrones*, edited by Helen Young, 59–76. New York, NY: Cambria, 2015.
Carroll, Shiloh. *Medievalism in A Song of Ice and Fire and Game of Thrones*. Medievalism, volume 12. Rochester, NY: D.S. Brewer, 2018.
Castle, Egerton. *Schools and Masters of Fence, from the Middle Ages to the Eighteenth Century*. London: Bell, 1885.
Cathala, Bruno, and Serge Laget. *Shadows Over Camelot Rulebook*. Days of Wonder, 2005.
Cembrzyński, Paweł. 'The Ecology of Mining. Human–Environmental Relations in the Medieval and Early Modern Mining in Central Europe'. *Kwartalnik Historii Kultury Materialnej* 67, no. 1 (2019): 17–39.

Champion, Erik. *Critical Gaming: Interactive History and Virtual Heritage*. Digital Research in the Arts and Humanities. Farnham: Ashgate, 2015.
Champion, Erik. 'Defining Cultural Agents for Virtual Heritage Environments'. *Presence* 24, no. 3 (2015): 179–86.
Chapman, Adam. 'Affording History: Civilization and the Ecological Epproach'. In *Playing with the Past: Digital Games and the Simulation of History*, edited by Matthew Kapell and Andrew B. R. Elliott, 61–73. New York, NY: Bloomsbury, 2013.
Chapman, Adam. *Digital Games as History: How Videogames Represent the Past and Offer Access to Historical Practice*. New York, NY: Routledge, 2016.
Chapman, Adam. 'Is Sid Meier's Civilization History?'. *Rethinking History* 17, no. 3 (2013): 312–32.
Chapman, Adam. 'Privileging Form Over Content: Analysing Historical Videogames'. *Journal of Digital Humanities* 1, no. 2 (2012): 42–6.
Chhabra, Deepak, Robert Healy, and Erin Sills. 'Staged Authenticity and Heritage Tourism'. *Annals of Tourism Research* 30, no. 3 (2003): 702–19.
Chiappelli A. 'Gli Ordinamenti Sanitari del Comune di Pistoia contro la Pestilenza del 1348', *Archivio Storico Italiano*, series 4, XX, 1887, 8–22. In *The Black Death*, edited by Rosemary Horrox, 194–203. Manchester: Manchester University Press, 1994.
Chris Jones, 'Is the Islamic State Medieval?', *Research the Headlines*, 18 September 2014, https://researchtheheadlines.org/2014/09/18/is-islamic-state-medieval/ (accessed 16 June 2018).
*Chronicon de Lanercost, MCCI–MCCCXLVI*, edited by Joseph Stevenson. Edinburgh: Edinburgh Printing Company, 1839.
Classen, Christoph, and Wulf Kansteiner. 'Truth and Authenticity in Contemporary Historical Culture: An Introduction to *Historical Representation and Historical Truth*'. *History and Theory* 48, no. 2 (May 2009): 1–4.
Clements, Pat. 'Authenticity'. In *Medievalism: Key Critical Terms*, edited by Elizabeth Emery and Richard Utz, 19–26. Cambridge: D. S. Brewer Editions, 2014.
Coakley, John. 'Mobilizing the Past: Nationalist Images of History'. *Nationalism and Ethnic Politics* 10, no. 4 (January 2004): 531–60.
Cohen, Jeffrey Jerome. *Of Giants: Sex, Monsters and the Middle Ages*. Minneapolis, MN: University of Minnesota Press, 1999.
Cole H., Lang, Tig. 'The Treating of Prince Henry's Arrow Wound, 1403'. *Journal of the Society of Archer Antiquaries* (2003): 95–101.
Constantine Porphyrogenitus. *De administrando imperio*, edited by Gyula Moravcsik, translated by R. J. H. Jenkins. Washington, DC: Dumbarton Oaks, 1967.
Continuum Heritage Attractions. *The Canterbury Tales*. Available at https://www.canterburytales.org.uk/ (accessed 26 February 2018).
Cook, Adam. 'Kingdom Come: Deliverance Beta – Dan Vávra Interview'. *Red Bull*, 2016. https://www.redbull.com/au-en/kingdom-come-deliverance-dan-vavra-interview.
Cooper, Victoria Elizabeth. 'Fantasies of the North: Medievalism and Identity in Skyrim'. Unpublished doctoral thesis, University of Leeds, 2016.
Copplestone, Tara Jane. 'But That's Not Accurate: The Differing Perceptions of Accuracy in Cultural-Heritage Videogames between Creators, Consumers and Critics'. *Rethinking History* 21, no. 3 (3 July 2017): 415–38.
Cosgrove, Denis. 'Modernity, Community and the Landscape Idea'. *Journal of Material Culture* 11, no. 1–2 (2006): 49–66.
Cosgrove, Denis. 'Prospect, Perspective and the Evolution of the Landscape Idea'. *Transactions of the Institute of British Geographers* 10, no. 1 (1985): 45–62.

Crawford, Chris. *Chris Crawford on Game Design*. Thousand Oaks, CA: Peachpit, 2003.
Cumming, Elizabeth S. 'Hole, William Fergusson Brassey'. Oxford Dictionary of National Biography. http://www.oxforddnb.com.ezproxy.is.ed.ac.uk/view/article/100749.
D'Arcens, Louise. *Comic Medievalism* Cambridge: Boydell and Brewer, 2014.
D'Arcens, Louise. 'Laughing in the Face of the Past: Satire and Nostalgia in Medieval Heritage Tourism'. *Postmedieval: A Journal of Medieval Cultural Studies* 2 (2011): 155–70.
D'Arcens, Louise, ed. *The Cambridge Companion to Medievalism*. Cambridge: Cambridge University Press, 2016.
D'Arcens, Louise. '"The Past Is a Different and Fairly Disgusting Country"'. In *Comic Medievalism Laughing at the Middle Ages*, 139–60. Woodbridge: Boydell and Brewer, 2014.
Daniel Floyd and James Portnow. 'Historical Games – Why Mechanics Must Be Both Good and Accurate'. *Extra Credits* 9, no. 6, 10 September 2014. Available online: https://www.youtube.com/watch?v=l8yl09GcI48 (accessed 10 May 2018).
Daniel Floyd and James Portnow. 'Strategic Uncertainty – Keeping Strategy Games Fresh'. *Extra Credits* 8, no. 18, 18 January 2017. Available online: https://www.youtube.com/watch?v=PJKTDz1zYzs (accessed 10 May 2018).
Darksword Armoury, 'The William Wallace Scottish Claymore Sword – Braveheart Sword (#1362)'. http://www.darksword-armory.com/medieval-weapon/medieval-swords/william-wallace-scottish-claymore-sword-braveheart-sword-1362/ (accessed 30 March 2018).
Davis, Natalie Zemon. '"Any Resemblance to Persons Living or Dead": Film and the Challenge of Authenticity'. *Historical Journal of Film, Radio and Television* 8, no. 3 (1988): 269–83.
Deacon, Jacob Henry. 'Prologues, Poetry, Prose and Portrayals: The Purposes of Fifteenth-Century Fight Books According to the Diplomatic Evidence'. *Acta Periodica Duellatorum* 4, no. 2 (2016): 69–90.
De Groot, Jerome. *Consuming History: Historians and Heritage in Contemporary Popular Culture*. New York, NY: Routledge, 2016.
de Lorris, Guillaume, and Jean de Meun. *The Romance of the Rose*. Translated by Charles Dahlberg. Princeton, NJ: Princeton University Press, 1971.
DeVries, Kelly and Robert Douglas Smith. *Medieval Military Technology*, 2nd edn. North York: University of Toronto Press, 2012.
Dey, Tapajit, Jacob Logan Massengill, and Audris Mockus. 'Analysis of Popularity of Game Mods: A Case Study'. In *Proceedings of the 2016 Annual Symposium on Computer-Human Interaction in Play Companion*, 133–9. New York, NY: ACM, 2016.
Domínguez, Ignacio X., Rogelio E. Cardona-Rivera, James K. Vance, and David L. Roberts. 'The Mimesis Effect: The Effect of Roles on Player Choice in Interactive Narrative Role-Playing Games'. *CHI '16: Proceedings of the 2016 CHI Conference on Human Factors in Computing Systems*, 3438–49. New York, NY: ACM, 2016.
Donnelly, Michael. *Scotland's Stained Glass: Making the Colours Sing*. Edinburgh: The Stationery Office /Historic Scotland, 2007.
Douglas, Christopher. '"You Have Unleashed a Horde of Barbarians!": Fighting Indians, Playing Games, Forming Disciplines'. *Postmodern Culture* 13, no. 1 (2002). doi:10.1353/pmc.2002.0029.
Douglas, Dante. '"Mordhau" and the Fantasy of an All-White Middle Ages'. *Vice*, 2019. https://www.vice.com/en_us/article/8xzpeg/mordhau-and-the-fantasy-of-an-all-white-middle-ages?__twitter_impression=true.

Douglas, L. 'Medieval Pregnancy Advice That Is Beyond Disturbing'. *Healthyway*, 5 April 2007. https://www.healthyway.com/content/medieval-pregnancy-advice-that-is-beyond-disturbing/ (accessed 13 October 2019).

Dow, Douglas M. 'Historical Veneers: Anachronism, Simulation, and Art History in Assassin's Creed II'. In *Playing with the Past: Digital Games and the Simulation of History*, edited by Matthew Wilhelm Kappell and Andrew B. R. Elliott, 215–32. New York: Bloomsbury, 2013.

Downes, Stephanie, and Helen Young. 'The Maiden Fair: Nineteenth-Century Medievalist Art and the Gendered Aesthetics of Whiteness in HBO's Game of Thrones'. *Postmedieval* 10, no. 2 (2019): 219–35.

Driver, Martha W. 'Historicity and Authenticity in Medieval Film'. In *The Medieval Hero on Screen: Representations from Beowulf to Buffy*, edited by Martha W. Driver and Sid Ray, 19–22. Jefferson, NC: McFarland, 2004.

Dukes-Knight, Jennifer. 'The Wooden Sword: Age and Masculinity in '*Táin Bó Cúailnge*''. *Proceedings of the Harvard Celtic Colloquium* 33 (2013): 107–122.

Dunsmore, Kevin. 'E3 2015: *Kingdom Come: Deliverance* Is *Skyrim* without Magic'. *Hardcore Gamer*, 26 June 2015. Available online: https://www.hardcoregamer.com/2015/06/26/e3-2015-kingdom-come-deliverance-is-skyrim-without-magic/155984 (accessed 22 April 2020).

Earl, Benjamin. 'Places Don't Have to Be True to Be True: The Appropriation of King Arthur and the Cultural'. In *Mass Market Medieval: Essays on the Middle Ages in Popular Culture*, edited by David Marshall, 102–12. Jefferson, NC: McFarland, 2007.

Egenfeldt-Nielsen, Simon. *Beyond Edutainment: Exploring the Educational Potential of Computer Games*. S.l.: Selbstverlag bei www.lulu.com, 2010.

Elema, Ariella. 'Trial by Battle in France and England'. Unpublished doctoral thesis, University of Toronto, 2012.

Elliott, Andrew B. R. 'Internet Medievalism and the White Middle Ages'. *History Compass* 16, no. 3 (March 2018): 124–41.

Elliott, Andrew B. R. *Medievalism, Politics and Mass Media: Appropriating the Middle Ages in the Twenty-First Century*. Cambridge: D.S. Brewer, 2017.

Elliott, Andrew B. R. 'Our Minds Are in the Gutter, But Some of Us Are Watching Starz: Sex, Violence and Dirty Medievalism'. In *Fantasy and Science Fiction Medievalisms: From Isaac Asimov to a Game of Thrones*, edited by Helen Young, 96–116. New York, NY: Cambria, 2015.

Elliott, Andrew B. R. *Remaking the Middle Ages: The Methods of Cinema and History in Portraying the Medieval World*. Jefferson: McFarland, 2011.

Elliott, Andrew B. R. and Matthew Kapell. 'Introduction: To Build a Past That Will "Stand the Test of Time"- Discovering Historical Facts, Assembling Historical Narratives', in Sid Meier's Colonization'. In *Playing with the Past: Digital Games and the Simulation of History*, edited by Matthew Kapell and Andrew B. R. Elliott, 1–29. New York, NY: Bloomsbury, 2013.

Ellison, Katherine; Martin, Nina. 'Lost Mothers: Severe Complications for Women During Childbirth Are Skyrocketing – And Could Often Be Prevented'. *ProPublica*, 22 December 2017. https://www.propublica.org/article/severe-complications-for-women-during-childbirth-are-skyrocketing-and-could-often-be-prevented.

Emrich, Alan. 'MicroProse' Strategic Space Opera is Rated XXXX!'. *Computer Gaming World* 110 (1993): 92–3.

Ende, Teresa, and Müller, Jürgen. 'En Garde! Duelldarstellungen in der bildenden Kunst und im Film'. In *Das Duell. Ehrenkämpfe vom Mittelalter bis zur Moderne*, edited by

Ulrike Ludwig, Barbara Krug-Richter, and Gerd Schwerhoff, 325–47. Konstanz: UVK Verlaggesellschaft, 2010.

Estonian Tourist Board. 'Talin Old Town'. *Visit Estonia: Official Tourist Information Website*. Available at https://www.visitestonia.com/en/where-to-go/tallinn/tallinn-old-town (accessed 26 February 2018).

Evans, Ruth. 'Gigantic Origins: An Annotated Translation of *De origine gigantum*'. *Arthurian Literature* 16 (1998): 191–211.

ExpertExpat. May 2017, comment on Erin Blakemore, 'This Nasty Medieval Remedy Kills MRSA'. *Smithsonian*. https://www.smithsonianmag.com/smart-news/nasty-medieval-remedy-kills-mrsa-180954808/.

Farrow, Robert and Ioanna Iacovides. 'Gaming and the Limit of Digital Embodiment'. *Philosophy & Technology* 27 (2013): 221–33.

Ferreday, Debra. 'Game of Thrones, Rape Culture and Feminist Fandom'. *Australian Feminist Studies* 30, no. 83 (2 January 2015): 21–36.

Field, P. J. C. *Malory: Texts and Sources*. Cambridge: D. S. Brewer, 1998.

Fife, Wayne. 'Semantic Slippage as a New Aspect of Authenticity: Viking Tourism on the Northern Peninsula of Newfoundland'. *Journal of Folklore Research* 41, no. 1 (2004): 61–84.

Finke, Laurie A., and Martin B. Shichtman. 'Inner-City Chivalry in Gil Junger's Black Knight: A South Central Yankee in King Leo's Court'. In *Race, Class, and Gender in 'Medieval' Cinema*, edited by Lynn Ramey and Tison Pugh, 107–22. Basingstoke: Palgrave Macmillan, 2007.

Fisher, Will. 'The Renaissance Beard: Masculinity in Early Modern England'. *Renaissance Quarterly* 54, no. 1 (2001): 155–87.

Fitzpatrick, KellyAnn. 'Game of Thrones: Neomedievalism and the Myths of Inheritance'. In *Neomedievalism, Popular Culture, and the Academy*, 103–40. Woodbridge: Boydell and Brewer, 2019.

Fitzpatrick, KellyAnn. *Neomedievalism, Popular Culture, and the Academy: From Tolkien to Game of Thrones*. Medievalism, volume XVI. Rochester, NY: D.S. Brewer, 2019.

Fogu, Claudio. 'Digitizing Historical Consciousness'. *History and Theory* 48, no. 2 (2009): 103–21.

Ford, Dom. '"eXplore, eXpand, eXploit, eXterminate": Affective Writing of Postcolonial History and Education in Civilization V'. *Game Studies* 16, no. 2 (2017). http://gamestudies.org/1602/articles/ford.

Forgeng, Jeffrey L. 'Owning the Art: The German *Fechtbuch* Tradition'. In *The Noble Art of the Sword: Fashion and Fencing in Renaissance Europe*, edited by Tobias Capwell, 164–75. London: Wallace Collection, 2012.

Foster, Tara. '"Kaamelott"'s Global Fifth Century'. *Arthuriana* 25, no. 1 (2015): 5–21.

*Four Middle English Romances: Sir Isumbras, Octavian, Sir Eglamour of Artois, Sir Tryamour*, edited by Harriet Hudson. Kalamazoo, MI: Medieval Institute Publications, 2006.

Frankel, Valerie Estelle. *Women in Game of Thrones: Power, Conformity and Resistance*. Jefferson, NC: McFarland, 2014.

Frasca, G. 'Simulation versus Narrative'. In *The Video Game Theory Reader*, edited by M. Wolf and B. Perron, 221–35. New York, NY: Routledge, 2003.

Fromme, Johannes. 'Computer Games as a Part of Children's Culture'. *Game Studies* 3, no. 2 (2003): 1–22.

Fugelso, Karl, and Carol L. Robinson, eds *Medievalism in Technology Old and New*. Studies in Medievalism XVI. Rocheter, NY: D.S. Brewer, 2008.

Fullerton, Tracy. Game Design Workshop: *A Playcentric Approach to Creating Innovative Games*. Boca Raton, FL: CRC Press, 2014.
Funk, John. 'Skyrim Mod Turns Dragons into Thomas the Tank Engine'. *Polygon*, 9 December 2013. Available online: https://www.polygon.com/2013/12/9/5192710/skyrim-mod-turns-dragons-into-thomas-the-tank-engine (accessed 22 April 2020).
Ganim, John. *Medievalism and Orientalism*. New York: Palgrave Macmillan, 2005.
Ganshof, François Louis. *Frankish Institutions under Charlemagne*. New York, NY: W.W. Norton, 1970.
Geary, Patrick J. *The Myth of Nations: The Medieval Origins of Europe*. Princeton, NJ: Princeton University Press, 2003.
Geary, Patrick. *Women at the Beginning: Origin Myths from the Amazons to the Virgin Mary*. Princeton, NJ: Princeton University Press, 2006.
Gee, James Paul. *What Video Games Have to Teach Us About Learning and Literacy*. New York, NY: Palgrave Macmillan, 2003.
*Gesta Henrici Quinti: The Deeds of Henry the Fifth*, edited and translated by Frank Taylor and John S. Roskell. Oxford: Clarendon Press, 1975.
Getz, Donald. 'Geographic Perspectives on Event Tourism'. In *A Companion to Tourism*, edited by Alan A. Lew, Michael Hall and Allen Williams, 410–22. Massachusetts: Blackwell Publishing Ltd., 2004.
Gibson, James. *The Ecological Approach Visual to Perception*. Boston, MA: Houghton Mifflin, 1979.
Given-Wilson, Chris. *Chronicles: The Writing of History in Medieval England*. London: Hambledon, 2004.
Goebel, Stefan. *The Great War and Medieval Memory*. Cambridge: Cambridge University Press, 2007.
Gonzalez, Susan. 'Director Spike Lee Slams 'Same Old' Black Stereotypes in Today's Films'. *Yale Bulletin & Calendar* 29, no. 21. Yale University, 2 March 2001.
Gottlieb, Owen and I. Schreiber. 'Designing Analog Learning Games: Genre Affordances, Limitations, and Multi-Game Approaches'. In *Rerolling Boardgames*, edited by E. MacCallum-Steward and D. Brown. Jeferson, NC: McFarland Press, Forthcoming.
Gottlieb, Owen. 'Design-Based Research: Mobile Gaming for Learning Jewish History, Tikkun Olam, and Civics'. In *Methods for Studying Video Games and Religion*, edited by Vít Šisler, Kerstin Radde-Antweiler, and Xenia Zeiler, 83–100. New York, NY: Routledge, 2017.
Gottlieb, Owen. 'Finding Lost & Found: Designer's Notes from the Process of Creating a Jewish Game for Learning'. *Gamevironments*, Special Issue: Jewish Gamevironments (2017) 42–65.
Gottlieb, Owen. 'Jewish Games for Learning: Renewing Heritage Traditions in the Digital Age'. In *Digital Judaism: Jewish Negotiations with Digital Media and Culture*, edited by Heidi Campbell, 91–109. Routledge Studies in Religion and Digital Culture. New York, NY: Routledge, 2015.
Gottlieb, Owen. 'Who Really Said What? Mobile Historical Situated Documentary as Liminal Learning Space'. *Gamevironments*, 5 (December 2016): 237–57.
Gottlieb, Owen and I. Schreiber. 'Prosocial Religion and Games: Lost & Found'. *Well Played: A Journal on Video Games, Value, and Meaning* 7 (2018): 17–41.
Graham, Shawn. 'Review of Evolving Planet [game]'. *Internet Archaeology* 42 (2016). Available online: https://doi.org/10.11141/ia.42.4 (accessed 28 March 2018).
Grattan, J. H. G., Singer, Charles. *Anglo-Saxon Magic and Medicine*. London: Folcroft Library Editions, 1952.

Graves, Robert. *I, Claudius*. London: Penguin, 2006.
Grayson, Nathan. 'Dragon Age III's Gaider On the Impracticality Of Sexism'. *Rock, Paper, Shotgun*, 2013. http://www.rockpapershotgun.com/2013/03/28/dragon-age-iiis-gaider-on-the-impracticality-of-sexism/.
Grayson, Nathan. 'Kingdom Come Owes Its Popularity to "Realism" and Conservative Politics'. *Kotaku Australia*, 2018. https://www.kotaku.com.au/2018/03/kingdom-come-owes-its-popularity-torealism-and-conservative-politics/.
Green, Monica. 'The Art of Medicine: Midwives and Obstetric Catastrophe', *The Lancet*, 372. https://www.thelancet.com/pdfs/journals/lancet/PIIS0140-6736(08)61467-1.pdf (accessed 14 July 2018).
Green, Monica. *Making Women's Medicine Masculine: The Rise of Male Authority in Pre-Modern Gynaecology*. Oxford: Oxford University Press, 2008.
Green, Monica. *The Trotula: An English Translation of the Medieval Compendium of Women's Medicine*. Philadelphia: University of Pennsylvania Press, 2002.
Green, Monica. *Women's Healthcare in the Medieval West*. New York: Ashgate, 2000.
Gregg, Joan Young. *Devils, Women, and Jews: Reflections of the Other in Medieval Sermon Stories*. New York, NY: SUNY Press, 1997.
Gregory, Philippa. *The White Queen*. London: Simon and Schuster, 2009.
Grmek, Mirko (ed.). *Western Medical Thought from Antiquity to the Middle Ages*, translated by Antony Shugaar. Cambridge, MA: Harvard University Press, 1998.
Hale, John R. *Artists and Warfare in the Renaissance*. New Haven, CT: Yale University Press, 1990.
Halewood, Chris and Kevin Hannam. 'Viking Heritage Tourism: Authenticity and Commodification'. *Annals of Tourism Research* 28, no. 3 (2001): 565–80.
Hamilton, William. *Blind Harry's Wallace*. Edinburgh: Luath Press Ltd, 1998.
Hanawalt, Barbara A. *Women and Work in Preindustrial Europe*. Bloomington, IN: Indiana University Press, 1986.
Härke, Heinrich. 'Anglo-Saxon Immigration and Ethnogenesis'. *Medieval Archaeology* 55 (2011): 1–28.
Harrison, L. S. *Public Commemorations of the Scottish Wars of Independence, 1800–1939*. PhD thesis, University of Edinburgh, Edinburgh, 2019.
Haydock, Nickolas A. 'Arthurian Melodrama, Chaucerian Spectacle, and the Waywardness of Cinematic Pastiche in *First Knight* and *A Knight's Tale*'. *Studies in Medievalism XII: Film and Fiction, Reviewing the Middle Ages*, edited by Tom Shippey, 5–38. Woodbridge: Boydell, 2003.
Haydock, Nickolas. *Movie Medievalism: The Imaginary Middle Ages*. Jefferson, NC: McFarland, 2008.
Hester, James. 'The Terminology of Medieval English Fight Texts: A Brief Overview'. In *'Can these Bones Come to Life?': Insights from Reconstruction, Reenactment, and Re-creation, Volume 1: Historical European Martial Arts*, edited by Ken Mondschein, 70–9. Wheaton, IL: Freelance Academy Press, 2014.
Higgin, T. 'Blackless Fantasy: The Disappearance of Race in Massively Multiplayer Online Role-Playing Games'. *Games and Culture* 4, no. 1 (2008): 3–26.
Higson, Andrew. '"Medievalism", The Period Film and the British Past in Contemporary Cinema'. In *Medieval Film*, edited by Anke Bernau and Bettina Bildhauer, 203–24. Manchester: Manchester University Press, 2009.
Hilbig, Benjamin E. 'Sad, Thus True: Negativity Bias in Judgments of Truth'. *Journal of Experimental Social Psychology* 45, no. 4 (2009): 983–6.

Hill, Melvin G. 'Tale of Two Fathers: Authenticating Fatherhood in Quantic Dream's Heavy Rain: The Origami Killer and Naughty Dog's The Last of Us'. In *Pops in Pop Culture*, edited by Elizabeth Podnieks, 159–76. New York, NY: Palgrave, 2016.

Hoadley, Christopher. 'Design-Based Research'. Presented at the ECT PhD Colloquium. New York University, 2013.

Hoadley, Christopher. 'Fostering Productive Collaboration Offline and Online: Learning from Each Other'. In *Internet Environments for Science Education*, edited by Marcia Linn, Elizabeth A. Davis, and Philip Bell, 145–74. Mahway, NJ: Lawrence Erlbaum Associates, Inc., 2004.

Hoadley, Christopher. 'Methodological Alignment in Design-Based Research'. *Educational Psychologist*, 39 (December, 2004): 203–12.

Hoeniger, R. (editor). 'Der Schwarze Tod', Berlin, 1882, Appendix III. 152–6. In *The Black Death*, edited by Rosemary Horrox, 158–63. Manchester: Manchester University Press, 1994.

Holo, Joshua. 'Rabbi Owen Gottlieb: Playing with Judaism in the Digital Age'. *Bully Pulpit Podcast: Torah with a Point of View*. Available online: https://collegecommons.huc.edu/bully_pulpit/judaism-in-digital-age/ (accessed 22 April 2020).

Houghton, Robert. 'Crusader Kings Too? (Mis)Representations of the Crusades in Grand Strategy Games'. In *Playing the Crusades*, edited by Robert Houghton. Engaging the Crusades 7. London: Routledge, Forthcoming.

Houghton, Robert. 'It's What You Do with It That Counts: Factual Accuracy and Mechanical Accuracy in Crusader Kings II'. *The Public Medievalist*, 30 September 2014. Available online: https://www.publicmedievalist.com/ckii-houghton/ (accessed 10 May 2018).

Houghton, Robert, ed. *Playing the Crusades*. Engaging the Crusades 7. London: Routledge, Forthcoming.

Houghton, Robert. 'Where Did You Learn That? The Self-Perceived Educational Impact of Historical Computer Games on Undergraduates'. *Gamevironments* 5 (2016): 8–45.

Houghton, Robert. 'World, Structure and Play: A Framework for Games as Historical Research Outputs, Tools, and Processes'. *Práticas Da História* 7 (2018): 11–43.

Hughey, Matthew. 'Cinethetic Racism: White Redemption and Black Stereotypes in 'Magical Negro' Films', *Social Problems* 25, no. 3 (2009): 543–77.

Icelandic Saga & Heritage Association. *Saga & Heritage Sites and Centers in Iceland*. Available at http://www.sagatrail.is/en/ (accessed 26 February 2018).

Ingold, Tim. *The Perception of the Environment*. London: Routledge, 2000.

Innes, Matthew. 'Charlemagne's Government'. In Charlemagne: Empire and Society, edited by Joanna Story, 71–89. Manchester: Manchester University Press, 2005.

Iwaniuk, Phil. 'The Obsessive Historical Accuracy of Kingdom Come: Deliverance, and How It Makes for a Better RPG'. *PCGamesN*, 2016. https://www.pcgamesn.com/kingdom-come-deliverance/kingdom-come-deliverance-historical-accuracy?amp.

Jansen, Dennis. 'How Fantasy Games Deal with Race: As Demonstrated by The Elder Scrolls'. *First Person Scholar*, 12 December 2018. Available online: http://www.firstpersonscholar.com/how-fantasy-games-deal-with-race/ (accessed 5 April 2019).

Jaquet, Daniel and Deluz, Vincent. 'Moving in Late Medieval Harness: Exploration of a Lost Embodied Knowledge'. *Journal of Embodied Research* 1, no. 1 (2018). Available online: https://jer.openlibhums.org/article/10.16995/jer.7/ (accessed 18 October 19).

Jaquet, Daniel. 'Combattre en armure à la fin du Moyen Âge et au début de la Renaissance d'après les livres du combat'. Unpublished doctoral thesis, Université de Genève, 2013.

Jóhanesson, Gunnar Thór et al. 'Icelandic Tourism: Past Directions – Future Challenges'. *Tourism Geographies* 12, no. 2 (2010): 278–301.
Johnson, Steven. *Everything Bad Is Good for You: How Today's Popular Culture Is Actually Making Us Smarter*. New York, NY: Riverhead, 2006.
Joinville, Jean. *The Life of St Louis*. London: Sheed and Ward, 1955.
Jones, Robert W. *Bloodied Banners: Martial Display on the Medieval Battlefield*. Woodbridge: Boydell, 2010.
Juul, Jesper. *Half-Real: Video Games between Real Rules and Fictional Worlds*. Cambridge, MA: MIT Press, 2005.
Kalay, Yehuda and John Marx. 'Architecture and the Internet: Designing Places in Cyberspace'. *First Monday Special Issue* 5 (2005). Available online: http://firstmonday.org/ojs/index.php/fm/article/view/1563 (accessed 28 March 2018).
Kanai, Seiji. *Love Letter Rulebook*. Alderac Entertainment Group, 2012.
Kapell, M. and A. Elliott eds *Playing with the Past: Digital Games and the Simulation of History*. New York, NY: Bloomsbury, 2013.
Karasu24. 'Enhanced Blood Textures'. *Nexus Mods Forums*. Available online: https://forums.nexusmods.com/index.php?/topic/457817-enhanced-blood-textures/page-36#entry4157769 (accessed 22 April 2020).
Kaufman, Amy S. 'Our Future Is Our Past: Corporate Medievalism in Dystopian Fiction'. In *Corporate Medievalism II*, Studies in Medievalism XXII, 11–20. Woodbridge: Boydell and Brewer, 2013.
Kaufman, Amy. 'Purity'. In *Medievalism: Key Critical Terms*, edited by Elizabeth Emery and Richard Utz, 199–206. Cambridge: D. S. Brewer, 2014.
Kears, Carl, and James Paz, eds *Medieval Science Fiction*. King's College London Medieval Studies, XXIV. London: King's College London, Centre for Late Antique & Medieval Studies, 2016.
Keen, Maurice. *Chivalry*. New Haven, CT: Yale University Press, 1984.
Keller, Hagen. 'Grundlagen ottonischer Königsherrschaft'. In *Reich und Kirche vor dem Investiturstreit: Vorträge beim wissenschaftlichen Kolloquium aus Anlass des achtzigsten Geburtstags von Gerd Tellenbach*, edited by Karl Schmid, 17–34. Sigmaringen: J. Thorbecke, 1985.
Kellett, Rachel E. '"... Vnnd schüß im vnder dem schwert den ort lang ein zů der brust": The Placement and Consequences of Sword-blows in Sigmund Ringeck's Fifteenth-Century Fencing Manual'. In *Wounds and Wound Repair in Medieval Culture*, edited by Larissa Tracy and Kelly DeVries, 128–49. Leiden: Brill, 2015.
Kelly, A. Keith. 'Beyond History Accuracy: A Postmodern View of Movies and Medievalism'. *Perspicuitas* (2004). http://www.perspicuitas.uni-essen.de/medievalism/articles/Kelly_Beyond%20Historical%20Accuracy.pdf.
King, Laura, and Gary Rivett. 'Engaging People in Making History: Impact, Public Engagement and the World Beyond the Campus'. *History Workshop Journal* 80, no. 1 (October 2015): 218–33.
'Kingdom Come: Deliverance – Historical Accuracy Isn't Whitewashing : Kingdomcome'. *Reddit*, 2018. https://www.reddit.com/r/kingdomcome/comments/7zgt4f/kingdom_come_deliverance_historical_accuracy_isnt/.
Kleinau, Jens Peter. 'Visualised Motion: Iconography of Medieval and Renaissance Fencing Books'. In *Late Medieval and Early Modern Fight Books: Transmission and Tradition of Martial Arts in Europe (14th–17th Centuries)*, edited by Daniel Jaquet, Karin Verelst, and Timothy Dawson, 88–116. Leiden: Brill, 2016.

Klíma, Martin, and Daniel Vávra. 'Statement by Daniel Vávra and Martin Klíma Regarding Racism/Nazism Accusations (Gamestar.De)'. *ResetEra*, 2018. https://www.resetera.com/threads/statement-by-daniel-vávra-and-martin-klíma-regarding-racism-nazism-accusations-gamestar-de.17259/.

Kline, Daniel T. 'Participatory Medievalism, Role-Playing, and Digital Gaming'. In *The Cambridge Companion to Medievalism*, edited by Louise D'Arcens, 75–88. Cambridge: Cambridge University Press, 2016.

Kline, Daniel T. 'Virtually Medieval: *The Age of Kings* Interprets the Middle Ages'. In *Mass Market Medieval Essays on the Middle Ages in Popular Culture*, edited by David W. Marshall, 154–70. Jefferson, NC: McFarland, 2007.

Kline, Daniel T., ed. *Digital Gaming Re-Imagines the Middle Ages*. Routledge Studies in New Media and Cyberculture 15. New York: Routledge, 2014.

Knight, Stephen. 'Parody and Archery: Re-Generating the Robin Hood Tradition'. In *Robin Hood in Outlawed Spaces: Media, Performance, and Other New Directions*, edited by Lesley Coote and Valerie B. Johnson, 191–208. Abingdon: Routledge, 2017.

Koziol, Geoffrey. 'Is Robert I in Hell?: The Diploma for Saint-Denis and the Mind of a Rebel King (Jan. 25, 923)'. *Early Medieval Europe* 14, no. 3 (2006): 233–67.

Krosnick, Jon A., and Stanley Presser. 'Question and Questionnaire Design'. In *Handbook of Survey Research*, edited by Peter H. Rossi, James D. Wright, and Andy B. Anderson, 2nd edn, 263–313. Emerald, 2010.

Kruger, Steven F. *The Spectral Jew: Conversion and Embodiment in Medieval Europe*. Minneapolis: University of Minnesota Press, 2006.

Kuefler, Matthew S. '"A Wyred Existence": Attitudes toward Children in Anglo-Saxon England'. *Journal of Social History* 24, no. 4 (1991): 823–34

LaMarre, Heather L., and Kristen D. Landreville. 'When Is Fiction as Good as Fact? Comparing the Influence of Documentary and Historical Reenactment Films on Engagement, Affect, Issue Interest, and Learning'. *Mass Communication and Society* 12, no. 4 (2009): 537–55.

Lange, Patricia G. 'Learning Real-Life Lessons From Online Games'. *Games and Culture* 6, no. 1 (2011): 17–37.

Larrington, Carolyne. 'Mediating Medieval(Ized) Emotion in Game of Thrones'. In *Authenticity, Medievalism, Music*, Studies in Medievalism XXVII, 35–42. Woodbridge: Boydell and Brewer, 2018.

Le Goff, Jacques. *Time, Work, and Culture of the Middle Ages*. Chicago: The University of Chicago Press, 1980.

Lee, John K. and Jeffrey Probert. 'Civilization III and Whole-Class Play'. *The Journal of Social Studies Research* 34, no. 1 (2010): 1–28.

Lees, Dominic. 'Cinema and Authenticity: Anxieties in the Making of Historical Film'. *Journal of Media Practice* 17, no. 2–3 (September 2016): 199–212.

Leftwich, Mariruth. 'New Intersections for History Education in Museums'. *Journal of Museum Education* 41, no. 3 (2 July 2016): 146–51.

Leung, Shing-On. 'A Comparison of Psychometric Properties and Normality in 4-, 5-, 6-, and 11-Point Likert Scales'. *Journal of Social Service Research* 37, no. 4 (2011): 412–21.

Lewis, Michael John. 'Identity and Status in the Bayeux Tapestry: The Iconographic and Artefactual Evidence'. *Anglo-Norman Studies* 29 (2007): 100–120.

Leyser, Karl. *Rule and Conflict in an Early Medieval Society: Ottonian Saxony*. Oxford: Blackwell, 1989.

Liberty Entertainment Group. 'The Early Days: Toronto's Camelot'. Casa Loma: *Toronto's Majestic Castle*. Available at http://casaloma.ca/camelot.html (accessed 26 February 2018).

London, British Library. MS Additional 39564.

London, British Library. MS Harley 3542, fols 82ʳ–85ʳ

Longan, Michael. 'Playing With Landscape: Social Process and Spatial Form in Video Games'. *Aether: The Journal of Media Geography* 2 (2008): 23–40.

Lubar, Stephen, and David Kingery. *History from Things: Essays on Material Culture*, edited by Stephen Lubar and David Kingery. Washington, DC: Smithsonian Books, 1995.

Lucat, Bertrand and Mads Haahr. 'What Makes a Successful Emergent Narrative: The Case of Crusader Kings II'. In *Interactive Storytelling*, edited by Henrik Schoenau-Fog, Luis Emilio Bruni, Sandy Louchart, and Sarune Baceviciute, 259–66. Cham: Springer, 2015.

Lynch, Andrew. *Malory's Book of Arms: The Narrative of Combat in 'Le Morte Darthur'*. Cambridge: Brewer, 1997.

MacDonald, C. 'The Haunting Remains of a Medieval Woman Who Had a Hole Drilled into Her Skull at 38 Weeks Pregnant and 'Gave Birth' After She Was Buried'. *Dailymail .com*, 10 December 2018. https://www.dailymail.co.uk/sciencetech/article-5547203 /Medieval-woman-hole-drilled-skull-38-weeks-pregnant-gave-birth-death.html (accessed 13 October 2019).

MacLean, Simon. 'Legislation and Politics in Late Carolingian Italy: The Ravenna Constitutions'. *Early Medieval Europe* 18, no. 4 (2010): 394–416.

Magnusson, Magnus. *Scotland: The Story of a Nation*. London: HarperCollins, 2000.

Make it York Ltd. Visit York: York's Official Visitor Information Service. Available at www.visityork.org (accessed 26 February 2018).

Malory, Thomas. *Le Morte D'Arthur*. 1485.

Malory, Thomas. *Le Morte Darthur*, edited by P. J. C. Field. Cambridge: Brewer, 2017.

Mantel, Hilary. *Wolf Hall*. London: Harper Collins, 2009.

Marcus, Alan S., Scott Alan Metzger, Richard J. Paxton, and Jeremy D. Stoddard. *Teaching History with Film: Strategies for Secondary Social Studies*. London: Routledge, 2018.

Marshall, David W. 'A World Unto Itself: Autopoetic Systems and Secondary Worlds in *Dungeons and Dragons*'. In *Mass Market Medieval: Essays in the Middle Ages in Popular Culture*, edited by David W. Marshall, 171–85. Jefferson, NC: McFarland and Co., 2007.

Martin, G. R. R. 'Introduction'. In *Mediations on Middle-Earth*, edited by Karen Haber, 1–5. New York, NY: St Martin's, 2001.

Martin Wainwright, A. 'Teaching Historical Theory through Video Games'. *The History Teacher* 47, no. 4 (2014): 579–612.

Maslen, R. W. 'Armour That Doesn't Work: An Anti-meme in Medieval and Renaissance Romance'. In *Medieval into Renaissance: Essays for Helen Cooper*, edited by Andy King and Matthew Woodcock, 35–54. Cambridge: D. S. Brewer, 2016.

Matthews, David. *Medievalism: A Critical History*. Cambridge: D. S. Brewer Editions, 2015.

Matthews, David. 'Middle'. In *Medievalism: Key Critical Terms*, edited by Elizabeth Emery and Richard Utz, 141–7. Cambridge: D. S. Brewer Editions, 2014.

McAvoy, Liz Herbert and Diane Watt eds *The History of British Women's Writing, 700–1500*. New York, NY: Palgrave MacMillan, 2011.

McCall, Jeremiah. 'Historical Simulations as Problem Spaces: Criticism and Classroom Use'. *Journal of Digital Humanities* 1, no. 2 (2012). http://journalofdigitalhumanities.org /1-2/historical-simulations-as-problem-spaces-by-jeremiah-mccall/.

McCall, Jeremiah. 'Teaching History with Digital Historical Games: An Introduction to the Field and Best Practices'. *Simulation & Gaming* 47, no. 4 (2016): 517–42.

McCall, Jeremiah and Adam Chapman. 'Discussion: Historical Accuracy and Historical Video Games (Part 1)'. *Gaming the Past*, 26 December 2017. Available online: https://gamingthepast.net/2017/12/26/discussion-what-is-historical-accuracy-in-an-historical-video-game-part-1/ (accessed 13 February 2018).

McLaughlan, Robert and Denise Kirkpatrick. 'Online Roleplay: Design for Active Learning'. *European Journal of Engineering Education* 29, no. 4 (2004): 477–90.

McLaughlan, Robert and Denise Kirkpatrick. 'Peer Learning Using Computer Supported Roleplay Simulations'. In *Peer Learning in Higher Education: Learning from and with Each Other*, edited by David Boud, Ruth Cohen, and Jane Sampson, 141–55. Hoboken, NJ: Taylor and Francis, 2014.

McMichael, Andrew. 'PC Games and the Teaching of History'. *The History Teacher* 40, no. 2 (2007): 203–18.

Medieval Times Dinner and Tournament. *Medieval Times Dinner and Tournament* (2018). Available at https://www.medievaltimes.com/about-medieval-times/index.html (accessed 26 February 2018).

Meyer, Stephen. 'Soundscapes of Middle Earth: The Question of Medievalist Music in Peter Jackson's Lord of the Rings Films'. In *Defining Medievalism(s) II*, Studies in Medievalism XVIII, 165–87. Woodbridge: Boydell and Brewer, 2009.

Middleton, William. *Guide to the National Wallace Monument*. Stirling: W. Middleton, 1909.

Mir, Rebecca and Trevor Owens. 'Modeling Indigenous Peoples: Unpacking Ideology in Sid Meier's Colonization'. In *Playing with the Past: Digital Games and the Simulation of History*, edited by Matthew Kapell and Andrew B. R. Elliott, 91–106. New York, NY: Bloomsbury, 2013.

Miss Cellania. 'The Historical Horror of Childbirth'. *Mental Floss*, 9 May 2013. http://mentalfloss.com/article/50513/historical-horror-childbirth (accessed 13 October 2019).

Mitchell, Piers. *Medicine in the Crusades*. Cambridge: Cambridge University Press, 2005.

Moberly, Kevin and Brent Moberly. 'Play'. In *Medievalism: Key Critical Terms*, edited by Elizabeth Emery and Richard Utz, 173–80. Cambridge: D. S. Brewer Editions, 2014.

Monagle, C., D'Arcens, L. '"Medieval" Makes a Comeback in Modern Politics: What's Going On?', *The Conversation*, 22 September 2014. https://theconversation.com/medieval-makes-a-comeback-in-modern-politics-whats-going-on-31780 (accessed 8 May 2018).

Mondschein, Ken. *Game of Thrones and the Medieval Art of War*. Jefferson, NC: McFarland, 2018.

Moore, Diane. *Overcoming Religious Illiteracy: A Cultural Studies Approach to the Study of Religion in Secondary Education*. New York, NY: Palgrave Macmillan, 2007.

Morris, Megan L. 'Chivalric Terrors', In *Defining Neomedievalism(s) II*, Studies in Medievalism XX, 61–78. Woodbridge: Boydell and Brewer, 2011.

Morton, Graeme. *William Wallace: A National Tale*. Edinburgh: Edinburgh University Press Ltd, 2014.

Murray, Janet. *Hamlet on the Holodeck: The Future of Narrative in Cyberspace*. New York, NY: The Free Press, 1997.

Nakamura, Lisa. 'Race in/for Cyberspace: Identity Tourism and Racial Passing on the Internet'. In *Reading Digital Culture*, edited by David Trend, 226–35. Keyworks in Cultural Studies 4. Malden, MA: Blackwell, 2001.

Nall, Catherine. *Reading and War in Fifteenth-Century England, from Lydgate to Malory*. Woodbridge: Brewer, 2012.
National Galleries Scotland. 'About the Portrait Gallery', accessed 15 November 2016. https://www.nationalgalleries.org/visit/about-the-portrait-gallery/.
National Records of Scotland. 'Wallace and Bruce Memorial: Edinburgh Castle', RF2/14.
Nelson, Janet L. *Charles the Bald*. London: Longman, 1992.
*Norstead: A Viking Village and Port of Trade*. Available at http://www.norstead.com/main.asp (accessed 26 February 2018).
North, Janice, Karl Alvestad, and Elena Woodacre, eds *Premodern Rulers and Postmodern Viewers*. New York, NY: Springer, 2018.
Nuryanti, Windu. 'Heritage and Postmodern Tourism'. *Annals of Tourism Research* 23, no. 2 (1996): 249–60.
Nutton, Vivian. *Ancient Medicine*. New York: Routledge, 2004.
O'Mara, Veronica. 'A Middle English Text Written by a Female Scribe'. *Notes and Queries* 37, no. 3 (1990): 396–8.
Ortega, Stephen. 'Representing the Past: Video Games Challenge to the Historical Narrative'. *Syllabus* 4, no. 1 (2015): 1–13.
Pagès, Meriem, and Karolyn Kinane, eds *The Middle Ages on Television: Critical Essays*. Jefferson, NC: McFarland, 2015.
Pagnotti, John and William B. Russell. 'Using Civilization IV to Engage Students in World History Content'. *The Social Studies* 103, no. 1 (2012): 39–48.
Paradis, Thomas W. 'Theming, Tourism, and Fantasy City'. In *A Companion to Tourism*, edited by Alan A. Lew, Michael Hall and Allen Williams, 195–209. Massachusetts: Blackwell Publishing Ltd., 2004.
Paradox Interactive. 'Dev Diary no.9: Lifestyles'. *Crusader Kings III*, 14 January 2020. Available online: https://www.crusaderkings.com/news/dev-diary-9-lifestyles (accessed on 22 April 2020).
Park, Chang Sup. 'Applying 'Negativity Bias' to Twitter: Negative News on Twitter, Emotions, and Patterson, Serina. 'Women, Queerness, and Massive Chalice: Medievalism in Participatory Culture'. In *Medievalism on the Margins*, Studies in Medievalism XXIV, 63–74. Woodbridge: Boydell and Brewer, 2015.
Political Learning'. *Journal of Information Technology & Politics* 12, no. 4 (2015): 342–59.
Pearce, Celia. 'Towards a Game Theory of Game'. In *First Person: New Media as Story, Performance, and Game*, edited by Noah Wardrip-Fruin and Pat Harrigan, 143–53. Cambridge, MA: MIT Press, 2004.
Peppiatt, Dom. 'Kingdom Come: Deliverance Is So Historically Accurate Historians Are Consulting The Dev Team'. *XboxAchievements.com*, 2016. https://www.xboxachievements.com/news/news-25767-Kingdom-Come--Deliverance-Is-So-Historically-Accurate-Historians-Are-Consulting-The-Dev-Team.html.
Perret, Michele. 'Travesties et Transsexuelles: *Yde, Silence, Grisandole, Blanchandine*'. *Romance Notes* 25 (1985): 328–40.
Peterson, Rolfe Daus, Andrew Justin Miller, and Sean Joseph Fedorko. 'The Same River Twice: Exploring Historical Representation and the Value of Simulation in the Total War, Civilization and Patrician Franchises'. In *Playing with the Past: Digital Games and the Simulation of History*, edited by Matthew Kapell and Andrew B. R. Elliott, 33–48. New York, NY: Bloomsbury, 2013.
'Pharos: Doing Justice to the Classics'. 2019. http://pages.vassar.edu/pharos/.
Phillips, Tom. '*Skyrim* mod replaces dragons with My Little Pony'. *Eurogamer*, 19 January 2012. Available online: https://www.eurogamer.net/articles/2012-01-19-skyrim-mod-replaces-dragons-with-my-little-pony (accessed 22 April 2020).

Pine, J. B., and J. H. Gilmore. *Authenticity: What Consumers Really Want?* Harvard: Harvard Business School Press, 2007.
Poellinger, Michele. 'Violence in Later Middle English Arthurian Romance'. Unpublished doctoral Thesis, University of Leeds, 2013.
Poole, Steven. *Trigger Happy: The Inner Life of Videogames*. London: Fourth Estate, 2000.
Poorna Shankar. 'Kingdom Come: Deliverance – The Tech Behind Henry's Quest'. *amespace.com*, 2018. https://www.gamespace.com/featured/kingdom-come-deliverance-the-tech-behind-henrys-quest/.
Poria, Yaniv et al. 'The Core of Heritage Tourism'. *Annals of Tourism Research* 30, no. 1 (2003): 238–54.
Porter, Pamela. *Medieval Warfare in Manuscripts*. London: British Library, 2000.
Prensky, Marc. *'Don't Bother Me Mom, I'm Learning!': How Computer and Video Games Are Preparing Your Kids for Twenty-First Century Success and How You Can Help*! St. Paul, MN: Paragon House, 2006.
Price, Brian. 'Yron & Steele: Chivalric Ethos, Martial Pedagogy, Equipment, and Combat Technique in the Early Fourteenth-Century Middle English Version of *Guy of Warwick*'. *Journal of Medieval Military History* 16 (2018): 159–88.
Prida, Jonas, ed. *Conan Meets the Academy: Multidisciplinary Essays on the Enduring Barbarian*. London: McFarland, 2013.
Pugh, Tison, and Angela Jane Weisl. *Medievalisms: Making the Past in the Present*. London: Routledge, 2013.
Purchese, Robert. 'Kingdom Come: Deliverance Review – History Is a Double-Edged Sword'. *Eurogamer*, 2018. https://www.eurogamer.net/articles/2018-02-20-kingdom-come-deliverance-review.
Ramey, Lynn Tarte. *Black Legacies: Race and the European Middle Ages*. Gainesville, FL: University Press of Florida, 2016.
Ramsey, Lee C. *Chivalric Romances: Popular Literature in Medieval England*. Bloomington, IN: Indiana University Press, 1983.
Robertson, Scott. 'Social Media and Civic Engagement: History, Theory, and Practice'. *Synthesis Lectures on Human-Centered Informatics* 11, no. 2 (23 May 2018): 1–123.
Robinson, Carol L. 'An Introduction to Medievalist Video Games'. In *Medievalism in Technology Old and New*, Studies in Medievalism XVI, 123–24. Rochester, NY: D.S. Brewer, 2008.
Robinson Carol L. and Pamela Clements, eds *Neomedievalism in the Media: Essays on Film, Television, and Electronic Games*. Lewiston, NY: Mellen, 2012.
Rogers, Charles. *The National Wallace Monument*. Edinburgh: John Menzies, 1860.
Rosenstone, Robert. 'The Historical Film as Real History'. *Film-Historia* 5, no. 1 (1995): 5–23.
Rosenstone, Robert. *History on Film: Film on History*. Harlow: Pearson, 2006.
Rosenwein, Barbara H. 'Friends and Family, Politics and Privilege in the Kingship of Berengar I'. In *Portraits of Medieval and Renaissance Living: Essays in Memory of David Herlihy*, edited by Samuel Kline Cohn and Steven A. Epstein, 91–106. Ann Arbor, MI: University of Michigan Press, 1996.
Rosenwein, Barbara H. *Negotiating Space: Power, Restraint, and Privileges of Immunity in Early Medieval Europe*. Ithaca, NY: Cornell University Press, 1999.
Rosenzweig, Roy, and David Thelen. *The Presence of the Past*. New York: Columbia University Press, 1998.
Rossignol, Jim. 'Czech Veterans Form New Studio, Warhorse'. *Rock, Paper, Shotgun*, 2011. https://www.rockpapershotgun.com/2011/07/26/czech-veterans-form-new-studio-warhorse/.

Rowlands, Alison. 'Witchcraft and Gender in Early Modern Europe'. In *The Oxford Handbook of Witchcraft in Early Modern Europe and Colonial America*, edited by Brian P. Levack, 449–67. Oxford: Oxford University Press, 2013.

Rubin, Rachel. *Well Met: Renaissance Faires and the American Counterculture*. New York: New York University Press, 2012.

Runestone Museum Foundation. *Runestone Museum*. Available at https://www.runestonemuseum.org/ (accessed 26 February 2018).

Ryan, Richard M., C. Scott Rigby, and Andrew Przybylski. 'The Motivational Pull of Video Games: A Self-Determination Theory Approach'. *Motivation and Emotion* 30, no. 4 (2006): 344–60.

Saed, Sherif. 'Kingdom Come Deliverance Has Sold 1 Million Copies'. *VG24/7*, 2018. https://www.vg247.com/2018/02/22/kingdom-come-deliverance-has-sold-1-million-copies/.

Salvati, Andrew J. and Jonathan M. Bullinger. 'Selective Authenticity and the Playable Past'. In *Playing with the Past*, edited by Matthew Wilhelm Kapell and Andrew B. R. Elliott, 153–67. London: Bloomsbury, 2013.

Samuel, Raphael and Thompson, Paul. 'Introduction'. In *The Myths We Live By*, edited by Raphael Samuel and Paul Thompson. London: Routledge, 1990.

San Nicolas Romera, C., M. A. Nicolas Ojeda, and J. Ros Velasco. 'Video Games Set in the Middle Ages: Time Spans, Plots, and Genres'. *Games and Culture* (2016): 1–22. https://doi.org/10.1177/1555412015627068.

Scacchi, Walt. 'Computer Game Mods, Modders, Modding, and the Mod Scene'. *First Monday* 15, no. 5 (May 2010). https://firstmonday.org/ojs/index.php/fm/article/download/2965/2526.

Seixas, Peter, and T Morton. *The Big Six of Historical Thinking*. Toronto: Nelson Education, 2013.

Seshadri-Crooks, Kalpana. *Desiring Whiteness: A Lacanian Analysis of Race*. New York and London: Routledge, 2000.

Shafir, Nir. 'Why Fame Miniatures Depicting Islamic Science Are Everywhere'. *Aeon*, 11 September 2018. https://aeon.co/essays/why-fake-miniatures-depicting-islamic-science-are-everywhere (accessed 1 October 2018).

Shaw, Adrienne. *Gaming at the Edge: Sexuality and Gender at the Margins of Gamer Culture*. Minneapolis, MN: University of Minnesota, 2014.

Shelagh Mitchell. 'The Armour of Sir Robert Salle: An Indication of Social Status?'. In *Fourteenth-Century England VIII*, edited by J. S. Hamilton, 83–94. Woodbridge: Boydell, 2014.

Shimshock, Robert. 'Developer Speaks Out Over Claim "Historical Accuracy" Pushes White Supremacy in Games'. *Breitbart*, 2015. http://www.breitbart.com/big-hollywood/2015/07/28/developer-speaks-out-over-claim-historical-accuracy-pushes-white-supremacy-in-games/.

Singer, Charles. *A Short History of Medicine*. New York: Oxford University Press, 1962.

Skoda, Hannah. *Medieval Violence: Physical Brutality in Northern France, 1270–1330*. Oxford: Oxford University Press, 2013.

Skowronek, Ewa, Andrzej Tucki, Edward Huijbens, and Marta Jóźwik. 'What Is the Tourist Landscape? Aspects and Features of the Concept'. *Acta Geographica Slovenica* 58, no. 2 (1 January 2018): 73–85.

Smailes, Helen E. 'A Pride of Lions: Noel Paton and the National Wallace Monument'. *Architectural Heritage* 25, no. 1 (2014): 85–106.

Smith, Adam. 'Cree Concerns Hammer Home Why Civ Needs to Reject Its Own Traditions'. Rock, Paper, Shotgun, 5 January 2018. Available online: https://www.rockpapershotgun.com/2018/01/05/civilization-vi-cree-nation-cultural-representation/ (accessed 5 May 2018).

Smith, Adam and Soren Johnson. 'Soren Johnson on Challenging the Norms of 4X Games'. Rock, Paper, Shotgun, 6 April 2018. Available online: https://www.rockpapershotgun.com/2018/04/06/soren-johnson-4x-strategy-interview/ (accessed 5 May 2018).

Smith, James L. 'Medievalisms of Moral Panic'. In *Medievalism and Modernity*, Studies in Medievalism XXV, 157–72. Woodbridge: Boydell and Brewer, 2016.

Spatz, Ben. *What a Body Can Do: Technique as Knowledge, Practice as Research*. London: Routledge, 2015.

Squire, Kurt D. 'Replaying History'. Bloomington: Indiana University, 2004.

Staiff, Russell et al. 'Introduction – Place, Encounter, Engagement: Context and Themes'. In *Heritage and Tourism: Place, Encounter, Engagement*, edited by Russell Staiff, Robyn Bushell and Steve Watson, 1–24. New York: Routledge, 2013.

Stanivukovic, Goran. '"The Blushing Shame of Soldiers": The Eroticism of Heroic Masculinity in John Fletcher's *Bonduca*'. In *The Image of Manhood in Early Modern Literature*, edited by Andrew P Williams, 44–54. London: Greenwood Press, 1999.

Stoddard, J. 'Film as a Thoughtful Medium for Teaching History'. *Learning, Media and Technology* 37, no. 3 (2012): 271–88.

Strickland, Matthew. 'Provoking or Avoiding Battle? Challenge, Judicial Duel, and Single Combat in Eleventh- And Twelfth-Century Warfare'. In *Armies, Chivalry and Warfare in Medieval Britain and France. Proceedings of the 1995 Harlaxton Symposium*, edited by Matthew Strickland, 317–43. Stamford: Watkins, 1988.

Stuart, Keith. 'The Last of Us, Bioshock: Infinite and Why All Video Game Dystopias Work the Same Way'. *The Guardian*, 1 July 2013. Available online: https://www.theguardian.com/technology/gamesblog/2013/jul/01/last-of-us-bioshock-infinite-male-view%5Cnhttp://www.guardian.co.uk/technology/gamesblog/2013/jul/01/last-of-us-bioshock-infinite-male-view?CMP=twt_gu (accessed 28 March 2018).

Stubbs, Jonathan. *Historical Film: A Critical Introduction*. Bloomsbury Film Genres Series. New York, NY: Bloomsbury Academic, 2013.

Sturtevant, Paul. 'Playing with the Middle Ages'. *The Public Medievalist*, 9 November 2014. Available online: https://www.publicmedievalist.com/playing-middle-ages/ (accessed 10 May 2018).

Sturtevant, Paul B. *The Middle Ages in Popular Imagination: Memory, Film and Medievalism*. New Directions in Medieval Studies. London: I.B. Tauris, 2018.

Suger. *The Deeds of Louis the Fat*, edited by Richard Cusimano and John Moorhead. Washington, DC: Catholic University of America Press, 1992.

Suits, Bernard, Thomas Hurka, and Frank Newfeld. *The Grasshopper: Games, Life, and Utopia*. Peterborough, ON: Broadview Press, 2014.

Sutherland, Jon N. *Liudprand of Cremona, Bishop, Diplomat, Historian: Studies of the Man and His Age*. Spoleto: Fondazione CISAM, 1988.

Talhoffer, Hans. 1459, Copenhagen, Det Kongelige Bibliotek, MS Thott.290.2°, fol. 2$^v$.

Tarason, Dominic. 'Assassin's Creed Origins Becomes Edutainment Feb 20th'. *Rock, Paper, Shotgun*, 13 February 2018. Available online: https://www.rockpapershotgun.com/2018/02/13/assassins-creed-origins-becomes-edutainment-feb-20th/ (accessed 5 April 2018).

Tauriq Moosa. 'Colorblind: On The Witcher 3, Rust, and Gaming's Race Problem'. *Polygon*, 2015. https://www.polygon.com/2015/6/3/8719389/colorblind-on-witcher-3-rust-and-gamings-race-problem.

Tekinbaş, Katie Salen and Eric Zimmerman. *Rules of Play: Game Design Fundamentals*. Cambridge, MA: MIT Press, 2003.

Terkenli, Theano S. 'Tourism and Landscape'. In *A Companion to Tourism*, edited by Alan A. Lew, Michael Hall and Allen Williams, 339–48. Massachusetts: Blackwell Publishing Ltd., 2004.

Terry, John T. R. 'Why ISIS Isn't Medieval'. *Slate*, 19 February 2015. http://www.slate.com/articles/news_and_politics/history/2015/02/isis_isn_t_medieval_its_revisionist_history_only_claims_to_be_rooted_in.html (accessed 14 August 2018).

*The Chivalric Biography of Boucicaut, Jean II Le Meingre*, translated by Craig Taylor and Jane H. M. Taylor. Woodbridge: Boydell, 2016.

The Design-Based Research Collective (DBRC). 'Design-Based Research: An Emerging Paradigm for Educational Inquiry'. *Educational Researcher* 32, no. 1 (2003): 5–8.

The National Wallace Monument. 'Stained Glass Windows'. Accessed 31 January 2017. http://www.nationalwallacemonument.com/the-monument/stained-glass-windows/.

Tolmie, Jane. 'Medievalism and the Fantasy Heroine'. *Journal of Gender Studies* 15, no. 2 (July 2006): 145–58.

Toolan, Michael. *Narrative: A Critical Linguistic Introduction*. 2nd edn London: Routledge, 2012.

Toswell, M. J. 'The Tropes of Medievalism'. In *Defining Medievalism(s)*, edited by Karl Fugelso, 68–76. Cambridge: Boydell and Brewer, 2009.

Tramell, Aaron. 'Misogyny and the Female Body in *Dungeons and Dragons*'. *Analog Game Studies* 2, no. 4 (2014). Available online: http://analoggamestudies.org/2014/10/constructing-the-female-body-in-role-playing-games/ (accessed 3 March 2018).

Traxel, Oliver M. 'Medieval and Pseudo-Medieval Elements in Computer Role-Playing Games: Use and Interactivity'. In *Medievalism in Technology Old and New*, Studies in Medievalism XVI. Rochester, NY: D.S. Brewer, 2008.

Trigg, Stephanie. 'Medievalism and Convergence Culture: Researching the Middle Ages for Fiction and Film'. *Parergon* 25, no. 2 (2008): 99–118.

Tuan, Yi-Fu. 'Place: An Experiential Perspective'. *Geographical Review* 65, no. 2 (1975): 151–65.

Tuhiwai Smith, Linda. *Decolonizing Methodologies: Research and Indigenous Peoples*. 2nd edn London and New York: Zed Books, 2012.

Tulloch, Rowan. 'The Construction of Play: Rules, Restrictions, and the Repressive Hypothesis'. *Games and Culture* 9, no. 5 (2014): 335–50. https://doi.org/10.1177/1555412014542807.

Turner, Frank M. 'Medievalism and the Invention of the Renaissance'. In *European Intellectual History from Rousseau to Nietzsche*, edited by Richard A. Lofthouse, 67–83. New Haven, CT: Yale University Press, 2014.

Tüzün, Hakan, Meryem Yılmaz-Soylu, Türkan Karakuş, Yavuz İnal, and Gonca Kızılkaya. 'The Effects of Computer Games on Primary School Students' Achievement and Motivation in Geography Learning'. *Computers & Education* 52, no. 1 (2009): 68–77.

Ubisoft. 'Discovery Tour by Assassin's Creed: Ancient Egypt'. *Assassin's Creed*. Available online: https://assassinscreed.ubisoft.com/game/en-gb/news/detail.aspx?c=tcm:154-319359-16&ct=tcm:154-76770-32 (accessed 5 July 2018).

Urry, John, and Jonas Larsen. *The Tourist Gaze 3.0. Theory, Culture & Society*. London: SAGE, 2011.

Utz, Richard. 'Academic Medievalism and Nationalism'. In *The Cambridge Companion to Medievalism*, edited by Louise D'Arcens, 119–34. Cambridge: Cambridge University Press, 2016.

Utz, Richard. *Medievalism: A Manifesto*. Amsterdam: Arc Humanities Press, 2017.

Vaccarino, Donald X. 'The Secret History of the Dominion 2 Editions'. *Board Game Geek*. Available online: https://boardgamegeek.com/thread/1648227/secret-history-domi nion-2nd-editions (accessed 10 September 2019).

Vaccarino, Donald X. *Dominion Rulebook*. Rio Grande Games, 2008.

Vadi, Filippo. *Arte Gladiatoria Dimicandi: 15th-Century Swordsmanship of Master Filippo Vadi*, translated by Luca Porzio and Gregory Mele. Union City, CA: Chivalry Bookshelf, 2003.

Various. 'Kingdom Come: Deliverance'. *Kickstarter*, 2018. https://www.kickstarter.com/pr ojects/1294225970/kingdom-come-deliverance/comments.

Various. 'What Do You Want NOT to See in Kingdome Come: Deliverance?' *Kingdom Come: Deliverance Community Forum*, 2014. http://forum.kingdomcomerpg.com/t/w hat-do-you-want-not-to-see-in-kingdome-come-deliverance/2106/240.

Vávra, Daniel. 'Tweet'. *Twitter*, 2015. https://twitter.com/DanielVavra/status/56968644534 4079872.

Veloria, Lorenzo. 'Kingdom Come: Deliverance Is a Historically Accurate *Skyrim*'. *GamesRadar*, 7 March 2016. Available online: http://www.gamesradar.com/kingdom-c ome-deliverance-historically-accurate-skyrim (accessed 22 April 2020).

Vernon, Matthew X. *The Black Middle Ages: Race and the Construction of the Middle Ages*. New York, NY: Palgrave, 2018.

Viking Queen. 'Viking/Medieval Markets in Norway, 2017'. *The Viking Queen: A Modern Viking Blog Written by an Ancient Soul*, 9 April 2017. Available at https://thevikingque en.wordpress.com/2017/04/09/vikingmedieval-markets-of-norway-2017/ (accessed 26 February 2018).

Viking Trail Tourism. 'Viking Trail: Your Road to Amazing Memories'. Newfoundland & Labrador. Available at http://www.vikingtrail.org/ (accessed 26 February 2018).

Ville de Provins. *35th Medievales de Provins: Humans and Beasts* (2017). Available at https://provins-medieval.com/en/ (accessed 26 February 2018).

Vosmeer, Mirjam and Ben Schouten. 'Interactive Cinema: Engagement and Interaction'. In *Interactive Storytelling*, edited by Alex Mitchell, Clara Fernández-Vara, and David Thue, 140–7. Cham: Springer, 2014.

Waitt, Gordon. 'Consuming Heritage: Perceived Historical Authenticity'. *Annals of Tourism Research* 27, no. 4 (2000): 835–62.

Waterton, Emma. 'Heritage Tourism and Its Representations'. In *Heritage and Tourism: Place, Encounter, Engagement*, edited by Russell Staiff, Robyn Bushell and Steve Watson, 64–84. New York: Routledge, 2013.

Watson, Steve. 'Country Matters: The Rural-Historic as an Authorised Heritage Discourse in England'. In *Heritage and Tourism: Place, Encounter, Engagement*, edited by Russell Staiff, Robyn Bushell and Steve Watson, 103–26. New York: Routledge, 2013.

Watson, Steve. 'Touring the Medieval: Tourism, Heritage and Medievalism in Northumbria'. In *Appropriating the Middle Ages: Scholarship, Politics, Fraud*, edited by T. A. Shippey and Martin Arnold, 239–62. Cambridge: Boydell & Brewer, 2001.

Watson, William R., Christopher J. Mong, and Constance A. Harris. 'A Case Study of the In-Class Use of a Video Game for Teaching High School History'. *Computers & Education* 56, no. 2 (2011): 466–74.

Watts, John. *The Making of Polities: Europe, 1300–1500*. Cambridge: Cambridge University Press, 2009.

Wear, A., Conrad, L., Neve, M., Porter, R., Nutton, V. *The Western Medical Tradition: 800 BC to AD 1800*. Cambridge, MA: Cambridge University Press, 1995.

Weisl, Angela Jane. *The Persistence of Medievalism: Narrative Adventures in Contemporary Culture*. New York, NY: Palgrave Macmillan, 2003.

Werner, Karl Ferdinand. 'Missus-marchio-comes: Entre l'administration centrale et l'administration locale de l'empire carolingien'. In *Histoire comparee de l'administration (IVe-XVIIIe siècles): actes du XIVe Colloque historique franco-allemand, Tours, 27 mars –1er avril 1977*, edited by Werner Paravicini and Karl Ferdinand Werner, 191–239. München: Artemis Verlag, 1980.

Werner, Karl Ferdinand. 'Untersuchungen zur Frühzeit des französischen Fürstentums (9.–10. Jahrhundert)'. *Die Welt als Geschichte* 18 (1958): 256–89.

West-Harling, Veronica Ortenberg. 'Medievalism as Fun and Games'. *Studies in Medievalism* XVIII (2009): 1–16.

Whelchel, Alex. 'Using Civilization Simulation Video Games in the World History Classroom'. *World History Connected* 4, no. 2 (2007). https://worldhistoryconnected.press.uillinois.edu/4.2/whelchel.html.

White, Richard. *King Arthur in Legend and History*. London: Routledge, 1997.

White, William J. 'The Right to Dream of the Middle Ages Simulating the Medieval in Tabletop RPGs'. In *Digital Gaming Re-Imagines the Middle Ages*, edited by Daniel T. Kline, 15–28. Routledge Studies in New Media and Cyberculture 15. New York, NY: Routledge, 2014.

Wilkins, D. *Concilia Magnae Britanniae et Hiberniae*, 4 vols, 1739, II. 745–6. In *The Black Death*, edited by Rosemary Horrox, 271. Manchester: Manchester University Press, 1994.

Wiltshire, Alex. 'How Crusader Kings 2 Makes People Out Of Opinions'. Available online: https://www.rockpapershotgun.com/2016/11/11/crusader-kings-2-characters/ (accessed 10 May 2018).

Wipo. 'The Deeds of Conrad II'. In *Imperial Lives and Letters of the Eleventh Century*, translated by T. E. Mommsen and K. F. Morrison, 52–100. New York, NY: Columbia University Press, 1962.

'Witch', *Dominion Strategy*. Available online: http://wiki.dominionstrategy.com/index.php/Witch (accessed 10 March 2018).

Wood, I. N. *The Merovingian Kingdoms*, 450–751. London: Longman, 1994.

Woodward, David. 'Reality, Symbolism, Time, and Space in Medieval World Maps'. *Annals of the Association of American Geographers* 75, no. 4 (1985): 510–21.

Wright, Andrea. 'A Sheep in Wolf's Clothing? The Problematic Representation of Women and the Female Body in 1980s Sword and Sorcery Cinema'. *Journal of Gender Studies* 21, no. 4 (2012): 401–11.

Wright, David. April 2015, Comment on Helen King, 'Why I Wasn't Excited About the Medieval Remedy That Works Against MRSA'. *The Conversationalist* (blog), 9 April 2015. https://theconversation.com/why-i-wasnt-excited-about-the-medieval-remedy-that-works-against-mrsa-39719#comment_641009.

Wymer, Kathryn. 'A Quest for the Black Knight: Casting People of Color in Arthurian Film and Television'. *The Year's Work in Medievalism* 27 (2012). https://web.archive.org

/web/20150919063457/http://ejournals.library.gatech.edu/medievalism/index.php/studies/article/view/13/31.

Wysocki, Matthew. 'It's Not Just the Coffee That's Hot: Modding Sexual Content in Video Games'. In *Rated M for Mature: Sex and Sexuality in Video Games*, edited by Matthew Wysocki and Evan W. Lauteria, 194–209. London: Bloomsbury, 2015.

Young, Helen Victoria. '"It's the Middle Ages, Yo!": Race, Neo/Medievalism, and the World of Dragon Age'. *The Year's Work in Medievalism* 27 (2012). https://sites.google.com/site/theyearsworkinmedievalism/all-issues/27-2012.

Young, Helen Victoria. *Race and Popular Fantasy Literature: Habits of Whiteness*. London: Routledge, 2015.

Young, Helen Victoria. 'Whiteness and Time: The Once, Present and Future Race'. In *Medievalism on the Margins*, Studies in Medievalism XXIV, 39–50. Woodbridge: Boydell and Brewer, 2015.

Young, Helen Victoria. *Race and Popular Fantasy Literature: Habits of Whiteness*. London: Routledge, 2015.

Zimmerman, Eric and Katie Salen. *Rules of Play: Game Design Fundamentals*. Cambridge, MA: MIT Press, 2004.

Žižek, Slavoj. *The Žižek Reader*, edited by Elizabeth Wright and Edmond Wright. Malden, MA and Oxford: Wiley, 1999.

Zucconi, Laura, Ethan Watrall, Hannah Ueno, and Lisa Rosner. 'Pox and the City: Challenges in Writing a Digital History Game'. In *Writing History in the Digital Age*, edited by Jack Dougherty and Kristen Nawrotzki, 198–206. Ann Arbor, MI: University of Michigan Press, 2013.

# Filmography

*Braveheart*, dir. Mel Gibson, Paramount Pictures (1995).
*Kautokeino Opprøret [The Kautokeino Rebellion]*. Norway: Borealis Production; Filmlance International AB, Metronome Productions, Rubicon TV AS, 2008.
*Merlin*, 'The Dragon's Call', Season 1, Episode 1, (2008) [TV programme] BBC One, 20 September.
*The Last Kingdom*. Season 1, episode 2, 'Episode 2'. BBC Two, 17 October 2015.
*The Last Kingdom*. UK: BBC, 2015–present.
*The Vikings*, 'The Wanderer', Season 3, Episode 2, (2015) [TV programme] History Channel, 26 February.
*Veiviseren [The Pathfinder]*. Norway: Filmkameratene A/S, Norway Film, 1987.
*Vikings*. Ireland: MGM Television, History Channel, 2013–present.
*Wolf Hall*. United Kingdom: BBC Worldwide, 2015.

# Ludography

*Age of Empires II: The Age of Kings*. Microsoft, 1999.
*Assassin's Creed*. Ubisoft, 2007.
*Assassin's Creed Origins*. Ubisoft, 2017.
*Baldur's Gate*. Interplay Entertainment, 1998.
*Baldur's Gate II: Shadows of Amn*. Black Isle Studios, 2000.
*Biblios*. IELLO, 2016.
*Carcassonne*. Rio Grande Games, 2000.
*Citadels*. MultiSim, 2000.
*Civilization VI*. 2K Games, 2016.
*Civilization*. MicroProse, 1991.
*Counter Strike*. Valve Corporation, 2000.
*Crusader Kings II*. Paradox Interactive, 2012.
*Crusader Kings III*. Paradox Interactive, 2020.
*Dota 2*. Valve Corporation, 2013.
*Europa Universalis IV*. Paradox Interactive, 2013.
*Jewish Time Jump: New York*. Gottlieb, Owen, and Jennifer Ash, 2013.
*Kingdom Come: Deliverance*. Deep Silver, 2018.
*Kingdom Come: Deliverance*. Warhorse Studioes, 2018.
*Lost & Found*. Gottlieb, Schreiber, Murdoch-Kitt, 2017.
*Lost & Found: Order in the Court – the Party Game*. Gottlieb and Schreiber, 2017.
*Master of Orion*. MicroProse, 1993.
*Medieval: Total War*. Activision, 2002.
*Medieval II: Total War*. Sega, 2006.
*Mordhau*. Triternion, 2019.
*Pandemic*. Z-Man Games, 2008.
*S.T.A.L.K.E.R.: Clear Sky*. GSC Game World, 2008.
*Settlers of Catan*. Kosmos, 1995.
*Shadows Over Camelot*. Days of Wonder, 2005.
*Team Fortress* series. Valve Corporation, 1999–2007.
*The Elder Scrolls V: Skyrim*. Bethesda Softworks, 2011.
*The Sims 3*. Electronic Arts, 2009.
*The Witcher*. CD Projekt, 2007.
*The Witcher 3: Wild Hunt*. CD Projekt, 2015.
*Thief: The Dark Project*. Eidos Interactive, 1998.
*Tournay*. Pearl Games, 2011.

# Mods cited

Apachii. 'ApachiiSkyHair'. *Nexus Mods*. Last updated 19 November 2017, https://www.nexusmods.com/skyrim/mods/10168.

Apollodown. 'Civil War Overhaul'. *Nexus Mods*. Last updated 11 November 2016, https://web.archive.org/web/20161109184105/http://www.nexusmods.com/skyrim/mods/37216.

BellaGail. 'Better Females by Bella'. *Nexus Mods*. Last updated 12 December 2011, https://www.nexusmods.com/skyrim/mods/2812.

Caliente, 'Caliente's Beautiful Bodies Edition -CBBE-'. *Nexus Mods*. Last updated 31 December 2015, https://www.nexusmods.com/skyrim/mods/2666.

Chesko. 'Frostfall'. *Nexus Mods*. Last updated 22 December 2016, https://www.nexusmods.com/skyrim/mods/11163.

DanielUA. 'True Medieval Economy'. *Nexus Mods*. Last updated 16 January 2018, https://www.nexusmods.com/skyrim/mods/72896.

dDefinder1. 'Enhanced Blood Textures'. *Nexus Mods*. Last updated 26 October 2015, https://www.nexusmods.com/skyrim/mods/60.

hothtrooper44. 'Immersive Armors'. *Nexus Mods*. Last updated 4 November 2015, https://www.nexusmods.com/skyrim/mods/19733.

hothtrooper44, Ironman500, Eckss. 'Immersive Weapons'. *Nexus Mods*. Last updated 8 April 2013, https://www.nexusmods.com/skyrim/mods/27644.

IcePenguin. 'A Quality World Map and Solstheim Map - With Roads'. *Nexus Mods*. Last updated 11 December 2016, https://www.nexusmods.com/skyrim/mods/4929.

Isoku. 'Wet and Cold'. *Nexus Mods*. Last updated 28 October 2016, https://www.nexusmods.com/skyrim/mods/27563.

JoshNZ. 'Animated Prostitution - *Skyrim* – WIP'. *Nexus Mods*. Last updated 28 February 2014, https://www.nexusmods.com/skyrim/mods/10748.

LogRaam. 'The Eyes of Beauty'. *Nexus Mods*. Last updated 20 October 2015, https://www.nexusmods.com/skyrim/mods/13722.

MGE. 'WARZONES 2015 – Civil Unrest'. *Nexus Mods*. Last updated 24 April 2015, https://www.nexusmods.com/skyrim/mods/9494.

NebuLa1. '*Skyrim* HD – 2K Textures'. *Nexus Mods*. Last updated 27 September 2015, https://www.nexusmods.com/skyrim/mods/607.

Witcher5688. 'Credo- Medieval *Skyrim* Overhaul'. *Nexus Mods*. Last updated 31 March 2017, https://www.nexusmods.com/skyrim/mods/49133.

# Index

Page numbers followed with "n" refer to endnotes.

Aarseth, Espen   180
Aberth, John   6
ABM. *See* agent based modelling (ABM)
accuracy   1, 3–5, 15, 29, 34, 44, 52, 55, 153, 189
   Henriksen, Vera   22–3
   historical   1–6, 23, 28, 30, 34, 55, 92, 142–6, 164, 170, 188
accurate   1, 15, 16, 63, 188
   historical   4, 35, 44, 161, 170
Ace, Mimi   143
Ackerman-Lieberman, Phillip   143, 144, 151
*Administrando Imperii*   202
agency   22–5, 31–2
   player   187–8, 190, 192, 193, 200, 202
agent based modelling (ABM)   181
*Age of Empires II: The Age of Kings*   191–2
aggressive expansion   195, 197
ahistorical play   196–9
Albina/Albion   108, 112, 113
Alexandria   133–4
Alvestad, Karl C.   6–7
amputation   59–60
anachronism   7, 33, 93, 162
Anderson, Andy B.   193
Anglo, Sydney   96
Anglo-Saxon   60, 64, 65
   game   177–80, 182
armour   49, 92–7, 100, 166, 169, 170
arms   39, 92–4, 96, 98, 100
Arnott, Megan   7
artefacts   143
   medieval   121, 122, 126–8, 131
Arthur, King   54
artwork   106, 107, 110–13, 115
*Assassin's Creed*   4, 186, 188, 192
Atkinson, Stephen   93, 97, 100
audiences   84–5
Austen, Jane   81

authentic   77, 78, 81, 83–4
authenticity   1, 3–5, 15–16, 23, 29, 44, 52, 53, 55, 75, 156, 161–2, 188, 189
   assessment   77
   constructed   5, 149–50
   as fidelity to written texts   81–2
   historical (*see* historical authenticity)
   of historical film and TV   74, 79
   of historical media   74–86
   of material culture   79–80, 166–8
   in a medieval fantasy   167
   negativity bias   84, 86
   online survey   76
   sanitized history   82–4
   and *Spelet om Heilag Olav* (*The Drama of Saint Olaf,* Gullvåg)   21–2
   through dialogue, reflection and deeper study   156–8
   through negotiation and dialogue   158–9
   tourism and   122, 124–5, 127, 129–32, 134
authentic representation   78–80, 83

*Bald's Leechbook*   64
*Baldur's Gate II: Shadows of Amn*   188, 192
Barbarossa, Frederick   191
Barnett, Teresa   46
Battle of Stirling Bridge   52
BBC   81
Beavers, Sian   7
Bellis, Joanna   97
beneficial objectives   190, 192–7, 199–201
Bildhauer, Bettina   6
Birka   129
Birkeland, Inger   17
Bjerck, Heim Bjartman   15, 24
Björko   129, 135

Black, Daisy  7
body  168–9
Bohemia  30, 31, 33, 34
Bonagura, Tori  143
Boothby, Richard  55
Borre  18
BOS. *See* Bristol Online Surveys  76
Boucicaut. *See* Jean II le Maingre
Bradford, John  60
*Braveheart* (1995)  51
Breivik, Anders Behring  20
Bristol Online Surveys (BOS)  76
Britain/Brutus  108
Bronte, Emily  81
Brown, G. Baldwin  43
Bruce, Robert the  45–50, 52–4
built heritage  125–8, 130, 131, 135
  types  126
Bullinger, Jonathan M.  161
bureaucracy  110, 112
Burkart, Eric  95

Caldwell, David  44, 46, 54
Canada  132
card games  106–15
carnivalesque  109, 131
Carroll, Shiloh  6
Castle, Egerton  94
challenge objectives  190, 192–3, 197–9
Chapman, Adam, spatial agency of  30, 31
character  30–2, 59, 60, 66, 67, 114, 168–9, 181–3, 196, 198
Chaucer, Geoffrey  93
Chhabra, Deepak  130, 132
childbirth  61–2
*Civilization*  186, 188, 190, 193, 196, 199, 201
*Civilization VI*  191, 193–5
Clements, Pat  110
clothing  32, 80, 166, 169
Clynn, John  62
collaboration  141, 146
colonialism  4
combat
  in fight books and on film  93–7
  in middle English romance  97–100
  mods  165–6
competitive-cooperative game  142, 160 n.6

computer games  176, 186–202
*Conan the Barbarian* (Howard)  167
contemporary medievalism  3, 5–8
Cooper, Victoria  7
cooperation  141, 152
Cosgrove, Denis  174, 175
Costner, Kevin  66
costumes  79–80, 85, 100
courtly love  113, 115
craft  60, 111
Crawford, Chris  177
Croatia  126
Cromwell, Thomas  79
*Crusader Kings II*  196–202
  objectives  197–9
  players of  196
*Crusader Kings III*  201, 202
cultural landscape  17, 25
*CurseForge*  163
Cursitor, Stanley  47, 55

D'Arcens, Louise  65, 127
dark ages  3, 106–9, 112
DBR. *See* design-based research (DBR)
Deacon, Jacob Henry  7
de Graeme, John Sir  46
De Groot, Jerome  186
democratization  2–3
design-based research (DBR)  159
Dey, Tapajit  163, 164
*dinar, dinarim* (pl)  150–3
*Dominion* (2008, Vaccarino)  106–13
  expansion packs  106–7, 109, 112
  fantasy  111–12
  medievalism  111–12
  medievalist mythology  108
  second edition  107
  victory points  107, 112
Driver, Martha  100
Dubrovnik  126
duel  97, 98
Dukes-Knight, Jennifer  54
dwelling perspective  175, 176, 183

Edinburgh Castle  43, 47, 55
Edward I  54
Elder, Bruegel the  175, 176, 178, 180, 183
*The Elder Scrolls V: Skyrim. See Skyrim*

Elliott, Andrew B. R.   2, 3, 6, 20, 29, 33, 44, 55, 59, 65, 171, 187
Ende, Teresa   93
England   126, 177
   'medieval' maps of   128
   environmental mods   165–6
Erskine, David Steuart   46
Estonia   130
*Europa Universalis IV*   201
European Middle Ages   34–6, 68
events   135, 142
   medieval   130–1, 134
*Excalibur* (1981)   94
experience   2, 15–16, 22–4, 32, 121, 122, 130

fantasy   111, 112
   gritty   165, 170
   medieval   166, 167, 169
female bodies   168–9
fencing   93–5
Fife, Wayne   132
fight books   91–2, 98–100
   representations of combat in   93–7
fighting manual. *See* fight books
Finnish   17
*First Knight* (1995)   99
first Scottish War of Independence (1296-1328)   43, 49
Fisher, Will   110
Forgeng, Jeffrey   96
France   129, 130
Freeman, Morgan   66–7
Fustat (Old Cairo)   142, 146–50

game(s)
   card   106–15
   defined   107
   fantasy   111, 112
   historical   74, 76–9
   historical accuracy in   143–6
   historical authenticity in   146–50
   for learning   140–1
   maps in   167
   mechanics   196, 198
   medievalism in   111–12, 115–16
   play   106, 108, 111, 114, 115, 142–3, 188, 189, 197
   structure of   142–3
   tabletop   105, 115, 141
*Game Modding*   163
game objectives   187, 190–3, 199–202
   classifying   190–3
   *Crusader Kings II*   197–9
   influential   193–6
*Game of Thrones*   1, 2, 4, 60, 92, 94, 98–100
*Game of Thrones and the Medieval Art of War* (Mondschein)   92
game tools   186, 189, 190, 202
game world   178–80
Ganim, John   67–8
Geary, Patrick   113
gender   2, 115–16
   balance   76
   bias   18
   and landscape   22–3
   role   17–18, 24, 113, 115
German fight books   93, 95
*Gesta Chuonradi II Imperatoris*   202
Gibson, James   179
Gibson, Mel   54
Godøystraumen   23–4
Gottlieb, Owen   7
Graham, Shawn   181
Grand Strategy Games   189, 190, 199–202
   *Crusader Kings II*   196–9
   influential objectives in   193–6
gritty fantasy   165, 170
gritty medievalism   169, 170
*Guide to the National Wallace Monument* (Middleton)   51
Gullvåg, Olav   18–19, 21–3

*halacha*   152, 153
Halewood, Chris   124, 129, 131, 134
Hannam, Kevin   124, 129, 131, 134
Härke, Heinrich   177
Harper, April   7
Harrison, Laura S.   7
*The Harvesters* (Elder)   175, 176, 178–80, 183
Hary, Blind   45, 54
Hastings, Adrian   17
Haydock, Nickolas   6, 30, 93
Heidegger, Martin   175, 182
*Heimskringla* (Sturluson)   16–17, 19, 21, 23–4

Helgesen, Anne 15, 20, 21, 23–4
Henriksen, Vera 18–21
  accuracy 22–3
Henry V of England 60
heritage 80, 124, 125, 132
  experiences 80
  sites 124
  tourism 124–8, 132, 146, 149
Higson, Andrew 110
Hiriart, Juan 7
historical accuracy 1–6, 23, 28, 30, 34, 55, 92, 142, 164, 170, 188
  pursuit of 143–6
historical authenticity 5–6, 28–35, 79, 92, 134, 189
  defining and pursuing 146–50
  and the Middle Ages 35–6
  in visual media for audiences 84–5
historical combat. *See* historical fighting
historical fighting 90–2
  in books 93–7
historical film and TV 74, 78–9
historical games 74, 76–9
  players of 188, 189, 192, 197–9
historical media, authenticity of 74–86
historical play 196–9
historical violence 92
history 74, 78, 80, 124
*History and the Media* 2, 6
Hivju, Erik 21
Holsinger, Bruce 66
*Holy Grail* (Gillam and Jones) 63
Houghton, Robert 7–8, 161
Howard, Robert E. 167
Hroch, Miroslav 17

Iceland 128, 129, 132
Icelandic Saga and Heritage Association 128
*I, Claudius* (2006, Graves) 81
identity 20, 30, 34, 35, 53, 55, 132, 134
imaginary identifications 30
immersion mods 165, 166
Immersive Armors 166
inauthentic 77, 80, 83, 84, 86
inauthenticity 4–5, 74, 75, 77–9, 82–6, 124
influence of games 187
Ingold, Timothy 174–6, 178–81, 183

inhabiting 178–80
*Ironclad* (2011) 94, 99
ISIS 66
Islam 65–70
  barbarity of 66
Islamophobia 65

Jaquet, Daniel 93
Jauss, Hans Robert 29
Jew 105
*Jewish Time Jump: New York* 150, 156
Joinville, Jean de 59
Jones, Chris 66, 68
Jones, Robert 99
Jorvik Viking Centre 127–8
Jorvik Viking Festival 130
Judaism 140, 141, 143
judicial combat 98

Kalay, Yehuda 179
Kanai, Seiji 113–15
Kapell, Matthew 45, 187
*The Kautokeino Rebellion* (2008) 17
Kellett, Rachel 93, 100
*ketubah* 151
Khan, Genghis 191
Kickstarter campaign 28, 31, 33
King 19, 21, 24, 30–1, 45, 54, 59, 90–1, 94, 96, 98, 99, 113–15, 131, 186, 195, 197, 201
King, Helen 64
*King Arthur* (2005) 4
*Kingdom Come: Deliverance* 7, 28–35
*Kingdom of Heaven* (2005, Scott) 68, 69, 90, 99
King Robert I (Robert the Bruce) of Scotland 45–50, 52–4
Kings 161, 186, 196–202
Kirkpatrick 188
Klíma, Martin 34, 35
Kline, Daniel T. 110, 134
Koshar, Ruby 17
Kuman 34

Lacan, Jacques 30
landscape 15–18, 23–5, 175–6
  gender and 22–3
  tourist gaze and 123–5
L'Anse aux Meadows 132, 133

*la porta di ferro* 90, 91
*La posta di falcone* 90
Larsen, Jonas 123, 130
*The Last Kingdom* 60, 82–3, 169
Le Baker, Geoffrey 99
Lee, Spike 66
legal 62, 140–1, 143, 157, 170
Le Goff, Jacques 69
Le Guin, Ursula K. 167
Leitch, Megan G. 97
Liberi, Fiore dei 90, 96
Liechtenauer, Johannes 93, 95
Likert Scale 76, 77
Løkka, Nanna 18, 24
Longan, Michael 174
*The Lord of the Rings* (Jackson) 4, 167
Losnegård, Rolf 20
*Lost & Found* 140–7, 150, 154, 155, 159
*Lost & Found: Order in the Court – the party game* 141, 143, 156–9
*Love Letter* (2012, Kanai) 106, 113–15
Lynch, Andrew 98, 99

MacCannell, Dean 124
McLaughlan, R. G. 188
Magnusson, Magnus 44
Maimonides, Moses 140, 150, 152, 156
'Maimonides' Dream' 150–6
Maingre, Jean II le 94
Malory, Thomas 92, 93, 97, 98, 100
Mantel, Hilary 81
maps 167–8
market 129, 131, 132, 134, 135
martial art 90, 92, 93, 95, 100
*The Martial Arts of Renaissance Europe* (Anglo) 93
Martin, George. R. R. 92, 167
Marx, John 179
masculinity 54–5
Maslen, Robert 97
Massengill, Jacob Logan 163, 164
*Master of Orion* 193
material culture 79–80, 85, 143, 150–2, 166–8
medieval 2, 3, 59, 62, 66, 68–70, 125–8, 135
  authenticity 162
  cartography 167
  cities 130

events 130–1, 134
fairs 134–5
film 66
medicine 58–70
Medieval Days festival 130, 132
*Medieval II: Total War* 4, 190, 192, 194, 195
medievalism 2–3, 15–20, 22–5, 66–8, 111, 112, 115
  books for 6
  contemporary 3, 5–8
  gritty 169, 170
*Medievalism, Politics and Mass Media* (Elliott) 2, 6, 65
*Medievalism and Orientalism* (Ganim) 67–8
medievalist media 5
medieval landscape 121–2, 128–9
  inventing 131–5
medieval medicine 58–70
medieval romance 92, 97, 100, 112, 114, 115
*Medieval Science Fiction* (Kears and Paz) 6
Medieval Times Dinner and Tournament 121
*Medieval: Total War* 199, 200
Medieval Week festival 130, 134
'Medieval' York 126, 127
memory 16–18, 22, 25, 44, 54, 130
*Menneske og Helgen Olav Haraldsson* (*Olaf Haraldson: Man and Saint*, Gullvåg) 19
*Merlin* 60
the Middle Ages 1, 2, 4–5, 35–6, 59, 61–70, 111, 162, 170–1, 194
middle English romance 97–100
Middleton, William 51
military 21, 55, 110, 189, 191, 192, 194–6, 200
Miller, Sean 35
*Mishneh Torah* 140, 142, 143, 150–1, 153, 156
Moberly, Brent 115
Moberly, Kevin 115
Mockus, Audris 163, 164
mod(s) 162–71
  historically accurate 170
  immersion 165, 166

nudity 168–9
modding 162, 170
modern media 59
Moesgård 131
Monagle, Clare 65
Mondschein, Ken 92
monument 18, 19, 44–6, 48, 51–4
Moore, Diane 141
Morris, William 125
*Morte Darthur* (Malory) 97–8
motivation 69, 77, 80, 193, 194, 198, 201, 202
movies/TV references 77, 80, 81
Müller, Jürgen 93
museum 4, 7, 67, 125–9, 131–4, 186
Muslims 65–70

Nall, Catherine 100
*Nasjonal Samling* 18–19
nationalism 4, 17, 20, 43, 70
National Wallace Monument 44, 46, 48, 51, 52, 54
negativity bias 84, 86
*Neomedievalism in the Media* 2
Nessa, Solveig 19
*Nexus Mods* 163, 164, 168
nineteenth-century 68, 165
non-linear role-playing game (RPG) 31, 32
non-player characters (NPCs) 32, 181, 182
Nora, Pierre 18
Norstead Viking village 132
North America 132, 134, 135
Norway 131
    landscape 15–18, 23–5
    medievalism 15–20, 22–5
Norwegian 17, 20
NPCs. *See* non-player characters (NPCs)
nudity mods 168–9
Nuryanti, Wiendu 124

objectives, game 187, 190–3, 199–202
    classifying 190–3
    *Crusader Kings II* 197–9
    influential 193–6
Oftebro, Nils Ole 21
Okkenhaug, Paul 19
Olaf II Haraldsson 19, 21

Olaf I Tryggvason 23, 24
Olsen, Kjell 17
orientalism 68
*Outlaw King* (2018) 94

paper map 167–8
Paradis, Thomas W. 124, 126
'Paranoid' characters 196
Parks Canada site 132, 133
participation 2, 3, 115, 124, 130, 176
personality traits 196
*The Physician* (2013) 68–9
plague 62–3
player 188–9, 192, 195, 197–9
    agency 187–8, 190, 192, 193, 200–2
*Playing with the Past* 2
Plokhy, Serhii 17
Poellinger, Michele 99
popular culture 92, 94, 100
popular medievalism 2–3
Poria, Yaniv 124, 132
power 29, 31, 35, 60, 63, 66–7, 69, 79, 94, 108, 112, 114, 115, 187, 193–6
progression objectives 191–3, 195, 197, 199, 200
props 79–80, 85
Provins Medieval Festival 130
pseudo-historical 161–2, 164, 166
Pugh, Tison 15, 16
Python, Monty 63

'A Quality World Map' 168

race 2, 28–30, 35–6
racial anxiety 30
racial identity 35. *See also* Whiteness
*Ragnhildsdrøm* 15–18, 20, 24
Ramsey, Lee 98, 99
*Raudr inn rammi* (the Powerful) 23
realism 161, 162, 164, 165, 180, 188, 189
    environmental 166
    unpopular 169–70
realistic objectives 202. *See also* game objectives
*Red Sonja* (1985) 55
reflection 156, 159
rehabilitation 18
religion 140–1, 191
religious law 141

religious legal systems   141
*Remaking the Middle Ages* (Elliott)   59
remembering   24, 134
Renaissance   65, 66, 69, 92
representation   29–30, 36
*Robin Hood* (2010)   4
*Robin Hood: Prince of Thieves* (1991, Costner)   61, 66–7
Rogers, Charles   44
roleplay   188, 190, 195, 196, 198–200
romance   90–2, 97–100, 112, 114–15
romantic medievalism   165
Rørvik, Ronald   15
Rosenstone, Robert   82
Rosenzweig, Roy   74
Rubin, Rachel   134
rulers   194–6, 199–202
rulership   194–6, 198, 202
rules   32, 158, 186–9
Runestone museum   133

Salen, Katie   177
Salten   23
Salvati, Andrew J.   161
Sami   17, 20
Samuel, Raphael   44
satellite map   168
Scacchi, Walt   162
Schreiber, Ian   156
science   191
*Scotichronicon*   54
Scott, George Gilbert   125
Scott, Ridley   90
*Season of the Witch* (2011)   63
Second World War   18–19
Seshadri-Crooks, Kalpana   29, 30
sets   79–80, 85
*The Seventh Seal* (1957)   63
*Shadows Over Camelot* (2005)   112
Shafir, Nir   67
Sharia law   141
Shaw, Adrienne   115
*The Ship Without a Dragon* (Henriksen, 1990-1992). *See Skipet uten drage*
*The Sigrid-trilogy* (Henriksen, 1961-3)   18, 19, 22
Silva, Eduardo Bonilla   31
*The Silverhammer* (Henriksen, 1961)   19
*The Sims* (Wright)   182
*The Sims 3*   201

simulation games   181–2
Singer, Charles, medieval medicine of   58–9, 61
single combat fight   98–9
Sivertsen, Birger   16
*Sjebneveven: Om Sagaen kvinner* (*Fate: About the Saga Women*, Henriksen)   18
*Skipet uten drage* (*The Ship without a Dragon*, 1990-2, Henriksen)   18, 20, 22
Skjerstad   22–4
Skoda, Hannah   92
Skowronek, Ewa   121, 136 n.6
*Skyrim*   162, 164–7, 169, 170
    'Enhanced Blood Textures'   165–6
social media   2
source-based historical modding   170
spatial agency   31
Spatz, Ben   95
spectrality   112
*Spel*   19
*Spelet om Heilag Olav* (*The Drama of Saint Olaf*, Gullvåg)   18, 19
    authenticity and   21–2
Staiff, Russell   123
Stanivukovic, Goran   54
statue   43, 46–9, 51, 55
Stiklestad   17–19, 21–2, 24
Stockholm   129
St Olaf. *See Olaf II Haraldsson*
Stolz-Swilling, Tobias   32, 33
Stuart, Keith   177
Sturluson, Snorri   16–19, 23, 24
Sturtevant, Paul B.   6, 69
sustainable governance   141
Swayze effect   184 n.24
Sweden   126, 129, 130
swords   54. *See also* Wallace Sword

tabletop   105, 115–16
*Táin Bó Cúailnge*   54
Talhoffer, Hans   95
Taliban   66
Tallinn   130
*Tamagotchis*   182
taskscapes   175–8, 180, 181
technology   2, 176
'The Temporality of the Landscape' (Ingold)   175–6

Terkenli, Theano  122
Terry, John  66
Thelen, David  74
thematic analysis  76, 84
*Thief: The Dark Project*  188
Thompson, Paul  44
time  158–9
Tolkien, J. R. R.  110, 135, 167
Toswell, M. J.  106
tourism  123, 135
   and authenticity  122, 124–5, 127, 129–32, 134
   built heritage  125–8, 130, 131, 135
   heritage  124–8, 132, 146, 149
   marketing  137 n.7
   Viking  128–9
tourist  123
tourist gaze  122, 126–8, 130–3, 135
   and landscape  123–5
*The Tourist Gaze* (Urry)  123
tourist landscape  122
   variable aspects of  136 n.6
tournament  96
trade  108, 109, 111, 132, 198
Trammel, Aaron  111
treason  113–14
Trigg, Stephanie  44
Tuan, Yi-Fu  179
Tudor  110–11
*Tudors*  1
Tumblr  28
Tu Youyou  64

UNESCO World Heritage Sites  126
United Kingdom  125
United States  135
unpopular realism  169–70
Urry, John  123, 130

Vaccarino, Donald X.  106–13
Vadi, Filippo  96
Vávra, Daniel  28, 32–5
*Veiviseren* (*Pathfinder*, 1987)  17, 20
Verne, Lyder  15, 20, 21, 23–4
victory objectives  190–5, 197, 200
video games  174, 177–80, 183
Viking  16, 18, 128–9, 132
   markets  131, 134
   tourism  129, 132–4

Viking Age  2, 15–18, 21, 24, 128, 133, 135
Viking Land Tour  129
Viking port of trade  132
*Vikings*  1, 59, 83–4
Viking Ship Museums  126–7
violence  62, 63, 66, 69, 92, 177
Visby  126, 130, 134
Visitestonia.com  126
*Vita Ludovici regis*  202

Waitt, Gordon  149, 159
*Wallace* (Blind Hary)  45, 54
Wallace, William Sir  43–5, 191
The Wallace Memorial  48, 50
Wallace Sword  7, 43–5
   accuracy and authenticity  52, 55
   depictions of  46–55
   impact of  53–5
   myth  45–6, 51
Warhorse Studios  28
Warnecke, Sylvia  7
Waterton, Emma  125
Watson, Steve  123, 125, 127
weapons  32, 43, 46, 55, 93–5
Weisl, Angela Jane  15, 16, 109
West-Harling, Veronica Ortenberg  115
Westminster Abbey  126
Whiteness  29, 30
*The White Queen*  81
William Wallace campaign  191–2
witchcraft  111
*The Witcher*  188
*Wolf Hall*  79–81
Wollenberg, Daniell  20
women  115–16
Wong, Annie  143
world building  107, 112, 113, 167–8
*The World Without End*  60
Wright, Andrea  55
Wright, David  64
Wright, Will  182
Wysocki, Matthew  168

York Minster  126
Young, Helen  7, 165, 170

Zimmerman, Eric  177

www.ingramcontent.com/pod-product-compliance
Lightning Source LLC
Chambersburg PA
CBHW062135300426
44115CB00012BA/1939